ASSESSING
TEACHER
COMPETENCY

ASSESSING TEACHER COMPETENCY

Five Standards-Based Steps
to Valid Measurement
Using the CAATS Model

Judy R. Wilkerson
William Steve Lang

Foreword by Richard C. Kunkel

CORWIN PRESS
A SAGE Publications Company
Thousand Oaks, CA 91320

For information:

Corwin Press
A Sage Publications Company
2455 Teller Road
Thousand Oaks, California 91320
www.corwinpress.com

Sage Publications Ltd.
1 Oliver's Yard
55 City Road
London EC1Y 1SP
United Kingdom

Sage Publications India Pvt Ltd.
B 1/I 1 Mohan Cooperative Industrial Area
Mathura Road, New Delhi 110 044
India

Sage Publications Asia-Pacific Pte Ltd.
33 Pekin Street #02-01
Far East Square
Singapore 048763

Printed in the United States of America

Library of Congress Cataloging-in-Publication Data

Wilkerson, Judy R.
Assessing teacher competency: Five standards-based steps to valid measurement using the CAATS model / Judy R. Wilkerson, William Steve Lang.
    p. cm.
Includes bibliographical references and index.
ISBN 1-4129-4119-9 or 978-1-4129-4119-8 (cloth)
ISBN 1-4129-4120-2 or 978-1-4129-4120-4 (pbk.)
    1. Teachers—Certification—United States. 2. Teacher effectiveness—United States.
I. Lang, William Steve. II. Title.

LB1771.W55 2007
379.1'57—dc22

2006026356

This book is printed on acid-free paper.

07 08 09 10 11 10 9 8 7 6 5 4 3 2 1

Acquisitions Editor:	Faye Zucker
Editorial Assistant:	Gem Rabanera
Typesetter:	C&M Digitals (P) Ltd.
Cover Designer:	Audrey Snodgrass
Graphic Designer:	Karine Hovsepian

Contents

List of Abbreviations and Acronyms

ACEI: Association of Childhood International

AERA: American Educational Research Association

APA: American Psychological Association

CF: conceptual framework

ESE: exceptional student education

ETS: Educational Testing Service

FEAP: Florida Educator Accomplished Practices

HEA: Higher Education Act

IEP: individual educational plan

INTASC: Interstate New Teacher Assessment and Support Consortium

IRA: International Reading Association

KSDs: knowledge, skills, and dispositions

LEA: local education agency

LEP: limited English proficiency

NAEYC: National Association for Education of Young Children

NBPTS: National Board for Professional Teaching Standards

NCATE: National Council for Accreditation of Teacher Education

NCLB: No Child Left Behind

NCME: National Council for Measurement in Education

NCSS: National Council for Social Studies

NCTAF: National Commission on Teaching and America's Future

NCTE: National Council for Teachers of English

NCTM: National Council of Teachers of Mathematics

NRC: National Research Council

SCDE: school, college, or department of education

SEA: state education agency

SPA: Specialty Professional Association

TEAC: Teacher Education Accreditation Council

TWSM: Teacher Work Sample Methodology

VRF: Validity, Reliability, and Fairness

List of Tables, Figures, and Boxes

Tables

**5. CAATS STEP 3: WRITING TASKS DESIGNED TO
MAXIMIZE VALIDITY AND RELIABILITY   135**

Boxes

7. CAATS STEP 5: CREDIBLE DATA 219

8. THE TROUBLE WITH TRIBBLES: STANDARD SETTING FOR PROFESSIONAL CERTIFICATION   281

Boxes

Tables

9. USING TEACHER SCORES FOR CONTINUOUS IMPROVEMENT   309

Boxes

Tables

Figures

A Step-by-Step Guide to Competency Assessment Aligned With Teacher Standards

The CAATS Model for Improved Teacher Assessment

CAATS STEP 1: ASSESSMENT DESIGN INPUTS—DEFINE PURPOSE, USE, PROPOSITIONS, CONTENT, AND OTHER CONTEXTUAL FACTORS

CAATS Step 1A: Define the purpose(s) and use(s) of the system.

CAATS Step 1B: Define the propositions or principles that guide the system.

CAATS Step 1C: Define the conceptual framework or content (s) of the system.

CAATS Step 1D: Review local factors that impact the system.

Worksheets

Worksheet #1.1: Purpose, Use, Propositions, Content, and Context Checksheet

Worksheet #1.2: Purpose, Use, Content, Draft

Worksheet #1.3: Propositions

Worksheet #1.4: Contextual Analysis

CAATS STEP 2: DEVELOP A VALID SAMPLING PLAN

CAATS Step 2A: Define purpose, use, propositions, content, and other contextual factors.

CAATS Step 2B: Develop a valid sampling plan.

CAATS Step 2C: Create or update tasks aligned with standards and consistent with the sampling plan.

CAATS Step 2D: Design and implement data aggregation, tracking, and management systems.

CAATS Step 2E: Ensure credibility and utility of data.

Worksheets

Worksheet #2.1: Organizing for Alignment (Version 1)

Worksheet #2.1: Organizing for Alignment (Version 2)

Worksheet #2.2: Our Critical Skills

Worksheet #2.3: Visualizing the Competent Teacher

Worksheet #2.4: Critical Task List

Worksheet #2.5: Sorting Formative and Summative Tasks

Worksheet #2.6: List of Summative Assessments by Competency Type

Worksheet #2.7: List of Summative Assessments by Levels of Inference

Worksheet #2.8: List of Summative Assessments by Points in Time

Worksheet #2.9: Matrix of Standards by Competency Type

Worksheet #2.10: Matrix of Critical Tasks by Competency Type and Benchmark

Worksheet #2.11. Aligning Tasks With NCATE Thematic Portfolios

CAATS STEP 3: WRITING TASKS DESIGNED TO MAXIMIZE VALIDITY AND RELIABILITY—CREATE OR UPDATE TASKS ALIGNED WITH STANDARDS AND CONSISTENT WITH THE SAMPLING PLAN

CAATS Step 3A: Determine the task format for data aggregation.

CAATS Step 3B: Create new tasks or modify existing tasks.

CAATS Step 3C: Conduct first validity study.

CAATS Step 3D: Align tasks with instruction.

Worksheets

Worksheet #3.1: Proficiency Level Descriptions

Worksheet #3.2: Task Design

CAATS STEP 4: DECISION MAKING AND DATA MANAGEMENT—DESIGN AND IMPLEMENT DATA AGGREGATION, TRACKING, AND MANAGEMENT SYSTEMS

CAATS Step 4A: Determine how data will be aggregated.

CAATS Step 4B: Set standards for minimal competency.

CAATS Step 4C: Select and develop a tracking system.

CAATS Step 4D: Develop implementation procedures and materials.

Worksheets

CAATS STEP 5: CREDIBLE DATA—ENSURE CREDIBILITY AND UTILITY OF DATA

CAATS Step 5A: Create a plan to provide evidence of validity, reliability, and fairness.

CAATS Step 5B: Implement the plan conscientiously.

Worksheets

Foreword

For over thirty years, colleagues and I have been working to design, develop, and implement systems of assessment that can be used by those involved in teacher education to do two things: (1) help us improve our programs in a thoughtful and data-based way and (2) help us account for our actions and programs through student performance in a convincing, evidence-based way.

This book, written by Wilkerson and Lang, was designed and written to assist with these important tasks. It was written from the knowledge of educational and psychometric policy and driven by many years of valued learning by its authors.

I clearly recall discussions about how important it was to assess what we do in teacher education at national professional meetings, college faculty meetings, and graduate classes at universities across this country. I recall in the 1960s, we were all talking about Bloom's Taxonomy and levels of questions used in the classroom. We felt that in general, the cognitive domain was measurable. However, the common statement mentioned then and today whenever someone mentioned David Krathwohl's Affective Domain was, "Oh, that's important but we can't measure that." Both topics were seen as important in teacher education, but few of us had the knowledge and skills to assess them, especially when considering validity and reliability.

This book is an important course correction to that drift. Yes, the cognitive domain is important and it can be measured, and YES, we can measure the affective domain with validity and reliability as well.

Wilkerson and Lang clearly are responding to national attention to this important topic brought by the National Commission on Teaching and America's Future, the National Council for Accreditation of Teacher Education, the Council of Chief State School Officers through their work with the Interstate New Teacher Assessment and Support Consortium (INTASC) Standards, along with the National Board for Professional Teacher Standards' system.

We have watched work in many states, such as Connecticut, California, Ohio, Indiana, and Florida, establish standards and methodologies to assess these standards in teacher preparation. This is neither a new topic nor one that has been viewed as fact and conclusively solved.

As of late, the continued growth of attention to standards in the dispositional realm has compounded this task. In the early years of INTASC and the 1980s redesign of the National Council for Accreditation of Teacher Education (NCATE), I clearly remember discussions that used language of dispositions and affective interest in evidence of teacher competencies in areas other than cognitive knowledge.

I recall the zeal of those who mocked up the first draft of dispositions for INTASC standards. Many of them were also involved in the 1980s redesign of NCATE, and the zeal was ever present because of the importance of this task to our nation and its schools.

NCATE and many state program reviews now focus on a professional education unit assessment system. As more and more teams apply these standards with academic rigor, increased attention is focused on the important qualities of validity and reliability in the unit assessment system.

A clear example of this is found in the mid 1990s work in Indiana. A quality group of educational stakeholders, banded together through the Indiana Professional Standards Board, wanted dispositions to be an important part of their standards, assessment and program review. I remember long and hard conversations with Dr. Marilyn Scannell (Executive Director of the IPSB) and Phil Metcalf of the Indiana State Teachers Association, who was the Chairman of the Board at that time. This discussion was very sensitive and important in regard to strenuous standards and assessment development in a state with a sizable population of quality educators and citizens with generally conservative beliefs. This was only one example of many meetings across the country with strong teacher association leadership demanding solid educational standards for program reviews. The big question then, and still remaining today in professional standards development, is, "How might such standards be addressed and how might this be done in a valid and reliable way?" Wilkerson and Lang clearly contribute a solid response to that question.

In *Assessing Teacher Competency: Five Standards-Based Steps to Valid Measurement Using the CAATS Model*, the authors have recognized this history and worked with many stakeholders in Florida and around the country. They have had their fingers and toes stepped on from time to time, and through perseverance have produced a publication that offers a valid step-by-step procedure that is based on sound principles of measurement, program evaluation, accreditation, and public policy.

This book is being published at a time when there is a strong backdrop of public interest, public policy, and even public demand that all call for the evidence of important outcomes as critical to our nation and its schools. No Child Left Behind (NCLB), a bipartisan national policy framework, calls for increased attention to assessing teacher competency and doing so with strong research-based methods.

Along with a primary focus on testing the students of our nation's teachers, *Assessing Teacher Competency: Five Standards-Based Steps to Valid Measurement Using the CAATS Model* is being published at a time when the U. S. Government also shows a strong interest in the topic of quality teacher preparation. Witness the presence of The Institute of Education Science and the National Institute for Child Health and Human Development, both with increased attention to the importance of individual student data guiding decisions on instruction at all levels.

Wilkerson and Lang give us a solid foundation and strong design to help think through the use of data collected on teacher preparation program graduates that impact the entire national mosaic. Our nation is growing in its agreement that every child must be taught by a quality teacher. There is a vitally important link between teacher preparation and the performance of those teachers and their students. This book provides a strong underpinning to both improve teacher competencies and to prove those competencies in both the cognitive and affective areas.

I strongly believe you will agree with these hopes when you read Wilkerson and Lang's *Assessing Teacher Competency: Five Standards-Based Steps to Valid Measurement Using the CAATS Model* and follow the clear steps it proposes.

—Richard C. Kunkel
Professor, Educational Leadership and Policy Studies,
Former Executive Director, National Council for Accreditation of Teacher Education

Preface

The national demand for assessing teacher competency using teacher standards is clear and compelling.

In the starkest terms, the failures of policies and practices, whether in federal or state government, in university preparation programs, or in school districts, are being shouldered by children. This is unconscionable. . . . It is unacceptable, as a matter of public policy, to hold students to academic standards that some of their teachers are unable to help them meet. It is time for full public disclosure. States and school districts should ensure that every teacher in every classroom has met *teaching standards* aligned with K–12 learning standards. The Commission believes it is time to make *accountability for results* a reality for everyone involved. The chain of accountability should include states, teacher preparation programs, and school districts. They all should be held responsible for *enforcing high standards* for all entrants to teaching coming from *all forms of teacher preparation*. All links in the chain should *deny teaching appointments to unlicensed and unqualified individuals.* [emphases added] (National Commission on Teaching and America's Future, 2003, "No Dream Denied")

Linda Darling-Hammond (2003) reminds us that it is possible to meet the teacher supply challenge and still prepare highly qualified teachers. She establishes as prerequisites the completion of high-quality traditional or alternative certification programs, the inclusion of both content and pedagogical preparation, and the adoption of standards based on teacher preparation research. She cites research that supports, among other things, frequent and substantial evaluation, benchmarks for competence, and high exit standards tied to state standards for teaching. She concludes that such standards should be enforced, at least in part, by state certification requirements and policy. She also concludes that teacher preparation and support is one of three major strategies that can improve teacher retention:

> A great unfinished task in American education is to create conditions for better support of new teachers, encompassing hiring procedures, protected initial assignments, steady provision of mentor and other support, *and improved evaluation to help novices.* (Preparation and Support) [emphasis added]

The above citations serve as a backdrop for this book. All too often in education we spend an inordinate amount of time planning instruction and then dealing with assessment as an afterthought. Here, we will reverse the tradition. We believe it is critically important that teacher preparation and staff development programs offered in colleges and school districts assess teacher candidates and teachers using systematic processes based on recognized teacher standards, that they identify the assessments needed to ensure that teachers have met those standards, and that they develop instruction targeted at helping teachers succeed in demonstrating the standards. Designing instruction first and assessing as an afterthought places the cart before the horse. Pilots don't take off without knowing where they are going to land the plane. They have a flight plan. We will propose a comprehensive planning process, rooted in the standards of teaching, as the key to successful assessment. This process allows professional educators to commit to excellent assessment through effective planning in order to focus their vision of high-quality teaching.

The model described in this book is aimed at protecting children from unqualified teachers, regardless of entry route. We believe that it is possible to define the critical tasks of teaching, based on standards. These tasks can be embedded in courses and district-based training programs and ensured in ways that make sense through frequent and substantial evaluation with benchmarks for competence and high standards for exit. If we plan and implement this well, the public can count on each of us to do our jobs and have confidence that teachers can do their jobs.

The assessment model in this book is targeted primarily at the preservice, minimally skilled teacher; however, it is also a starting point for moving beyond the entry level teacher to advanced teaching. We note, throughout the book, aspects that translate well into district-based preparation programs that will assist teachers in improving their practice and move toward national certification. The NBPTS and INTASC Standards are not all that dissimilar!

The book is divided into 10 chapters, with the core in Chapters 3 to 7. We begin with two introductory chapters. In the first, we establish the expectations and options for accountability and teacher assessment, continuing our discussion of NCTAF, NCLB, Title II of the Higher Education Amendments of 1998, and then adding additional findings from the National Research Council's Committee on Assessment and Teacher Quality. We also include a brief review of related literature. We provide a lengthy discussion of standards, establishing as a basis for our work not only the standards that define teacher competency but also the standards that define high quality assessment. We conclude that chapter with an overview of various assessment options. The second introductory chapter is all about portfolios and our recommendations for assessment systems in general, including those that are portfolio based. We acknowledge the utility of portfolios for advanced certification, as in the case of the National Board of Professional Teaching Standards, but we raise serious questions about the way in which portfolios are currently being used to assess initial certification candidates. We identify five conflicting paradigms that account for this and propose five recommendations (one each) to address the conflicts. We continue with eight requirements and caveats for accountability in portfolio design. We then provide 10 recommendations for assessment system design in general (totaling 23 recommendations). We end the chapter with an introduction to the five-step model that is the purpose of this book.

The heart of this book is the five chapters in the middle—Chapters 3 through 7—which establish the steps and substeps of the CAATS model—Competency Assessments Aligned with Teacher Standards. The model (and chapter headings) calls for clearly delineating the assessment design inputs, planning with a continuing eye on valid assessment decisions, writing tasks designed to maximize validity and reliability, decision making and data management, and credible data. In each of these five chapters, readers will be presented with the following:

- A quick summary or refresher of where we have been so far
- An introduction to the CAATS step to set the stage
- "Before Moving On . . ."—Questions to invoke early thinking about the content of the chapter
- "Chapter Definitions and Guiding Questions"—to clarify reading and aid understanding
- A detailed discussion of how to implement the step with examples and important points in highlighted text
- An alignment of the steps with the "gold" standard of assessment design (1999 AERA, APA, NCME *Standards of Educational and Psychological Testing*)
- A "Wrap-Up" summary of the chapter
- "Story starters" for preparing readers to answer the "nay-sayers" in their departments
- Activities, worksheets, and/or examples to work through the steps of the model

After the step-by-step discussion of our model, we conclude with three more chapters. Chapters 8 and 9 provide some technical information on cut-score or standard setting, and a measurement model that can provide useful information for validity, reliability, bias studies, gain score calculations, rater adjustments, and further research.

Throughout the book we help readers address the need for assessment credibility from a psychometric standpoint—as a matter of integrity. We understand and acknowledge the fear of high-quality assessment that exists in our society, so we have attempted to write in an easy style, using humor as a tool. Even our technical chapters are intended to be as user-friendly and to-the-point as we can make them. But our message is hopefully very clear. We maintain throughout the book that it is important to make sure that we are truthfully measuring what we intend to measure and what we need to measure (validity), that we do so in a trustworthy and consistent way (reliability), and that our instruments and procedures are fair and unbiased (fairness).

In the last chapter of the book, Chapter 10, we discuss the potential for legal challenges that are tied to a failure to attending to psychometric integrity, and we end with a 2005 court case in which a non-standards-based decision (not valid) made without due process (not fair) caused the teacher preparation institution to lose.

This book is based in part on our role in designing a state assessment system for alternative certification in Florida. We have used this model, as it evolved, in helping Florida school districts and teacher preparation programs nationwide in designing their assessment systems. Audiences that may find this work useful include all those involved in assessing teacher competency:

- Teacher educators (college of education and school district based) preparing teachers through traditional or alternative routes
- Colleges of education preparing for accreditation and program approval

- School system administrators responsible for evaluating teachers and providing professional development activities for them
- State department personnel seeking to improve their oversight of certification preparation programs and requirements
- National policymakers who want every child to learn
- Graduate students learning about measurement and program evaluation
- Measurement professionals who want to work with teacher educators
- School board members or elected officials who want to understand what a valid and reliable, performance-based teacher assessment system can be

Although this book is not written specifically for teachers, its practical discussions, worksheets, and assessment design techniques can be useful to classroom teachers hoping to create their own instruments to help diagnose competency-based problems in their own classrooms. Readers interested in measuring teacher affect, or dispositions, are referred to our other work in that area.

Acknowledgments

It is difficult to mention all the contributors to this book, but we will attempt to thank a few. We gratefully acknowledge the staff of the Florida Department of Education who gave us so many opportunities over the past 15 years to learn and practice our trade through our work in designing the Florida Alternative Certification Program Assessment System and the Florida Teacher Education Program Approval System—David Ashburn, Bethany Bowman, Ava Byrne, Betty Coxe, Beverly Gregory, Barbara Harrell, Eileen McDaniel, and Karen Wilde. Staff of the American Association of Colleges of Education, particularly Judy Beck and Brinda Albert, have supported our workshops offered over the past five years at the association annual meetings, where we learned from our hundreds of eminent colleagues and "students." We remember with fondness our early collaborators on the design of the system—Lou Carey of the University of South Florida, Catheryn Weitman of Barry University, and Susan Woods of Florida State University. Our journal editors gave us a forum for our ideas and the wisdom of peer reviewers—Gene Glass of *Educational Policy Analysis Archives,* Larry Rudner of *Practical Assessment, Research, and Evaluation,* and Richard Smith of *Journal of Applied Measurement.* John Mike Linacre, author of *Winsteps and FACETS* software, was always there for us when we needed advice on data analysis advice.

Finally, and most important of all, we would never have had the courage to engage in this project without our tireless and talented Corwin Executive Editor, Faye Zucker.

Corwin Press thanks the following reviewers for their contributions to this book:

Martha Gage, Director, Teacher Education & Licensure
Kansas State Department of Education, Topeka, Kansas

Lin Kuzmich, Educational Consultant
KCS, Inc., Loveland, Colorado

Pearl Solomon, Associate Professor of Teacher Education
St. Thomas Aquinas College, Sparkill, New York

Marilyn Troupe, Director
Education Professional Standards Board, Division of Educator Preparation, Frankfort, Kentucky

Elaine Wilmore, Professor
Dallas Baptist University, Dallas, Texas

About the Authors

 **Judy R. Wilkerson** is Associate Professor of Research and Assessment at Florida Gulf Coast University, where she teaches graduate and undergraduate courses in measurement, evaluation, and research. As in this book and all of her research, she focuses her efforts with students on providing a highly pragmatic approach, based in theory, with the goal of instilling a commitment in them to assess K–12 learning. Her PhD is in Measurement and Research from the University of South Florida, where she served for 15 years as Director of Program Review, leading college and university efforts in accreditation. Her career has been dedicated to standards-based assessment of programs and teachers, beginning with the creation of an evaluation model for accreditation in 1987, which she implemented in several states. From 1990 to 2005, she served as the primary consultant for higher education to the Florida Department of Education, where she drafted the standards for the initial approval of teacher education programs, designed the program approval process, and provided technical assistance to colleges of education in evaluation of teachers and programs statewide. She has consulted nationally on NCATE accreditation and worked with state associations of teacher educators on accreditation related issues. She has also consulted with school districts in Florida on assessment systems for teachers. She was lead designer of the assessment system for the Florida Alternative Certification Program, now used in over 40 of the 68 school districts in the State.

 **William Steve Lang** is Associate Professor of Educational Measurement and Research at the University of South Florida, St. Petersburg, where he teaches graduate courses in measurement, statistics, and research. He, too, focuses his teaching on making meaningful and pragmatic uses of the disciplines he teaches. He earned his PhD from the University of Georgia in 1984. He has taught as a public school teacher in South Carolina and Georgia and as a college faculty member in South Carolina, Georgia, and Florida. He has published on a variety of applications in educational testing and works extensively with the Rasch model of item response theory. He began working extensively with Judy Wilkerson when she joined the faculty of the St. Petersburg Campus in 2001. Since that time, they have collaborated in all aspects of their research and service efforts with the Florida Department of Education, Florida school districts, and teacher education programs nationwide. They are working together to build two teacher assessment scales—one on teacher competencies, the subject of this book, and another on dispositions. Their work in both areas is standards driven.

1

Expectations and Options for Accountability and Teacher Assessment

*I*n this chapter, we will provide an introduction to the remainder of the book by summarizing expectations for accountability from various important national studies and the literature. Included will be the National Commission on Teaching and America's Future (NCTAF), the Higher Education Act (HEA), No Child Left Behind (NCLB) legislation, and a study from the National Research Council's (NRC's) Committee on Assessment and Teacher Quality (2001). The studies will point to the need for a systematic evaluation process for teachers and will lead us into the use of standards as a road map for assessment design. We will identify all of the standards to be used in this book and tell why they are important. We will address the requirements of a conceptual framework including the definition proposed by the National Council for Accreditation of Teacher Education (NCATE), and we will conclude with a brief discussion of six assessment options.

THE CHALLENGE FROM THE NATIONAL COMMISSION ON TEACHING AND AMERICA'S FUTURE

In January 2003, the National Commission on Teaching and America's Future released its second report on the challenges faced by children in the schools. Titled *No Dream Denied: A Pledge to America's Children* (NCTAF, 2003), the report continues the work previously written about *Doing What Matters Most: Investing in Quality Teaching* (1997), and provides a discussion and set of recommendations on building quality teacher preparation, accreditation, and licensure efforts as the foundation on which the nation needs to rest its hopes for change. We began our Preface with a quote from that report. In *No Dream Denied,* the Commission also admonishes us that:

> It is well past the time to abandon the futile debate over "traditional" vs. "alternative" teacher preparation. The key issue for the Commission, and the nation, is not *how* new teachers are prepared but *how well* they are prepared and supported, whatever preparation pathway they may choose. Developing high quality teachers is the responsibility of all who take on the task of teacher preparation, whether in colleges and universities, in programs sponsored by school districts, or in nonprofit organizations. Because all routes lead to the classroom no matter who sponsors them; all who take those paths should meet the same standards for teaching quality. (p. 19)

While teacher preparation program faculty and school district personnel can engage in endless debates about what good teaching is, the Commission had the wisdom to say that we already have defined good teaching after a decade of policy development, experience, research, and classroom practice that has resulted in consensus. This consensus is articulated by both the Interstate New Teacher Assessment and Support Consortium Principles (INTASC, 1992) and the National Board for Professional Teaching Standards Core Propositions (NBPTS, 1986), with the former defining good teaching at the beginning level and the latter defining it at the advanced or accomplished level. The Commission synthesizes the work of these two bodies in the following manner (Note: In Box 1.1 we have inserted the numbers in parentheses in the text that reflect our alignment of the Commission's statements with the INTASC Principles/NBPTS Core Propositions):

Box 1.1. NCTAF Statement About Great Teachers Aligned With INTASC and NBPTS

Great teachers have a deep understanding of the subjects they teach (1/2). They work with a firm conviction that all children can learn (3/1). They know and use teaching skills (7/2) and a complete arsenal of assessment strategies to diagnose and respond to individual learning needs (8/3). They know how to use the Internet and modern technology to support their students' mastery of content. They are eager to collaborate with colleagues, parents, community members, and other educators (10/5). They are active learners themselves, cultivating their own professional growth throughout their careers (9/4). They take on leadership roles in their schools and profession (9/4). Finally, they are models, instilling a passion for learning in their students (5/1).

SOURCE: Adapted from NCTAF, 1997.

The Commission went on to identify six dimensions of quality teacher preparation programs, and we provide them in Box 1.2:

Box 1.2. NCTAF List of Dimensions of Quality Teacher Preparation Programs

1. Careful recruitment and selection of teacher candidates
2. Strong academic preparation for teaching
3. Strong clinical practice to develop effective teaching skills
4. Entry-level teaching support in residencies and mentored induction
5. Modern learning technologies
6. Assessment of teacher preparation effectiveness

SOURCE: Adapted from NCTAF (1997).

In this book, we will focus on the sixth recommendation about assessment. The Commission explicated this dimension in the statement provided in Box 1.3:

Box 1.3. NCTAF Explanation of Assessment of Teacher Preparation Effectiveness

Programs that assess the performance of their teacher candidates are in a better position to improve. Assessment of teacher preparation means that teacher candidates are evaluated by more than final exams in their courses, the "comps" required by their degree programs, or by other graduation requirements. Ongoing formative assessments should encourage teachers to continually reflect on their learning and how it will be applied and improved in the classroom. (p. 20)

SOURCE: NCTAF (1997).

In their discussion of accountability for teacher preparation at the federal, state, and local levels, the Commission advises that documentation efforts need to include the extent to which graduates have mastered the qualities of a highly qualified beginning teacher that were identified in the synopsis of INTASC Principles and NBTPS Propositions quoted above. In addition, they should provide evidence of pupil learning that has occurred as a result of their instruction. This is precisely what is required in the Standards of the National Council for Accreditation of Teacher Education (NCATE), which embeds the INTASC Principles in its accreditation requirements. So, for initial teacher preparation, NCATE monitors the implementation of these Principles in colleges of education, often in partnership with the states. The states apply these Principles in their joint reviews of colleges of education, which can have a carryover effect in their approval of alternative certification programs in the districts, thereby impacting licensure and certification of all new teachers. The NBPTS Propositions provide the foundation for continuing assessment of teachers in staff development activities, graduate coursework, or regular annual review as they progress to a level of accomplishment warranting national recognition. This, too, is often an endeavor supported by state departments of education.

In terms of licensure or certification, the Commission defines it as the state's legal vehicle for establishing competence for members of professions, including teaching. In the strategy for ensuring teacher quality that the Commission outlined in the 1996 report, licensure played a key role. The Commission continues to advocate that all teachers should be licensed on the basis of demonstrated performance, including tests of subject matter knowledge, teaching knowledge, and the teaching skills that reflect the core competencies of a highly qualified beginning teacher. They conclude that more must be done if licensure is to gain the respect it holds in other professions:

> Most states test prospective teachers, but many are still not using true perfor-mance-based assessments that provide valid measures of teaching compe-tence. In short, teacher licensure tests simply don't measure up; many are weak indices of the depth of knowledge and skills all teachers must have. States also differ substantially in how they set passing scores. States have raised teaching standards substantially in the past decade; now they need to improve the mea-sures of teaching competence that make standards credible. (p. 23)

Among the action steps proposed at the conclusion of the chapter on teacher preparation is the call to "develop and use widely accepted standards and cut scores on licensing exams that are driven by a rigorous definition of teaching quality; develop multiple measures for licensure composed of rigorous tests of content knowledge, performance-based assessments of teaching skill, and portfolios docu-menting both content knowledge and teaching skill" (p. 25).

TITLE II OF THE HIGHER EDUCATION ACT AMENDMENTS OF 1998

The 1996 release of NCTAF's *Doing What Matters Most: Investing in Quality Teaching* (1997) received a great deal of attention nationally, including some vocal opposition to teacher education. The criticisms focused on three categories of concern:

- The current preparation of teachers is inadequate;

- Teacher education should be guided by strong standards (as proposed by NCTAF); and

- Formal teacher education is unnecessary, as characterized by NCTAF critics.

Members of Congress decided to jump on the bandwagon through the initiation of national directives (Earley, 2000). They found the opportunity to do so with the reauthorization (Earley, 2001) of the Higher Education Act, or HEA. This act was initially introduced by President Lyndon Johnson in the 1960s and was periodically reauthorized by Congress, making it a natural place for governmental intervention. However, because the federal government is limited in its ability to impose college-level curriculum or to set state licensure standards for educators, the Congress had to focus on the teacher preparation category of concern.

Congress used the 1996–1998 amendment process as an opportunity to abolish Title V of the Act, which was previously used to strengthen teacher preparation, replacing it with the new Teacher Quality section known as Title II. The new Title II established (1) grant programs for partnerships between K–12 schools and institu-tions of higher education and for states to improve teacher quality, and (2) new accountability requirements for states and institutions that prepare teachers. This latter requirement is the accountability provision driving much of the teacher education monitoring and reform process in today's colleges of education. Title II requires that any teacher preparation institution that receives funds through HEA for any purpose submit to Congress an annual report on its efforts to improve the quality of teaching.

The provisions in Title II are designed to gather information on, and rank within states, institutions that prepare teachers. As Miller (2001) points out, the reasoning behind these provisions is to urge college and university presidents to direct energy and resources toward improving the teacher education programs on their campuses. Consequently, each year that the law is in effect, colleges and universities must report the following information to their state:

- The pass rates of students who have completed a teacher education program on each of the state's licensure examinations
- The number of students enrolled in teacher education programs
- The number of hours each teacher education student is required to complete in practice teaching and the faculty-student ratio in this part of the program
- Whether or not the college or university's teacher education program is approved or accredited by the state
- Whether or not the state has identified the institution's teacher education program as low performing
- Supplemental information of the institution's choice

Strong sanctions are associated with Title II. Institutions failing to report can be fined $25,000. States are required to develop criteria to flag low-performing colleges and universities and provide them with technical assistance. Institutions that do not show improvement may lose eligibility to receive federal grants to support educator professional development and may not enroll a student in its teacher education program who receives student financial aid under Title IV of HEA.

State departments of education need to compile all data submitted by colleges and universities. In addition, the state is expected to:

- Describe its licensure requirements and all assessments that are used as part of the teacher credentialing process.
- Explain the extent to which there is alignment between the teacher education licensure requirements and K–12 content standards.
- Report the qualifying scores and percentage of candidates who pass each teacher licensure exam for each program in the state.
- Provide the number of licensure waivers granted by the state disaggregated by teaching subject and by high- and low-poverty school districts.
- Describe any alternative routes to teaching in the state and the percentage of students in these programs who pass the licensure exams.
- Provide the criteria used to approve a teacher education program unit.
- Provide information about any and all subject matter examinations teachers or future teachers must take.

This was the first of two major laws designed to generate major educational reform in this country. The second was *No Child Left Behind* (NCLB), which followed three years later.

NO CHILD LEFT BEHIND (NCLB) LEGISLATION

We will start this explanation of the No Child Left Behind (NCLB) legislation with the introduction and overview provided by the U.S. Department of Education on their Web site (http://www.ed.gov/nclb/overview/intro/factsheet.html) (U.S. Department of Education, 2004):

> President Bush has made education his number one domestic priority. On January 23, 2001, he sent his No Child Left Behind plan for comprehensive education reform to Congress. At that time, he asked members of Congress to engage in an active bipartisan debate on how we can use the federal role in education to close the achievement gap between disadvantaged and minority students and their peers. The result, the *No Child Left Behind Act of 2001*, embodies the four principles of President George W. Bush's education reform plan: stronger accountability for results, expanded flexibility and local control, expanded options for parents, and an emphasis on teaching methods that have been proven to work.
>
> The agreements will result in fundamental reforms in classrooms throughout America. This is the most sweeping reform of the Elementary and Secondary Education Act (ESEA) since it was enacted in 1965. It redefines the federal role in K–12 education to help improve the academic achievement of all American students.

The U.S. Department of Education provides the definitions in Box 1.4 related to highly qualified teachers in its March 2004 Fact Sheet www.ed.gov/nclb/methods/teachers/hqtflexibility.html:

Box 1.4.   USED Definitions Related to Highly Qualified Teachers

- *Highly Qualified Teachers*: To be deemed highly qualified, teachers must have 1) a bachelor's degree, 2) full state certification or licensure, and 3) prove that they know each subject they teach.

- *State Requirements*: NCLB requires states to 1) measure the extent to which all students have highly qualified teachers, particularly minority and disadvantaged students, 2) adopt goals and plans to ensure all teachers are highly qualified, and 3) publicly report plans and progress in meeting teacher quality goals.

- *Demonstration of Competency*: Teachers (in middle and high school) must prove that they know the subject they teach with 1) a major in the subject they teach, 2) credits equivalent to a major in the subject, 3) passage of a state-developed test, 4) HOUSSE (for current teachers only, see below), 5) an advanced certification from the state, or 6) a graduate degree.

- *High, Objective, Uniform State Standard of Evaluation (HOUSSE)*: NCLB allows states to develop an additional way for current teachers to demonstrate subject-matter competency and meet highly qualified teacher requirements. Proof may consist of a combination of teaching experience, professional development, and knowledge in the subject garnered over time in the profession.

SOURCE: U.S. Department of Education, 2004.

Readers of this book may have divergent opinions about the NCLB legislation. District personnel are pleased with the doors opened to alternative routes to certification in order to fill critical shortages of teachers in the schools, but many education professionals at the district and college levels are concerned about the likelihood of having "highly qualified teachers" in every classroom when we all know that on day one of their alternative certification program they cannot be highly qualified in terms of pedagogy. It is not our intent to engage in debates surrounding these issues; we only assert that there is a need to assure a minimum level of skill and an opportunity for continued growth regardless of initial certification route.

We will use the attributes of quality assessment of children as the baseline for the federal perspective on the attributes of quality assessment of teachers. These attributes are operationally defined under Title I, Part A, Subpart 1, and include seven examples of uses of funds under this Title. (Money talks.) We have added boldface italics to the ones most parallel to the processes outlined in this book for teacher educators (traditional and alternative route):

- developing challenging state academic content and student academic achievement standards and aligned assessments in subjects areas other than those required under Title I;
- developing or improving assessments of English language proficiency;
- *ensuring the validity and reliability of state assessments;*
- *refining state assessments to ensure continued alignment with the state's standards and to improve the alignment of curricula and instructional materials;*
- *developing multiple measures to increase the reliability and validity of state assessment systems;*
- *strengthening the capacity of local educational agencies (LEAs) and schools to improve student achievement;*
- *expanding the range of accommodations available to students with limited English proficiency and students with disabilities to improve the rates of inclusion of such students; and*
- *improving the dissemination of information on student achievement and school performance.*

The uses of funds for states that are provided for in the law are included in Box 1.5:

Box 1.5.   Funding Targets for Assessment of Children

- Improving the quality, validity, and reliability of state assessments
- Using multiple measures of student academic achievement
- Charting the progress of students over time
- Developing comprehensive academic assessment instruments, such as performance and technology-based academic assessments, to evaluate student achievement

---

It is our assertion that teacher educators, teacher training programs, colleges of education, and districts, all need to model assessment processes for new teachers. What is good for the goose is good for the gander. While we regret that similar funding priorities have not been established for teacher training, the message is clear with regard to students, and it is the same in our own teacher education standards. We need to use multiple assessments.

- These assessments need to be:
  - Aligned with standards
  - Targeted at improving both student achievement and overall school performance
  - Inclusive of accommodations for special populations (both exceptional student education and students with limited English proficiency)
  - Performance based and comprehensive (with use of technology as a tool)
- The data need to be aggregated and reported so that it is possible to analyze and show growth over time.
- These assessments need to be valid and reliable for scientifically based decisions (which is mentioned three times in Title I).

NATIONAL RESEARCH COUNCIL— THE COMMITTEE ON ASSESSMENT AND TEACHER QUALITY

A study commissioned by the National Research Council (2001) examined the role of licensure tests in improving teacher quality. The researchers concluded that even a set of well-designed tests is inadequate to measure all of the prerequisites for a competent beginning teacher. They wrote:

> Initial teacher licensure tests are designed to identify candidates with some of the knowledge and skills needed for minimally competent beginning practice. The tests currently used measure basic skills, general knowledge, content knowledge, and knowledge of teaching strategies. They are designed to separate teacher candidates who are minimally competent in the areas assessed from those who are not. Initial teacher licensure tests do not provide information to distinguish moderately qualified from highly qualified teacher candidates nor are they designed to test all of the competencies relevant to beginning practice. (p. 165)

The Committee concluded that, "Because a teacher's work is complex, even a set of well-designed tests cannot measure all of the prerequisites of competent beginning teaching. Current paper-and-pencil tests provide only some of the information needed to evaluate the competencies of teacher candidates" (p. 165). They recommended that, "It is crucial that states use multiple forms of evidence in making decisions about teacher candidates. Licensure systems should be designed to rely on a comprehensive but parsimonious set of high-quality indicators" (p. 166).

In the very end of their report, the Committee asked "How can innovative measures of beginning teacher competence help improve teacher quality?" They stated:

Several new and developing teacher assessment systems use a variety of testing and assessment methods, including assessments of teaching performance. These include multiple measures of candidates' knowledge, skills, abilities, and dispositions. In these systems, assessments are integrated with professional development and with ongoing support of prospective or beginning teachers . . .

The conclusions and recommendations of the Council are revealing in the call for new assessment systems, including broad-based indicators of teacher competence that are not limited to tests but are performance-based systems instead. We quote directly from their report in Box 1.6.

Box 1.6. NRC Conclusion and Recommendations Regarding Need for New Teacher Assessment Systems

Conclusion:

- New and developing assessment systems warrant investigation for addressing the limits of current initial teacher licensure tests and for improving teacher licensure. The benefits, costs, and limitations of these systems should be investigated.

Recommendations:

- Research and development of broad-based indicators of teacher competence, not limited to test-based evidence, should be undertaken; indicators should include assessments of teaching performance in the classroom, of candidate's ability to work effectively with students with diverse learning needs and cultural backgrounds and in a variety of settings, and of competencies that more directly relate to student learning.

- When initial licensure tests are used, they should be part of a coherent developmental system of preparation, assessment, and support that reflects the many features of teacher competence. (pp. 171–172)

WHAT A FEW OTHERS HAVE SAID: A BRIEF REVIEW OF THE LITERATURE ON TESTING AND LICENSURE

Much has been written about the shortcomings of licensure tests in sorting the qualified from the unqualified teacher (Frels, Cooper, & Reagen, 1984; Pascoe & Halpin, 2001; Zirkel, 2000) and the need for including performance tasks with licensure tests to measure teacher competence (Lee & Owens, 2001; Mehrens, 1991; Nweke & Noland, 1996; Rebell, 1991). McKibbin (2001) noted that the most powerful training systems operationalize the training task into component tasks that must be demonstrated. This parallels the recommendations for establishing some evidence of validity in the *Standards* promulgated by the American Educational Research Association, the American Psychological Association, and the National Council on Measurement in Education (AERA, APA, and NCME, 1999). The notion of a task-based system of teaching and assessing was further supported in an analysis of teacher education programs and pathways to certification (Darling-Hammond & Youngs, 2002). In that study, the authors identified some of the core tasks of teaching, such as the ability to make subject matter knowledge accessible to students, to plan instruction, to meet the needs of diverse learners, and to construct a positive learning environment. They concluded that many teachers do not feel that their programs adequately prepared them for certain teaching tasks, and they make the link between preparedness, core tasks, and retention.

It should be clear from the above that we need to do a better job of assessing teachers and that licensure tests are not adequate measures. It is this performance task-based approach to assessment that is at the core of what we will describe in the chapters that follow. Again, we remind our readers that we are not recommending that observations, paper-and-pencil tests, or portfolios be eliminated from the decision-making structure—only that the task-based approach be carefully considered as a relevant major addition to assessment processes that have room to improve.

All good teaching and assessment begins with a vision, based on our beliefs and values, about what we hope to achieve. This vision, combined with established expectations, provides a conceptual framework.

STANDARDS: THE ROAD MAP TO ACCOUNTABILITY AND SCIENTIFICALLY BASED PERFORMANCE ASSESSMENT

The Principal Sets of Standards Governing Our Work

The two standards-setting groups providing a road map for this book and the design of an assessment system for teacher training are the National Council for Accreditation of Teacher Education (NCATE) and a Joint Committee of the American Educational Research Association, the American Psychological Association, and the National Council of Measurement in Education. They have written respectively the *Professional Standards for the Accreditation of Schools, Colleges, and Departments of Education* (2002) for the accreditation of colleges and schools of education and the *Standards for Educational and Psychological Testing* (1999), which guides the development of all measurement and assessment processes.

In this "how to" book, our model for the design of teacher assessment systems brings these two critical sets of standards together under a single umbrella. First, though, we need to explain a little about the two sets of standards, since some readers may not be equally familiar with both of them, and they are *equally* important in what we do in the assessment world for beginning teachers (NCATE), as well as all teacher and K–12 students (AERA, APA, and NCME).

We note in passing here that we have provided some attention to the Core Propositions of the National Board of Professional Teaching Standards (NBPTS) as well, since much of this model can be applied to assessment systems for career advancement. Earlier in this chapter, we demonstrated that there is a strong alignment between the INTASC Principles and NBPTS Propositions; hence, we will not continually repeat these comparisons. Suffice it to say here that a modified and less intense process is possible for advanced programs.

National and State Pedagogical and Content Standards

The groups to which colleges of education are held accountable include not only the state departments of education that license teachers but also the National Council for Accreditation of Teacher Education (NCATE) and all of its affiliated standards-setters—the specialty professional associations (SPAs). The SPAs include associations such as the National Council of Teachers of Mathematics (NCTM), the National Council for Social Studies (NCSS), the National Council for Teachers of English (NCTE), the Association of Childhood International (ACEI), the International Reading Association (IRA)—just to name a few. NCATE is recognized by the U.S. Secretary of Education as the national professional accrediting agency for schools, colleges, and departments of education (SCDEs) that prepare teachers. The Council for Higher Education Accreditation, a private organization that oversees accrediting agencies, also recognizes NCATE. The Teacher Education Accreditation Council (TEAC) is another rising accreditation agency; however, NCATE requirements are more closely aligned with the states and are, therefore, presented in this book. At present, 48 of the 50 states have partnerships with NCATE for the accreditation of teacher preparation programs.

In addition to the teacher standards, most states also have written K–12 content standards that articulate what K–12 students need to know and be able to do. It is logical to assume that if children are expected to learn it; teachers must learn it first. So, colleges of education across the country have to ensure compliance with state program approval requirements as well as national accreditation requirements and all that are encompassed by both—pedagogical and content standards for both teachers and students. Districts are plagued by a different set of standards. NCLB with its requirement for "highly qualified teachers" and national achievement goals parallel program approval standards for teacher education.

There are often significant differences among the standards, and this can be problematic for designers of assessment systems. The assessment of teacher dispositions is an example of this. NCATE, through its use of the INTASC Principles, requires the assessment of teacher dispositions. Similarly, NBPTS has embedded dispositions in its Propositions. The first core proposition, for example, is dispositional in nature: teachers are *committed* to students and their learning. We have come to realize that teachers who do not value a given skill probably will not apply it in the classroom after graduation from a college of education. If you do not think it is useful to plan a lesson, you won't. Some states, however, such as Florida, ignore dispositions in their state standards. In Step 2 of the model proposed in this book, we will discuss in depth how to address the volume of standards with which we must deal. In a nutshell, it is a whole lot. For now, we note that both colleges and districts need to get a handle on the voluminous standards that have been written and make intelligent decisions about which ones to use.

At the core of the NCATE and SPA processes are the INTASC Principles, so throughout this book we will refer to them as the central set of professional competency standards used to define and evaluate beginning teacher competence. In its publication titled, "Next Steps: Moving Toward Performance-Based Licensing in Teaching," INTASC (1995) stated with clarity its expectation that the Principles be used as the basis for a performance-based teacher licensure assessment system. They wrote:

> These assessments must be good representations of the actual tasks, knowledge, and skills needed for teaching and of what good teachers actually do in a learning setting . . . [They must] replace existing course-counting strategies with licensing based on successful completion of performance-based assessments . . . Implied in a performance-based licensing and accreditation system is the expectation that *more rigorous and meaningful assessments for licensing will be created and used for all candidates* (i.e., no one will be licensed without having accomplished all of the necessary demonstrations of readiness to practice). (p. 5)

INTASC (1995) went on to describe the redesign of licensing in a series of points that concluded with the following two:

> Redesign licensing regulations so that they rely on the acquisition of identified areas of knowledge and skill and the successful completion of comprehensive, high-quality assessments of knowledge and performance. These assessments would take place in part during the teacher preparation sequence and an associated internship experience, and in part in common examinations.
>
> Ensure that all candidates are evaluated according to the same standards of knowledge and performance, eliminating differences in standards that have emerged due to the current array of differential licensing programs. The presumption of performance-based licensing is that, while preparation programs may differ in how they organize courses and other learning experiences, all entrants must demonstrate on common assessments that they have mastered the essential knowledge and skills necessary for responsible practice. (p. 6)

The call from INTASC, then, is clear. Beginning teachers need to be assessed over time, throughout their program of study—whether it be college or district-based—using multiple measures that are required for all candidates. This is not a flexible system of assessment. Instruction can be flexible and individualized, but assessments cannot.

Unit Accreditation and Operational Standards

In addition to the standards that define the content beginning teachers must know and be able to teach (SPA standards) and the pedagogical and professional expectations (INTASC), NCATE also has a set of six standards that governs the accreditation decision. These standards are preceded by a requirement to articulate the unit's own conceptual framework, including its own vision of what teachers should know, be able to do, and believe. Standards 1 and 2 focus on candidates' knowledge, skills, and dispositions and the unit assessment system, requiring not only that teacher education institutions be able to provide evidence that candidates have learned what the pedagogy and content standards require, but also that there is a system in place to ensure this. The standards are quoted in Box 1.7:

> **Box 1.7. NCATE Assessment and Evaluation Standards**
>
> *Standard 1:* Candidates preparing to work in schools as teachers or other professional school personnel know and demonstrate the content, pedagogical, and professional knowledge, skills, and dispositions necessary to help all students learn. Assessments indicate that candidates meet professional, state, and institutional standards.
>
> *Standard 2:* The unit has an assessment system that collects and analyzes data on the applicant qualifications, candidate and graduate performance, and unit operations to evaluate and improve the unit and its programs. (p. 10)

NCATE Standard 2 outlines expectations about how to determine competence through a unit assessment system:

> The unit has an assessment system that collects and analyzes data on the applicant qualifications, candidate and graduate performance, and unit operations to evaluate and improve the unit and its programs. (p. 21)

This standard, like all of the NCATE *Standards*, is subdivided into elements evaluated using a rubric that establishes target, acceptable, and unacceptable unit proficiencies. For the assessment system, selected target expectations are provided in Box 1.8:

> **Box 1.8. Excerpts From NCATE Target Expectations for the Unit Assessment System**
>
> - The unit . . . is implementing an assessment system that reflects the conceptual framework(s) and incorporates candidate proficiencies outlined in professional and state standards.
> - The unit continuously examines the validity and utility of the data produced through assessments.
> - Decisions about candidate performance are based on multiple assessments at multiple points before program completion.
> - The unit conducts thorough studies to establish fairness, accuracy, and consistency of its performance assessment procedures.

Thus, paramount among the assessment system requirements is the expectation that units take responsibility for ensuring that the decisions made are credible. These requirements translate directly to the critical cornerstones of good measurement and testing—validity, reliability, and fairness.

Many states, too, have program approval standards that, like the NCATE *Standards*, deal with the success of the unit from a variety of perspectives. State standards are also sometimes applied to approval of alternative certification programs in the districts. The legitimate and important focus that NCATE and the states have introduced for technically sound assessment, combined with district and college needs to have legally defensible as well as credible decisions, make the next set of standards critically important in the design of teacher assessment systems. This other set of standards is described in the next section.

Technical Standards for
Measurement of Teacher Competency

A joint committee of the American Educational Research Association, the America Psychological Association, and the National Council on Measurement in Education wrote the *Standards for Educational and Psychological Testing* (AERA, APA, & NCME, 1999). This set of standards overrides just about everything related to validity and reliability on your bookshelf written before that date. They are the legally acknowledged standards that define the issues we need to consider to develop valid, reliable, and fair tests.

Tests, as defined in the *Standards*, include not only objective (e.g., multiple choice) formats (that can be completed on a scanned form and scored by a computer) but also performance assessments, sometimes called alternative assessments. Even portfolios technically can be classified as tests. The factor used to determine whether an assessment is technically a test is how the results will be used. If it is a high-stakes assessment (graduate or not graduate, complete or fail to complete, college or district-based), these *Standards* apply. The *Standards* address issues such as test design, validity, reliability, fairness, and certification testing. We will talk about them extensively in this book, and you will see them integrated throughout the steps of the model proposed in this book to help ensure that the process used in designing assessment systems will meet the technical standards of validity, reliability, and absence of bias.

For districts, the AERA, APA, and NCME *Standards* definitely apply, and these *Standards* apply not only to teacher assessment through alternative certification but also to continuing performance appraisal systems for teachers and, yes, even the preparation districts provide for K–12 students to take state standardized tests. The fact that they remain relatively unknown by practitioners is a really big "Oops!" If we are ever challenged in a court of law by one of our students—teacher candidate, fully credentialed teacher, or K–12 student—for an unfair decision based on a bad assessment, it is these *Standards* that will inform the court's decision, especially if the challenge comes from a protected class (e.g., female, minority, or handicapped). We talk a little more about legal challenges based on these *Standards* in the final chapter of this book. For now, we will summarize some major threats to validity in most K–20 assessment systems.

SOME MAJOR THREATS TO VALIDITY
IN MOST CURRENT ASSESSMENT SYSTEMS

We noted a little earlier that validity has become an important focus in the review of assessment systems by NCATE and the states. The AERA, APA, and NCME (1999) *Standards* help us determine how to develop systems in ways that maximize our chances of making valid decisions. We will discuss this throughout the chapters elaborating our model. For now, it is important to recognize that many systems being developed nationwide get started on the "wrong foot." Reliability, too, is an issue, but it is not addressed in depth in this book, although we note briefly that reliability without validity is meaningless (Cureton, 1950). One could ask how assessment systems have gotten so far off track. The answer appears rather simple.

The hodgepodge or haphazard evidence collected without the use of design frameworks or blueprints to meet NCATE *Standards* and/or state laws and rules makes meeting psychometric requirements virtually impossible. There are three critical flaws in the typical assessment process. Each poses a major threat to validity and is described in Box 1.9:

Box 1.9.   Three Critical Flaws in the Typical Assessment Process

- *Evidence drawn from a collection of class assignments or district workshops:* This evidence is used for a purpose for which it was not intended (i.e., summative assessment of standards-based competency). Course assignments, tests, and workshop activities are typically designed to meet individual course or staff development objectives and do not constitute the kind of job-related consistent evidence called for by INTASC to ensure high-quality beginning teachers. Instead, they serve only as a record of participation or achievement useful in colleges to derive a course grade for a transcript and in districts to accumulate points for staff development requirements. Typically, they are not designed to serve as a measure of meeting a standard.

- *Collections of artifacts, self-selected by the student or teacher:* This evidence is often chosen solely on the basis of a tangential relationship to a standard, or reflective/showcase portfolios of teachers' best work, which usually fail to stand the test of construct representativeness or domain sampling, since sampling (through a test blueprint) was not the design starting point. Again, these do not fulfill the expectations outlined by INTASC.

- *Decisions made about teacher competency based on a self-assessment through reflection (a college favorite!):* This evidence does not stand the test of job-relatedness. In service, teachers rarely analyze their work against teaching standards once they are in the classroom full time, and few school districts require reflections to be turned in and reviewed by building administrators. For the third time, this strategy is nonresponsive to the call from national groups such as INTASC.

So, from the outset, some fundamental tenets of establishing validity outlined in the standards are violated.

CONCEPTUAL FRAMEWORKS: PULLING IT ALL TOGETHER

NCATE Standards

In the case of teacher training, the standards of our profession, which are derived from the research in our field, define the external expectations that translate into conceptual frameworks (CF). Internal expectations also are used in developing a part of the conceptual framework, just as school districts define their own missions and values. In this book, we focus on combining externally defined and internally defined standards in the assessment system. The NCATE *Standards* describe the conceptual framework as the underlying structure of the unit that sets forth its vision and provides a theoretical and empirical foundation for everything the unit does, just as the mission and values statements of a district do. The precise language of the NCATE conceptual framework requirement is provided in Box 1.10:

> **Box 1.10. The NCATE Conceptual Framework**
>
> The conceptual framework(s) establish the shared vision for a unit's efforts in preparing educators to work effectively in P–12 schools. It provides direction for programs, courses, teaching, candidate performance, scholarship, service, and unit accountability. The conceptual framework is knowledge-based, articulated, shared, coherent, consistent with the unit and/or institutional mission, and continuously evaluated. (p. 10)

AERA, APA, and NCME Standards

A conceptual framework that meets AERA, APA, and NCME *Standards*, and, therefore, is applicable to colleges and school districts alike, is somewhat more narrowly defined. However, it does bear great resemblance to the first two standards in the NCATE requirements, as cited earlier in this chapter. Before reading the language of the AERA, APA, and NCME *Standards*, we remind our readers that the term *test* is used throughout the *Standards* to include all forms of formalized assessment that result in a significant decision impacting such things as treatment, employment, or graduation. These could include psychological tests as well as educational paper-and-pencil tests of knowledge (e.g., certification exams), performance assessments (both products and demonstrations), surveys, interview protocols, and so forth. In the following quote, we note that the concept of creating and using a conceptual framework is the beginning point for validity and includes how the scores will be interpreted in terms of high and low amounts of what is being measured (e.g., competent or not), the use or decision to be made (e.g., certification), and finally the actual things being measured (i.e., the construct). So, these *Standards* help us tie together what NCATE (and good practice in general) requires, with the official language quoted in Box 1.11.

> **Box 1.11. The AERA, APA, NCME Conceptual Framework**
>
> Validation logically begins with an explicit statement of the proposed interpretation of test scores, along with a rationale for the relevance of the interpretation to the proposed use. The proposed interpretation refers to the construct or concepts the test is intended to measure. . . . To support test development, the proposed interpretation is elaborated by describing its scope and extent and by delineating the aspects of the construct that are to be represented. The detailed description provides a conceptual framework for the test, delineating the knowledge, skills, abilities, processes, or characteristics to be assessed. (p. 9)

So, both NCATE and AERA, APA, and NCME say essentially the same thing. If you figure out what you need to decide, what you are going to measure (what the teachers need to learn and demonstrate), and how you are going to measure it, then validity is built in.

INTASC Principles: Where NCATE and AERA, APA, and NCME Standards Converge

NCATE's Standard 1 elaborates on one of the conceptual framework structural elements—candidate proficiencies—and sets the stage for NCATE Standard 2 with the following language:

Candidates preparing to work in schools as teachers or other professional school personnel know and demonstrate the content, pedagogical, and professional knowledge, skills, and dispositions necessary to help all students learn. Assessments indicate that candidates meet professional, state, and institutional standards. (p. 10)

In their supporting explanation for this standard, NCATE asserts that it has aligned its unit and program standards with the INTASC Principles, referencing colleges to their use in assessment designs.

Making Sense of Conceptual Frameworks

The linkages here are obvious. Definitions from AERA, APA, and NCME and from NCATE of what teacher educators need to do are essentially the same: we need to define the knowledge, skills, and dispositions (KSDs) we want teachers to have (our conceptual framework) and then we need to measure them systematically (our assessment system). In other words, INTASC tells us where to start with KSDs, although we need to add in those of other standard-setting groups—our state and the national professional organizations, as well as our own personal and institutional versions—and then we need to measure teacher competence against those standards in some systematic way. If we want to do this well and safely, we can do so with the standards established for how we measure competence technically, as articulated by AERA, APA, and NCME, and making sure that our decisions are credible—valid, reliable, and fair—not to mention useful. The literature and the call from major influential groups and legislation such as NCTAF, NRC, and NCLB all tell us the same thing—use high-quality multiple assessments, including performance-based tasks.

Our Conceptual Framework: What We Value

We believe in balanced and appropriate assessment, grounded in modern theory and relevant standards, but practical and useful. In articulating our own conceptual framework, we include the following conceptualizations of assessment in Box 1.12:

Box 1.12. Our Conceptual Framework for Assessment

- *Assessment as Learning:* It is possible, and even advisable, to use assessment not just as a device for measuring what teachers have learned but also as a frame for their continued improvement. While we do not support teaching to the test when standardized paper-and-pencil tests are the target, we do support using performance-based tasks that provide the operational definition of critical skills as the basis for instruction. If tasks are truly critical to successful performance, then it is appropriate to have students (or teachers) try to complete them successfully more than one time, with instructional support and feedback provided between tries. The final result, then, is the assessor's confidence that the teacher has learned how to perform the critical skill and can be expected to do it again, repeatedly, in different contexts. The teacher has learned by doing.

- *Assessment by Design:* It is important to know precisely what you want to see teachers do and design assessments based on that vision. Assessments should be

(Continued)

(Continued)

created with regard to a specific vision that is carefully articulated and planned. This can occur by using frameworks that help establish a balanced and appropriate design. Failure to design adequately can lead to inaccurate decisions about capability and therefore be invalid.

- *Assessment for Decision Making:* There is no need to accumulate data that will not be used. Assessments all need to contribute to the overall decision to be made. Asking the same question in different formats, or repeating the same task over and over for different assessors (e.g., the 45 lesson plans required and assessed as summative results in most teacher preparation programs), does not lead to information needed to make a judgment about licensure. Instead, we need to assess (and count) only what we really need. Redundancy can be problematic from many perspectives, not the least of which is frustration and wasted time and resources.

- *Assessment as Flexible Accountability:* A certain amount of flexibility is needed in the assessment process. Some tasks will not be appropriate to some individuals; some tasks can be completed without extensive instruction, particularly in the alternative certification world. It is acceptable to vary criteria within a task to meet differing needs in college classrooms and school districts. When such flexibility is desired, it needs to be built into the system in ways that do not sacrifice psychometric integrity. Alternative tasks, for example, need to be checked for coverage of standards. They need to be equated to ensure that they are measuring the same thing the same way.

- *Assessment Through Performance:* The best way to know if people can do something is to have them do it. Multiple-choice tests may be the best way to determine if an examinee knows something—whether it be facts about science or available methods to teach science. The best way to know if teachers can deliver science in ways students can learn science is to have them deliver science content and assess the results in terms of student learning.

- *Assessment Governed by Standards:* No man is an island. There are standards to which K–12 students are held accountable and standards to which teachers are held accountable. Assessment systems need to be built around those standards and not what individuals want to do because they are "experts." The Greeks and Romans learned the tough lesson of what hubris can do to a culture.

- *Assessment as Modeling:* If teachers in the schools are not good assessors, it is because we have not assessed them well ourselves as teacher educators. Teachers teach as they were taught and assess as they were assessed. If we lead them to believe that it is okay to have a slapdash approach to measuring standards and for faculty members or staff developers to do what they want, they will not be ready to work as a team in a standards-based environment in their own school and classroom. If we want them to use alternative assessments, we need to model how to do that with the best alternative assessments we can build. If we want them to use multiple measures that lead to a decision in which data are aggregated in a meaningful way, we need to create and use such measures ourselves.

ASSESSMENT OPTIONS

We now turn to an in-depth discussion of the options available for a system that uses multiple measures, since national policy and professional literature seem to be clearly pointing us in that direction. The full ranges of measures identified by an institution become the components or core of a comprehensive assessment system. These components will, of necessity, need to fit the purpose of the system, which we will address in much greater depth in subsequent chapters. For now, though, we discuss the variety of components that system designers can consider. Included among the choices are those listed in Box 1.13:

Box 1.13.   Assessment Options—Six Choices

- Records of training completed
- Test and exam scores
- Observations of performance
- Portfolios of assessable artifacts
- Job-related tasks and work sample products
- K–12 students work samples

Below is a brief discussion of each of the above types of knowledge and skill competency assessments, all of which are currently widely used and deserve some special comments. While we will present some of the obstacles encountered when each of these is used as the predominant form of assessment, we note from the outset that we advocate for each of these strategies when they are combined into an appropriate and balanced system of assessments. We will introduce portfolios in this chapter, but we note now that we dedicate the entire next chapter to this often misunderstood and misused assessment method.

Records of Training Completed

Virtually every college of education requires a minimum GPA and a minimum set of required courses to graduate, and virtually every school district keeps records on staff development completed by practicing teachers. The record of completion of these training opportunities provides an important measure of what the teachers know and, to some extent, what they can do. Clearly, this is a measure of quality control and a vehicle to ensure that teachers have had adequate opportunity to acquire the knowledge and skills required in the profession. For colleges progressing through NCATE accreditation, these opportunities must be explicitly described. They are documentation of what specific knowledge is gained in each course as it relates to national standards of content.

As a measure used exclusively, however, transcript analysis and other records of completion lack a great deal, even once the content is clearly articulated. Instructors vary in grading consistency and cheating is a real possibility; quality of coursework varies; syllabi and transcripts are often not absolute indicators of what happened in courses. Staff development, too, varies widely and often consists largely of opportunities to listen or participate in discussions, with limited opportunity to produce a scorable product documenting actual knowledge and skill acquisition.

In the university context, the notion of academic freedom often works against consistency of syllabi, course materials, and classroom experiences. Nevertheless, a GPA of 1.5 or the omission of critical coursework in the subject matter tells us that a teacher is clearly not qualified to teach, just as repeated missed opportunities to participate in staff development activities provide us with the same message. Conversely, a GPA of 4.0 and all the right courses, or a long list of workshops or other professional development activities, is a fairly good indication that the teacher has some potential. The generalizability of decisions based on transcripts is woefully lacking.

Test and Exam Scores

There is no substitute for the paper-and-pencil test to measure teachers' knowledge in terms of the content to be taught, the theories to be applied, and the strategies from which to choose. Tests are the most common format for assessing teacher knowledge. Tests may be developed by individual faculty, colleges, school districts, state agencies, or test publishers. The degree to which one needs to be concerned about psychometric issues is directly proportional to the weight the tests will have in deciding which teachers are credentialed. Course exams will not require special evaluations for validity and reliability (although it is always a good idea!), but entrance exams or comprehensive finals required for a diploma or teacher certification exam are a different matter.

Whatever weight is applied to them, paper-and-pencil tests have limited use in providing evidence of what teachers can do with children. Only observations of performance or reviews of work products can give us the information we need about skill application and integration of complex concepts. If we want to know whether a teacher can create a classroom management plan, write a lesson plan or a test, or write a note home to parents, products are clearly the best strategy to use. If we want to assess how well plans are implemented, we must observe the teacher in the classroom. Thus, paper-and-pencil tests, particularly standardized certification exams, when used to the exclusion of other important strategies, have been challenged in the courts. Typically the validity of the measures and the cut scores chosen are the targets in tests that have not been carefully validated to ensure that only the candidates who fail to meet standards of minimum competence are kept out of the profession (Mellnick & Pullin, 2000).

Observations of Performance

As we noted in the previous section, there is no substitute for observing a teacher in the classroom. Clearly, if we want to know whether a teacher communicates effectively with learners, is sensitive to diversity, and can manage a classroom or deliver a lesson, observation is the best strategy to do this. Observations only can be used, though, to measure a very limited set of skills in a snapshot fashion. They are not useful to determine the extent to which the teacher can foster students' learning, create sound assessment systems, accommodate for diverse children, or interact positively with colleagues and parents. Institutions and states have trouble when they overuse observation to the exclusion or near exclusion of other assessment strategies. Observation instruments are subjective and are prone to tapping behaviors that may not be critical to teacher performance (e.g., enthusiasm) and, therefore, are fodder for litigation (Hazi, 1989; McGinty, 1996). This is especially true when the observation is not videotaped. Finally, observation systems that seem to measure well tend to quickly become complex and time consuming to administer and score (Flanders, 1970).

Portfolios of Assessable Artifacts

Many colleges and districts are making extensive use of portfolios of examples of finely tuned work, typically selected by the teacher. Despite their growing popularity, the legal and psychometric issues, combined with time-consuming development and evaluation processes, have made the utility of these portfolios questionable within the certification context. While there is no doubt that portfolios are unparalleled in their potential to help students of all ages learn, their use for accountability purposes is highly suspect (Barrett, 2004; Wilkerson & Lang, 2003), unless they are merely a packaged set of prescribed and evaluated work. In this latter case, the portfolio as a vehicle for learning loses its meaning to record keeping. This is often a conflict of purpose, as will be discussed in our next chapter.

The concerns expressed about portfolios for certification are in no way meant to be interpreted as a criticism of National Board Certification. That is a different context used for a different population with a different purpose driving the system. Minimal competence has already been established for this population, which is capable of more broadly constructed measures that require less comprehensive coverage of the content assessed. NBPTS processes have also been subjected to rigorous and very expensive test development that is not typically available to institutions of higher education or even states. We do, however, in this book encourage readers to consider this assessment system design model as useful for building local training and assessment models that will help teachers progress through NBPTS certification and other advancement opportunities.

Job-Related Tasks and Work Sample Products

The AERA, APA, and NCME *Standards* provide a useful discussion of the meaning of performance assessments, particularly in a job-related area, in Chapter 3 on *Test Development and Revision.*

One distinction between performance assessments and other forms of tests has to do with the type of response that is required from the test takers. Performance assessments require the test takers to carry out a process such as playing a musical instrument or tuning a car's engine or to produce a product such as a written essay. Performance assessments generally require the test takers to demonstrate their abilities or skills in settings that closely resemble real-life settings. For example, an assessment of a psychologist in training may require the test taker to interview a client, choose appropriate tests, and arrive at diagnosis and plan for therapy. Performance assessments are diverse in nature and can be product-based as well as behavior-based. Because performance assessments typically consist of a small number of tasks, establishing the extent to which the results can be generalized to the broader domain is particularly important. The use of test specifications will contribute to tasks being developed so as to represent systematically the critical dimensions to be assessed, leading to a more comprehensive coverage of the domain than what would occur if test specifications were not used. Further, both logical and empirical evidence are important to document the extent to which performance assessments—tasks as well as scoring criteria—reflect the processes or skills that are specified by the domain definition. When tasks are designed to elicit complex cognitive processes, logical analyses of the tasks and both logical and empirical analyses of the test takers' performance on the tasks provide necessary validity evidence. (pp. 41–42)

Several important points come from this lengthy citation, and they will form the basis for subsequent discussions, including the 10 recommendations that serve as a foundation for our design model introduced at the end of the next chapter. They are summarized in Box 1.14.

Box 1.14. Performance Assessment in the AERA, APA, NCME *Standards*

- The term *performance assessment* includes both products and activities that must be performed in live settings.
- Real settings, or simulated ones, are necessary.
- Test specifications (or blueprints or frameworks) are necessary to ensure adequate coverage of the domain—in this case the job of teaching.
- Scoring criteria are necessary for everything assessed formally.
- Not everything needs to be tested, but nothing important should be omitted. There is no set number of tasks, but there must be enough to make the decision about whether or not critical skills have been acquired and demonstrated.
- Logical (or judgmental) and empirical analyses are necessary for validity—logical during the design stage and both logical and empirical once performance data are available.

In teacher certification then, the types of tasks we might need to determine job capability are both product based and behavioral or observational in nature. Although we discussed observation separately above, because it is often not viewed as a task, we will now transition to use of the term *task* to include both products and performances, consistent with the AERA, APA, and NCME *Standards*.

What do we mean by job-related tasks? Some examples are provided in Box 1.15.

Box 1.15. Examples of Job-Related Tasks

- Unit test or semester exam
- Lesson plans
- Alternative assessment
- Classroom management plan
- Accommodations plan or Individual Educational Plan (IEP)
- Folder of parent communications
- Observation of classroom environment

Some tasks will be short term while others will be long term. For example, creating a unit exam would be a short-term product, but assessing an individual child over time to provide remediation would take a longer period. Both could result in a written product.

Interacting with children in the classroom, treating diverse populations equitably, and maintaining a supportive learning environment all would require an observation. The ability to communicate expectations to children and parents would require a product. Task by task, the method has to match the job function as defined in the conceptual framework.

The task-based products have tangible results (e.g., a record of accommodations, a lesson plan to teach critical thinking skills, a classroom management plan, a portfolio of K–12 student work, an assessment with mastery analyzed and follow-up suggested, a semester and unit plan, a folder of communications with parents, a case study showing results of improvement with one child). All of these require specific scoring criteria and examples of acceptable and unacceptable products. The observations, too, require instruments on which decisions can be recorded.

As we think about creating teacher assessment systems for certification programs designed in colleges and school districts, the citation and subsequent analyses above lead to some conclusions about advantages and disadvantages for both types of designers. Clearly, it is easier for school districts to develop and use assessments that are truly reflective of, and performed in, real job settings, since their entire training program is on the job. They often, however, are painfully distracted from adequate coverage by the routine demands of the job, and this is exacerbated by the newcomers' need to survive. So, districts will not be tempted to test everything, as colleges are; they will have trouble with doing a bare minimum. Planning for continuing professional development, however, is a natural for districts.

For colleges, the need to use many measures is not a problem, since they have more time and energy to do training and assessment of teachers. Thinking about ranges of difficulty and increasing complexity is easier, but not the norm. Colleges will be distracted by the desire to include everything—job related or not—and will have difficulty in focusing on decisions that are more or less critical to the ultimate decision about certification. Colleges are often consumed in their assessment systems with reflection, making it more important than other critical dimensions of teaching—such as measuring the effect of teaching on K–12 learning.

The major measurement issues of test specifications or blueprints, developing rubrics, scaling, and conducting validity studies will be difficult for both houses. Colleges may be somewhat more comfortable in these areas than districts when they work with measurement personnel; districts may recognize the need for this more clearly, facing court challenges more frequently.

K–12 Student Work Samples

K–12 student work samples are really a subset of the job-related tasks described above. They have become an important add-on or even a driving force in some college programs. The Teacher Work Sample Methodology (TWSM), developed at Western Oregon University, is the most well-known example. In this approach to looking at teacher ability, assessors look specifically at the results of teaching. In some models, such as TWSM, local factors in the school, lesson planning, and pre/post assessment or gain scores are reviewed in mini-portfolios developed by the teacher. Student products may not be included, but charts and graphs showing the results for each student are provided, along with reflections on what worked and what did not work in the unit.

To describe this model, we provide the following excerpt from *Connecting Teaching and Learning: A Handbook for Teacher Educators on Teacher Work Sample Methodology,* published jointly by Western Oregon University, AACTE, and ERIC in 2002. The foreword poses the question, "Is there a way in which teacher preparation can accelerate the development track, providing candidates with tools that focus their attention on the instructional needs and progress of their students?" The text answers the question as follows:

> Some years ago, in the context of Oregon's extensive state framework for articulation of K–12 and teacher education standards, researchers and faculty at Western Oregon University set out to find answers to that question. These educators outlined an approach in which teacher candidates are explicitly taught and practice a model that links pre-instructional planning, conduct of the instructional process, and subsequent reflection with a strong emphasis on assembling and analyzing data about their students' learning and growth.

Graduation requirements include two work samples, both of which are for two- to five-week units, with the second prepared largely independently by a candidate. Elements and specifications for the work sample follow in Table 1.1.

Table 1.1.   Elements and Specifications of the TWSM Approach

Elements	Specifications
Sample of Work	The sample of teacher and pupil work studied must be of sufficient length and scope to permit the assessment of multiple dimensions of a teacher's work and to make the learning outcomes pupils are to accomplish of genuine importance to their long-term progress in learning.
Targets for Learning	The learning outcomes to be accomplished by pupils are to be carefully delineated and are to vary in complexity and kind (e.g., concept acquisition and the solution of multistep problems).
Measures of Learning	Key learning outcomes are to be accompanied by a description of the pre- and post-institutional measures to be used in assessing the progress pupils make in working toward their accomplishments; instructional planning is to reflect findings from pre-instructional assessment.
Descriptors of Process	Information is to be collected and reported on the conditions and processes of instruction provided by a teacher during the course of the work sampled.
Descriptors of Context	Information is to be collected and reported on the classroom, school, and community contexts in which teaching and learning occur.
Analysis of Learning Gains	The learning gains made by pupils as a consequence of instruction are to be provided on a pupil-by-pupil basis and summarized for selected groups of children (e.g., pupils starting the unit with little versus a great deal of related knowledge, or pupils who have English as a second language versus those who do not).
Reflection and Next Steps	Candidates are to provide a reflective analysis of their teaching and accomplishments with pupils in light of the information reported in the sample of work as a whole and identify their need for continued professional development.

SOURCE: Adapted from Girod (2002).

The tasks illustrated in Table 1.2 are required in Western Oregon University's Teacher Work Sample.

#	Task Description
Table 1.2. Tasks in the TWSM Approach	
1	Describe the unit of study to be sampled and the curriculum context in which it rests.
2	Map the classroom and school context in which the sample of teaching and learning is to be taken, giving particular attention to the number and characteristics of pupils for whom one is responsible.
3	Given (1) and (2), identify the learning outcomes one's pupils are to accomplish through the unit of study.
4	Given (1) through (3), develop the measures to be used in assessing the accomplishment of these outcomes.
5	Administer a pre-instruction version of these measures to determine where pupils are with respect to what they are expected to learn.
6	Using information obtained through all of the above, prepare an instruction/ management/assessment plan for helping *all* pupils reach the learning outcomes desired.
7	Implement this contextually adapted instructional plan, with supervisors' attention directed to classroom management; the alignment and integration of curriculum, instruction, and assessment; the appropriate use of best teaching practices; mastery of subject matter taught; and demonstration of interpersonal sensitivity and professionalism.
8	Assess the post-instructional accomplishment of pupils and calculate the *growth* in learning achieved for each pupil.
9	Summarize, interpret, and report the growth in learning for each pupil in one's class and for selected groups of pupils. Relate the progress made in learning to the context in which teaching and learning occurred.
10	Reflect on what would be done differently if the unit were taught again and what has been learned from the unit about needs for continued.

SOURCE: Adapted from Girod (2002).

The advantage of the TWSM model is that it helps teachers see assessment within the context of planning and the local school. When the model is used as intended, it becomes a focal point for the curriculum, and teachers become accustomed to linking instruction and assessment. On the less positive side, it presents a single model of assessment—gain scores—which often is not appropriate to instructional outcomes and assessment methods. Not everything is appropriate to the pre/post test model, and many higher order outcomes can fall by the wayside for the inability to apply that model. For example, students' creation of a research paper or preparation for a debate does not lend itself to pre/post testing.

Other models, such as the one being used in alternative certification in Florida, start from the same point—effect on K–12 learning—but break up and expand the measures in a different way. The Florida Alternative Certification Program (Florida Education Standards Commission, 2002) assessment system includes eight impact tasks, each focusing on a different aspect of K–12 impact. Teachers begin their work with the development of a classroom management plan before school starts to establish a positive environment from day one. As they learn more about their students from school records and surveys, they plan to accommodate any special needs and then track those accommodations throughout the semester. They select one student who needs special assistance throughout the semester, assuring that the student makes much needed progress, working with his or her family and with their colleagues to make this happen. The teacher keeps a constant eye on who in the class learns and who does not, always on the lookout for unintended discrepancies in performance among protected populations. The teacher focuses on teaching students to think critically and creatively in each of the content areas and showcases the teacher's own accomplishments through the accomplishments of the students in a K–12 student portfolio. The specific tasks, each of which is accompanied by a set of explicit directions and a scoring rubric, are as shown in Table 1.3.

The Florida approach expands on the teachers' use of a variety of assessment approaches, giving the teacher a more in-depth perspective on the use of assessment tools. However, falling short on the repetition of the process and the focus on integration with instruction, teachers may see it less as part of the complex process of classroom instruction and assessment, missing some of the connections afforded by working through single units as in the TWSM model. Perhaps the best solution is a combination of the two methods!

Table 1.3. Student Impact Tasks in the Florida Alternative Certification Assessment System	
Task Name	*Brief Description*
Classroom Management System	The teacher creates a system to manage the classroom. The system includes rules; expected behaviors; procedures; and organization of space, time, and materials. Students are involved in the planning process.
A Demographic Study of Your Students and a Plan to Meet Their Needs	The teacher compiles descriptive group data about students in the school and about specific students in his or her classes, presenting school and class data in chart form. The teacher analyzes these data and, after consultation with an Exceptional Student Education (ESE) specialist and counselor in the school, the teacher documents the adaptations that he or she will need to meet the individual needs of students.
Student Attitudes About School and Learning	The teacher administers a survey to students to determine their attitudes about self-concept, reading/learning, autonomy, environmental mastery, family, and school. The teacher analyzes the results of the survey and develops strategies to motivate and support students. The product includes the analysis and the strategies along with a report of their effectiveness.
Individual Planning for Intervention	The teacher participates in an Individual Education Plan (IEP), Academic Improvement Plan (AIP), or Family Services Plan (FSP) as part of a team conference aimed at the instructional planning or intervention for an ESE

Task Name	Brief Description
	student, Limited English Proficiency (LEP) student, or a student identified as needing intervention. The teacher participates in alternative strategy planning or recommendations for the student and takes responsibility for implementation of a portion of the IEP or student intervention plan, keeping a running record of the progress or success of the intervention.
Documentation of Diversity Accommodations	The teacher documents the adaptations that he or she has made to meet the individual needs of students.
Case Study of a Student Needing Assistance	The teacher works with a student, the student's parent or guardian, and colleagues throughout the semester to improve the student's performance. This could be the student identified in Task 05C. The teacher keeps records of family and colleague contact targeted at improving the student's performance. The teacher also assesses that student's performance, reports results to all involved parties, and maintains records of the results and the discussions/reports of performance.
Demonstration of Positive Student Outcomes	The teacher demonstrates a positive impact on student learning in a major specified unit using multiple measures to determine mastery of objectives by individual students and the class as a whole.
Portfolio of Student Work	The teacher creates a showcase portfolio of student work over a semester or year. This portfolio includes samples of work from eight students in the teacher's class who have exceeded and/or met expectations with regard to targets for critical, creative, or higher-level thinking, and two who were difficult to teach. The work samples from students also show that they have acquired and used knowledge in four content areas. The teacher explains why each sample was selected and provides copies of the prompts used to generate the work (tests, lesson plans, or task instructions.)

SOURCE: Adapted from Florida Department of Education (2002).

Ⅴ WRAP-UP

In this chapter, we reviewed various expectations regarding accountability and teaching assessment, ranging from national legislation to the work of major think-tanks. We noted that standards are the thread that ties accountability and assessment together, and we focused on several important sets of standards that help define our measurement construct and product—NCATE *Standards*, INTASC Principles and SPA standards for what teachers should know and be able to do, and AERA, APA, and NCME *Standards* for testing and measurement. We looked at conceptual frameworks from the standard setters, as well as our own as authors. We then established standards as a road map for assessment design, bringing together content/pedagogical standards, accreditation standards, and measurement standards. Finally, we reviewed some of the pros and cons of various assessment options, including tests, products, performances, and assessments of impact on K–12 learning. We also described in some detail the importance of using job-related tasks in measuring teacher competence.

CAATS CHAPTER 1—ACTIVITY #1
What's Happening in Your State and School?

Explanation:

You can use the following questions to examine some important issues that will help frame the assessment design process. These questions should be addressed by school leaders.

1. Find out what legislative requirements, state mandates, and local research studies may impact accountability and teacher assessment in your state. What about your institution or school district? Make a list of sources and obtain a copy for your resource files.

2. Does your state, district, or college have competency-based standards that are required to help define the content? Are the competencies you have identified important enough to you to say that you would deny graduation or a continuing contract to a teacher whose competence is questionable?

3. Is there a union contract that will affect your work? How does it define assessment of teaching effectiveness? Does it require validity and reliability of the assessments?

4. What level of faculty and administrator awareness of, and support for, the assessment program can you expect? Make a list of persons and resources that will be available to help you build your program.

5. What level of faculty and administrator resistance or other constraints do you anticipate? What resistance can you identify to measuring competencies in your department? Make a list of persons and resource needs that will be problematic for your work.

6. How much time and energy do you want to spend on assessment?

CAATS CHAPTER 1—ACTIVITY #2

Questionnaire for Faculty Views on Competency Assessment

Explanation:

This is a questionnaire for all faculty in the unit or school. It will help identify strengths and weaknesses in terms of assessment and values about assessment.

1. Why should we measure competencies? What will be the purpose of our system?

2. Should we use the INTASC indicators as part of our system? Other standards?

3. What aspects of our conceptual framework or mission statement describe knowledge and skills? Do we want to assess them?

4. How will we use the data we collect? Will we deny a teacher a teaching license if we do not find that teacher has the competencies we value?

CAATS ACTIVITIES

CAATS CHAPTER 1—ACTIVITY #3
Assessment Belief Scale

Explanation:

You can use this scale to "take another assessment literacy check" in your school. If many faculty get low scores, assessment literacy is a problem that you will face throughout this process. Some staff or faculty development may be needed. Check out some of the writings of Rick Stiggins and Jim Popham on this topic. After you score yourself, tally the scores of the entire group. You may want to plan a discussion of the results.

We provide the scoring key here, but it should not be distributed to the faculty in advance!

Scoring Key

Agree: 2, 3, 4, 5, 6, 9, 10, 11

Disagree: 1, 7, 8, 12, 13, 14, 15, 16

Turn to next page to complete the survey.

CAATS CHAPTER 1—ACTIVITY #3
Beliefs About Assessment

Name: _____

Please decide if you agree or disagree with each of the following statements about assessment. Mark your answers as "A" for "agree" and "D" for "disagree."

1	A	D	Planning for instruction is more important than planning for assessment.
2	A	D	It's impossible to be a great teacher without formally and informally assessing student progress constantly as you teach.
3	A	D	Just about everyone has had the experience of taking a test with confusing or unfair items because teachers rarely analyze their tests.
4	A	D	The best teachers make their own assessments instead of using the ones that come with the book.
5	A	D	Even the most experienced teachers need rubrics to maintain scoring consistency.
6	A	D	It's virtually impossible for a teacher to plan a content valid assessment without using tables of specification, blueprints, or test grids.
7	A	D	The best use of portfolios is to showcase student work.
8	A	D	Good teachers believe that education would improve if we just threw away all tests and concentrated on instruction.
9	A	D	I am looking forward to measuring how much my students have learned.
10	A	D	If given a choice between spending my time on designing a lesson and writing an alternative assessment, I would spend my time on the assessment.
11	A	D	Assessment is one of the most rapidly developing areas of education and good teachers keep up with new developments.
12	A	D	Traditional tests should only be used to measure lower-level thinking.
13	A	D	Essays are easy to use and grade, so they should be used a lot.
14	A	D	I don't need to worry about all this accountability stuff; it's not my problem.
15	A	D	Tests are the best way to know what kids and teachers know.
16	A	D	Alternative assessments take too long to grade, so I don't like to use them.

CAATS ACTIVITIES

CAATS CHAPTER 1—ACTIVITY #4
Assessment Options

Explanation:

Conduct a focus group in your school or district. Discuss the strengths and weaknesses of each of the assessment options, and attempt to reach consensus on how useful the option is to you on a scale of 1 to 5, with 5 being critically important and 1 being useless.

#	*Assessment Option*	*Ratings*	*Discussion Notes*
1	Standardized tests	5 4 3 2 1	
2	Classroom or workshop tests	5 4 3 2 1	
3	Job-related teacher products such as lesson plans and classroom management plans	5 4 3 2 1	
4	Observations of performance	5 4 3 2 1	
5	Products showing K–12 learning and growth	5 4 3 2 1	
6	Portfolios for growth (reflection, learning, etc.)	5 4 3 2 1	
7	Portfolios for accountability	5 4 3 2 1	

2

Portfolios

To Be or Not to Be? That IS the Question!

$\mathcal{I}$n this chapter, we will discuss portfolios as assessment devices in some detail, since many colleges and school districts are relying heavily on portfolios as tools for decision making about teacher competence. Portfolios have many positive attributes, but their use as an accountability-based assessment method is questionable. We dedicate an entire chapter to this issue because it is so important and so often misunderstood. We begin with some research on the use of portfolios for assessment, followed by a discussion of a set of conflicting paradigms that we believe are at the root of the problem of portfolio misuse. We then turn to some ideas and a graphic model we have developed collaboratively with Helen Barrett of the University of Alaska that can help sort out the problems and solve them in terms of useful and appropriate assessment. We conclude this chapter with a set of caveats about portfolio use in assessment, a list of recommendations we have previously identified for assessment system design, and an introduction to the five-step design model that is the main subject of this book.

THE PORTFOLIO: PANACEA OR PANDORA'S BOX?

Portfolios, both paper and electronic, have become hot topics in standards-based performance assessment. Salzman, Denner, and Harris (2002) report that almost 90% of schools, colleges, and departments of education (SCDEs) use portfolios to make decisions about candidates, and almost 40% do so as a certification or licensure

---

AUTHORS' NOTE: Portions of this chapter were previously published as an article in *Education Policy Analysis Archives,* an open-access, refereed education journal available at http://epaa.asu.org.

Accountability portfolios

Accountability portfolios contain evidence collected to show that standards have been achieved or met. They are summative in nature and prepared more for the institution than for the individual's purposes and needs. The student may learn by compiling the portfolio, particularly through reflection, but that is not the ultimate purpose. The institution has to prove it is doing a good job!

Guiding Question: "What artifacts will help my institution prove I learned?"

requirement. These portfolios are called accountability portfolios. In our own study of teacher preparation programs in Florida, we found that virtually every institution in the state is using portfolios in some way to help make certification decisions (Wilkerson & Lang, 2003). In fact, portfolios seem to be viewed by many as the panacea of performance assessment. It is hard to go to national meetings without being greeted by software professionals who have designed electronic portfolio products that they claim will help SCDEs meet state and national standards for accreditation and program approval. The National Board certification model for certifying accomplished teachers has successfully implemented a portfolio assessment process, but it is an expensive undertaking designed for advanced teachers. It is not intended to measure minimal competency.

For many teacher educators, particularly those involved with initial certification, the jury is still out on portfolio assessment. Some have not yet reached a conclusion about whether to use portfolios for accountability purposes. Others are reconsidering this decision, having determined that the time involved for both faculty and candidates is excessive. Hence, there is a need to clarify the issues being raised nationwide. Much of this consternation is caused by a general confusion about the purposes of portfolios, with those being drawn to them for accountability thinking largely about showcase or growth portfolios. These two types of portfolios exist for different purposes and for good, but different, reasons.

Showcase portfolios

Showcase portfolios are used to share best work, so that creators can take pride in their accomplishments and/or showcase their work to parents or prospective employers.

Guiding Question: "What artifacts can I have my students assemble in a folder or computer file that will make them feel proud of themselves or impress someone else?"

As measurement professionals, we are frequently asked if portfolio assessment can be used as an appropriate and safe vehicle to make summative decisions in a certification context. Are they good measurement? Our answer is this: "No, unless the contents are rigorously controlled and systematically evaluated," as is the case in the National Board process. As Ingersoll and Scannell (2002) pointed out, portfolios are not assessments, but are instead collections of candidate artifacts that present examples of what candidates can do. The contents need to be evaluated individually as part of the candidate's overall performance record using a database format. Making them electronic does not change that fact and does not make them meet the requirements of any of the organizations or documents, cited in our previous chapter, that called for a consistent set of assessment evidence that is highly related to job performance.

Without proper attention to the psychometric requirements of sound assessment, teacher educators may find themselves on a slippery slope. SCDEs, school districts, and states have to make sure that assessment devices are created and used properly, and that costs time and money. Otherwise, they may make bad decisions and face legal complaints that can have severe consequences—expensive trials and court imposed interventions—not to mention institutional reputation and the potential for even more burdensome legislation and rules.

Looking at this issue from a different viewpoint, in medicine, society would not dream of allowing physicians to be licensed based on their own selection of showcased successes. We recognize that many critical failures could be hidden behind their selected portfolio entries, and such failures could certainly prevent them from being "safe" practitioners. Medical licensure requires the identification and systematic assessment of a solid set of skills. Pilots, too, must pass a series of carefully constructed performance tests. We do not want to fly on an airplane where we forgot to measure how safely the pilot could land the plane. Maybe a bump or two is okay, but bruised or dead bodies are not. Landing is part of minimal competence. Two bumps, three bumps, 20 bumps? One bruised passenger in hurricane-force winds?

> **Growth portfolios**
>
> Growth portfolios contain evidence collected over time so that users can determine if growth is as expected, greater than expected, or less than expected. They are formative in nature and help us determine next steps—keep going, change direction, remediate, quicken the pace.
>
> *Guiding Question: "What artifacts will help me track improvement over time?"*

In portfolio assessment systems that allow candidates to choose their own artifacts with limited guidance, minimal competency with regard to standards is difficult to establish. Such portfolios are useful, however, for showcasing work for job interviews or for demonstrating growth over time for self-assessment. Both also can be sources of pride and self-esteem. When used for accountability purposes, though, the growth or showcase portfolio results in just too many "test forms" to establish either validity or reliability. When faculty or school district administrators fail to adequately align the artifacts selected by teacher candidates with specific aspects of standards that define performance requirements, the range of material may preclude adequate standards-based decisions. When assessors fail to assess artifacts with solid, standards-based rubrics, it is difficult to interpret what their decisions mean and make appropriate inferences about what teachers know, can do, and believe.

PORTFOLIOS AS CERTIFICATION "TESTS": LESSONS FROM STANDARDS AND HISTORY

According to the definition of *tests* in the 1999 AERA, APA, and NCME *Standards for Educational and Psychological Testing*, forms of testing may include traditional multiple-choice tests, written essays, oral examinations, and more elaborate performance tasks. Hence, portfolios that are comprised of written reflections (a form of an essay) and products representative of the teacher candidate's skills and performance fall under a professionally acceptable definition of *test*. At another level, in a legal analysis of testing and certification issues, Pullin (2001), too, lumps together traditional tests and alternative assessments. Finally, the use of portfolios in high-stakes testing in states such as Georgia and Vermont lend further credibility to the classification of portfolios as a "test." Hence, even if one does not typically think about a portfolio as a test, the classification of portfolios as a test is appropriate.

When Vermont implemented its K–12 statewide portfolio assessment system in 1988 as the first attempt in the United States to use portfolio assessment as a cornerstone of a statewide assessment, the results in these areas were clear and strong. The studies by the RAND Corporation and the Center for Research on Evaluation,

Standards, and Student Testing—CRESST (Koretz, 1994)—clearly indicated that teachers thought that portfolios were helpful as informal classroom assessment tools but that they, too, were worried about their use for external assessment purposes. The majority of teachers surveyed agreed or strongly agreed that portfolios help students monitor their own progress. However, the vast majority did not believe it would be fair to evaluate students on the basis of their portfolio scores.

Questions about using portfolios in high-stakes assessments have also been raised in the teacher certification arena. The Georgia Teacher Performance Assessment Instrument (TPAI), initiated in 1980, included a portfolio component and an observational component as an interview. The TPAI was initially success-fully challenged by a teacher (Kitchens) for the validity of its observational com-ponent, which was found to include behaviors that were difficult to measure (e.g., enthusiasm). However, in the aftermath of the Kitchens case, the opposition to TPAI that grew was around the portfolio process, which was again found to be far too time consuming for a beginning teacher and not a valid measure of teacher performance because the portfolios were being judged on the basis of form rather than substance. The $5,000,000 "mammoth measurement tool" was laid to rest (McGinty, 1996).

Despite findings such as these, though, portfolios continue to be a major compo-nent of teacher assessment systems in SCDEs. The American Association of Colleges of Teacher Education (AACTE) conducted a survey of member institutions in fall 2001 (Salzman, et al., 2002) on teacher education outcomes measures. The pur-pose of the study was to identify and describe what SCDEs are doing to meet the requirements for outcomes assessment for unit accreditation and program approval (teacher certification). They concluded that institutions are responding to more rigorous standards and to national and state mandates for accountability through multiple types of outcome measures, including portfolios. Results from the 370 responding institutions indicated that portfolios are used as an outcome measure by 319 (87.9%) of the responding institutions. Responses further indicated that 64 (20.1% of the institutions) do so in response to a state mandate while 269 (84.3%) do so as part of an institutional mandate. Portfolios were noted as required for certifi-cation or licensure by 123 (38.6%) institutions and not required by 159 (49.8%) for licensure. Data were missing from 37 (11.6%) of the respondents. Most units (305 or 95.6%) reported that the portfolio requirements were developed by the unit.

There is a school of thought that advocates strongly for portfolios. *With Portfolio in Hand*, edited by Nona Lyons (1998), contains several important chapters advocat-ing for portfolios. Even in these chapters, the caveats exist. For example, although Moss proposes that validity issues related to assessment of teaching be rethought to allow for the benefits of portfolio assessment, she concludes with suggestions from classical measurement theory. On the one hand, she proposes an integrative or hermeneutic approach to portfolio assessment in which raters engage in a dialogue to reach consensus about ratings, but she acknowledges that this is a time-consuming approach for which substantial empirical work is needed to explore both the possi-bilities and limitations. Even with this proposed new approach, Moss acknowledges the need to ensure the relevance, representativeness, and/or criticality of the per-formances and criteria as well as job-relatedness, social consequence studies, lack of bias, reliability, and most other aspects of psychometrics. Dollase (1998), while advocating for portfolios in teacher certification, also acknowledges the severity of the issue of time in terms of the "doability" of the approach.

ASSESSMENT ILLITERACY, PARADIGM SHIFTS, AND CONFLICTING PURPOSES

Most U.S. colleges of education are experiencing some difficulty in sorting out how to build their assessment systems. School districts are faced with state statutes demanding performance-based accountability. Why is this so? At present, it appears that colleges of education nationwide are baffled by the great mystery of validity. As we travel from institution to institution and from state to state, we find consistent blank stares when we ask if anyone has considered validity. The validity problem in teacher assessment begins with a common confusion about assessment purpose.

Stiggins and Popham have both eloquently and repeatedly described the state of assessment illiteracy in this country (Popham, 2004; Stiggins, 1998, 2000). We, too, believe that this helps to explain the consternation. We add to that our concern about conflicting paradigms—not just paradigm shifts, but conflict, particularly about purpose.

The paradigmatic shift from process to performance or results, as exhibited in most national, regional, state, and professional standards-setting agencies, has caused the need for different approaches to the accreditation review process. Most accreditation agencies and legislatures are now looking for evidence of the achievement of student learning outcomes and improvement resulting from institutionally diagnosed deficiencies. This is true at the regional level in Southern Association of Colleges and Schools (SACS, 2001), which uses the outcomes and quality enhancement terminology. It is even in the title of their Standards—*Principles of Accreditation: Foundations for Quality Enhancement.* Others may vary their language and style, but the message is clear. In the business, engineering, nursing, and other professional accreditation agencies, the requirement for outcomes and improvement is also applied. Syllabi are reviewed, but results and growth drive the process.

It is the conflicting paradigms, however, that make the shift all the more difficult. We have identified five sources of conflict, each of which we will discuss briefly in the following subsections of this chapter. We list them first in Box 2.1.

Box 2.1. Five Conflicting Paradigms for Assessment

1. Formative vs. summative assessment

2. Program approval vs. accreditation

3. Regulatory vs. professional perspectives

4. Freedom vs. accountability

5. Constructivism vs. positivism

The Conflict of Formative vs. Summative Assessment

Formative assessment or evaluation, by definition, occurs during a program for the purpose of modifying and improving results based on data while learning is

Formative assessments

Formative assessments are used primarily to conduct a kind of status check during which we make decisions about what immediate improvements in instruction are needed so that our students can achieve our goals better.
They occur during instruction and may be formal or informal, traditional or alternative in nature.

Guiding Question: "How can we track students' growth in ways that allow us to help them learn what they missed?"

occurring. Summative assessment or evaluation occurs at the end to make a final decision about learning or some other attribute.

On the one hand, we need to make summative decisions about teacher candidates in order for them to graduate and be certified. But is everything needed for graduation also needed for certification, and does everything need to be a demonstration of teacher standards? No and again no. We also need to make decisions that will establish a path for continued growth and reflective analysis of our successes and challenges. These twists and turns in how we view the use of each assessment lead to different decisions about the formative or summative nature of the assessment. So, many of our important assessments have both a formative and a summative purpose. These purposes can be in conflict with each other and can cause confusion and disruption among the faculty as they select the assessments that become a part of their assessment system for accreditation and program approval purposes. Add to that, as a summative decision, when children are at stake, the results must be highly positive—perfect, if possible, for the children's sake. However, from a formative perspective, improvement is not possible if everything is perfect.

Most faculty and district personnel, living in the world of their own courses and workshops, see rather routine tasks as summative in nature, because they result in a record of participation (grade or staff development credits of some sort), even though the task provides little information about the potential for the teacher to perform well on the job in job-related tasks after certification. Diaries, journals, research article critiques, original research papers, and even micro-teaching events are typical examples of these graded events in college-based programs that are summative for the purpose of course completion and formative for the purpose of teaching.

When assessment designers have to choose the tasks they want in their assessment systems, they experience the conflict of having to make the formative vs. summative decision. If the task is formative for certification and licensure, they often feel that their contribution to the unit is weakened. This is not true, but the perception that it is true makes it a difficult reality that needs to be faced in designing assessment systems driven by purpose and use.

Summative assessments

Summative assessments help us draw conclusions about what students actually learned from our instruction. Summative assessment occurs after instruction has concluded and is typically formal but can be either traditional or alternative in nature.

Guiding Question: "Did students learn what we taught?"

On the staff development side in the districts, trainers are brought in to conduct workshops, which are often disconnected. The products from these workshops may be summative for the workshop but may not be conceptualized as part of a system or process designed to assess how much the teacher can actually do as it relates to specific job requirements. In Box 2.2, we present our recommendation on how to manage this conflict.

> **Box 2.2. Recommendation Regarding the Conflict of Formative vs. Summative Assessment**
>
> Acknowledge that an individual assessment may be formative for one purpose but summative for another. Usage dictates the decision. Both are important. Resist the temptation to denigrate formative assessment. Develop assessment systems that make appropriate and balanced use of both forms of assessment, with formative assessment providing diagnostic support for summative assessments.

The Conflict of Program Approval vs. Accreditation

Colleges of education need to respond to accreditation and approval requirements that are based on different purposes, and these purposes often remain undifferentiated. School districts in some states are now also being required to seek approval of their alternative certification programs. School boards provide their own set of pressures and expectations that can be similar to those of accreditation agencies. As consultants, we have seen this for years in Florida and other states. Deans and faculty talk about "NCATE" and mean both the national accreditation agency and the state's department of education. There are NCATE Coordinators, not NCATE/DOE Coordinators, here and elsewhere, and this can be a schizophrenic job.

State departments of education approve programs so that colleges of education and school districts have some say in the certification or licensure decision about their program completers. From that perspective, the college or district must certify a level of minimum competence on the part of the candidate in its shared role with the state in protecting the public from unqualified practitioners (AERA, et al., 1999; Wilkerson & Lang, 2003). This dictates a yes/no decision, where everything that is important is okay. Improvement is not the goal; protection is. State expectations focus on the consistency of teacher qualifications.

Accreditors want candidates to be proficient, but there is no requirement that every graduate be acceptable to the accreditation agency. NCATE conceptual frameworks focus on the unique aspects of graduates of an accredited program. For accreditation, colleges need data to show that (1) most candidates demonstrate proficiencies or learning outcomes and (2) that the data provide measures of performance leading to the potential for improvement and growth. The local state department of education, too, wants improvement, but the focus is far more on the individual graduate. So, on the one hand, candidates need to have a perfect record for certification (state's view), but on the other, there needs to be room for growth so that they, and their institution, can improve (NCATE's need). While both types of agencies review results for teachers on the same or similar sets of teaching standards, they look at them through a different lens because their purposes are different. Parallels to this at the district level are limited.

Making the situation even more complex, college faculties do not want to think about minimal competence, because, by virtue or human nature, they want to believe they are preparing teachers better than anyone else, especially districts using alternative routes. District personnel similarly have difficulty in aiming for minimal competence in a world where *every* teacher must be "highly qualified" even if it is their first day in the classroom. The NCATE conceptual framework and years of defining vision and purpose for other institutional and accreditation purposes feed this value, just as the law does for districts. Thinking about graduation and licensure requirements focused on minimal qualifications and protection of the public is, to put it bluntly, distasteful, if not politically dangerous. However, the AERA, APA, and NCME *Standards* make it clear that in credentialing decisions, job-related competency is precisely the role that assessment needs to play. Perhaps the crisis cited by the National Commission on Teaching and America's Future (NCTAF) and others who worry about the failures of American schooling is a direct result of failing to focus on the measurement of minimum competence, as defined by the agreed-upon details of good teaching.

Despite these differences in purpose, colleges often attempt to meet both sets of requirements with the same data housed in the same containers, typically in a portfolio (often electronic) of teacher-selected work. The conflicting paradigms of ensuring minimal competence (protecting the public from unqualified practitioners) from the state perspective, preparing unique practitioners from the NCATE perspectives, and ensuring highly qualified teachers from the national perspective create a potential validity conflict. The model of the reflective portfolio of self-selected evidence is then emulated in some school districts, where practitioners learned the technique in the colleges in which they studied.

Both of these conflicting paradigms—formative vs. summative evaluation and program approval vs. accreditation, then, result in the same issue—perfect but imperfect at the same time. In Box 2.3 we present our recommendation on how to manage this conflict.

Box 2.3.   Recommendation Regarding the Conflict of Program Approval vs. Certification

Acknowledge that state certification and program approval decisions are based on minimal competence and sameness while accreditation decisions focus on improvement and uniqueness.

Acknowledge that these two decisions require a different visualization of the teacher—one who gets by and one who excels. Develop assessment systems that make appropriate and balanced use of both visions. The data in these systems need to be aggregated to yield two sets of data, as appropriate to the accreditation/approval decision. This may require that some criteria in a rubric contribute to one decision and some to the other, or it could be that some tasks are in one system and others in another, or that there are different levels of proficiency identified in summative task or program completion decisions (different cut scores), or some other strategy. One way or another, some data will show "individual candidate perfection" and other data will show need for "candidate and program growth."

The Conflict of Regulatory vs. Professional Perspectives

This conflict is possibly the "quiet killer" in the set of assessment issues faced by teacher education programs housed in colleges and districts. The business community, which influences and serves in the legislatures, is driven by a different personal/ professional perspective or ethic than the one they are requiring of the educational community. As the world of Deming, Baldrige, and the Carnegie Foundation (Lunce, Lunce, & Maniam, 2002) invade college campuses and school districts, the focus on quality improvement and the challenges in schooling improvement and striving to be better reign supreme in an objective and economic reality. And so they should if one reads *A Nation at Risk* (National Commission on Excellence in Education, 1983). But in the world of legislative control of education, the "highly qualified" mandates require that all teachers exceed the standard of minimal competency. In testing, both K–12 and teacher training, meeting the standard can generate rewards; not meeting the standard can generate punishments. More money, graduation, and recognition vs. reduced funds, nonpromotion, and ignominy prevail. Passing the test or meeting Title II requirements are the target. Students and schools are graded and accredited.

Hence the conflict within business and legislators coming from business backgrounds is both internal (within themselves) and external (in the schools where the requirements are realized.) What the business community really expects and what the teachers really want is the improvement model, but what they are requiring is the minimal competency model, because no one wants to admit that some teachers are less than ideal or that any child could be left behind. If we do not admit that some are better than others, however, we never find the data we need to improve the system. Instead, the public schools learn to cheat so everyone can pass and create the Lake Wobegon Effect (Cannell, 1989). We teach to the test, we eliminate students from reports, or, worse, we cause exceptional education children to struggle in inappropriate ways. A parallel version of cheating is now pervasive in higher education.

Linacre (2004) provides a useful graphic representation of the true business model from Lele and Sheth (1991), which he then applies to educational measurement in Figures 2.1 and 2.2.

In business, we know who the customers are, but in education we often confuse ourselves about the customers. If we give the customer candidates all A's, how does that impact the customer children? If we design our items to maximize the variable, some of the customer candidates will do less well than other customer candidates

Figure 2.1. Six Key Characteristics of "Winning" Businesses

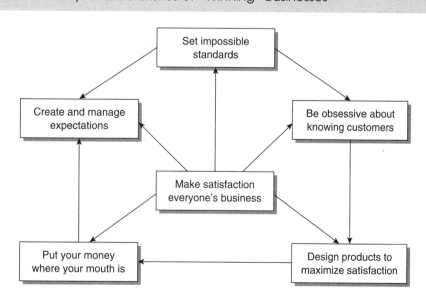

SOURCE: Redrawn from Figure 3.1, Lele & Sheth (1991).

Figure 2.2. Six Key Characteristics of "Winning" Measurement Projects

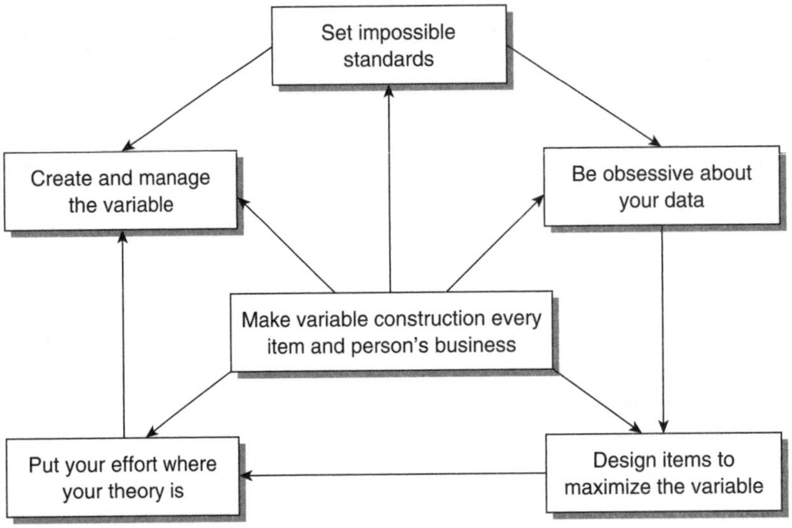

SOURCE: Lele & Sheth (1991).

and be less satisfied, and will we find ways to improve our product to meet the needs of the business/legislative mandates?

We can compare these graphics with one used during NCATE Board of Examiner Training (Gollnick, 2006) in Figure 2.3, an example of data aggregation on internship evaluation as part of our thinking about setting (or not setting) impossible standards.

Note that almost everyone meets the standard; variability is minimal; opportunities for improvement are hard to find. The data clearly fit the competency model,

Figure 2.3. NCATE Training Example of Aggregated Data

Sample Internship Evaluation Results				
	Focused Attention Needed	*Progressing Toward Expectations*	*Meets Expectations*	*Exceeds Expectations*
Professional Responsibility			100%	
Understanding Learners	2%	5%	93%	
Command of Subject Matter			98%	2%
Teaching Practice		3%	93%	4%
Classroom Management	1%	4%	95%	
Technology		7%	88%	5%
Community and Professional Involvement		2%	98%	

but not the program improvement model, although the purpose here is improvement and not just documentation of competency. The standard is clearly not "impossible to achieve," as in the business model. As we think about teachers in the schools, we ask ourselves, is this reflective of our general impression of all the teachers we see? Probably not, but, for Title II purposes, it works well. For the external business community looking at what we do, from their seats on the Board of Trustees or in the State Legislature, they reflect on their own experiences with weak teachers of their own children and see us as self-aggrandizing or having lost touch with reality. In Box 2.4, we present our recommendation on how to manage this conflict.

> **Box 2.4. Recommendation Regarding the Conflict of Regulatory vs. Professional Perspectives**
>
> Acknowledge that standards represent ideal expectations. Without high standards individuals and groups can become complacent, failing to "shoot for the stars." Perfection is an ideal and not a reality. Set impossible standards to allow for growth, and develop educational assessment systems that "live" in the real business world of Total Quality Management (TQM). Encourage the identification of differences between the best, the average, and the worst need, so that improvement can thrive.

The Conflict of Freedom vs. Accountability

In this book, we describe a five-step model for designing assessment systems that calls for the identification and evaluation of critical, job-related tasks. The model suggests that faculty and school district personnel acknowledge that not everything they do is critical for making a certification decision, even if it is critical to good instruction and learning the material they teach. This observation is linked to what we noted in the first conflict—formative vs. summative assessments. We will suggest later in this book the use of common task formats with a common rubric format and scale for summative assessments. Finally, we will suggest that, where appropriate and feasible, assessment designers create and use an overall ability scale, using item response theory, to create useful data for improvement purposes to help address the second and third conflicts, both of which really converge into a conflict over perfectionism vs. acceptance of (or even welcoming) imperfection. Use of such a task-based system requires that faculty sacrifice a small amount of their freedom and agree to work for the common good as part of a larger team making a collective judgment about teacher candidate ability.

The clear conflict in paradigms here is whether faculty should or can be asked to do something in the same way as their colleagues. Academic freedom would say no; accountability would say yes. If two or three faculty cannot even agree on a common textbook, will they agree on a common assessment task and a common format?

This causes the institution to grapple with some difficult questions about where academic freedom applies and where it does not. Faculty have become used to accepting the number of credit hours and scheduling of their courses; they agree to annual review and performance appraisal processes; they often agree to departmental syllabi and district curricula for accreditation purposes. Much will depend on the strength and credibility of academic leadership in the unit. In some institutions, this may be the easiest conflict to resolve; in others, it is a Rock of Sisyphus that brings each faculty discussion to a screeching halt. In Box 2.5 we present our recommendation on how to manage this conflict.

> ### Box 2.5. Recommendation Regarding the Conflict of Freedom vs. Accountability
>
> Acknowledge that all freedom has its limits. We cannot drive 100 mph or commit murder. Freedom needs to be limited when it affects the common good. Common rubrics and formats are like speed limits; they are necessary for safety. If the assessment system is designed to certify teachers, the "common good" is defined by what protects and helps children the most. Develop assessment systems that lead toward valid and reliable decisions about teacher competency; common rubrics and formats make that possible.

The Conflict of Constructivism vs. Positivism

Paulson and Paulson (1994) outlined the differences between constructivism and positivism in terms of assessment of teacher candidates more than 10 years ago. Their focus was on portfolios, but the comparison helps to bring meaning to some of the other conflicts discussed above. They defined the two types of portfolios and the differences between them as follows:

> *Positivist portfolio:* "The purpose of the portfolio is to assess learning outcomes and those outcomes are, generally, defined externally. Positivism assumes that meaning is constant across users, contexts, and purposes . . . The portfolio is a receptacle for examples of student work used to infer what and how much learning has occurred." (p. 36)

> *Constructivist portfolio:* "The portfolio is a learning environment in which the learner constructs meaning. It assumes that meaning varies across individuals, over time, and with purpose. The portfolio presents a process, a record of the processes associated with learning itself; a summation of individual portfolios would be too complex for normative description." (p. 36)

Paulson and Paulson (1994) concluded that there are critical differences (and tensions) between these two approaches. While the positivist approach puts a premium on the selection of items that reflect outside standards and interests, the constructivist approach puts a premium on the selection of items that reflect learning from the student's perspective.

Beyond those differences, and in terms of the conflicts we have identified earlier, we conclude the following:

- Teacher education institutions need to meet both of these purposes because of licensure/certification requirements, the need to demonstrate candidates' potential for continued growth and development, and the need to collect data for program improvement—all of which are consistent with the purposes outlined by the National Research Council. (2001)

- The positivist approach has the following characteristics:
  - It is more geared toward summative evaluation, program approval, accountability, and program improvement.
  - It is useful for licensure or certification because there is a requirement that learning be held constant, providing a common core against which

demonstration of required competencies can be measured. There is a common data set, each piece of which can be scored separately with a rubric established for a final decision about competence. This helps to establish minimal competency that makes the practitioner "safe to teach." It defines "the floor below which teacher candidates cannot fall."

- For accountability purposes, there must be externally driven feedback from an instructor that the standard or competency for which the artifact is intended to serve as evidence was indeed successfully demonstrated. Such feedback is best provided through a scoring instrument or rubric, with a decision about proficiency reached

- Because it is not the showcase personal portfolio of self-selected works, candidates can more readily accept the inclusion of artifacts that are not perfect, understanding that the use here is to identify areas for program growth to help their successors in the program. The reflective process is controlled to identify these areas of improvement, which are standards-based and prescribed.

- The burden of proof and decision making rests with the faculty.

- The constructivist approach has the following characteristics:

  - It works well for showcasing, for formative evaluation and continued learning by individual candidates, for accreditation focused on continuous improvement, for the business ethic of setting high standards, and for establishing freedom for both students and faculty.

  - It also allows for a self-directed reflective process that incorporates plans for growth and establishes a mindset that such plans are important. Data aggregation at the unit level for program improvement is not necessary. Candidates learn to celebrate their successes and identify for themselves the places in which they choose to grow.

  - The burden of proof and decision making rests with the teacher and/or is shared with the faculty.

It has become important that we learn to differentiate between at least three types of portfolios, so that institutions can choose the model or models best suited to their needs and conceptual frameworks:

- Student-centered portfolios in which candidates demonstrate deep learning and showcase their work. E-portfolios work best; but paper portfolios still work.

- Institution-centered portfolios in which candidates provide required documentation of competency, the results of which are reported as aggregated data at the task level and across tasks at a "portfolio" level. Again e-portfolios work best; but paper portfolios still work, especially in smaller institutions.

- Data management systems, including institutional portfolios, showing the results of assessments (aggregated data) with samples of candidate work for demonstration purposes.

To provide for the level of freedom and data collection implied by these three types of portfolios, we propose the use of three different systems that work together, as illustrated in Figure 2.4, originally developed by Helen Barrett.

Figure 2.4. Assessment Systems and Electronic Portfolios: Balancing Accountability and Learning

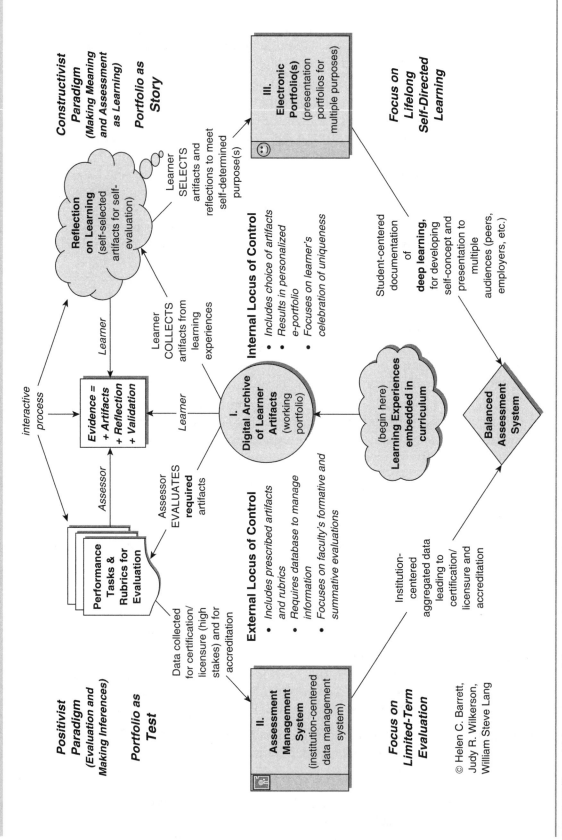

Positivist Paradigm (Evaluation and Making Inferences)

Portfolio as Test

Constructivist Paradigm (Making Meaning and Assessment as Learning)

Portfolio as Story

Reflection on Learning (self-selected artifacts for self-evaluation)

Learner SELECTS artifacts and reflections to meet self-determined purpose(s)

III. **Electronic Portfolio(s)** (presentation portfolios for multiple purposes)

Focus on Lifelong Self-Directed Learning

interactive process

Learner

Evidence = + Artifacts + Reflection + Validation

Learner COLLECTS artifacts from learning experiences

Internal Locus of Control
- Includes choice of artifacts
- Results in personalized e-portfolio
- Focuses on learner's celebration of uniqueness

Student-centered documentation of **deep learning,** for developing self-concept and presentation to multiple audiences (peers, employers, etc.)

Assessor

Learner

Assessor EVALUATES required artifacts

I. **Digital Archive of Learner Artifacts** (working portfolio)

(begin here) **Learning Experiences embedded in curriculum**

Balanced Assessment System

Performance Tasks & Rubrics for Evaluation

Data collected for certification/licensure (high stakes) and for accreditation

External Locus of Control
- Includes prescribed artifacts and rubrics
- Requires database to manage information
- Focuses on faculty's formative and summative evaluations

Institution-centered aggregated data leading to certification/licensure and accreditation

II. **Assessment Management System** (institution-centered data management system)

Focus on Limited-Term Evaluation

© Helen C. Barrett, Judy R. Wilkerson, William Steve Lang

SOURCE: http://electronicportfolios.org/systems/balanced.htm

NOTE: This is copied directly from the original

- An archive, preferably digital, of learners' work

- A learner-centered portfolio, preferably electronic, "using the learner's authentic voice"

- An institution-centered database and archive of selected student work to collect faculty-generated assessment data based on tasks and rubrics

Looking at this concept map at the bottom center of the graphic, we begin with learning and assessment experiences that are embedded in the curriculum. Those experiences should produce work that can be stored in an archive of artifacts that is often called a *working portfolio.*

On the left side of the graphic, the positivist paradigm of evaluation and making inferences, or the "Portfolio as Test," is described. This is the model we have previously presented. The artifacts in the archive (the required tasks in the assessment system) are evaluated by an assessor, based on the performance tasks and rubrics. These data are collected for certification or licensure and sampled for accreditation or program approval. The results are stored in the assessment management system, which is an institution- or district-centered data management system. In colleges, an institutional portfolio can be created from this archive. This process results in aggregated data leading to certification or licensure for the individual teacher and supports program evaluation as well. The focus of this process in on more limited-term evaluation, with an external locus of control which:

- Includes prescribed artifacts and rubrics.

- Requires a database to manage information.

- Focuses on assessor's summative evaluations.

- May include reflections written by teachers for purposes other than accountability (i.e., demonstration of learning and/or growth).

On the right side of the graphic, the constructivist paradigm of making meaning and assessment as learning, or the "Portfolio as Story," as described by Paulson and Paulson, is presented. The artifacts in the archive are collected from the learning experiences. Through the process of reflecting on his or her own learning, the teacher selects artifacts and reflection for self-evaluation based on self-determined purposes. The process results in teacher-centered documentation of deep learning, for developing self-concept, and presentation to multiple audiences (e.g., peers or employers). The focus of this process is on continuous, self-directed learning, with an internal locus of control which:

- Includes choice of artifacts.

- Results in personalized portfolio.

- Focuses on learner's celebration of uniqueness and growth.

- Includes reflections to document and explain growth.

In Box 2.6 we present our recommendation on how to handle this conflict.

> **Box 2.6. Recommendation Regarding Conflict of Constructivism vs. Positivism**
>
> Acknowledge that portfolios are only useful when the purpose and process match. Like all good assessment, there are varying approaches to design, and there is nothing wrong with using more than one design. Develop assessment systems that make appropriate uses of portfolio assessment, using highly structured portfolios for accountability and reflective portfolios for showcasing and growth. The accountability portfolio needs to be accompanied by a data management system and rigorous structure. The reflective portfolio does not do so. Both can be collected in an all-encompassing working portfolio, which is easily managed with currently available software.

In this section, we summarized five conflicting paradigms and provided a recommendation to help resolve each conflict at the end of the relevant discussion. In total, there were five recommendations for the five conflicts. We now continue with a set of eight recommendations that expand on this last recommendation regarding portfolios. After that, we will provide one more set of 10 recommendations—for assessment design in general—and we conclude this chapter with our proposed solution for implementing all of these recommendations (all 23 of them!) with our five-step assessment system design model—the real subject of this book and the next five chapters. We tell you this now, so that you know some solutions are on the way!

RECOMMENDATIONS FOR USE OF PORTFOLIOS IN ACCOUNTABILITY CONTEXTS

By way of summary of the issues we have raised regarding portfolios, we continue with an overarching set of 10 recommendations for both colleges and districts that decide to implement an assessment system that includes accountability portfolios (Wilkerson & Lang, 2003). We have organized these recommendations in the form of requirements for tests and caveats for portfolios, as shown in Table 2.1 (on the page opposite).

TEN RECOMMENDATIONS FOR ASSESSMENT SYSTEM DESIGN

Having looked at portfolios in some depth and all of the requirements for developing assessment systems, it is time to summarize with some specific recommendations for assessment system design and then introduce the model that comprises the remainder of this book. Based on our analysis of the field, and most particularly the *Standards for Educational and Psychological Testing* (AERA, et al., 1999), which define the requirements for good assessment, we have previously offered (Wilkerson & Lang, 2003) the following list of 10 recommendations.

1. *Identify the construct to be measured.* In this case, the *Standards* provide an example of a construct as "performance as a computer technician." This can easily be converted for teacher educators as "performance as a teacher." (Chapter 1, p. 9, Validity)

#	*Requirement for Tests*	*Caveats for Portfolios*
	Table 2.1. Recommendations for Portfolios Used as Tests	
1	The knowledge and skills to be demonstrated in the portfolio/test must be essential in nature. They must represent important work behaviors that are job related and be authentic representations of what teachers do in the real world of work.	If the portfolio is used as a test itself containing new or original work created outside of courses and workshops, rather than just a container of evidence of course-embedded tasks, the portfolio must stand the test that it is job related and authentic. The SCDE or district should be prepared to defend how portfolio preparation as a stand-alone activity is a critical job function that teachers perform on a routine basis, similar to lesson planning, communication with students and parents, assessment, teaching critical thinking skills, etc. In the case of electronic portfolios, if the product is used to demonstrate a standard or expectation on technology that relates to using technology in the classroom, the SCDE or district will need to justify that the preparation of the portfolio is equivalent to what teachers do with technology in the classroom. This may be difficult from an authenticity perspective.
2	The entire portfolio/test (assessment system) must meet the criteria of representativeness, relevance, and proportionality.	If the portfolio is a container of evidence used as a summative assessment for the certification/graduation decision, the SCDE or district must be prepared to defend the contents of portfolios submitted by all teachers or teacher candidates for the representativeness, relevance, and proportionality of contents against the requirements of the teaching profession, e.g., the standards being assessed from national and state agencies, as well as the institution itself (conceptual framework). If the portfolio is a specific piece of evidence itself, then its place within the assessment system must be included in the analysis of representativeness, relevance, and proportionality. All criteria used to evaluate the portfolio must be relevant to the job. Criteria such as neatness and organization are particularly suspect, unless they can be directly tied to the potential for poor performance in the classroom. The SCDE or district will need to prove that sloppy or disorganized teachers cannot be effective teachers.
3	There must be adequate procedures and written documents used to provide notice to candidates of the requirements, the appeals process, and the design (fairness) of the appeals process.	The SCDE or district must have adequate documentation in place that tells teachers how and when to prepare the portfolio, how it will be reviewed, who is allowed to help them and how much help they can receive, the consequences of failure and the opportunities for remediation, and what their due process rights and procedures are if they wish to challenge the review results.

(Continued)

(Continued)

#	Requirement for Tests	Caveats for Portfolios
4	There must be adequate instructional opportunities provided to candidates to succeed in meeting the requirements of the portfolio/test and to remediate when performance is inadequate.	The SCDE or district should embed portfolio preparation, including the contents of the portfolio, into its instructional program (i.e., coursework or workshops). Any requirements outside of the program could be subjected to a claim based on instructional/curricular validity. The entire team needs to buy into and support portfolio preparation activities and provide remedial opportunities for components that are found lacking.
5	There must be a realistic cut score for determining if the performance is acceptable. This cut score must differentiate between those who are competent to enter the profession and those who are not.	This is the most difficult aspect of portfolio design. The SCDE or district will need to identify the specific score or characteristics that sort teachers into the dichotomous categories of competent and not competent based on their portfolios.
6	Alternatives must be provided to teachers or teacher candidates who cannot successfully complete requirements, or the SCDE or district must be able to demonstrate why no alternatives exist.	If the portfolio is a container of evidence, the alternatives must relate to specific pieces of evidence. The SCDE or district must ensure, however, that alternatives do not detract from the representativeness, relevancy, and proportionality criteria. If the portfolio is used as evidence of a specific standard, such as reflection, then an equivalent alternative should be identified if at all possible.
7	The results of the portfolio evaluation (scoring) and the extent to which protected populations are equally or disproportionately successful must be monitored.	If the SCDE or district finds that a disproportionate number of protected populations (minorities, handicapped, women) do not successfully complete the portfolio assessment process, the SCDE or district must prepare to defend its use of the portfolio in terms of all of the above requirements 1 through 6 and show why no alternatives exist or are offered to the protected classes.
8	The process must be implemented and monitored to ensure reliable scoring and to provide for adequate candidate support.	Tests of reliability must be performed and samples of candidate work and faculty scoring must be reviewed on a regular basis to ensure that procedures and scoring are not "drifting" and to minimize measurement error. Raters need to be trained and updated on a regular basis. Directions need to be clear. Portfolios across candidates need to be comparable in difficulty. Rater mood and fatigue need to be carefully monitored. Safeguards against cheating need to be implemented. The sufficiency of items in the portfolio must be adequate. Records should also be kept of all exceptions made, alternatives provided, due process proceedings, and faculty/candidate training.

SOURCE: Wilkerson and Lang (2003).

2. *Define the purpose.* Chapter 14 describes the requirements for credentialing. If the teacher preparation unit or the school district is advising the state on whether or not to license or certify, then this chapter applies. The *Standards* clarify that credentialing decisions are valid when they protect the public from unqualified practitioners, which then becomes the purpose. (Chapter 1, Validity)

3. *Determine the use.* Institutions and districts need to decide if they will deny graduation or long-term certification to a teacher candidate based on the results of the assessment. Some states require this use; others do not require such a high-stakes decision. Districts need to determine whether they will fire a teacher based on the results of the assessment. In Florida, this is required. (Chapter 1, Validity)

4. *Identify the measurable conceptual framework.* Both NCATE and the *Standards* refer to observation of knowledge, skills, and dispositions when discussing a conceptual framework, so the framework can be all the teacher standards that define competency in these three categories. (Chapter 1, Validity)

5. *Develop a blueprint or framework to guide the design process.* Chapter 3 clarifies the need to build an assessment system, like any test, based on the domains to be measured—the conceptual framework. This is the reverse of what most teacher preparation institutions and districts do. They start with what they have and hope it fits. (Chapter 3, Test Development and Revision)

6. *Keep checking validity—both construct and content.* Ensure that the system being built measures teacher performance through job-related tasks (construct validity). Also show evidence that the set of assessments adequately represents the most important elements of the domains to be measured—with not too much and not too little and nothing irrelevant targeted for any given standard (content validity). Look for confirmation that the tasks are both critical and authentic. (Chapter 1, Validity)

7. *Build assessments that can be studied for internal consistency.* Rater agreement is important, but so are other sources of measurement error. A common scale on various tasks may help provide an adequate number of "items" to check for reliability. (Chapter 2, Reliability)

8. *Develop systems to ensure fairness toward all those candidates assessed.* This includes the policies and procedures to implement and monitor the system, specified checks for bias in the way tasks are written, and differential results for protected populations. (Chapters 7 to 10 on Fairness in Testing)

9. *Check the consequences of the decisions.* Show evidence that (1) remediation attempts are appropriate and (2) the decisions made reduce to a minimum the number of poor teachers being certified ("false positives") and the number of good teachers being excluded ("false negatives"). (Chapter 1, Validity)

10. *Build it once, and revise it.* Many institutions attempt to build parallel systems for each individual set of the many sets of standards to which they are held accountable. This is less of a problem for districts. Institutions should align the standards from the beginning and develop a single system to measure all of the standards. The system may aggregate branches or tracks to fit multiple purposes, but all standards and all purposes should be considered at one time. Districts will need to consider multiple assessment systems within their staff development areas. The certification system should be correlated with, and

lead naturally to, the induction program. Then revise based on experience; changes in standards; changes in institutional/district mission/programs; and/or problems identified related to validity, reliability, and fairness. (Chapter 3, Test Development and Revision)

A RECOMMENDED, STANDARDS-BASED MODEL

There is no magic number of assessments that will make for a good assessment system. While there is extensive discussion in the accreditation and measurement literature about the need for multiple measures, the term *multiple* is left open to one's imagination. NCATE's recent attempt to provide relief to institutions attempting to meet standards documents from specialty professional associations that number 100 to 150 pages each would lead one to the conclusion that about seven is enough. If, on the other hand, one listens to the AERA, APA, and NCME *Standards*, which say that the number is defined by a job analysis, then it becomes important to determine what knowledge and how many skills a teacher needs to have to be effective. With that decision made, one then needs to turn to how these skills can be combined into assessment tasks that can be successfully completed by teachers and consistently evaluated by assessors. Whether or not this can be accomplished in an average of seven assessments can only be determined by how extensive those individual assessments are and how many mini-assessments are embedded within the seven big ones. In the section on K–12 student work samples in Chapter 1, we provided two examples of how many small tasks can be merged into a series of comprehensive tasks that could become a thematic portfolio.

Ingersoll and Scannell (2002) advocate for a continuous system of assessment in which assessment data are collected throughout a teacher's training program and then stored in a database for easy retrieval and use. The authors of the INTASC Core Standards also promote assessments during the program and during an internship. The set of thematic portfolios might provide for a good balance between the new NCATE SPA process and the important advice from Ingersoll and Scannell. Our primary advice to readers is to use as many assessments as they need to do the job—no more, no less—regardless of whether they are based in colleges or districts.

Where we differ from the Ingersoll and Scannell recommendations, however, is the source of the assessments. They begin with an analysis of curriculum; we begin with an analysis of the job. They allow for a wide variety of assessment formats; we advocate for a single format that leads to a scale. Neither approach is right or wrong. The choice is based on several factors:

- Perceived need to adhere to AERA, APA, and NCME *Standards*
- Primary context of the system—credentialing vs. improvement
- Ability to lead and manage the data collectors (faculty and district personnel)

In Chapters 3 through 7, we will describe an approach we have built in Florida that is task based and developed from a job analysis. It is offered as a model so that readers can visualize a product emerging from the approach we recommend. An overview of the model follows.

OVERVIEW OF COMPETENCY ASSESSMENTS ALIGNED WITH TEACHER STANDARDS (CAATS) MODEL

The CAATS model consists of five steps. They are less linear than they appear, since designers constantly need to revisit the systems they are building. Ideas change; standards change; people change.

CAATS Step 1: Define Purpose, Use, Propositions, Content, and Other Contextual Factors

In this step, designers begin by determining why they need an assessment system (assessment purpose), the decisions they will need to make (use), what givens underlie their work (propositions), and what they want to know (assessment content). Each purpose and use is conceptualized and evaluated separately as a matter of validity. At the end of this step, designers analyze all the local factors that would affect the system (e.g., conceptual framework, resources, faculty resistance/cooperation), since these factors can impede or help them in their work.

CAATS Step 2: Develop a Valid Sampling Plan

A critical next step is the identification of all relevant standards and the alignment of standards with each other into content domains. This is the beginning of the job analysis, and common threads that run through all of the sets of standards are identified and aligned. When considered together, as a kind of content domain or a set of content domains, one can clearly see the similarities and differences between and among the perceptions of what is important from each group of professionals. To the extent possible, the identified standards should be expressed in taxonomies or frameworks and *not* by the institution's crosswalk of courses with standards.

Designers should also develop a condensed version of the standards, or critical skills, to be used by the institution as part of its conceptual framework. Next, faculty members should visualize the competent teacher performing the critical skills and the standard, brainstorm a series of product and performance-based tasks that the teacher must do to demonstrate the skills, and then sort the tasks into formative and summative so that only the most important tasks remain in the decision-making structure. Once the list is complete, a series of design frameworks can be used to ensure that the list provides for a balanced and appropriate sampling plan that will lead to valid inferences about teacher competency in a way that is feasible for the college or district.

CAATS Step 3: Create or Update Tasks Aligned With Standards and Consistent With the Sampling Plan

A common format for all tasks is recommended in order to make data aggregation across tasks easier. Clear directions and rubrics need to be written, preferably with a common rating scale that includes an equal number of points on the scale. Then evidence of content validity should be gathered to ensure that the tasks are representative of the construct and its conceptual framework, proportional, and in fact job-related. This evidence should be gathered through analyses at multiple levels (tasks, criteria, and decision rules) by internal and external experts (stakeholders or expert judge panels). Evidence that adequate instruction is provided for each task needs to be gathered.

CAATS Step 4: Design and Implement Data Aggregation, Tracking, and Management Systems

The data must be accumulated and managed for decision making, so decisions need to be made about how this will be done and what the standards for minimal competency (cut score) should be. Other levels of competency may also be considered, but this is optional. Tracking systems, record keeping, and other procedural details are necessary to do this.

Consensus around the system needs to be built and supported. Reward systems could include anything that makes faculty or other assessors more amenable to the accountability requirements. A maintenance program is necessary and should be created to include training of assessors, collection of scored examples showing different levels of proficiency, orientation of teachers being assessed, alternative strategies or tasks for teachers who need them, advising materials (including due process), and an appeals process. Formal review times to update and improve the tasks and the system should be established in advance. Identified people or committees responsible for data collection in a timely and regular fashion are also important for the valid implementation of the system.

CAATS Step 5: Ensure Credibility and Utility of Data

There are increasing calls for ensuring the credibility of assessments, including validity, reliability, and fairness. Assessment designers should make use of the *Standards for Educational and Psychological Testing* (AERA, et al., 1999), including blueprints; a focus on job-relatedness; and evidence of validity (particularly content validity), reliability, and fairness. Judgmental as well as empirical data should be gathered.

V̇ WRAP-UP

In the first chapter, we provided the overview of assessment design, outlining the major components or methods that can be used in an assessment system—records of training completed, tests and exams, observations of performance, portfolios, job-related tasks, K–12 students work samples, and dispositional measures. We noted some pros and cons of using each, particularly as the single or predominant method, and we advocated for using a combination of these methods.

In this chapter we focused on portfolios, introducing five paradigmatic conflicts that cause tension in the assessment world: formative vs. summative evaluation, program approval vs. accreditation, business or legislative personal/professional perspectives vs. accountability through Title II requirements, faculty academic freedom vs. accountability, and constructivism vs. positivism. We made recommendations about how to address each conflict. We provided a graphical model of how to think about two types of portfolios—one for accountability to meet institutional or district needs and one for growth to meet individual teacher needs—and we suggested eight caveats and requirements for those who use portfolios for accountability purposes.

We then presented 10 recommendations for assessment system design based on our understanding of the measurement standards. We ended with an overview of the CAATS model, which will be the subject of the next five chapters—Chapters 3 through 7.

A Note About Chapters 8 and 9

Before moving on to the model itself in the next five chapters, we need to tell you one more thing that you will soon discover (or may have already discovered). Among the most important things you will need to decide is how you will sort out those teacher candidates who should be certified and those who should not. Some folks call this a cut score; some call it standard setting. This can be a complex issue, but we have tried to make it a simple one in the CAATS model. To understand our approach and rationale, you may need to read a user-friendly chapter on this topic. We have included such a chapter (Chapter 8) after the chapters describing the five steps of the model. That helps us to avoid interrupting our flow with too many technical details.

The same is true about *psychometric integrity* (validity, reliability, and fairness). We will need to have a measurement model to use to generate the numbers we decide to use. You will see that we advocate for the Rasch model of item response theory as the best approach. As with cut scores, we have provided a technical chapter addressing the basics of the Rasch model after the CAATS steps—Chapter 9.

For both cut scores and Rasch, we encourage you *not* to be totally sequential in your reading. Get a feel for what is in Chapters 8 and 9, so you will know when best to refer to them. The best time to read them in some depth will depend on your needs and interests, but we think that they should help you most with Chapters 6 and 7 on CAATS Steps 4 and 5.

CAATS CHAPTER 2—ACTIVITY #1
Review Your Feelings

Explanation:

Go back to the questionnaire you completed in Chapter 1. Have any of your feelings changed based on your reading of this chapter? Record your new thoughts below.

_____

_____

_____

_____

_____

_____

_____

_____

_____

_____

_____

_____

_____

CAATS CHAPTER 2—ACTIVITY #2

Thinking About Conflicting Paradigms

Answer each of the following questions alone. Compare your answers with those of your colleagues.

1. Examine one assessment to which you are particularly attached. Argue for it as formative and then summative. Which argument do you think is stronger?

2. Identify one thing you expect your teachers to do because it is standards related and critically important for a minimally competent teacher. Identify something else your teachers do that helps define them as different from teachers from other programs or districts.

3. Identify one thing that you think only an initially certified teacher who is truly exceptional could do well that other teachers could not do well.

4. Argue for and against all faculty and workshop personnel using the same rubric format in terms of the price of freedom.

5. In your mind, what is the most important purpose a portfolio can serve? How does that relate to accountability—same or different?

CAATS CHAPTER 2—ACTIVITY #3
Getting Your Action Plan Started

Explanation:

It's time to get the big picture planning process started. This activity will introduce you to the steps of the CAATS model. Use it as an advance organizer. Fill in the details of this plan *as you read the remaining chapters of this book.* Each chapter is a step in the model. You also will have a set of worksheets provided at the end of each chapter to help you chart your course. The plan below provides you with an introduction to the details of the model.

For now, who are your key players? What committees and groups will be involved? What are the critical deadlines for the college, accreditation agency, district, and/or state that will drive the details of this plan?

Coordinator: _____

Committee(s): _____

_____

_____

_____

Critical Deadlines: _____

Please refer to the chart opposite.

Step	Activity/Action	Personnel	Target Date
Step 1: Define purpose, use, propositions, content, and other contextual factors.			
A. Define the purpose(s) and use(s) of the system.			
B. Define the propositions of the system.			
C. Define the conceptual framework or content of the system.			
D. Review local factors that impact the system.			
Step 2: Develop a valid sampling plan.			
A. Organize standards into content domains.			
B. Visualize the minimally competent teacher			
C. Brainstorm summative tasks.			
D. Sort out formative tasks from summative tasks.			
E. Build assessment frameworks.			
Step 3: Create or update tasks aligned with standards and consistent with the sampling plan.			
A. Determine the task format for data aggregation.			
B. Create new tasks or modify existing tasks.			
C. Conduct first validity study.			
D. Align tasks with instruction.			
Step 4: Design and implement data tracking and management systems.			
A. Determine how data will be aggregated.			
B. Set the standards for minimal competency.			
C. Select and develop a tracking system.			
D. Develop implementation procedures and materials.			
Step 5: Ensure credibility and utility of data.			
A. Create a plan to test for validity, reliability, and fairness on a regular basis.			
B. Implement the plan.			

In the last chapter, we presented an overview of the five steps of our design model for building assessment systems. We call the model "Competency Assessment Aligned with Teacher Standards," or CAATS. We laid the groundwork for the model in terms of the national call for accountability and creativity in teacher assessment and a series of conflicting paradigms that have called into question the use of portfolios in an accountability context. We established a variety of recommendations that we will now follow in the next five chapters, each of which describes one step in the CAATS model.

The first chapter of this series, and the four that follow it, will each present one step of the model and some worksheets to help you implement the model at your institution or school district. As you no doubt noticed, there was an Action Plan at the end of Chapter 2 to help you with broad planning. You may want to keep filling in that plan to lay out your actions, personnel, and timelines, progressing through these five chapters.

Ingersoll and Scannell (2002) use the words *truthfulness* and *trustworthiness* of data to describe validity and reliability. If, as ethical practitioners, we recognize the utility of these descriptors, then it becomes incumbent on us to try to gather evidence of validity and reliability in appropriate ways. We will discuss some options for how to do this both judgmentally and empirically in the chapter on CAATS Step 5. For now, suffice it to say that we are setting you up for success in CAATS Step 5, and we are beginning that process in the chapter on CAATS Step 1. We are on the path to psychometric integrity, and we begin by defining why and what we are assessing in our own local contexts.

3

CAATS Step 1

Assessment Design Inputs

*I*n order to start the design process of assessing teacher competence in a way that is likely to yield valid and useful results, it is important to analyze relevant inputs. Of course, standards will be high on the list! At this critical step in the design process, we consider lessons learned in our previous chapters in order to make informed decisions about the inputs.

All assessment processes and instruments are only as good as their utility for making necessary decisions. Assessment design, therefore, begins with a clear articulation of the reason(s) or purpose(s) of the assessment and the anticipated results or use(s) of the data we hope to obtain. After all, if we don't have a clear vision of why we are assessing or what we will do with the results, we are wasting a lot of time and energy on a useless process. We all have certain beliefs about teaching and assessment, and those beliefs need to be articulated and agreed on in the form of propositions to avoid misunderstandings and conflicts as we progress through the process. We then need to ensure that we collect the right data and enough of it to serve the purpose and use the results for effective decision making in accordance with our values about what is important and how it can be measured. We do that by

> **CAATS Step 1: Define purpose, use, propositions, content, and other contextual factors.**

deciding what content (including standards) we will embed in our assessment system. We need to plan in advance what we really want to know about teachers and how we will eventually use the scores in our system. Our planning efforts need to be conducted based on our own strengths, weaknesses, resources, and barriers—our own context. The more complex or important (high stakes) the use of the assessment, the more planning we need to do. This is the essence of CAATS Step 1. Without a clear understanding of these fundamental conceptual inputs to the assessment system, progress can be hindered.

Consider the glossary definitions and questions throughout this chapter to guide your work in this step, where we will do four things. Each is a substep of CAATS Step 1.

CAATS Step 1A: Define the purpose(s) and use(s) of the system.

CAATS Step 1B: Define the propositions or principles that guide the system.

CAATS Step 1C: Define the conceptual framework or content(s) of the system.

CAATS Step 1D: Review local factors that impact the system.

Before Moving On . . .

1. Since you are reading this book, you probably expect to use the assessment system to make decisions about certification or progression in a teacher's career. Correct? Do you want to do more? If so, jot down some ideas about what you want from this system.

2. Do you believe that teachers should be denied certification or lose their jobs if they do not have the vital skills needed for teaching? If yes, what are some of those skills? If not, why not?

3. On a scale of 1 to 10 with 10 being high, how important is assessment? Justify your answer.

4. Everyone has an expected troublemaker. In your department, who (or what) are you most worried about when you think about assessing teachers? Who (or what) will be your greatest help? How will you combat the evil and profit from the good?

5. Think back over your career and/or schooling and remember an experience you had when you were unclear why you had to do something. You couldn't figure out the purpose or how what you did would affect you. How did you feel?

6. Define *highly qualified* for initial certification teachers and accomplished teachers. How can you tell the difference?

\V

CAATS STEP 1A: DEFINE THE PURPOSE(S) AND USE(S) OF THE SYSTEM

The Importance of Purpose and Use

In this model, we will use *purpose* as the reason we create an assessment or an assessment process—the end and not the means. Remember our question from above: "Why are we assessing teachers?" Purpose drives everything else, including how we use the data for decision making and, consequently, the extent to which we worry about issues like validity. This fundamental importance of purpose holds true no matter what kind of assessment we are designing—whether it is the kind of assessment we do in a K–20 classroom or the kind of assessment we use for making decisions about licensure or gaining national accreditation. As obvious as this seems to be, it is surprising that there are so many K–20 teachers who miss this simple concept, but that is why so many children come home from school frustrated and crying, "Mom, I don't know what the teacher wants or why I have to do this or if it will count for my grade and hurt me." It is also why so many college students gather in college corridors and dorms uttering similar complaints.

By beginning with purpose and use, we begin to construct an assessment system that meets standard of validity. The other parts of this step, especially pro-positions and content, add to the validity standards, but purpose and use are at the core of validity. A long time ago, you probably memorized the statement that, "A test must be valid for the purpose for which it is intended." As you watch schools being graded based on state tests that were intended to diagnose student learning, you may be thinking about that timeless definition with some nostalgia!

As the importance of our instruments increases in terms of uses for decision making (i.e., high-stakes decisions such as counseling out of a program or firing), so does the importance of making sure we are measuring the right things in the right ways (i.e., interpreting our results or scores correctly and for the right purpose). We can be less concerned or rigorous in terms of valid-ity about an informal observation used only for coun-seling than we should be about an evaluation of the teacher's skill in managing a classroom used for a deci-sion about certification or licensure.

> ### Competency
> We use the word competency in this book to mean knowledge and skills—Bloom's cognitive domain. Competency may be defined differently by various groups. Competency, as assessed for certification, can be at a minimal level or restricted to subject matter knowledge, while competency for career advancement (e.g., NBPTS or promotion) can be at a much higher level.
>
> *Guiding Question: "What does the teacher need to know and be able to do?"*

> ### Purpose
> The purpose is the reason for establishing an assessment system. It is the end, not the means.
>
> *Guiding Question: "Why are we assessing our teachers?"*

Different Strokes for Different Folks for Different Purposes

From the outset, we need to think about the wide variety of purposes that can exist in an assessment design. Some will be more important than others, and we are not limited to having just one purpose. We will have choices about the types of assessment methods, and these choices will be governed by purpose and use. Among the choices are formative or summative assessments, informal or formal assessments, showcase or growth portfolios, and accountability assessments. It is important to under-stand some of the differences.

Purpose and Use in the Accountability Context

The more complex or important the assessment, the more planning we need to do and the more types of assessments we may chose to use. The selection will vary based on our assessment purpose.

> ### Content
> The content is the set of topics or matter with which we are going to work. Content includes, at a minimum, the standards for teaching—institutional or district, state, and national. The content defines precisely what material will be assessed and requires good sampling procedures once defined.
>
> *Guiding Question: "What will we assess?"*

In Table 3.1, we align some assessment purposes with appropriate types of assessment, scoring requirements, and possibilities for use. These, too, serve as a backdrop for our work on competency assessment aligned with teacher standards. To become accustomed to thinking about the relationships of assessment type, purpose, and use, we provide the following set of examples. The purpose and use also dictate decisions about assessment methods, scoring procedures, and the eventual output. It is useful to begin thinking about the assessment instruments even at this early stage, and this is modeled in Table 3.1.

Type	Sample Purpose	Use	Possible Methods	Scoring	Output
Table 3.1. Making Various Assessment Types Work in Practice					
Formative for knowledge of skills (informal and formal)	Quick check of understanding	Adjust instruction for the class	Informal: Observations, informal activities, homework; Formal: quiz	Check for specific behavior or completion and/or score and provide informal feedback— no grades	Informal: Notes or comments; Formal: Checklist of early progress
Formative for attitudes (informal and formal)	Quick check of motivation	Adjust instruction or work with an individual child	Informal: Observation of class demeanor; Formal: Survey, self-report, interview	Keep track mentally; score but don't grade	Informal: Discussions; Formal: Intervention report
Summative	Ensure learning	Remediate if necessary but hope to continue with next unit	Test or project	Scoring key or rubric for a grade	Aggregated raw scores or standard scores
Growth	Prepare for continuing growth	Plan next steps together	Reflective portfolio	Scoring rubric or qualitative feedback	Progress chart or gain score
Showcase	Impress parents or employers	Show others	Showcase portfolio	None	Discussions
Accountability	Ensure competence for entry into the teaching profession	Make a credentialing decision	Tests, products and performances, dispositional measures	Scoring keys and rubrics	Test scores, performance ratings, or standard scores

In accountability contexts (the purpose of this book), sometimes we want to make decisions only about individual teachers; other times we want to look at the results for many teachers in a group (program or school). Typically, when we are looking for decisions at the individual level, we hope for the opportunity to diagnose and remediate. At the group level, however, the focus may be on assuring that we are "on track" and finding and fixing programmatic aspects that are not as good as expected for the benefit of future teachers. These purposes have different implications for how we structure the assessment, data aggregation, and decision-making processes.

> ### Use
>
> The use of the system is the decision or set of decisions to be made about teachers. It defines what will be done with the data collected.
>
> *Guiding Question: "What decisions will we make with our data?"*

Some purposes for assessing competencies within the accountability context, then, are as follows:

- Certify or license a teacher
- Ensure a common set of knowledge and skills in a population (e.g., reflective practice)
- Improve the performance of individual teachers
- Improve teacher training
- Maximize children's opportunities to learn from competent teachers
- Receive national accreditation
- Encourage teachers to seek National Board certification

The main assessment system purpose for most teacher educators (college or district-based) is most likely to be certification or licensure. This carries with it the need to identify candidates or alternative certification teachers with knowledge- and skill-based problems that could impact their role with children and consequently the children's opportunities to learn. In Box 3.1 is an example of a purpose statement that is typical for certification or licensure decisions. It can be used for assessors making such a decision, either in colleges of education or school districts. You could write other purpose statements, as modeled in Boxes 3.2 and 3.3, for anything on the list above, or anything else, for that matter, but remember, as the purpose varies, so do the use, assessment method, and scoring procedures.

Box 3.1. Sample Statement of Purpose #1

To protect the public from unqualified practitioners by determining whether the teachers assessed have demonstrated the essential competencies (knowledge and skills), as defined in the standards of _____. These competencies are necessary for safe and appropriate practice and certification in the State of _____.

In the context of continuing professional development, a different purpose might drive the system—one of teacher improvement at the individual level. Box 3.2 provides an example for that purpose.

Box 3.2. Sample Statement of Purpose #2

To assist each teacher to acquire an increasing level of knowledge and skills in both the essential competencies (knowledge and skills) of the State of ___ and the mission of _____ District. These competencies are necessary for high-performing educators in this district who can reflect on their own performance and make maximum use of the knowledge and skills acquired.

The uses of the data are likely to include decisions about both candidates or teachers and about program quality. In terms of candidate or teacher evaluation, assessors need to decide if they will deny graduation to a candidate or let go a teacher who repeatedly demonstrates cognitive deficits. In consideration of program evaluation, the assessors can also use the data as a self-check when the data are aggregated in ways that allow assessors to pinpoint areas in which they can improve programs. A third purpose is provided in Box 3.3.

Box 3.3. Sample Statement of Purpose #3

To identify program areas that can be improved in order to better train teachers.

Some examples of how data can be used and how a statement about use can be written are provided in Boxes 3.4 and 3.5.

Box 3.4. Sample Data Uses: Decisions About . . .

- Entry into the profession (i.e., graduation and licensure)
- Advising or remediation based on individual weaknesses only (i.e., an individual professional development plan)
- Continuation or advancement in the profession (e.g., rehire, promotion, or merit raise)
- Improvement of program structure (e.g., more focus on reflection)
- Compliance with accreditation requirements (e.g., NCATE)

Box 3.5. Sample Statement of Use

Aggregated data are used to determine, in part, if teachers are eligible to graduate and/or to receive the state certificate or license (or to continue employment in the district). Additional licensure requirements required for the licensure decision include a grade point average of ___, a passing score on the state certification exam, and a background clearance check conducted by the state Department of Law Enforcement.

In this context, if the usage decision does include the possibility of denying graduation or rehire, then the assessment developers need to spend much more time on designing their system to ensure that it has psychometric integrity, which includes the many faces of validity (of which social consequences is but one). Step 5 of the CAATS model will be particularly important to these users. For those who only intend to provide informal feedback to teachers, then the low-stakes nature of the system allows for much slack in its design. By making the usage decision early in the process, assessors have the opportunity to think about how comprehensive their approach should be.

More on Accountability-Based Systems: State Program Approval

Some of our freedoms are limited by the purpose of the system and how we have to use the data for decision making. So, carefully thinking about how we will use the data for decision making is critically important. The starting point for defining purpose and use in the system for state approval is with the context of credentialing within the state. The context will also define some of the characteristics of the system. The two predominant contexts are outlined in Table 3.2.

Table 3.2. Contexts in the State System for Certification			
Context of System	*Purpose of System*	*Use of System*	*Characteristics of System*
Context #1: State has total control of certification—little to no reliance on SCDEs or districts	Check learning and gather information for improvement	Program completion and improvement	Fluid, much use of formative data, less need for rigorous structure and common tasks
Context #2: State has given significant control to SCDEs and districts to determine qualifications for credentialing	Protect the public from unqualified practitioners	Allow teacher to graduate/complete or not—a cut score required	Rigid, requires summative data and consistent tasks and structure

In this book, we will be describing a model that is most useful for the second context in which the state has delegated part of its authority to credential (license or certify) teachers to the trainers, whether they be district based or college based. In such scenarios, the results of the program are combined with a certification exam and a background check for the license or certificate to be granted. The certification exam could be state developed or from a testing company (e.g., ETS's Praxis). The status of the teacher as a program completer indicates to the licensing authority that if the completer has demonstrated the knowledge and/or skills needed to teach in that state, and given positive results in other requirements (e.g., the test and background check), the completer should be granted the license or certificate. The state values what the trainers have confirmed.

In this scenario (row 2 of Table 3.2), we maintain that a rigid structure of summative tasks is needed to ensure the quality of the data (validity, reliability, and fairness issues). This is not to say that a system with much fluidity cannot coexist with the rigid system. This is very much the subject of our chapter on portfolios and conflicting paradigms (Chapter 2). These two systems simply serve different purposes, are used differently, and have different content and characteristics. It does mean, though, that the fluid system cannot exist alone. The decisions about "safe to teach based on standards" and "likely to be successful based on program/district values" are different, and they are likely to be based on different data. Examples are provided in Table 3.3.

Table 3.3. Examples of What We Can Say About a Teacher in a Data-Based Decision-Making Process		
Decision	*Statement About Teacher*	*Data Source*
Decision #1—"safe to teach based on standards"	"This teacher has demonstrated all of the standards and is competent to teach in this state/district."	Completion of required tests and tasks (including both products and observations), which could be housed in an accountability portfolio
Decision #2—"likely to be successful based on our values" (or consistent with INTASC dispositions)	"This teacher is likely to be a lifelong learner or committed to social justice or an ethical/reflective practitioner."	Completion of reflective portfolio with reflection or dispositions measures
Decision #3—"likely to be successful based on values that are consistent with INTASC Principles"	"This teacher values the standards-based skills required of good teachers and is likely to use what s/he has learned."	Completion of disposition assessment instruments

Note that, as we have previously stated in our portfolio chapter, there can be overlap between the data sources. There can be reflections in the tasks, and some of the tasks can be in the portfolio. Even the tasks used for Decision #1 could be housed in a portfolio after being assessed by faculty, but this would not be a self-selected portfolio assessed all at once for the first time.

AERA, APA, and NCME (1999) *Standards*
and CAATS Step 1A

Standard 1.2:

The test developer should set forth clearly how test scores are intended to be interpreted and used. The population(s) for which a test is appropriate should be clearly delimited, and the construct that the test is intended to assess should be clearly described.
   CAATS Steps Influenced: 1A, 1C, 1D, 3A

Standard 1.23:

When a test use or score interpretation is recommended on the grounds that testing or the testing program per se will result in some indirect benefit in addition to the utility of information from the test scores themselves, *the rationale for anticipating the indirect benefit should be made explicitly.* Logical or theoretical arguments and empirical evidence for the indirect benefit should be provided. Due weight should be given to any contradictory findings in the scientific literature, including findings suggesting important indirect outcomes other than those predicted.
   CAATS Steps Influenced: 1A

Standard 3.2:

The purpose(s) of the test, definition of the domain, and the test specifications should be stated clearly so that judgments can be made about the appropriateness of the defined domain for the stated purpose(s) of the test and about the relation of items to the dimensions of the domain they are intended to represent.
   CAATS Steps Influenced: 1A, 1C, 2E, 5A

Standard 13.1:

When educational testing programs are mandated by school, district, state, or other authorities, the ways in which test results are intended to be used should be clearly described. It is the responsibility of those who mandate the use of tests to monitor their impact and to identify and minimize potential negative consequences. Consequences resulting from the uses of the test, both intended and unintended, should also be examined by the test user.
   CAATS Steps Influenced: 1A, 5A

Discussion

These *Standards* give some flavor of the importance of clear statements about purpose and use in the psychometric requirements. Note that in Standard 1.23, the thrust is on indirect benefit. We connect that to the continuous improvement purpose often associated with this type of assessment system and required for NCATE accreditation and the quality improvement mission in many districts.

NOTE: Emphases added for clarity.

Proposition

Propositions are what we believe to be true that influence the way we will develop the assessment system. They are the agreed-upon givens we hold to be self-evident. They are based on our values and beliefs about teaching and assessment.

Guiding Question: "What are the fundamental truths about teaching and assessment that guide our thinking?"

CAATS STEP 1B: DEFINE THE PROPOSITIONS OR PRINCIPLES THAT GUIDE THE SYSTEM

It is hard to imagine or identify the teacher who has not written a statement of philosophy at one point in his or her training or career. Values clarification is a starting point for much of our work. In assessment design, such clarification is again a starting point. Here, we will call it *propositions* or principles that guide the system. These statements are what we believe to be true and therefore guide what we are willing to do.

Examples of the types of propositions that might guide a standards-based competency assessment system are included in Box 3.6.

Box 3.6. Sample Propositions

- Certain competencies (knowledge and skills) are critical to effective teaching.
- These competencies can be identified and measured.
- National standards and local missions and values serve as a baseline for these competencies.
- Measures of competency can be developed based on the standards identified and appropriate test construction theories.
- Teachers who have demonstrated competency on the measures are likely to be better teachers, who can have a higher impact on K–12 learning.
- Teachers who have not demonstrated competency on the measures are likely to be poorer teachers who may cause harm to children.
- Different assessment processes and data are needed for different decisions.

The *Standards* do not include a specific standard on propositions, but the need for creating and using propositions is contained in the narrative explanation of validity with the statement outlined in the Standards Box on the opposite page.

CAATS STEP 1C: DEFINE THE CONCEPTUAL FRAMEWORK OR CONTENT(S) OF THE SYSTEM

So What Is Assessment Content?

In this context, we will use "content" to mean the information we want to obtain from the assessment system—the set of topics or matter with which we are going to work. Since this is a standards-based process, the standards are obviously the starting point for content. Identifying the relevant standards and then sampling from them is the crux of the system.

AERA, APA, and NCME (1999) *Standards*

Discussion of Propositions Relevant to CAATS Step 1B

The decision about what types of evidence are important for validation in each instance can be clarified by developing a *set of propositions* that support the proposed interpretation for the particular purpose of testing. For instance, when a mathematics achievement test is used to assess readiness for an advanced course, evidence for the following propositions might be deemed necessary: (a) *that certain skills are prerequisite* for the advanced course; (b) that the *content domain of the test is consistent with these prerequisite skills;* (c) that test scores can be generalized across relevant sets of items; (d) that test scores are not unduly influenced by ancillary variables such as writing ability; (e) *that success in the advanced course can be validly assessed;* and (f) *that examinees with high scores on the test will be more successful in the advance course than examinees with low scores on the test* . . . The validation process evolves as these propositions are articulated and evidence is gathered to evaluate their soundness. (pp. 9–10)

Discussion

Examples from the discussion of propositions from AERA, APA, and NCME served as a basis for the examples we created above.

NOTE: Emphases added for clarity.

As we think about the standards and any other sources of content, it is also useful to begin thinking about how to classify the content to ensure adequate sampling. Some things are prerequisite to others in most taxonomies, so this will help us achieve a balanced and appropriate set of assessment tasks to measure our content. Equally important is continuing our thinking about assessment methods, so that we can begin to visualize the types of assessment instruments we will have in our system. So, in this substep of the CAATS model, we define our conceptual framework based on the content we will require and the taxonomies we will use to analyze it for assessment system design. The inputs here, then, are standards and taxonomies, and these will result in the need for specific assessment methods, just as purpose and use influence them.

NCATE Standard 1 clearly provides us with one very useful classification system or taxonomy, and it is consistent with those used in theory. NCATE makes use of the INTASC Principles (standards) and classifies teacher requirements as knowledge, skills, and dispositions. We will address dispositions in our work on DAATS (Disposition Assessments Aligned with Teacher Standards)—a parallel five-step design model (Wilkerson & Lang, in press), but we mention it here in terms of the overall taxonomy.

The focus on knowledge, skills, and dispositions correlates well with Bloom's taxonomy in the cognitive (knowledge and skills) and affective (dispositions) domains. As useful as Bloom's taxonomy is, though, there are other taxonomies that help us think about teacher competency and the requisite assessment methods. The Stiggins (1998) taxonomy, for example, is more "assessment-ready" than the Bloom (Bloom & Krathwohl, 1956) domain levels. In Table 3.4, we provide an alignment of various taxonomies and note the assessment methods that fit each type.

As each of these important types of information about what teachers need to know, be able to do, and believe is operationally defined and classified in Step 2 of the process, the assessment system begins to come together. We will use frameworks to help us get there so that we have balance and coverage in our system.

Table 3.4.	Information Types, Taxonomic Classifications, and Assessment Methods			
Type of Information	*General Examples*	*Specific Examples*	*Taxonomies*	*Assessment Methods*
Knowledge	Facts, principles, theories, concepts	Definition of iambic pentameter; the list of the elements and requirements for an effective lesson	Bloom's cognitive domain—lower level thinking (knowledge and comprehension) Gagne's verbal information Stiggins's knowledge and simple understanding	Tests: Selected and constructed response
Skills	Applications of knowledge (higher order thinking in Bloom's cognitive domain)	An original poem in iambic pentameter; an original unit plan on poetry	Bloom's cognitive domain—lower level thinking (application, analysis, evaluation, synthesis) Torrance and Williams's critical thinking. Gagne's intellectual skills Stiggins's deep reasoning, products, and skills	Tests Authentic tasks—both products and performances
Dispositions	Values, attitudes, beliefs	Attitude toward mathematics (including anxiety); belief that all children can learn and should be given equal opportunity to do so	Bloom's and Stiggins's affective domain	Observations Self-reports
Psychomotor Skills	Skills that require the use of actions or movement	Piano recital of Chopin's Raindrop Prelude; basketball game.	Bloom's psychomotor Stiggins's skills Gagne's motor skills	Performance tasks

Standards as the Link Between Purpose, Use, and Content

It is time to begin thinking about the details of what we will assess—the specific knowledge and skills we will use to define the construct of teacher performance. A preliminary step that can prevent much worry and aggravation later is to identify all the content-related inputs into the system. Since this is a standards-based system, it makes sense to start with the standards as our beginning for defining content. While we do not have to determine precisely how we will measure the selected content at this point (that is part of Step 2 of the CAATS model), we already know the general types of assessment methods we will use. Now we add to that the standards that form our inputs and get a general sense of their scope. We also need to think about the relationships between external standards and internal values and beliefs (the local conceptual framework or mission).

When we described the conceptual framework in the previous chapter and talked about defining the construct and its content, this is what we had in mind. At its most simplistic level, the construct is teacher performance, with the content articulated in the INTASC Principles.

The required standards will vary, depending first and foremost on the state in which the institution or district is located. Since the ultimate purpose of the assessments in most states is to ensure competence leading to the awarding of a professional teaching certificate or license (a teaching credential), then the tasks have to be designed in such a way as to ensure that the teacher can teach the way the state expects and what the state expects K–12 students to learn.

In some states, such as Wisconsin, there are state-developed standards for competencies. Other states rely on the national standards exclusively. National standards include not only the INTASC Principles but also standards from the specialty professional associations affiliated with NCATE, such as the National Council for Teachers of English, Association for Childhood International, and Council for Exceptional Children, etc. Twenty sets of SPA standards are now aligned with the INTASC Principles, and many states have also aligned their standards with INTASC. NBPTS, too, has defined a set of Core Principles that are related to the INTASC Principles.

As part of the accreditation process in colleges and as part of the day-to-day human resource function of many school districts, locally defined competencies (or a conceptual framework) have also been developed. In these cases, it is hard to imagine a set of locally defined competencies that are not highly correlated with the national standards. Planning, assessment, classroom management, and learning environment, diversity, and so forth, are always in there somewhere!

So, standards can be drawn from a number of sources, as listed in Box 3.7.

Box 3.7.   Sources of Standards

- INTASC Principles or NBPTS Standards
- National professional association standards
- State standards for teachers and for children
- College conceptual framework
- District standards or mission
- School mission and values statement

Whether institutions and districts choose standards or mission-based competencies, the specific indicators of those competencies need to be clearly set forth. The INTASC knowledge and performance indicators, like the Standards of the National Board of Professional Teaching Standards, are a sufficient set for those standards. However, locally defined values, such as social justice, would need to be operationally defined in terms of indicators or behaviors that can be observed as the basis for instrument development. If faculty cannot visualize what a teacher exhibiting the competency looks like, then it cannot be measured. For example, how is a "lifelong learner" visible unless one follows the graduate for a lifetime?

Let's start putting purpose, use, and content together. Table 3.5 aligns some common purposes with potential uses and content at the standards level.

| Table 3.5. Aligning Purpose, Use, and Content in a Standards-Based Context |||
Purpose	*Use*	*Content*
Certify or license a teacher	Decision about acceptance or denial of entry into the profession via program completion (traditional or alternative routes)	Standards on the certification exam (e.g., INTASC Principles or state teacher competencies)
Ensure a common set of knowledge and skills in a population (e.g., reflective practice)	Decisions about program structure (e.g., course content, sequence, and grades/credits)	Locally defined unit/district standards (e.g., conceptual framework, goals, or mission)
Improve the performance of teachers	Decisions about strengths and weaknesses of individual teachers related to eligibility to continue in program or job	Mastery or performance standards or goals for an individual or a group (e.g., individual remediation plan or performance appraisal system)
Improve teacher training	Decisions about strengths and weaknesses of programs to identify needs for program changes	Objectives or standards for a course or training materials
Maximize children's opportunities to learn from competent teachers	Decisions about effect of teacher training on K–12 student achievement	State K–12 standards
Receive national accreditation	Decisions about compliance with standards	Accreditation standards
Encourage teachers to seek NBPTS certification	Decisions about support structures (training, release time, aides, modified appraisal system)	NBPTS Propositions

Assessment designers will need to develop a unified approach, but it may have different subapproaches or paths to fit each master's requirements. At times these paths will converge, but at other times they will diverge. These paths, or subsystems, will be based on different purposes and will lead to different decisions using different content and standards. A college or district, for example, may determine that all of its program completers are qualified (certification decision), but there is still ample room for improvement (program evaluation decisions).

AERA, APA, and NCME (1999) *Standards*
and CAATS Step 1C

Standard 1.2:

The test developer should set forth clearly how test scores are intended to be interpreted and used. The population(s) for which a test is appropriate should be clearly delimited, and *the construct that the test is intended to assess should be clearly described.*
    CAATS Steps Influenced: 1A, 1C, 1D, 3A

Standard 3.1:

Tests and testing programs should be developed on a sound scientific basis. Test developers and publishers should compile and document adequate evidence bearing on test development.
    CAATS Steps Influenced: 1C, 2E, 3C

Standard 3.2:

The purpose(s) of the test, definition of the domain, and the test specifications should be stated clearly so that judgments can be made about the *appropriateness of the defined domain for the stated purpose(s) of the test and about the relation of items to the dimensions of the domain* they are intended to represent.
    CAATS Steps Influenced: 1A, 1C, 2E, 5A

Standard 14.4:

When empirical evidence of predictor-criterion relationships is part of the pattern of evidence used to support test use, the criterion measure(s) used should reflect the criterion construct domain of interest to the organization. *All criteria should represent important work behaviors or work outputs, on the job or in job-relevant training, as indicated* by an appropriate review of information about the job.
    CAATS Steps Influenced: 1C, 2B, 5A

(Continued)

(Continued)

AERA, APA, and NCME (1999) *Standards*
and CAATS Step 1C

Standard 14.8:

Evidence of validity based on test content requires a thorough and explicit definition of the content domain of interest. For selection, classification, and promotion, the characterization of the domain should be based on job analysis.
    CAATS Steps Influenced: 1C, 2E

Standard 14.9:

When evidence of validity based on test content is a primary source of validity evidence in support of the use of a test in selection or promotion, a close link between test content and job content should be demonstrated.
    CAATS Steps Influenced: 1C, 2E

Standard 14.10:

When evidence of validity based on test content is presented, *the rationale for defining and describing a specific job content domain in a particular way* (e.g., in terms of tasks to be performed or knowledge, skills, abilities, or other personal characteristics) should be stated clearly.
CAATS Steps Influenced: 1C, 2E

Standard 14.14:

The content domain to be covered by a credentialing test should be defined clearly and justified in terms of the importance of the content for credential-worthy performance in an occupation or profession. A rationale should be provided to support a claim that the knowledge of skills being assessed are required for **credential-worthy performance** in an occupation and are *consistent with the purpose* for which the licensing or certification program was instituted.
    CAATS Steps Influenced: 1C, 2E, 3C, 5A

Discussion

Note the focus on scientifically based and job-related content. Here we use the INTASC and other standards to meet that criterion (or NBPTS for advanced). There also continue to be strong linkages between purpose and content in these *Standards*. Of particular importance here, though, is that Chapter 14 of the *Standards* sets the stage for using content validity studies correlating tasks and job performance as the major form of validity evidence, if we do a good job here in the definition of content (and the conceptual framework).

NOTE: Emphases added for clarity.

CAATS STEP 1D: REVIEW LOCAL FACTORS THAT IMPACT THE SYSTEM

Once the purpose(s), use(s), and content are determined, it is important to analyze all the local factors that would impact the system (e.g., state requirements for college or district role in certification, internal resources, availability of external resources, faculty resistance/cooperation, time available, NCATE status). In the case of measuring dispositions, contextual factors for the institution or district may include a variety of local issues, including the institution or district's own degree of commitment to assessment and the time and resources available locally. Critical here is determining the affect of the faculty and district personnel. Do they think measuring performance through a collective process is important? If not, the measures developed will probably form a loosely connected system that yields limited data for improvement at the candidate or program levels.

Context

The context defines and describes the conditions that surround us and influence our work. They may be institutional, state, or national. Some contextual factors are helpful and some are not.

Guiding Question: "What are the factors that will help or hinder implementation of the envisioned assessment system?"

The sometimes fatal stumbling block that administrators have to face in assessment system design is the conflict between academic freedom and accountability. We wrote about that as one of our conflicting paradigms in Chapter 2. College faculty and district administrators hold tightly to their ability to control their own context as individuals and as authority figures within their own locus of control. They are not often amenable to controlling forces that attempt to direct them to change the ways they have always done business. How many times have you heard a statement like the following?

- "My syllabus is my right; the grades I give are my bond."
- "This is my school; I will decide who I want to hire and fire based on my rules and experience."

Yet, technically, when we credential people for employment in the public service, legislative requirements, legal decisions, and public expectations hold us to a different standard—one of compliance that assures protection. It is no longer our rights that count; it is the rights of the children in the schools. This is a very tough message to deliver.

The result of this conflict over locus of control is a reliance on consensus building and compromise. Faculty agree to contribute to the decision-making process by telling what they do and allowing it to be put into a crosswalk. Districts make adaptations in their ongoing procedures to allow for the newness of the inductees. But, in the end, these adaptations, compromises, and crosswalks fall short of a system that can lead to a valid decision. This becomes painfully obvious when we compare the expectations outlined in the AERA, APA, and NCME *Standards* with the crosswalking practice (which will be discussed in the next chapter).

Beyond this sometimes near terminal stumbling block, there are four other contextual factors to consider:

- Structural elements of the conceptual framework (e.g., mission and goals)
- Resources available to support instrument development and assessor (faculty and district personnel) training

- Willingness to dedicate the time necessary to assess and make decisions based on the data

- A population that may be tested or have access to the assessments

On this latter, the population, it is important to ensure that the population consists of the teachers who are in the program from beginning to end. It is not advisable to create assessments that would be provided prior to entry into the program (e.g., from a community college program or from another school district) unless teachers have the opportunity to make up those assessments without being penalized in any way.

We also need to make sure that the population to be tested is the one that is targeted in the assessment purpose. It would be a misuse of the assessment instruments if they were used at the wrong career stage. For example, assessments designed for initial certification should not be the same as assessments used for promotional opportunities in a career ladder.

AERA, APA, and NCME (1999) *Standards*
and CAATS Step 1D

Standard 1.2:

The test developer should set forth clearly how test scores are intended to be interpreted and used. *The population(s) for which a test is appropriate* should be clearly delimited, and the construct that the test is intended to assess should be clearly described.
    CAATS Steps Influenced: 1A, 1C, 1D, 3A

Standard 6.3:

The rationale for the test, recommended uses of the test, support for such uses, and information that assists in score interpretation should be documented. *Where particular misuse of a test can be reasonably anticipated, cautions against such misuses should be specified.*
    CAATS Steps Influenced: 1D

Discussion

Context is an appropriate place to define who can and cannot participate in this assessment system, ensuring fairness for all involved.

NOTE: Emphases added for clarity.

V⁷ WRAP-UP

In this chapter we studied the first of five steps of a design model for competency assessments aligned with teacher standards. We noted that unless the assessors are careful about defining the purpose, use, propositions, and content of the system, within the context in which they operate, the design process will be seriously flawed from the start, and the validity of decisions made about teachers will be questionable and dangerous. The key aspects of purpose, use, propositions, and content are as follows:

- *Purposes* will vary based on need. Institutions and districts may have dual or triple purposes—such as teacher certification, program improvement, teacher or pupil growth, fulfillment of mission. Each purpose and use is conceptualized and evaluated separately as a matter of validity.

- *Uses* also dictate what will be done with the data. Some examples of decisions are: certify a teacher or allow him or her to graduate, identify program weaknesses and improve a program, identify weaknesses and make improvements in unit-defined areas of importance (e.g., conceptual framework or mission), just advise teachers who are having difficulties.

- *Propositions* are based on values and what we believe in. They are the underlying framework that drives the system just as our personal philosophy causes us to act the way we do.

- *Content* can be defined in many ways, but in the case of accreditation, it is reasonable to be consistent with NCATE Standard 1 in terms of the type of information we need to gather. Classification by type of information and use of a recognized taxonomy helps us to foresee the types of assessment methods that will be used in the system. The specific requirements in pedagogical and content standards, combined with the institutional conceptual framework or district mission, provide the actual content to be assessed. This would require organizing content in terms of the knowledge, skills (intellectual and sometimes psychomotor skills), and dispositions required of teachers by various groups—national (professional), state, and institutional. We will discuss the standards in much more detail in the next chapter on CAATS Step 2.

- *Context* also sets the stage for us. External factors cause us to have the strengths (or weaknesses) to do (or not do) what we plan.

We will conclude this discussion of purpose, content, and use with some simple statements of starting points for identifying the minimum requirements of a certification-based system in Table 3.6.

Table 3.6.	Minimum Requirements for a Certification-Based System
Purpose	At a minimum, the system ensures teacher competence in order to protect the public from unqualified practitioners.
Use	The data from the system are used to determine who should be allowed to teach and who should not.
Propositions	Teacher knowledge and skill can be assessed, and it is important to do so.
Content	State and national professional standards.
Context	Accountability for performance is here to stay.

Story Starters

Starter #1:

Professor/Teacher Tiredovitawl stomps into your office and says:

"I'm sick to death of all of this accountability stuff [not really the word she chose], and I'm going to teach what I want. This is America, and you are encroaching on my First Amendment rights and academic freedom. My students will learn what I think is important, and I don't care what anybody else says. I have tenure, and you can't make me."

You say. . . . .

Starter #2:

Mrs. Kidzstink was certified in the glorious state of Hellacious. She passed the certification exam, but she really does not like children, cannot plan a lesson to save her life, will never assess learning, and cannot think critically—much the less teach kids to do so. Her teacher preparation program is state-approved but it missed certain critical parts of the design process. What were they? How do you know?

Starter #3:

Mr. Righteous sought a teaching license 100 years ago. He successfully passed an examination of his morality after questioning by members of a local school board. He agreed to start teaching every day with an appropriate devotional. He would not date nor be seen with a female companion (except at Sunday School) unless she was unmarried and at least 16 years old. His contract contained a morality clause that he would be fired if observed violating this rule. After a trial of two years, the school district would provide Mr. Righteous a permanent teaching certificate for the state. How can school districts separate cultural norms from teaching competence—or can they? What cultural aspects of your current time and place are included in teacher standards for your state and local school districts?

CAATS STEP 1—WORKSHEET #1.1

Purpose, Use, Propositions, Content, and Context Checksheet

Explanation:

Complete this worksheet as your starting point for designing a competency assessment process. Check all that apply and add your own, as needed. Consider this a rough draft.

Purpose:

_____ Certify or license teachers

_____ Identify teachers with competency-based problems likely to harm children

_____ Ensure a common set of values in a population

_____ Improve the performance of individual teachers

_____ Improve teacher training

_____ Impact the value systems of children (e.g., motivation to learn)

_____ Receive national accreditation

_____ Other _____

_____ Other _____

Use:

_____ Advising or remediation only (low stakes)

_____ Program improvement (low stakes)

_____ Entry into the profession (graduation and licensure—high stakes)

_____ Continuation in the profession (rehire—high stakes)

_____ Other _____

_____ Other _____

(Continued)

CAATS WORKSHEETS

(Continued)

Propositions or Principles:

_____ Certain competencies (knowledge and skills) are critical to effective teaching.

_____ These competencies can be identified and measured.

_____ National standards and local missions and values contribute to the identification of competencies.

_____ Measures of competency can be developed based on the standards identified and appropriate test construction theories.

_____ Teachers who have demonstrated competency on the measures are likely to be better teachers, who can have a higher impact on K–12 learning.

_____ Teachers who have not demonstrated competency on the measures are likely to be poorer teachers, who may cause harm to children.

_____ Other _____

_____ Other _____

Content:

_____ INTASC Principles

_____ Locally defined values

_____ State, district, school standards

_____ National professional association standards

_____ Other _____

_____ Other _____

Context:

Faculty support level _____

Fiscal resources available _____

Personnel resources available _____

Time available _____

NCATE status _____

Other _____

CAATS WORKSHEETS

CAATS STEP 1—WORKSHEET #1.2
Purpose, Use, and Content Draft

Explanation:

Write out a formal statement of your purpose(s). For each purpose, also write a statement about how you will use the data and what the content of the assessment system will be. These should now be aligned. (Feel free to borrow from ours!) You may have more than three; use as many worksheets as you need or develop your own format.

	Set #1	*Set #2*	*Set #3*
Purpose: Why are we assessing our teachers?			
Use: What decisions will we make with our data?			
Content: What will we assess (e.g., standards)?			

CAATS WORKSHEETS

CAATS STEP 1—WORKSHEET #1.3
Propositions

Explanation:

Write out a formal list of the propositions that will guide your work. Answer the question: What are the fundamental truths about teaching and assessment that guide our thinking? (Feel free to borrow from ours!)

1. _____

2. _____

3. _____

4. _____

5. _____

6. _____

7. _____

8. _____

9. _____

10. _____

CAATS STEP 1—WORKSHEET #1.4
Contextual Analysis

Explanation:

Write out a formal statement of the context within which your assessment system will be built. Answer the question: what are the factors that will help or hinder implementation of the envisioned assessment system?

Factors that help:

_____

_____

_____

_____

_____

_____

Factors that hinder:

_____

_____

_____

_____

_____

_____

CAATS WORKSHEETS

Where We Have Been So Far

In the previous chapter we discussed Step 1 of the CAATS model, which centered around assessment design inputs. These inputs include **purpose, use, propositions**, and **content**, as the primary inputs, moderated by other **context** factors. We also talked a little about **validity**, reminding our readers that decisions based on assessments can only be valid if made for the purposes for which they were intended. That took us into the realm of using the data. We noted that there are many possible purposes for an assessment system, and the use has to be adjusted to accommodate all purposes. We gave many examples, two of which are repeated here:

- If our purpose is to certify or to endorse a transcript so that the state has our assurance that a teacher should be certified, then the data must lead to a yes/no decision about certification.

- If our purpose is to enhance the skills of teachers district-wide to prepare them for promotions or NBPTS certification, then the data must help us make decisions that will focus on program improvement targets (e.g., new or better workshops or decisions about other resource issues). This purpose will require scores that can be aggregated.

We concluded that for the system to have meaning and utility, the data have to be used for appropriate decisions, given the purpose(s) of the system. If the data are useless, or if the data are used for the wrong purpose, the system will not lead to valid decisions about teachers.

Quite naturally, the content of the assessment process has to match the purpose and use—NBPTS issues were related to NBPTS certification, and state teacher competencies (or INTASC Principles) are the main content for initial certification decisions. If the decisions are based on the wrong content (e.g., INTASC for promotion and NBPTS for initial certification), we again have a system that will not lead to valid decisions about teachers.

We ended our CAATS Step 1 discussion with a recognition that we do not do our work in a vacuum; our belief system, as articulated in propositional statements, and our local context influence everything we can and cannot do. We concluded that our "prime directive" (for those who remember *Star Trek*) and the primary focus of this book is the high-stakes purpose of an assessment system—protecting the public from the unqualified practitioner. Such was our "Lesson #1" on validity. We now continue our work on validity in CAATS Step 2 with a series of detailed planning procedures, all based on sampling the content identified in CAATS Step 1.

4

CAATS Step 2

*Planning With a Continuing
Eye on Valid Assessment Decisions*

$\mathcal{W}$hen we face our task of assessment design with integrity, we soon come to realize that the concept of validity is the most important thing we need to think about. Like a little puppy, it never leaves our side. Sadly, most measurement textbooks leave us kind of hanging and frustrated by offering little practical advice about how to collect evidence of validity—just a bunch of definitions and formulae. In this chapter, we will continue to tackle the problem head-on and hands-on, as a thread that winds through the model. By the time we reach CAATS Step 5, where we address psychometric integrity directly, we will find that we have really covered most of the ground we needed to cover by designing our system carefully.

> **CAATS Step 2: Develop a valid sampling plan.**

In CAATS Step 1, we identified the content, or the "what" of the assessment process. We clarified that the "what" in a standards-based system is, at a minimum, the standards themselves. The standards articulated by others, as well as our own locally developed standards and values, make up the locally defined conceptual framework. In this chapter, we look at what we do to use our conceptual framework in designing the assessment system and its instruments. We now leave the world of broad-based planning and enter the world of the nitty-gritty details. CAATS Step 2 is all about alignment and the sampling that results from that alignment. This is a time-consuming step, but if you miss it, nothing else you do will ever really matter.

We will begin by ensuring that we have identified all relevant standards, and we align them into **content domains** that are comprised largely of the **indicators** for each of the aligned standards. This is the beginning of the **job analysis**, and common threads that run through all of the **standards sets** are identified and aligned. When they are considered together, as a kind of content domain or a set of content domains, one can clearly see the similarities and differences between and among the perceptions of what is important from each group of professionals. Designers should also develop a condensed version of the standards, or **critical skills**, to be used by the institution as an operational definition of its conceptual framework. Next, faculty members should **visualize the competent** teacher performing the critical skills and demonstrating the standard, **brainstorm** a series of **product- and performance-based tasks** that the teacher must do to demonstrate the skills, and then sort the tasks into **formative and summative** tasks so that only the most important tasks remain in the decision-making structure. Once the list is complete, a series of **design frameworks** can be used to ensure that the list provides for a **balanced and appropriate sampling plan** that will lead to valid **inferences** about teacher competency in a way that is feasible for the college or district.

Note that we will use the Florida standards as an example of state standards. One must consider state standards when licensure is an issue because they drive the state process.

Throughout the chapter are some terms, definitions, and guiding questions that we add to our vocabulary as we progress through this step.

In this step we will do five things:

CAATS Step 2A: Organize standards into content domains.

CAATS Step 2B: Visualize the competent teacher.

CAATS Step 2C: Brainstorm a set of summative tasks (sampling plan).

CAATS Step 2D: Sort tasks into formative and summative assessments.

CAATS Step 2E: Build assessment frameworks.

Before Moving On . . .

1. Have you thought about a conceptual framework (CF)? If so, what's in it? If not, do you plan on developing one? Does your vision of a CF incorporate what others have said (both standards as well as research literature) or just what you think is important?

2. There are lots of standards out there. Do you consider this a good thing or a bad thing? Why? Wouldn't the world be a better place if we just had a set of national standards that fit all teachers at all levels of development in all content areas?

3. What does a competent teacher look like when standing in front of a group of students? Jot down what you see in your mind's eye.

4. Are the tasks you are currently using to assess teachers more formative or summative in nature? Do you think you have too many to use for decision making about your purpose? Are some missing?

5. Do you have a sense that your current assessments are balanced and appropriate? Or are they lumped together in one area (e.g., planning) or one time period (e.g., internship or observation time)? Are your assessments predominantly observational or product based?

P.S.: Don't forget to keep working on that action plan from Chapter 2!

CAATS STEP 2A: ORGANIZE STANDARDS INTO CONTENT DOMAINS

All Those Standards Sets

As we noted previously, whatever combination of standards are used in a state, there are typically multiple sets of standards that need to be used in the assessment system, and these should have all been located in CAATS Step 1C (content). In a standards-based system, we have to start with the standards. But what do we do with them once they are all located? There are so many standards that we need to organize them for use. We can think about this as the analysis and synthesis levels of Bloom's cognitive taxonomy. We have to pick them apart and then put them back together again in a meaningful way to get a handle on them so we can use them for decision making!

Most institutions have found that there is extensive, and frustrating, overlap between and among the sets of standards. For example, most standards-setting organizations have something about knowledge of content, planning, assessment, improvement, communication, learning environment, learning and development theory, and so forth. Institutions that want to conserve their energy and make maximum use of their time will begin by aligning the required standards with each other. This is the time to decide whether you will approach the development process looking at the glass as half empty or half full. If you see it as half empty (those pessimists among us), you may be angry and frustrated at the time it takes to align standards. If, on the other hand, you take the optimistic path (glass as half full), you will soon recognize that combining standards by topics across agencies provides a rich and valuable resource for developing tasks that are standards aligned and likely to lead to valid decisions about what teachers know and can do. But how can this be done?

We recommend that the institution or state collect all the relevant sets of standards and identify the key themes, categories, or, what we call, *base standards* to use as an organizing framework for the alignment process. The INTASC Principles provide a natural organizing structure, since so many of the state and professional standards use them directly or in some reformatted way. Another logical option is to use the state standards as an organizing framework. In the next section, you will see the set we defined as base standards, and you may wish to use the same set. We organized them in a politically correct way—alphabetically!

> **Standards Sets**
>
> Lots of groups have written or rewritten standards. Each set of standards written by one group is a standards set. Examples include INTASC, Florida Accomplished Practices, and National Council of Teachers of Mathematics.
>
> *Guiding Question:*
> *"Whose standards count for me?"*

> **Alignment**
>
> Alignment is a judgmental process by which we analyze two sets of like elements (e.g., standards) and position together the ones that are similar. Because it is a judgmental process, not all people will agree on every alignment.
>
> *Guiding Question: "Does the standard I am reading sound a lot like another standard or standards? Is this just wordsmithing?"*

Organizing for Alignment

In our own application of the system we describe herein, we chose this latter option, aligning by state standards (the Florida Educator Accomplished Practices or FEAPs), taking the best of both worlds—state and national—by using alphabetical order and number of our Florida standards. We have worked with 12 base standards to create a chart aligning the two. Table 4.1 illustrates that process.

Table 4.1. Base Standards as a Summary Statement of National and State Standards		
Sample Standards Alignment		
Base Standard	*INTASC Principle*	*Florida Educator Accomplished Practice*
Assessment	Principle #8: The teacher understands and uses formal and informal *assessment* strategies to evaluate and ensure the continuous intellectual, social, and physical development of the learner.	#1—*ASSESSMENT:* The preprofessional teacher collects and uses data gathered from a variety of sources. These sources include both traditional and alternate assessment strategies. Furthermore, the teacher can identify and match the students' instructional plans with their cognitive, social, linguistic, cultural, emotional, and physical needs.
Communication	Principle #6: The teacher uses knowledge of effective verbal, nonverbal, and media *communication* techniques to foster active inquiry, collaboration, and supportive interaction in the classroom.	#2—*COMMUNICATION:* The preprofessional teacher recognizes the need for effective communication in the classroom and is in the process of acquiring techniques which she/he will use in the classroom.
Continuous Improvement	Principle #9: The teacher is *a reflective practitioner* who continually evaluates the defects of his/her choices and actions on others (students, parents, and other professionals in the learning community) and who actively seeks out opportunities to grow professionally.	#3—*CONTINUOUS IMPROVEMENT:* The preprofessional teacher realizes that she/he is in the initial stages of a lifelong learning process and that *self-reflection* is one of the key components of that process. While her/his concentration is, of necessity, inward and personal, self-reflection, working with immediate colleagues and teammates, and meeting the goals of a personal professional development plan.
Critical and Creative Thinking	Principle #4: The teacher understands and uses a variety of instructional strategies to encourage students' development of *critical thinking,* problem solving, and performance skills.	#4—*CRITICAL THINKING:* The preprofessional teacher is acquiring performance assessment techniques and strategies that measure higher order thinking skills in students, and is building a repertoire of realistic projects and problem-solving activities designed to assist all students in demonstrating their ability to think creatively.

Sample Standards Alignment		
Base Standard	*INTASC Principle*	*Florida Educator Accomplished Practice*
Diversity	Principle #3: The teacher understands how students differ in their approaches to learning and creates instructional opportunities that are adapted to *diverse learners.*	#5—*DIVERSITY:* The preprofessional teacher establishes a comfortable environment which accepts and fosters diversity. The teacher must demonstrate knowledge and awareness of varied cultures and linguistic backgrounds. The teacher creates a climate of openness, inquiry, and support by practicing strategies such as acceptance, tolerance, resolution, and mediation.
Ethics		#6—*ETHICS:* Adheres to the Code of Ethics and Principles of Professional Conduct of the Education Profession in Florida.
Human Development and Learning	Principle #2: The teacher understands how children *learn and develop,* and can provide learning opportunities that support their intellectual, social, and personal development.	#7—*HUMAN DEVELOPMENT AND LEARNING:* Drawing upon well-established human development/learning theories and concepts and a variety of information about students, the preprofessional teacher plans instructional activities.
Knowledge of Subject Matter	Principle #1: The teacher understands the central concepts, tools of inquiry, and structures of the discipline(s) they teach and can create learning experiences that make these aspects of *subject matter* meaningful for students.	#8—*KNOWLEDGE OF SUBJECT MATTER:* The preprofessional teacher has a basic understanding of the subject field and is beginning to understand that the subject is linked to other disciplines and can be applied to real-world integrated settings. The teacher's repertoire of teaching skills includes a variety of means to assist student acquisition of new knowledge and skills using that knowledge.
Learning Environment	Principle #5: The teacher uses an understanding of individual and group motivation and behavior to create a *learning environment* that encourages positive social interaction, active engagement in learning, and self-motivation.	#9—*LEARNING ENVIRONMENTS:* The preprofessional teacher understands the importance of setting up effective learning environments, and has techniques and strategies to use to do so, including some that provide opportunities for student input into the processes. The teacher understands that she/he will need a variety of techniques and work to increase his/her knowledge and skills.

(Continued)

(Continued)

Sample Standards Alignment		
Base Standard	*INTASC Principle*	*Florida Educator Accomplished Practice*
Planning	Principle #7: The teacher *plans* instruction based upon knowledge of subject matter, students, the community, and curriculum goals.	#10—*PLANNING:* Recognizes the importance of setting high expectations for all students, the preprofessional teacher works with other professionals to design learning experiences that meet students' needs and interests. The teacher candidate continually seeks advice/information from appropriate resources (including feedback), interprets the information, and modifies her/his plans appropriately. Planned instruction incorporates motivational strategies and multiple resources for providing comprehensible instruction for all students. Upon reflection, the teacher continuously refines outcome assessment and learning experiences.
Role of the Teacher	Principle #10: The teacher fosters relationships with school *colleagues, parents,* and agencies in the larger community to support students' learning and well being.	#11—*ROLE OF THE TEACHER:* The preprofessional teacher communicates and works cooperatively with *families and colleagues* to improve the educational experiences at the school.
Technology		#12—*TECHNOLOGY:* The preprofessional teacher uses technology as available at the school site and as appropriate to the learner. She/he provides students with opportunities to actively use technology and facilitates access to the use of electronic resources. The teacher also uses technology to manage, evaluate, and improve instruction.

Note that we have printed in boldfaced italics the words that caused us to align the INTASC Principle to our base standard and FEAP. The similarities are quite obvious, and the keyword identification strategy really helps with the alignment process.

Worksheet #2.1 provides a form you can use to do the same kind of alignment in your state or district. We have provided two formats for you—one using our base standards, and one open-ended, in which you can create your own base standards. You might choose to reorder them based on your state standards or the order of the INTASC Principles. You could also change the keywords. For Florida's ethics and technology base standards, you might choose something that fits your state or your own additions to the base standards list drawn from INTASC and Florida.

"A Rose Is a Rose" or More of the Same

Fortunately, as we noted above, "a rose is a rose," and there is a great deal of overlap between various sets of standards. In the previous section, we demonstrated the alignment of INTASC and Florida generic standards of pedagogy and professionalism, applicable to all certification areas. The alignment process extends to some extent to the content-specific standards as well. By design, NCATE is now requiring the specialty professional associations, or SPAs, to align their content-focused standards with the INTASC Principles, as we mentioned in the previous chapter. There is variability among the results, with some SPAs more closely aligned. Examples of SPAs that are well aligned with the INTASC Principles include the Council for Exceptional Children (CEC) and the Association for Childhood Education International (ACEI), which address special education and elementary education. Other SPAs adhere to other formats. For example, the National Council for Social Studies (NCSS) adheres to themes; other SPAS are somewhere in-between.

> **Hint! A Word to the Wise:** As you go through each step of the CAATS model, keep careful records of all of your work. This is an integral part of the requirements of the AERA, APA, and NCME Standards and your collection of validity evidence.

The extent of overlap can easily be demonstrated through continuation of the alignment process, as is shown in Table 4.2, where three commonly accepted aspects of good teaching are aligned for Florida's Accomplished Practices, INTASC Principles, and ACEI, CEC, and National Association for Education of Young Children (NAEYC—primary) guidelines. SPAs such as NCSS would not be able to be aligned this way, but in these cases, typically everything aligns with content knowledge (INTASC #1).

Table 4.2. Using Base Standards to Organize and Align National and State Standards

Base Standard	INTASC #	ACEI #	CEC #	NAEYC #	Florida #
Assessment	8	4	8	3	1
Content	1	2	1, 4	4	8
Critical Thinking	4	3c	4	4d	4
Planning	7	3	7	4	10

?
Content Domains

Content domains consist of each grouping of standards that have been aligned because they are all similar and convey the same basic set of ideas.

Guiding Question: "Does this set of standards and indicators hang together to form a body of content that can be assessed?"

?

When considered together, as a kind of content domain, one can clearly see the similarities and differences between and among the perceptions of what is important from each group of professionals. To demonstrate the similarities, the precise standards language for two standards—assessment and critical thinking—(with some language in bold for emphasis) is provided in Boxes 4.1 and 4.2.

Box 4.1. Various Standards on Assessment

- **INTASC:** The teacher understands and **uses formal and informal assessment** strategies to evaluate and ensure the continuous **intellectual, social, and physical development** of the learner.

- **ACEI:** Candidates know, understand, and **use formal and informal assessment** strategies to plan, evaluate, and strengthen instruction that will promote continuous **intellectual, social, emotional, and physical development** of each elementary student.

- **CEC:** Assessment is integral to the decision making and teaching of special educators, and special educators **use multiple types of assessment information** for a variety of educational decisions. Special educators use the results of assessments to help identify exceptional learning needs and to develop and implement **individualized instructional** programs, as well as to adjust instruction in response to the ongoing learning progress . . .

- **NAEYC:** Candidates use **multiple**, systematic observations, documentation, and other responsible **assessment strategies** as an integral part of their practice.

- **Florida:** The preprofessional teacher collects and **uses** data gathered from a variety of sources. These sources will include both **traditional and alternate assessment strategies**. Furthermore, the teacher can identify and match the students' instructional plans with their **cognitive, social, linguistic, cultural, emotional, and physical needs**.

Box 4.2. Various Standards on Critical Thinking

- **INTASC:** The teacher understands and uses a variety of instructional **strategies** to encourage students' development of **critical thinking, problem solving, and performance skills**.

- **ACEI:** Development of critical thinking, problem solving, and performance skills—Candidates understand and use a variety of teaching **strategies** that encourage elementary students' development of **critical thinking, problem solving, and performance skills**.

- **CEC:** Special educators possess a repertoire of evidence-based instructional **strategies** to individualize instruction for individuals with ELN. Special educators select, adapt, and use these instructional strategies to promote positive learning results in general and special curricula, and to appropriately modify learning environments for individuals with ELN. They enhance the learning of **critical thinking, problem solving, and performance skills** of individuals with ELN, and increase their self-awareness, self-management, self-control, self-reliance, and self-esteem. Moreover, special educators emphasize the development, maintenance, and generalization of knowledge and skills across environments, settings, and the lifespan.

- **NAEYC:** Building Meaningful Curriculum: Candidates use their own knowledge and other resources to design, implement, and evaluate meaningful, challenging curriculum that promotes comprehensive developmental and learning outcomes for all young children.
  - Security and self-regulation
  - **Problem-solving and thinking skills**
  - Academic and social competence

- **Florida**: The preprofessional teacher is acquiring performance assessment techniques and **strategies** that measure **higher order thinking skills** in students and is building a repertoire of realistic projects and **problem-solving** activities designed to assist all students in demonstrating their ability to **think creatively**.

Most of the standards could be correlated in a similar fashion, extending the matrix in both directions—vertically and horizontally—with more base standards and more state or national standards sets. The point is that there is substantial overlap among standards sets, and we need to take advantage of this to the extent possible.

Finally, one more alignment needs to be made in the content areas where the overlap with INTASC Principles is weak, such as in social studies. In this case, a separate table should be created matching state and national standards for each content area of this type. The table might look like our example in Table 4.3 for social studies, again using Florida as an illustrative state, but demonstrating this time an alignment that requires even more judgment and creativity—the alignment is not straightforward and might be completed differently by different analysts. Here we illustrate an opportunity to show alignments that do not provide a one-to-one correspondence, sometimes repeating for different standards and sometimes not showing any alignment. In such cases, the domain being defined becomes significantly larger because of different viewpoints about what is important from national and state-level decision makers (and test writers!).

As you examine Table 4.3, note that if we find discrepancies such as this in comparing national and state standards, there is a burden on colleges to address both. Much thought has gone into the preparation of national standards, and it would not be ethical to ignore them. These standards are important for children in the schools and for teachers who may move to another state. This places a heavy, but important, burden on teacher educators.

> **Indicators**
>
> Indicators are statements or sub-parts that give specific examples or meanings to standards. We would call them sub-standards, but that might be misinterpreted!
>
> *Guiding Question: "What are the details of the standards that help me understand what the standards are intended to mean?"*

Table 4.3. Example of Aligning National and Content Standards	
National Standards for Social Studies (NCSS)	*Florida's State Content Standards for Social Studies*
1.1 Culture and Cultural Diversity	5.0 Knowledge of American History
1.2 Time, Continuity, and Change	4.0 Knowledge of World History 5.0 Knowledge of American History
1.3 People, Places, and Environment	1.0 Knowledge of Geography
1.4 Individual Development and Identity	
1.5 Individuals, Groups, and Institutions	
1.6 Power, Authority, and Governance	3.0 Knowledge of Political Science
1.7 Production, Distribution, and Consumption	2.0 Knowledge of Economics
1.8 Science, Technology, and Society	
1.9 Global Connections	4.0 Knowledge of World History
1.10 Civic Ideals and Practices	3.0 Knowledge of Political Science
	6.0 Knowledge of Social Science and its Methodology

Why Bother?

This is obviously something that takes a lot of time and thinking, and that is why many assessment designers would like to skip the alignment step. That is not a good idea. Not only will it save us time in the long run to align standards in this way, but we are also taking another big step forward toward validity. Standards typically have indicators that flesh out the depth and breadth of the intent of each standard. When we combine those indicators into one long list, we have a rich set of behaviors from which to choose. In measurement terms, we have a domain from which we can sample. The domain defines the various behaviors a teacher needs to have on the job. In the case of social studies in Florida, the domain will be even richer.

This is the beginning of what we refer to as a *job analysis*, a cornerstone of validity. After all, if we are preparing teachers for a job, we need to make sure that we know what that job entails and then assess them on all the important aspects of that job. The standards, in essence, help us define those aspects, so this is not as daunting a task as it sounds. Teachers need to convey content, plan lessons, assess progress, etc. All of these tasks are embedded clearly in the standards. They are the common threads that run through all of the sets of standards because the literature has identified several important characteristics of effective teaching consistently over time. While there is much hairsplitting in the field

---

Job Analysis

A job analysis requires that we identify all of the important things a teacher is expected to know and do to be able to perform the job well.

Guiding Question: "What does a teacher have to do on the job to ensure that children learn?"

about the details, essentially the 10 Principles written by INTASC identify those critical competencies for pedagogy but not content.

The need, then, is to analyze and synthesize the details (indicators) into some kind of composite list of what we will call *critical skills* that become the institution or district's own set of most valued job requirements. We will look at an example of how this can be done, using the indicators for the critical thinking base standard, as articulated in Florida and two national groups (INTASC and ACEI). The indicators are provided in Boxes 4.3 to 4.5, and the critical skills we extracted are located in Box 4.6.

Critical Skills

Critical skills are the aspects of performance that a teacher should not be able to miss. They are the most valued aspects of job performance. A critical skill for pilots is landing the plane. The pilot who can't land the plane should not be a pilot.

Guiding Question: "What do the teachers absolutely have to do, and if they can't do it, they shouldn't be teachers?"

Box 4.3. INTASC Principle #4: Critical Thinking Indicators

1. The teacher understands the cognitive processes associated with various kinds of learning (e.g., critical and creative thinking, problem structuring and problem solving, invention, memorization and recall) and how these processes can be stimulated. (Knowledge)

2. The teacher understands principles and techniques, along with advantages and limitations, associated with various instructional strategies (e.g., cooperative learning, direct instruction, discovery learning, whole group discussion, independent study, interdisciplinary instruction). (Knowledge)

3. The teacher knows how to enhance learning through the use of a wide variety of materials as well as human and technological resources (e.g., computers, audio-visual technologies, videotapes and discs, local experts, primary documents and artifacts, texts, reference books, literature, and other print resources). (Knowledge)

4. The teacher values the development of students' critical thinking, independent problem solving, and performance capabilities. (Dispositions)

5. The teacher values flexibility and reciprocity in the teaching process as necessary for adapting instruction to student responses, ideas, and needs. (Dispositions)

6. The teacher carefully evaluates how to achieve learning goals, choosing alternative teaching strategies and materials to achieve different instructional purposes and to meet student needs (e.g., developmental stages, prior knowledge, learning styles, and interests). (Performances)

7. The teacher uses multiple teaching and learning strategies to engage students in active learning opportunities that promote the development of critical thinking, problem solving, and performance capabilities, and that help students assume responsibility for identifying and using learning resources. (Performances)

8. The teacher constantly monitors and adjusts strategies in response to learner feedback. (Performances)

9. The teacher varies his or her role in the instructional process (e.g., instructor, facilitator, coach, audience) in relation to the content and purposes of instruction and the needs of students. (Performances)

10. The teacher develops a variety of clear, accurate presentations and representations of concepts, using alternative explanations to assist students' understanding and presenting diverse perspectives to encourage critical thinking. (Performances)

Box 4.4. ACEI Standard 3C: Critical Thinking Indicators

1. Candidates understand cognitive processes associated with various kinds of learning and how these processes can be stimulated.

2. They also understand principles and techniques, advantages and limitations, associated with appropriate teaching strategies (e.g., cooperative learning, direct instruction, inquiry, whole group discussion, independent study, interdisciplinary instruction).

3. Candidates know how to enhance learning through use of a wide variety of materials as well as collaboration with specialists, other colleagues, and technological resources, and through multiple teaching and learning strategies that will promote development of critical thinking, problem solving, and performance capabilities.

Box 4.5. Florida Accomplished Practice #4: Critical Thinking Indicators

1. Provides opportunities for students to learn higher-order thinking skills.

2. Identifies strategies, materials, and technologies which she/he will use to expand students' thinking abilities.

3. Has strategies for utilizing discussions, group interactions, and writing to encourage student problem solving.

4. Poses problems, dilemmas, and questions in lessons.

5. Assists students in development and use of rules of evidence.

6. Varies her/his role in the instructional process (instructor, coach, mentor, facilitator, audience, critic, etc.) in relation to the purposes of instruction and the students' needs, including linguistic needs.

7. Demonstrates and models the use of higher-order thinking abilities.

8. Modifies and adapts lessons with increased attention to the learners' creative thinking abilities.

9. Encourages students to develop open-ended projects and other activities that are creative and innovative.

10. Uses technology and other appropriate tools in the learning environment.

11. Develops short-term personal and professional goals relating to critical thinking.

Box 4.6. Sample of Locally Developed Critical Skills for Critical Thinking

- The teacher models critical/creative thinking in the classroom.
- The teacher encourages students to think creatively/critically.
- The teacher focuses significant portions of instruction at the application and higher levels so that children demonstrate critical/creative thinking and problem solving.

In Boxes 4.3 through 4.5, we have listed the indicators for three sets of standards, but the list keeps on growing as we add more. Well, obviously, that is a whole lot of indicators, and the list clearly becomes unmanageable quickly. This is why we recommend the creation of a set of locally defined critical skills, as we have done in Box 4.6.

This locally developed interpretation could serve as a component of the conceptual framework required for NCATE and a basis for creating assessment devices for any system. If carefully constructed, the critical skills list can provide a synthesis of important skills so that the design of assessment tasks is facilitated. It is easier to cover 3 to 5 critical skills adequately than to cover 10 to 50 adequately, and there may be as many as 50 indicators when all aligned standards are combined. In our example above, in just three standards sets, we listed 24 indicators, including Florida, INTASC, and ACEI only. We can never lose total sight of the long list, since it will help us flesh out the details of some of our tasks, but to get a sense of what we really value, there is no substitute for our own list. That is really a key principle behind the need for a conceptual framework. The "laundry list" keeps us honest about assessing the breadth of what the standards-setters had in mind. Worksheet #2.2 provides a sample space for the development of the college or district's set of critical skills.

> **Conceptual Framework**
>
> The conceptual framework is the content and philosophy that guide teaching and assessment. It is drawn from standards, research, professional experience, and vision. See detailed explanation in Chapter 1.
>
> *Guiding Question: "What do I want to include in my system?"*

Once the standards are aligned with each other and the critical skills are identified, the job of developing assessment tasks becomes easier, making this effort worthwhile. We can now assure our design team that their work will satisfy the requirements of all the standards setting organizations with one unified effort. While the tasks they are going to create are likely to change over time and with experience, at least we have saved the horrible work of trying to design separately for each set of standards, over and over again. Frustration naturally grows with each new start on the same job and, therefore, should be avoided by the analysis and synthesis of standards.

Beyond reducing the frustration from restarts, use of aligned standards helps us to profit from the wisdom of different groups that have attempted to answer the same questions and introduced both similar and different viewpoints. Perhaps the best news, though, from an assessment standpoint, is that once the standards are aligned or grouped in this way, we have defined an assessment or content domain that can be taught and assessed. Critical thinking then becomes one of our domains, and we are again moving toward creating a system that can lead to valid decisions about teachers' competence.

In Box 4.7, we provide some advice on how to number your indicators. This is an important step that can save much frustration as you work with your system. Some standards-setters do not number; others use letters; still others use numbers. Using a consistent approach, designed in advance for computer analysis, is where you need to aim.

Box 4.7. Numbering Your Indicators

Make sure the standards and indicators throughout your system are numbered in a consistent way. For example, the Florida Educator Accomplished Practices are numbered 1 through 12, but there are no numbers for the indicators. We prefer decimal notation with leading zeros. For our first FEAP, the sequence would be 1.01, 1.02. 1.03, and so on. FEAP #2 indicators are numbered 2.01, 2.02, 2.03, and so on. The use of leading zeros allows sorting in a database and will help greatly as you move through the design process. It's a whole lot easier than reading or typing the full text each time!

To this point, we have been encouraging you to follow specific planning strate-gies to prepare for valid inferences or judgments about teacher competency. You may be starting to wonder about a common strategy you may be using to design your standards-based assessment system. We will call it crosswalking, and we will show you why it is ineffective and potentially harmful.

Crosswalks and Standards

Many colleges and districts begin their work on developing an assessment system by building crosswalks of what they have in their courses that relate in some way to the pedagogical, professional, and content standards. This can be an effective strategy for content standards, but not for pedagogical and professional.

For those who are not familiar with the crosswalking process, crosswalks are typically charts or tables that align courses (or assignments in courses or staff devel-opment workshops) and standards. In Table 4.4, we provide an example. The assessments (e.g., lesson plan, classroom management plan, role playing activity, case study) are placed in the cells corresponding to the standards (rows) for which they might provide evidence. The columns place these assessments in their respec-tive courses.

Table 4.4. Crosswalk of Assessments by Standard (Rows) and Delivery Location (Columns)					
	Course/ Workshop 1	*Course/ Workshop 2*	*Course/ Workshop 3*	*Course/ Workshop 4*	*Etc.*
INTASC 1 or NBPTS 1	Lesson Plan	Research Project			
INTASC 2 or NBPTS 2		Lesson Plan		Case Study	
INTASC 3 or NBPTS 3	Role Play	Lesson plan		Lesson Plan	
INTASC 4 or NBPTS 4	Lesson Plan	Lesson Plan	Lesson Plan	Lesson Plan	
And so forth					

So, why are we against starting here when virtually everyone in the country is doing this? Both Chapter 3 ("Validity") and Chapter 14 ("Testing in Employment and Credentialing") of the AERA, APA, and NCME 1999 *Standards* give us the same strong message. To have any hope of achieving validity in the decision-making process when it involves credentialing for a job, the only place to start is with a thorough job analysis. We must begin by asking ourselves what the minimally competent (or advancing) employee has to be able to do. That is the next substep (CAATS Step 2B) in this model. To answer that question, we must know what the teacher is expected to do—all those standards we just finished aligning. When we begin with what we want to teach them in our classes or staff development programs (or worse what we have taught them for the past quarter century), we are literally putting the cart before the horse and letting our individual intuitions, needs, and traditions, even when discussed collaboratively, drive the system. The result is that often there are important components missing and some assessments overused (e.g., lesson plan).

The decisions that are made when some standards are not covered well or some assessments do not really fit the standard are what Messick (1995) called *construct under-representation* and *construct irrelevant variance*. The former means there just is not enough assessment; the latter means that some of it is not appropriate to the standard, so we are measuring the wrong domain. There are other forms of construct irrelevant variance that are related to reliability (e.g., raters are inconsistent or students are not motivated), but these two threats to validity are now considered to be among the most serious and serve as cornerstones of the AERA, APA, and NCME standard on validity.

Construct Under-Representation

Construct under-representation occurs when we do not have enough data to make a decision about the construct because we haven't sampled well.

Guiding Question: "Do I have enough stuff to decide well?"

Another problem with starting with crosswalking is that we provide more emphasis than we should on some minor assignments or activities. They seem to take on a life of their own, as each faculty member or trainer has to prove how much he or she does to meet the standards. Resistance then grows to creating anything new, as we are lulled into believing that we already have plenty—so why do more? But, if we think about the issues in the previous paragraph, we may see lots of some things while we see not enough of others. Typically, the most frequent assessment that suffers or is lost is the one that looks at results for K–12 learning.

A third problem that often surfaces is that designers tend to over-crosswalk in their zealous attempts to prove how valuable everything they do is; they like to say that every assignment or activity covers every standard—or almost every standard. They become sloppy in their work, and the whole crosswalking process can become rather meaningless. We have seen countless crosswalks where every course or training session and every assignment or activity covers almost every standard. In reality, though, they rarely do. We need to be careful about saying that we are making informed decisions about standards-based competency when we are really just giving it just a lick and a promise.

Construct Irrelevant Variance

Construct irrelevant variance is any extraneous factor that distorts the meaning or interpretation of a score. A common form of this variance is measuring the wrong thing.

Guiding Question: "Have I mixed some other stuff into the decision I am trying to make?"

One common example of the over-crosswalking issue is in lesson or unit plans. True, they can cover all or most standards when carefully constructed, but they rarely do, and they become terribly difficult to evaluate standard-by-standard when we try. A good example of this problem is thinking that assessment is demonstrated in a lesson plan when all the teacher does is say that there will be a quiz. Saying that there will be a quiz does not give us useful information about whether or not this teacher can write a quiz, modify a quiz, or use the results of the quiz to make decisions about teaching and learning. In Box 4.8 we summarize the three key points we have made thus far about crosswalks.

Box 4.8.   Why Shouldn't We Do Crosswalks? A Summary

1. Crosswalks start in the wrong place—what we have instead of what we need (job analysis). So things we need, but don't do, slip through the cracks.

2. Crosswalks encourage an overemphasis on the unimportant—formative is equated with summative. Empty cells are painful.

3. Crosswalks cause us to view standards alignment as a measure of self-worth—personal credit is accumulated by taking credit for teaching/assessing all standards in all work, but we can't assess it all well! We lull ourselves into thinking we have assessed things we haven't.

It is our assertion that when we start with the old paradigm of crosswalking syllabi and standards, and not with a critical job analysis that outlines the major tasks a teacher has to perform to teach every child, we will never succeed at achieving validity and we cannot make that all-important decision about "safe to teach" with any degree of credibility. The crosswalking approach is based on starting with what we have, rather than what we need, and that is what makes it so very dangerous. Once the crosswalk is done, we become more and more invested in the status quo and more and more resistant to changing it. We have already said that purpose, use, and content are the place to start, but we reiterate it here with our "Word to the Wise" note on the side. It is not quite a poem, but it does deliver our message.

The real question is whether or not a college or a district can survive the struggle when consensus is attempted but at some point the dean or superintendent says, "Enough is enough. We need to measure these things in these places to make this decision. Teach it anyway you want, but make the task-based decisions that lead up to the credentialing decision." But how do we get there if crosswalking is not the answer? Well, that is the subject of the next step.

We visualize the competent teacher performing the standards. It is the old WYSIWYG approach: "what you see is what you get." Or at least, it is what you want, and you know it, and that is a very good start. If you don't know what you want, how will you know if or when you get it?

⸮ ——— Crosswalks ———

Crosswalks are charts or tables that align courses (or assignments in courses or staff development workshops) and standards.

A Word to the Wise

If you always do
What you always have done,
You will always have
What you always had.

AERA, APA, NCME 1999 *Standards*
and CAATS Step 2A

Standard 1.6:

When the validation rests in part on the appropriateness of test content, the *procedures followed in specifying and generating test content* should be described and justified in reference to the construct the test is intended to represent. If the definition of the content sampled incorporates criteria such as importance, frequency, or criticality, these criteria should also be clearly explained and justified.

   CAATS Steps Influenced: 2A, 2B, 2C, 2D

Discussion

Since the construct of teacher performance is articulated in multiple sets of standards that are, at least in part, redundant, the content domains into which they are compiled in this step become an explicit part of the assessment design process through this procedure.

NOTE: Emphases added for clarity.

CAATS STEP 2B: VISUALIZE THE COMPETENT TEACHER BASED ON THE STANDARDS

Instead of crosswalking all those assignments with all those standards, we suggest you just close your eyes for a minute and visualize in your mind a good teacher teaching—doing what a specific standard says is important. What does that teacher look like? What is happening in the classroom? How did it get that way? Can you describe it in terms of a specific product or performance? Ask yourself one or both of the important questions in Box 4.9.

Box 4.9. Standards-Based Job Analysis Questions

"What does each standard look like in practice, when performed by a good teacher?"

or

"How can we see that the teacher has acquired the knowledge and skills called for in the standards at some minimal level of competence?"

The AERA, APA, and NCME *Standards* make it clear that the assessment tasks need to be based on a thorough job analysis. When you visualize the teacher performing the standards, that is exactly what you are doing. If you do this systematically, standard-by-standard, you will have met the requirement for a thorough job analysis. If, on the other hand, you are tied to crosswalks that have things in them that are appropriate to your own classroom-based instruction and assessment but are not typical of what a classroom teacher actually does in a K–12 setting, you are wandering away from the job-relatedness criterion. After all, how often do teachers write in their journals about what they learned that day? If something is not job-related, then, it should not be included in the system as a summative assessment. That does not mean it is irrelevant or unimportant for teaching teachers; it just should not be a summative assessment that translates into a teaching credential! The same situation holds true in district situations where routine paperwork takes on a life of its own in the assessment system.

How, then, can one begin to identify the set of tasks that is required of the competent teacher? There are several approaches one can use:

- Visualization: The process we just described—close your eyes and "see" the teacher.
- Poll or Survey: We can poll or survey district personnel and other stakeholders.
- Literature Review: What does research tell us?

We recommend the use of more than one approach, and the easiest way to start is with the visualization. What can you see a teacher doing, in your mind's eye, that looks like teaching critical thinking? Does the teacher need to be doing it with a group of students? Or is it something the teacher prepares at home and takes to school for use? Or is it both? Once you can see these teacher actions, you are well on the road to creating the task-based system you need.

If we were to practice this activity for critical thinking, we might see the effective behaviors provided in Box 4.10.

Box 4.10.   Effective Teacher Behaviors for Critical Thinking

- The teacher is asking the students questions that cause them to think about big issues.
- The teacher is giving them an assignment that requires research skills and probing.
- The teacher is preparing a lesson that has objectives at the application or higher level in Bloom's taxonomy.
- The teacher is looking for materials in the library or on the Internet that can be brought to class for students to use.
- The teacher is assigning work for students to do in groups or in the media center.

Sometimes it is also useful to imagine a poor teacher who is doing the opposite of demonstrating the standard. In this case, we might see the ineffective behaviors listed in Box 4.11.

Box 4.11.   Ineffective Teacher Behaviors for Critical Thinking

- The teacher has the class reciting definitions from rote memory.

- The teacher has the class filling in worksheets all day.

- The children are sitting quietly listening to an endless lecture, sleeping in their chairs.

Sometimes these visions help us refine the list. For example, we might add: "The teacher is using a variety of instructional techniques that model critical thinking skills for the students."

One of the greatest challenges faced by teacher educators attempting to measure the critical thinking standard centers around some confusion about who needs to think critically – student or teacher. The answer is: "the student." While the teacher has to be a good thinker to teach others to teach critical thinking, the buck stops with the child. It is impact on learning that counts here. Box 4.12 should help clarify the distinction.

Box 4.12.   It's About TEACHING Critical Thinking

You might say that an effective behavior you visualized for critical thinking is the teacher sitting at home writing in his or her journal about what happened during the day that worked or did not work. The teacher is analyzing the events and thinking critically about them. Be careful. There are two reasons why this is wrong:

1. The standard requires that the teacher be teaching children to think critically or model it. Sitting home alone writing in a journal is not the same thing.

2. The journal writing is worthwhile, but does every teacher have to do that to be a good teacher who can teach children to think critically? Probably not.

Until you start with that visualization of the competent teacher (and the incompetent one), you may continue to have more of the same without having benefited from your own wisdom and the wisdom of others. Remember: If you always do what you have always done, you will always have what you always had—our Word to the Wise on page 102. And maybe that is just not the right stuff after all. Maybe some of it is, some of it isn't, and some of it is just plain missing. Worksheet #2.3 provides space for you to go through the visualization process.

Now that you can see the teacher performing the standard, it is time to translate that vision into tasks. Not too many, and not too few—a construct representative sample.

AERA, APA, and NCME (1999) *Standards*
and CAATS Step 2B

Standard 1.6:

When the validation rests in part on the appropriateness of test content, the procedures followed in specifying and generating test content should be described and justified in reference to the construct the test is intended to represent. *If the definition of the content sampled incorporates criteria such as importance, frequency, or criticality, these criteria should also be clearly explained and justified.*
   CAATS Steps Influenced: 2A, 2B, 2C, 2D

Standard 14.4:

When empirical evidence of predictor-criterion relationships is part of the pattern of evidence used to support test use, the criterion measure(s) used should reflect the criterion construct domain of interest to the organization. *All criteria should represent important work behaviors or work outputs, on the job or in job-relevant training, as indicated by an appropriate review of information about the job.*
   CAATS Steps Influenced: 1C, 2B, 5A

Discussion

This is the first attempt in the model to operationalize the standard about frequency and criticality, since the visualization process moves us away from a reliance on non-authentic tasks that are rare or unimportant teacher actions. Using the visualization process, we help to ensure the job-relatedness aspect of the system—it is not what you do in your classes and workshops but rather what they do in their own classrooms that counts! Again, the worksheets will help you with the documentation requirement of Standard 1.6.

NOTE: Emphases added for clarity.

CAATS STEP 2C: BRAINSTORM A SET OF SUMMATIVE TASKS (SAMPLING PLAN)

All good assessment requires a sampling plan. The sampling plan is what helps us be sure that we have covered everything we need without having either too much or too little. After all, we cannot test everything, but neither do we want to miss anything that is really important. If we do not have a plan, there is no telling what we will have in the end. Architects make blueprints before they start putting down bricks and hammering studs. That way, they are sure that there will be enough doors and windows and that they will be in the right places and in the right quantities. Even with blueprints, sometimes there are mistakes that need adjustment—like a window partially in a closet that the architect did not notice. Assessment designers need to start with a plan, too, or they will end up with what we like to call "just a bunch of stuff"—too much of some stuff and not enough of other stuff. And, they need to be prepared to revise it as they find gaps and overages.

The beginning of the sampling plan is the vision of the competent teacher discussed in CAATS Step 2B. It is now time to think about how to create a set of tasks to operationalize those performances—both products prepared as part of teaching and skills demonstrated in the classroom context with children. How many tasks it will take to cover the domain and make the visualization assessable will vary from standard to standard, but it is hard to imagine the need for less than three tasks or more than 10, except possibly in content areas where there can be many, many standards representing knowledge in many areas. The tasks could be traditional paper-and-pencil tests, but they are more likely to be products and performances. The taxonomic classifications discussed in Step 1 will help guide the selection of assessment methods.

> ? ──── **Product- and Performance-Based Tasks** ────
>
> Tasks are the things we ask teachers to do to show evidence of their competence. They result in a tangible product (e.g., a classroom management plan) or a live performance (e.g., a class session in which children are working well together to learn).
>
> *Guiding Question: "What things can I have the teachers do to prove they can do the job?"* ?

Brainstorming works best here, probably on chart paper by a team representative of the faculty or district. The group can create a list of tasks that can be narrowed or expanded to ensure adequate representation of the domain. Assessment designers should anticipate going through a series of changes and refinements as tasks are identified, developed, aligned with standards, tested, evaluated, and refined. The process is never truly complete. For that reason, it is important to identify a manageable number of focused tasks that provide enough information without overwhelming test developers, test takers, and evaluators. The goal is to have enough to do the job well. In Boxes 4.13 and 4.14, we provide a set of tasks for assessing the teacher's ability to teach critical and creative thinking skills and another to assess ability to work with diverse populations.

Box 4.13. Sample Tasks to Measure a Teacher's Ability to Teach Critical Thinking

- Questioning using a taxonomy
- Lesson(s) to teach critical and creative thinking
- Portfolio of K–12 student work
- Critical thinking strategies and materials file

Box 4.14. Sample Tasks to Measure a Teacher's Ability to Work With Diverse Populations

- A demographic study of your students and a plan to meet their needs
- Documentation of diversity accommodations
- Individual planning for intervention
- Observation for diversity

Worksheet #2.4 provides a space for you to get started. Getting to that manageable number of just the right tasks is the next step. Frameworks help here to ensure a balanced and appropriate set of tasks in the sampling plan.

Sampling Plan

There are bunches of things a teacher could do to provide evidence of competence, and there are bunches of indicators collected in the domains made up of various standards. The sampling plan selects the most important tasks and indicators from the domains being assessed. It must include a representative sample from each domain. It would not be a good sampling plan if the teacher had to create 30 lesson plans and no assessments or if the teacher was assessed on only 3 of 30 indicators or 6 of 10 standards.

Guiding Question: "What tasks will I pick to cover all of the standards?"

AERA, APA, and NCME (1999) *Standards*
and CAATS Step 2C

Standard 1.6:

When the validation rests in part on the appropriateness of test content, the procedures followed in *specifying and generating test content should be described and justified in reference to the construct* the test is intended to represent. If the definition of the content sampled incorporates criteria such as *importance, frequency, or criticality*, these criteria should also be clearly explained and justified.

CAATS Steps Influenced: 2A, 2B, 2C, 2D

Discussion

This standard is repeated for the third time. Again, the process of brainstorming summative tasks based on the visualization process of Step 2B reinforces the job-relatedness aspect of the system. Later in the model (Step 5A), when we specifically address psychometrics, we will explore the use of a survey of stakeholders in which we ask them to rate the frequency, authenticity, and criticality of each task in the system. This will serve a major role in our gathering of validity evidence.

NOTE: Emphases added for clarity.

CAATS STEP 2D: SORT TASKS INTO FORMATIVE AND SUMMATIVE ASSESSMENTS

It is important to think through carefully which tasks should be used for formative purposes and which ones should be used for summative decision making. College faculties are often tempted to include everything they do, and this will lead to an unmanageably large system. District personnel, too, often have a routine in the workshops presented, sometimes based on available skills in the office. Sampling is critically important to achieve the desired use and interpretation. There are two key questions here.

- How much is enough—not too much and not too little—to assure a representative and thorough sample of all critical skills without overdoing it?

- What is really important, and what can just lead up to a more important task/decision?

If this were airline pilot school, one could make the following analogy: Landing the plane is important and needs to be measured. Finding the "bring me food" button (there probably is no such button) does not need to be assessed; the pilots will find it when they get thirsty or hungry. Some pilot instructors may think it is important because previous pilots have complained, or it was their most-used button when they were pilots, or they always forgot to get dinner before going to work. But it is not a critical skill.

One useful strategy for reducing the overall number of tasks is to think about how many are really needed for a summative decision. In cases where there is an abundance of tasks, more is not necessarily better. All assessment tasks are important, but not all are necessary for a summative decision. Here are two useful guidelines:

- Summative assessment tasks define minimal competency on a standard.
- Formative assessment tasks prepare candidates for summative assessments and provide evidence of improvement needs.

Assessment designers need to determine if some tasks provide practice for others and can be used as formative assessments, keeping the larger or more important later tasks as summative measures. This is difficult because it often involves ownership. Most faculty members and trainers will think all of their tasks are critical to the overall success of the mission. CAATS Steps 3 and 4, which address data aggregation, may help them understand that this is not necessarily the case.

Some examples will help to elaborate this concept. If we ask teachers to analyze standardized test reports, this, by itself, sounds like an important summative task. However, if we also ask them to develop an IEP based on a number of factors, including an analysis of standardized test results, then the IEP can become the summative task in the system with the first task of analysis only serving a formative function. The IEP task, however, needs to be written to include that analysis of standardized test reports, the quality of which is evaluated. The simple analysis task then becomes formative and is used in preparation for the IEP task. This type of analysis will help create a scope and sequence for the curriculum or training. Some other examples for our critical thinking standard are provided in Table 4.5.

Table 4.5. Sorting Formative and Summative Tasks	
Formative Tasks	*Summative Tasks*
Objective writing and classification exercise	Lesson plan, including questioning based on a taxonomy
Analysis of videotaped teacher questioning students	Critical-thinking strategies and materials resource file with applications used
Brainstorming, lateral thinking synectics, and other critical-thinking activities design	Lessons to teach critical thinking in the content areas
Self-analysis of teacher's own creative skills	Portfolio of K–12 student work in which students demonstrated critical thinking

Some questions can help us to make the formative vs. summative decision:

✓ How strong is the linkage between the task. the standard, and your expectations about minimal competency?

✓ How much common agreement is there among faculty and district personnel on the task?

✓ Is this task critical to good teaching?

✓ Is this task authentic?

✓ Can you keep track of the decisions in your database?

There is one final note to be made on the formative vs. summative assessment sorting process. The categorization of these tasks is somewhat akin to categorizing goals and objectives. One person's objectives may be another person's goals. Much will depend on the vision of the competent teacher and the opportunities available for assessment through coursework or mentoring relationships. The key here is to make sure that the summative tasks cover the standard and that the formative tasks do not provide duplicative information but rather help prepare the teacher for the summative tasks. Worksheet #2.5 will help take you through this process.

AERA, APA, and NCME (1999) Standards
CAATS Step 2D

Standard 1.6:

When the validation rests in part on the appropriateness of test content, the procedures followed in specifying and generating test content should be described and justified in reference to the construct the test is intended to represent. If the definition of the content sampled incorporates criteria such as *importance, frequency, or criticality*, these criteria should also be clearly explained and justified.

CAATS Steps Influenced: 2A, 2B, 2C, 2D

Discussion

This standard is repeated for the fourth and last time. Again, sorting out the formative tasks from the summative ones not only helps to reduce the redundancy and volume of the system but reinforces the criticality criterion.

NOTE: Emphases added for clarity.

CAATS STEP 2E: BUILD ASSESSMENT FRAMEWORKS

Framework Options

Assessment frameworks, or blueprints or charts, are useful in conducting the next review of tasks that have been identified and sorted through CAATS Steps 2C and 2D. Such charts are useful in filling gaps, reducing overloaded areas, and adding other elements of the assessment system that are not task based (e.g., GPA and standardized test scores). This step makes the set of assessment instruments and measures both manageable and complete, helping to ensure that the set of assessments and other tasks envisioned in the brainstorming session is appropriate, balanced, and manageable from a variety of perspectives. There are many types of frameworks possible. Some of the most important are:

> **Frameworks**
>
> Frameworks are two-way grids that help one conceptualize a balanced and appropriate set of assessments.
>
> *Guiding Question: "What do I have in my system that fits a selected set of planning criteria (e.g., timing, standards, Bloom's taxonomy)?"*

- Types of competency (knowledge, skills, dispositions, impact on K–12 learning)
- Level of measurement inference (high, medium, low)
- Timing (admission, pre-internship, internship, graduation, post-graduation)
- Assessment method (e.g., tests, products, observed performances, interviews, scales).

Table 4.6 provides some details on the types of frameworks, a brief description of each of them, and some examples of the rows (or columns) that could be

Table 4.6. Frameworks for Analyzing and Completing Task Lists		
Framework Type	*Description*	*Examples*
Assessment Method or Strategy	The instruments or data sources to be used	Tasks (products and performances) GPA Praxis or Certification Test Score Employer or Alumni Survey Rehire Study
Standards	The INTASC standards, base standards, or some other set of standards	Assessment Communication Critical Thinking, and so on
Conceptual Framework Elements	The institution's own set of descriptors of what a graduate is like	Caring Individual Competent Professional Reflective Practitioner Critical Thinker Problem Solver

(Continued)

(Continued)

Framework Type	Description	Examples
Competency Types	The elements of Standard 1 in the NCATE Standards (and the organizing structure of the INTASC Principles)	Knowledge Skills (professional and pedagogical, as well as psychomotor if applicable) Dispositions Impact on K–12 Learning
Levels of Inference	The levels of difficulty in making a judgment or decision about competency	Low Medium High
Points in Time	The "gates" when decisions about competency need to be made throughout a program (and afterwards) to ensure adequate and timely diagnosis and remediation for individuals and the program itself	Admission Pre-Internship Internship Pre-Graduation Post-Graduation

Inference Levels

Inference levels are controlled by the amount of difficulty in making a decision or judgment. They range from no judgment (low inference), as in a correct/incorrect response, to extensive judgment requiring professional expertise to interpret a response.

Guiding Question: "How hard will it be to make a decision about quality—or how much subjectivity is there in this decision?"

included in the framework for analysis purposes. Frameworks can be single dimensional—just rows—or two dimensional—one type in the columns and another in the rows. Three dimensional gets a bit complex! As you read Table 4.6, visualize the examples going down or across or paired into a single table. We will provide some examples later.

Each of these is important. If we do not plan using these frameworks, we can end up with a very lopsided system with too much of something in one category and not enough in another. For example, it is easy to overload knowledge and skills and skip over K–12 impact or dispositions. We can also have too many low inference assessments, never really making judgments that are difficult to make but important to use. Or, we can pile way too much in internship for a university supervisor or cooperating teacher to be able to manage. Balance and distribution are important here to build a system that has utility and practicality.

Some examples of the kinds of assessments that can be used for these framework types follow in Tables 4.7 through 4.9, in which we sort our summative assessments by competency type (Table 4.7), levels of inference (Table 4.8), and points in time (Table 4.9). Each of these approaches to sorting, as modeled in the tables, is accompanied by a worksheet at the end of the chapter (Worksheets #2.6 through #2.8).

Table 4.7.	Excerpt of Framework Using Competency Types
Knowledge	Test on Literacy Teaching Strategies Research Paper on Earth Science
Skills	Writing Sample and Interview Lesson Plan Plan to Accommodate ESE Children Record of Accommodations Student Teaching Evaluation Follow-Up Surveys
Dispositions	Thurstone Scale on INTASC Dispositions K–12 Focus Group on INTASC Dispositions
Impact	Portfolio of K–12 Work Showing Critical Thinking Analysis of Individual Child's Growth in a Content Area

Table 4.8.	Excerpt of Framework Using Levels of Inference
Low	Test on Literacy Teaching Strategies Thurstone Scale on INTASC Dispositions Follow-Up Surveys
Medium	Writing Sample and Interview Research Paper on Earth Science Lesson Plan Analysis of Individual Child's Growth in a Content Area Plan to Accommodate ESE Children Record of Accommodations
High	K–12 Focus Group on INTASC Dispositions Portfolio of K–12 Work Showing Critical Thinking Student Teaching Evaluation

Table 4.9.	Excerpt of Framework Using Points in Time
Admission	GPA and SAT Transcript Analysis Writing Sample and Interview Research Paper on Earth Science
Pre–Student Teaching	Test on Literacy Teaching Strategies Thurstone Scale on INTASC Dispositions Lesson Plan
Student Teaching	Plan to Accommodate ESE Children Record of Accommodations
Pre-Graduation	Student Teaching Evaluation
Post-Graduation	Follow-Up Surveys Rehire Studies

When building assessment frameworks, once these basic lists are developed, test developers need to select as many pairs as needed to think through their programs. Examples of framework pairs are:

- Competency type by level of inference
- Competency type by standards and/or conceptual framework elements
- Standard by assessment type
- Standard by timing
- Competency type by timing

In Tables 4.10 and 4.11, we provide non-comprehensive examples of the first two framework pairs (competency type by level of inference and competency type by standards).

Table 4.10.   Sample Framework by Competency Type (Columns) by Levels of Inference (Rows)

INTASC Taxonomy	Knowledge	Skills	Disposition	Impact
Low	Multiple Choice	Folio Artifacts	Belief Scale	Pre-Post Gain Scores
Medium	Essay	Group Project	Self-Report	Student Work Samples
High	Semester Unit Plan	Clinical Observation	K–12 Focus	Analysis of Interventions

Table 4.11.   Sample Framework by Competency Type (Columns) by INTASC Principles (Rows)

INTASC Principles		Knowledge and Skills	Impact	Disposition
#	Key Words			
1	Content Knowledge	Test Lesson and/ or Unit Plan	K–12 Work Portfolio	Observation Checklist K–12 Focus Group Teacher Questionnaire
2	Learning and Development	Test Lesson and/ or Unit Plan and/or IEP	Test Score Comparisons with Same Age/ Development	Teacher Belief Scale Teacher Questionnaire
3	Diverse Learners	Individual Educational Plan	IEP Results	Observation Checklist K–12 Focus Group

	INTASC Principles	Knowledge and Skills	Impact	Disposition
#	*Key Words*			
4	Critical Thinking	Lesson and/or Unit Plan	K–12 Work Portfolio	Teacher Questionnaire K–12 Focus Group
5	Motivation and Learning Environment	K–12 Attitude Scale	Use of K–12 Attitude Scale and Results	K–12 Focus Group Observation Checklist
6	Communication	Folder of Communications Interaction Observation	Real-Time Monitoring	Focus Group Observation Checklist
7	Planning	Lesson and/or Unit Plan	Readiness Test in Next Grade	Teacher Questionnaire K–12 Focus Group
8	Assessment	Objective Test Alternative Assessment	TWSM Remediation Plans and Results	Teacher Belief Scale K–12 Focus Group
9	Reflection and Professionalism	Ethics Test Lesson and/or Unit Plan	Results of Modified Lesson	Scenario Interview
10	Collegiality	Record of Work on School Improvement Team	Interviews with Co-teachers	Teacher Belief Scale Principal Interview

There is no need to be obsessive about completing the charts. Not every cell needs to have assessments in it, and single assessments can appear in multiple rows and columns. These are *just* planning tools that help ensure the appropriateness, balance, and feasibility of the complete assessment system. Again, we provide worksheets for you to use should you choose to develop these kinds of frameworks on your own (Worksheets #2.9 and 2.10).

A Special Case: Aligning Tasks With NCATE Requirements

Because the NCATE program review process requires data on candidates in five areas, the final alignment for colleges of education should be based on these requirements.

1. State licensure examinations of content knowledge;

2. At least one additional assessment of content knowledge;

3. An assessment of candidate ability to plan instruction, or (for nonteaching fields) to fulfill identified professional responsibilities;

4. The evaluation of clinical practice; and

5. An assessment that demonstrates candidate effect on student learning or (for nonteaching fields) the ability to create supportive learning environments.

Matching those areas to a system of critical tasks leading to licensure or certification in a state can be a challenge. The state may require more comprehensive coverage of the standards than NCATE does. The same is true of the specialty professional associations, which may require all of their standards to be covered. The question becomes how a teacher education unit can combine the short and long lists in a meaningful way. One solution is the development of a set of thematic portfolios. For example, in addition to evidence from the certification exam and data for course-based content knowledge tests (INTASC Principle #1), four portfolios, such as the ones modeled in Box 4.15, could be constructed from tasks in the assessment system.

Box 4.15. Four Sample Thematic Portfolios

- *Thematic Portfolio #1: Planning for Instruction (NCATE Requirement #3 Expanded)*

  In this portfolio, teachers demonstrate their ability to align curriculum, instruction, and assessment, providing evidence of many aspects of integrated planning. They identify objectives at multiple learning levels to ensure critical thinking, incorporate specific interdisciplinary targets, and use a variety of instructional strategies. This portfolio is broader than the third NCATE requirement but pulls together three important competencies, modeling best practice for teachers. This portfolio would include tasks targeted for INTASC Principles 4, 7, and 8 (critical thinking, planning, and assessment principles). Note that assessment spans across two portfolios—planning—and the results of planning—learning.

- *Thematic Portfolio #2: Interacting With Stakeholders (NCATE Requirement #4 Expanded)*

  In this portfolio, teachers demonstrate their ability to work with children and their parents, individually and in groups, verbally and in writing. The final internship evaluation is a part of this portfolio and includes products resulting from work with children and adults, as appropriate. This portfolio would provide specific tasks targeted for INTASC Principles 6 and 10 (communication and collegiality principles).

- *Thematic Portfolio #3: Supporting Learning in a Positive Environment (NCATE Requirement #5)*

  The third portfolio provides evidence of the ability of the teacher to help all children learn both through documentation of students' progress and through the creation of an environment that supports their growth as individuals and collectively. A variety of assessment techniques is used, all targeted at measuring student learning individually and/or in groups. This portfolio would include tasks targeted for INTASC Principles 2, 3, 5, and 8 (learning and development, diversity, learning environment, and assessment principles).

- *Thematic Portfolio #4: Becoming a Professional*

  In this portfolio, the teacher explores some issues related to professional behaviors and attitudes, begins collecting resource materials, and initiates plans for continuing improvement. This portfolio would include tasks targeted for INTASC Principle #9 (professionalism principle) as well as dispositions.

Worksheet #2.11 provides workspace for matching tasks to thematic portfolios should you decide to use this approach.

AERA, APA, and NCME (1999) *Standards*
and CAATS Step 2E

Standard 3.1:

Tests and testing programs should be developed on a *sound scientific basis.* Test developers and publishers should compile and document *adequate evidence bearing on test development.*
    CAATS Steps Influenced: 1C, 2E, 3C

Standard 3.2:

The purpose(s) of the test, *definition of the domain, and the test specifications* should be stated clearly so that judgments can be made about the appropriateness of the defined domain for the stated purpose(s) of the test and *about the relation of items to the dimensions of the domain they are intended to represent.*
    CAATS Steps Influenced: 1A, 1C, 2E, 5A

Standard 3.3:

The *test specifications should be documented*, along with their rationale and the process by which they were developed. The test specifications should *define the content of the test, the proposed number of items, the item formats*, the desired psychometric properties of the items, and the item and section arrangement. They should also specify the amount of time for testing, directions to the test takers, procedures to be used for test administration and scoring, and other relevant information.
    CAATS Steps Influenced: 2E, 5A

Standard 3.11:

Test developers should document the extent to which the content domain of a test represents the defined domain and test specifications.
    CAATS Steps Influenced: 2E

Standard 13.3:

When a test is used as an indicator of achievement in an instructional domain or with respect to specified curriculum standards, *evidence of the extent to which the test samples the range of knowledge and elicits the processes* reflected in the target domain should be provided. Both tested and target domains should be described in sufficient detail so their relationship can be evaluated. The analyses should *make explicit those aspects of the target domain that the test represents as well as those aspects that it fails to represent.*
    CAATS Steps Influenced: 2E, 3C

Standard 14.8:

Evidence of validity based on test content requires a thorough and explicit definition of the content domain of interest. For selection, classification, and promotion, the characterization of the domain should be based on a *job analysis.*
    CAATS Steps Influenced: 1C, 2E

(Continued)

(Continued)

AERA, APA, and NCME (1999) *Standards*
and CAATS Step 2E

Standard 14.9:

When evidence of validity based on test content is a primary source of validity evidence in support of the use of a test in selection or promotion, *a close link between test content and job content should be demonstrated.*
    CAATS Steps Influenced: 1C, 2E

Standard 14.10:

When evidence of validity based on test content is presented, the *rationale for defining and describing a specific job content domain in a particular way (e.g., in terms of tasks to be performed* or knowledge, skills, abilities, or other personal characteristics) should be stated clearly.
    CAATS Steps Influenced: 1C, 2E

Standard 14.14:

The *content domain to be covered by a credentialing test should be defined clearly and justified* in terms of the importance of the content for credential-worthy performance in an occupation or profession. A rationale should be provided to support a claim that the knowledge of skills being assessed are required for credential-worthy performance in an occupation and are consistent with the purpose for which the licensing or certification program was instituted.
    CAATS Steps Influenced: 1C, 2E, 3C, 5A

Discussion

We have just listed nine standards from three different chapters that all say essentially the same thing: build frameworks or blueprints or specifications to show how you are covering the standards that define the job of teaching in your tasks. Judging from the sheer repetition in the AERA, APA, and NCME *Standards*, the importance of this step should be evident.

NOTE: Emphases added for clarity.

∇ WRAP-UP

In this chapter we outlined a series of steps to take you through the planning process in a way that will maximize your opportunities to make valid decisions about teacher performance. CAATS Step 2 is designed to help you develop a valid sampling plan so that you avoid a hodgepodge of assessments that do not give you the answers you need about assessing teachers using standards.

You have read about organizing the standards into content domains to avoid the redundancy and frustration inherent in the multiple sets of standards, and to maximize their benefit to you in designing assessment tasks. You will see how this really works later. You have visualized the minimally competent (or advanced) teacher in order to begin the task identification process. You have brainstormed the tasks that fit your vision and then reduced them for efficiency's sake to include only those tasks that are summative in nature. You have begun to think about how to ensure that the overall assessment system is balanced in a variety of ways, covering not only the standards, but doing so in a way that touches on all the competency types you need to address, helps you make better decisions by using varied inference levels, spreads your work out over time, and other frameworks for organizing your system.

Before planning at a detailed level—the tasks themselves, let's make sure you have a set of tasks that is worth your time and energy. Before moving on to CAATS Step 3, fill in the rows for CAATS Step 2 of the action plan in Chapter 2 and, if you have not already done so, complete the worksheets at the end of this chapter!

Story Starters

Starter #1:

Professor/Teacher Paneinthebutt stomps into your office and says:

"There are just too many standards. I don't see any value in looking at all of them. I'll just stick to the top five and forget about the rest. Besides, everything I do in my curriculum is critical to good teaching, so I'm going to weight it all equally in my decisions, regardless of whether it is formative or summative in your eyes. The diary my students keep is just as important as your classroom management plan. A teacher who can't keep a good diary just shouldn't be a teacher. I write in my diary every day and reread it every Saturday night. I read the best parts to my grandchildren! I can tell a good teacher when I see one, and I just don't need to be this picky. Like I said before, I have tenure, and you can't make me."

You say. . . . .

Starter #2:

On the surface, Mr. Kidzartuph seems like he will be a great teacher. He has high test scores, dresses professionally, and is always on time. He took a workshop on planning and learned how to write a lesson plan. He uses what he learned every day in school. He turned in several for his performance appraisal, and they were great. He's really a quick study! But he just can't shift gears when things aren't working in the classroom. I fear that one day the kids will just tie him to a chair and set the room on fire. What did we miss when we assessed him?

CAATS STEP 2—WORKSHEET #2.1
Organizing for Alignment (Version 1)

Explanation:

Align your national standards with the state standards of your choice. Select some keywords to help you think about what the state and national standards have in common.

Base Standards	National Standards	State Standards

CAATS STEP 2—WORKSHEET #2.1
Organizing for Alignment (Version 2)

Explanation:

Align your standards with those of INTASC. You may also change the base standards if you prefer different keywords.

Base Standard	INTASC Principle	Your State or Local Standards
Assessment	*Principle #8:* The teacher understands and uses formal and informal ***assessment*** strategies to evaluate and ensure the continuous intellectual, social, and physical development of the learner.	
Communication	*Principle #6:* The teacher uses knowledge of effective verbal, nonverbal, and media ***communication*** techniques to foster active inquiry, collaboration, and supportive interaction in the classroom.	
Continuous Improvement	*Principle #9:* The teacher is ***a reflective practitioner*** who continually evaluates the defects of his/her choices and actions on others (students, parents, and other professionals in the learning community) and who actively seeks out opportunities to grow professionally.	
Critical and Creative Thinking	*Principle #4:* The teacher understands and uses a variety of instructional strategies to encourage students' development of ***critical thinking***, problem solving, and performance skills.	

(Continued)

(Continued)

CAATS STEP 2—WORKSHEET #2.1
Organizing for Alignment (Version 2)

Base Standard	*INTASC Principle*	*Your State or Local Standards*
Diversity	*Principle #3:* The teacher understands how students differ in their approaches to learning and creates instructional opportunities that are adapted to *diverse learners.*	
Human Development and Learning	*Principle #2:* The teacher understands how children *learn and develop*, and can provide learning opportunities that support their intellectual, social, and personal development.	
Knowledge of Subject Matter	*Principle #1:* The teacher understands the central concepts, tools of inquiry, and structures of the discipline(s) he or she teaches and can create learning experiences that make these aspects of *subject matter* meaningful for students.	
Learning Environment	*Principle #5:* The teacher uses an understanding of individual and group motivation and behavior to create a *learning environment* that encourages positive social interaction, active engagement in learning, and self-motivation.	
Planning	*Principle #7:* The teacher *plans* instruction based upon knowledge of subject matter, students, the community, and curriculum goals.	
Role of the Teacher	*Principle #10:* The teacher fosters relationships with school *colleagues, parents*, and agencies in the larger community to support students' learning and well being.	

(sidebar) **CAATS WORKSHEETS**

CAATS STEP 2—WORKSHEET #2.2
Our Critical Skills

Explanation:

List the skills you think articulate the content domain for an individual base standard. The form allows for up to 10 skills, which should be your maximum. Aim, though, for three to five skills per standard, and complete one of these worksheets for each of your base standards. Hit the highlights! Don't cover every detail.

NOTE: Skills begin with a verb (e.g., "communicate effectively with parents").

Base Standard: _____

Skill Number	*Skill Text*
Skill #1	
Skill #2	
Skill #3	
Skill #4	
Skill #5	
Skill #6	
Skill #7	
Skill #8	
Skill #9	
Skill #10	

CAATS WORKSHEETS

CAATS STEP 2—WORKSHEET #2.3
Visualizing the Competent Teacher

Explanation:

There are two steps for this worksheet. First, you will visualize the competent (and incompetent) teacher. Then you will seek the wisdom of others. Repeat this process for each base standard.

Base Standard: _____

Step 1: Close your eyes and think about a great teacher demonstrating this base standard. What do you see the great teacher doing? Start the first list. Now think about a really bad teacher. What is the bad teacher doing? Start the second list.

What do you see the really good teacher doing?

1. *The teacher is*_____.
2. *The teacher is*_____.
3. *The teacher is*_____.
4. *The teacher is*_____.
5. *The teacher is*_____.

What do you see the really bad teacher doing—or not doing?

1. *The teacher is NOT*_____.
2. *The teacher is NOT*_____.
3. *The teacher is NOT*_____.
4. *The teacher is NOT*_____.
5. *The teacher is NOT*_____.

Step 2: Now talk to some stakeholders and ask them to critique your list, adding their visualization to it. Then check out your list in the library or online. What does research about best practices tell you? Update the list one more time.

CAATS STEP 2—WORKSHEET #2.4
Critical Task List

Explanation:

List the tasks—both products and observed performances—that will provide evidence of the critical skills you think articulate the content domain for an individual base standard. Use your visualization process—what was the teacher doing? The form allows for up to 10 tasks, which should be your maximum. Aim, though, for three to five tasks per standard, and complete one of these worksheets for each of your base standards. Hit the highlights! Don't cover every detail.

Note: Tasks begin with a noun.

Examples:

> Record or observation of parent-teacher conference
> Lesson plan to teach critical thinking

Remember: These tasks must be job related—authentic and critical!

Base Standard: _____

1. _____

2. _____

3. _____

4. _____

5. _____

6. _____

7. _____

8. _____

9. _____

10. _____

CAATS WORKSHEETS

CAATS WORKSHEETS

CAATS STEP 2—WORKSHEET #2.5
Sorting Formative and Summative Tasks

Explanation:

Assess the tasks you identified by answering each of the following questions. Then place a "yes" or a "no" in the appropriate cell. At the end of the row, decide if the task should be formative or summative. When you are done, go back and number the tasks remaining as summative with the base standard and task number or letter as in this example: 01A (Base Standard 1, Task 1) or 02D (Base Standard 2, Task 4). This will help a lot later.

Questions:

- ✓ How strong is the linkage between the task and the standard and your expectations about minimal competency (or advanced competency)?
- ✓ How much common agreement is there among faculty and district personnel on the task?
- ✓ Is this task critical to good teaching?
- ✓ Is this task authentic?
- ✓ Can you keep track of the decisions in your database?

Task	Linkage	Agreement	Critical	Authentic	Manageable	Formative or Summative

CAATS STEP 2—WORKSHEET #2.6
List of Summative Assessments by Competency Type

Explanation:

Using the numbers you just added to your list of summative tasks on Worksheet #2.4 (the ones you decided to keep on Worksheet #2.5), now classify each task by competency type. You only need to write the numbers in the right column—unless you prefer to write the task names. You will be doing this a few times, so think about the decision carefully. NOTE: You may want to omit this worksheet and do Worksheet #2.9 instead.

Competency Type	Assessments
Knowledge	
Skills	
Dispositions	
Impact on K–12 Learning	

Do you have enough in every row? How is the balance? You can still make changes!

CAATS STEP 2—WORKSHEET #2.7

List of Summative Assessments by Levels of Inference

Explanation:

Now reclassify the tasks by level of inference, using numbers or task names in the right column. Think about how hard it will be to make judgments about the quality of the teacher's competence on the skills reflected in the product or in the performance.

Level of Inference	*Assessments*
Low	
Medium	
High	

Do you have enough in every row? How is the balance? You can still make changes!

CAATS STEP 2—WORKSHEET #2.8

List of Summative Assessments by Points in Time

Explanation:

Now reclassify the tasks by points in time. Try not to lump everything into internship (or any summative observation) or you will have a very unhappy rater and a teacher who has no early warning system. NOTE: This form works best in colleges.

Points in Time	*Assessments*
Admission	
Pre–Student Teaching	
Student Teaching	
Pre-Graduation	
Post-Graduation	

Do you have enough in every row? How is the balance? You can still make changes!

CAATS WORKSHEETS

CAATS STEP 2—WORKSHEET #2.9

Matrix of Standards by Competency Type

Explanation:

Now start putting the tasks into two-way matrices. Here combine what you did earlier on Worksheet #2.6 and combine that work with the standards alignment.

Standard	Knowledge	Skill	Disposition	Impact on K–12
INTASC #1				
INTASC #2				
INTASC #3				
INTASC #4				
INTASC #5				
INTASC #6				
INTASC #7				
INTASC #8				
INTASC #9				
INTASC #10				

Do you have enough in every row? How is the balance? You can still make changes!

CAATS WORKSHEETS

CAATS STEP 2—WORKSHEET #2.10

Matrix of Critical Tasks by Competency Type and Benchmark

Explanation:

In this chart, you have an opportunity to think about the timing of tasks that require children or skills demonstration. It is useful to help you balance the tasks.

Fill in the chart thinking about one standard at a time.

Benchmark/Time	Impact on K–12 Learning	Skills Demonstration	
	Field-Based Tasks (Practicum/ Internship)	*Field-Based Tasks (Practicum/ Internship)*	*Campus-Based Tasks (Course Work)*
End of Program (Final Internship Semester)			
Middle of Program (All Semesters Except First and Last)			
Beginning of Program (First Semester)			

Do you have enough in every row? How is the balance? You can still make changes!

CAATS WORKSHEETS

CAATS STEP 2—WORKSHEET #2.11
Aligning Tasks With NCATE Thematic Portfolios

Explanation:

Last one. See if you can organize the tasks into thematic portfolios for NCATE—colleges only of course. This worksheet helps align tasks with NCATE Requirements if the unit decides to use a thematic portfolio approach. A set of themes is suggested and correlated with the INTASC Principles. You can also make up your own themes, keeping them closely aligned with the NCATE list of evidence.

NCATE Evidence #	INTASC Principles Aligned	Thematic Portfolio Title	Tasks Incorporated
3	4, 7, 8	Planning for Instruction and Assessment	
4	6, 10	Interacting with Stakeholders	
5	2, 3, 5, 8	Supporting Learning in a Positive Environment	
Additional	9	Becoming a Professional	

NOTE: INTASC #1 could be assessed in course-based content exams but is not included in these portfolios.

Where We Have Been So Far

By now, it should be pretty obvious that we are planning for validity, that little puppy that never leaves our side. We have focused our thinking about assessment by clearly articulating the purpose(s), use(s), and content of the system in CAATS Step 1—all within our own local value system and operational context. Using our decisions about content, particularly about standards sets, we visualized the competent (or advanced) teacher performing on the job—a job analysis—and sought aid from our stakeholders and the literature. We looked at all the standards of interest together to form assessment domains from which we could sample, paired down the domains into a useful set of critical skills, articulated tasks that would serve as evidence of those skills, reviewed the tasks to sort out those that were predominantly formative or redundant, and used a variety of frameworks to help ensure a balanced and appropriate set of assessment instruments that covered the standards adequately. Our goal was just enough—not too much and not too little—because the job of writing up and using the tasks is a very time-consuming one.

We now have our marching orders—a "blueprint"—just like architects who are going to build a building. We know where the doors are (decision points or gates), what is on each floor (competency levels), how hard it will be to climb from one floor to the next (inference levels), and how the load is distributed (between products and performances). It is now time to move on to CAATS Step 3—developing the tasks to do the job.

5

CAATS Step 3

*Writing Tasks Designed to
Maximize Validity and Reliability*

The whole assessment system is only as good as the sum of its parts. Each task needs to be an assessment jewel. While that may be a bitter pill for some to swallow, it is a necessary one. When tasks are developed in a sloppy manner, the information they provide will be sloppy. For this reason, above all, we offer words of caution about not having too many tasks in the system. In CAATS Step 2, we actively discouraged assessment designers from shortcutting the system with just one task per standard, but we also actively discouraged throwing everything into the soup pot (with crosswalks).

> **CAATS Step 3: Create or update tasks aligned with standards and consistent with the sampling plan.**

In CAATS Step 3, we will create or modify tasks that can be combined into an assessment system that yields valid, reliable, and useful decisions about teachers. A **common format** for all tasks is recommended in order to make **data aggregation** across tasks easier. Clear **directions and rubrics** containing the language of target standards need to be written, preferably with a common **rating scale** with an equal number of points on the scale. Then evidence of **content validity** should be gathered to ensure that the tasks are representative of the construct and its conceptual framework, proportional, and in fact job related. Evidence that **adequate instruction** is provided for each task needs to be gathered, so that we are confident that all teachers have an opportunity to succeed.

Some terms you need to add to your vocabulary for this step are provided throughout this chapter.

In this step, we will complete four substeps:

CAATS Step 3A: *Determine the task format for data aggregation.*

CAATS Step 3B: *Create new tasks or modify existing tasks.*

CAATS Step 3C: *Conduct first validity study.*

CAATS Step 3D: *Align tasks with instruction.*

P.S.: Don't forget to keep working on that action plan from Chapter 2!

Before Moving On . . .

1. How do you feel about "winging it"? Do you believe that students (of all ages) should be given thorough directions or instructions before they are asked to complete a task? Justify your answer.

2. If you had a choice between a score that provided extensive feedback regarding what you did well and what you didn't and a score that was just a single number, which would you pick? Why?

3. Is it important to write a test that covers all of the main concepts in a unit, or is it okay to give a short test—say an essay—on a limited portion of the content? Why?

4. How do you feel about using stakeholders or experts to make sure you have done a good job in designing your work?

5. What happens when you test what you haven't taught?

CAATS STEP 3A: DETERMINE THE TASK FORMAT FOR DATA AGGREGATION

If Professor Globbel uses a holistic rubric on his task and Professor Analit uses a three-point rating scale on hers, and Professors Smartey and Knowall use their "best judgment" with no rubric at all, then combining their decisions to reach a summative decision about teacher competence and areas for improvement is very difficult. We will talk more about making summative decisions, also called cut scores (one piece of the data aggregation challenge), in Step 4. For now, we need to be prepared to aggregate the data in meaningful ways. If we are not prepared to do so, the ramifications of that difficulty play out in the overall validity, reliability, fairness, and utility of the decision-making process, and just plain keep on nagging at us!

Task

A task is something you ask a teacher to do to demonstrate competency. The task may be in the form of a written product (e.g., a lesson plan) or a skill (e.g., that lesson plan delivered).

Guiding Question: "What things can I ask a teacher to do to show competence—or lack thereof?"

What Happens When There Is No Common Format?

You may be headed toward an assessment system that will be virtually impossible to use effectively because you do not have a common format for scoring, and you will not be able to aggregate data in Step 4. In Box 5.1 we provide two examples of what the future may hold in store if you head down this path.

Box 5.1.   Examples of Data That Are Difficult to Aggregate and Use

Example of Results for a Teacher on Five Tasks:

- Task #1: 99%
- Task #2: 4 ratings of satisfactory and 1 rating of unsatisfactory
- Task #3: 5 ratings of excellent, 2 ratings of marginal, and 1 rating of unacceptable
- Task #4: 18 points
- Task #5: C–

Decision for the teacher: This teacher had a mixed result, doing better on some tasks than others. The teacher needs remediation on tasks 2, 3, and possibly 5 and probably should not be certified.

Problem: We don't know precisely what the teacher did wrong, or if there are any patterns in the problems that can be remediated. We don't even know what 18 points mean in terms of an overall score. How do we remediate or justify the certification decision?

❖

Example of Results Across Teachers on Task #1:

- Teacher #1: 99%
- Teacher #2: 65%
- Teacher #3: 83%
- Teacher #4: 76%
- Teacher #5: 77%

Decision for the program: Teachers had an average score of 80% on this task. No specific criteria are identified as problematic, so no improvement is necessary.

Problem: Three of the five teachers were below average, and we have no information on why. Was there a common problem—something all three of them were getting wrong—that could be fixed to improve the learning of future teachers being assessed on this task?

Can I Use Percents and Total Points? No, They Don't Cut It!

Total points and percents can mask a multitude of sins. We just saw two in terms of data aggregation in the previous examples. In Box 5.2 we provide a more specific illustrative example of why they simply do not work.

> ### Box 5.2. An Example of Why Percent Scores Don't Work for Standards-Based Decisions
>
> - **Task**: Unit assessment
> - **Rubric**: 5 criteria are rated on a three-point scale (3, 2, 1).
> - **Results**: 4 criteria are rated a 3 (target) and 1 criterion is rated a 1 (unacceptable). The unacceptable rating is for using the data to improve student learning. The teacher misinterpreted the data and made bad decisions about what to do next.
> - **Score**: $(4 \times 3) + (1 \times 1) = 13$ out of 15 points, or 87%, or B+.
> - **Conclusion**: Teacher has 87% mastery on INTASC #8 and a grade of B+ on the assessment task.
> - **Problem**: The teacher will hurt children. If the teacher were an airline pilot, s/he could not land the plane!

This is a clear example of why we can't calculate percent scores for tasks and have something meaningful. Matters get more ridiculous, of course, when we start calculating means and standard deviations for tasks across students or programs, which is what most of the e-portfolio software programs are now doing and what we just demonstrated in our previous example! Descriptive statistics of meaningless numbers are still meaningless. This is very much the same message we will provide in Chapter 8 on currently accepted approaches to cut scores.

Elements of a Common Task Format

As we continue down the path of creating a system that yields valid decisions about teacher competency—decisions that can be aggregated—we need to reach consensus on a common task format so that we will be able to aggregate the data for decision making and then apply both judgmental and empirical approaches to test the validity and the reliability of our decisions. We also want to make sure our students have the maximum opportunity to succeed on each task, so we need to tell them what we expect!

To reach our validity target, we recommend that each task has, at a minimum, the following components, which are listed below and described in Boxes 5.3 through 5.6 on the page opposite. Examples are provided under Step 3B.

- Standards alignment
- A brief description of the task for public consumption
- Comprehensive directions for task completion
- Detailed scoring rubrics or guides that include both criteria and a scale

Worksheets #3.1 and #3.2 are designed to help you settle on a scale and a format for your tasks. Examples of each of these task elements are provided in CAATS Step 3B. You may wish to hold off on completing the worksheets for this step until you have looked at those examples. For now, we have tried to show you why it is important to have a common format even if you are not sure yet what it might look like in practice.

Box 5.3.   Description of Standards Alignment

This should be a correlation with all relevant standards, at the indicator level where feasible. This includes the state standards for pedagogy (if any), the state content standards if relevant to the task, the INTASC (or NBPTS) Propositions, the standards of the relevant specialty professional association affiliated with NCATE, and the critical skills or elements of the conceptual framework and/or local mission, as applicable. The task itself should include a listing of these by number. When creating this alignment, ask yourself this question:

**"Will the assessor be able to 'see' evidence of this indicator
in the actual work of the teacher?"**

If such evidence is not clearly visible in this task (as opposed to other tasks in the system), then it should not be included. This is not a test of importance of the standards or the task. It is a test of whether or not an individual task provides evidence of the indicators and standards.

Box 5.4.   Description of a Task Description

This should be a brief description of the task, from one to several sentences in length, including what the teacher is expected to produce or perform. It helps to make public the assessment system. If you list just the full set of task descriptions in one single document, it provides readers with a clear description of the results of the job analysis you completed.

Box 5.5.   Description of Directions

Vague instructions lead to a wide range of student work, much of which is not what the assessors expected and contributes to considerable construct irrelevant variance because of reliability problems. If teachers and assessors have different understandings of expectations, the work will be done differently and scored differently, and this will not be a reflection of what the teachers know and can do. Detailed instructions designed to maximize candidates' chances to produce what is needed well and to minimize frustration must be incorporated into each task, point by point, to improve reliability and, consequently, validity.

Box 5.6.   Description of a Scoring Rubric

For each task, there must be a rubric that provides the explicit criteria to be used by all assessors. This, too, helps to reduce construct irrelevant variance caused by reliability issues. The criteria should be directly linked to both the directions in the task and the standards and indicators they are designed to demonstrate. Everyone needs to know what is expected and how it will be scored.

AERA, APA, and NCME (1999) *Standards*
and CAATS Step 3A

Standard 1.2:

The test developer should set forth clearly how *test scores are intended to be interpreted and used*. The population(s) for which a test is appropriate should be clearly delimited, and the construct that the test is intended to assess should be clearly described.

CAATS Steps Influenced: 1A, 1C, 1D, 3A

Standard 3.14:

The *criteria used for scoring test takers' performance* on extended-response items should be documented. This documentation is *especially* important for performance assessments, such as scoreable portfolios and essays, *where the criteria for scoring may not be obvious to the user.*

CAATS Steps Influenced: 3A, 3B

Standard 5.9:

When test scoring involves human judgment, *scoring rubrics should specify criteria for scoring*. Adherence to established scoring criteria should be monitored and checked regularly. Monitoring procedures should be documented.

CAATS Steps Influenced: 3A, 3B

Standard 8.8:

When score reporting includes assigning individuals to categories, the *categories should be chosen carefully and described precisely*. The least stigmatizing labels, consistent with accurate representation should always be assigned.

CAATS Steps Influenced: 3A

Discussion

In this CAATS substep we hope you have made a decision to use a common scoring format, since the *Standards* tell us repeatedly that we need to have consistent and clear criteria that lead to a supportable and useful decision. Without clear rubrics, we cannot aggregate the data at an individual teacher level in order to interpret our results in meaningful ways or meet any of these *Standards*.

NOTE: Emphases added for clarity.

CAATS STEP 3B: CREATE NEW TASKS OR MODIFY EXISTING TASKS

Basic Concepts About Tasks

Having described the basic components needed for a set of summative tasks that can be aggregated for decision making about individual candidates and overall program quality, we now provide some suggestions on how to create new tasks or modify those that are already in existence. Some tasks, of course, are likely to come from the existing curriculum. Others will be new. Several design features can be incorporated into sets of tasks:

- The tasks can have a range of complexity and a range in duration of time to complete. Careful planning allows for an appropriate balance of low and high inference tasks that can be completed throughout teachers' training programs. Planning with the use of frameworks is a primary focus of the second step in the CAATS model.

- Teachers can become increasingly sophisticated in their ability, through readings, instructional activities, and then completion of each task. Instruction and staff development need to be aligned with assessment activities to provide adequate opportunities for all teachers to succeed.

- Teachers can build the foundation for continued professional development by starting their personal collection of strategies and materials and by analyzing their status on standards upon completion of tasks in the system.

- While there may be components of tasks that might not be routine job functions (e.g., a written analysis of results), each task, on the whole, should reflect an important job-related activity correlated with the standards about teaching (see next section).

- A common scale will allow simpler and better analysis of overall performance using modern measurement methodologies, as described in CAATS Step 4.

- Teachers can become accustomed to reflecting on the results of their work and being held accountable for K–12 student learning. Reflection and analysis have a place in the task-based system, although they should not be the major focus of it. Job performance is the major focus, with nothing more important than the results of a teacher's work on K–12 learning.

Hints and Advice About Writing Tasks

Using the descriptions and explanations for the parts of a summative task from CAATS Step 3A, assessment designers can follow the sequence and examples below to create or modify tasks using the recommended format.

1. **Start with the name, number, and description of the task to make sure everyone is thinking about the same thing. Here are some pointers:**
   - Assign a number or code to the task, so that you can have something easy to use later when you are discussing or analyzing the task. You may have done this already on Worksheet #2.4 of CAATS Step 2. Here are two possibilities:

- Number consecutively from 001 to 999 (you will have probably fewer than 100, but leading zeros allow you to sort in databases and spreadsheets).

- Code tasks by the key standard or principle to which they relate and then a sequence after that. This adds some meaning to your numbers. For example, for INTASC Principle #4, you might number all tasks in that series with a leading 04 and then 01 to 99 or A to Z. (We recommended numbers in CAATS Step 2, but we will model letters here.)

- Prepare your readers (students, colleagues, accrediting agents, district and state level personnel) for the essentials of the task in both the name and description from the beginning. Readers should be able to visualize the teacher's work before you get into the details of instructions and rubrics.

- Be sure to include all the parts or elements of the product or performance, including the specific pieces you expect the teachers to submit in the description.

In Box 5.7 we provide examples for three tasks.

Box 5.7. Examples of Three Critical Tasks With Numbers, Names, and Descriptions Used in the Florida Alternative Certification Program Assessment System

04A: Lesson(s) to Teach Critical and Creative Thinking Using a Taxonomy: The teacher develops a lesson or lessons on facilitating students' use of critical and creative thinking skills. The lessons include objectives and questions classified according to Bloom's taxonomy. The final product consists of the lesson plan(s), an analysis of results and prospective changes, the assessment instrument, and two samples of student work (one where the student performed as expected and one where the student did not).

04B: Portfolio of K–12 Student Work: The teacher creates a showcase portfolio of student work over a semester or year-long period. This portfolio includes samples of work from students in the teacher's class who have exceeded and/or met expectations with regard to targets for critical, creative, or higher-level thinking and those who have not met expectations (at least on an initial evaluation). The product is the portfolio with five work samples, associated performance tasks/tests, and reflections.

04C: Critical Thinking Strategies and Materials File: This is a semester-long project in which the teacher collects strategies and materials to promote critical/creative thinking and problem solving, and annotates each strategy regarding how it was, or will be, used in teaching the content. The product is the file of annotated strategies and materials. At least two strategies must be collected using technology resources.

SOURCE: Adapted from Florida Department of Education (2002).

---

2. **Next, align the task with the most important (visible) standards and indicators, remembering only to pick the ones you think you will be able to see in the teacher's performance or product. Here are some pointers:**

- Make sure the standards and indicators are numbered in a consistent way, since some may not have numbers at all. For example, the INTASC Principles are numbered 1 through 10, but there are no numbers for the indicators. We numbered the INTASC indicators for Principle #1 as follows: 1.1, 1.2, 1.3, and so on. Principle #2 indicators are numbered 2.1, 2.2, 2.3, and so on. If you are going to sort these in a database, use leading zeros (01.1, 02.1, and 03.1). The same system would work for state standards or your own institutional/district standards. You have many choices about how to do this. You also can make your coding even more meaningful if you want to do so. For example, you could number the INTASC Principles with an additional code to reflect whether the indicator is for knowledge, skill (performance), or disposition (e.g., 01K01, 01S04). This step only has to be done once, and it will help with all subsequent tasks, so it is worth a little extra planning time and effort.

> **Reminder**: Do you remember how we said earlier that the task descriptions provide a quick summary of your job analysis? Do the task descriptions in Box 5.7 provide a clear vision of what a teacher who can teach critical thinking should be able to do to demonstrate that ability in job-related ways?

- Using the numbering system, select the standards and indicators that will be readily observable in teachers' work. Look for the best fit of the task and standards.

- Avoid the temptation to overselect. It is unlikely that you will be able to see everything in a single task. Overselection often results in a loss of reliability, not to mention confusion and "assessment exhaustion." When you are making your selections, think about how you could use the official language of the standard and indicators selected to write the directions and scoring criteria. If you can use the language or intent of the indicator, that means you are measuring this aspect of the standards, and it also helps you make sure that the decisions are valid for the standard being assessed. Stick closely to the agency's intent (not your personal beliefs about what is important) in interpreting the meaning of the standard.

- Your alignment should reference all of the indicators by number, using your own numbering system; we used ours. As back-up for audit purposes, keep a list of the indicators in their full text form and make a table that shows where you incorporated them in the directions and rubric. In Box 5.8 is a detailed example that should help you see how this process works.

> **Remember**: The more high stakes your decision and the higher up in the food chain of accountability you are (e.g., state department of education), the more precise you should be about doing this kind of alignment.

We now turn to providing some detailed examples of how the alignment process works with a high-stakes and difficult task. It is not easy, but, in the long run, it adds tremendous credibility (a.k.a. validity) to the assessment system. If tasks are limited in number, the level of work exemplified here is possible. Boxes 5.8 through 5.13 model the alignment process in an assessment we developed for the Florida Alternative Certification Program Assessment System (2002). In our view, it is the most critical task in the system because it taps that all important attribute of a high quality

> **Criteria**
>
> Criteria are the aspects of a performance task that will be judged in the scoring rubric. They help separate high-quality and low-quality work.
>
> *Guiding Question: "What will I look for to judge the quality of this task?"*

teacher preparation program—impact on K-12 learning. The task is called, "Portfolio of K-12 Work." In this task, teachers present examples of the work of their students showing mastery of content and application of critical thinking skills.

In Box 5.8, Part I of our example includes your "public" alignment—just the numbers. In our example, we have aligned the task with the INTASC Principles, as well as the national standards for elementary and special education (ACEI and CEC). We complete the alignment with Florida standards, so that we assure the validity of our process for state-based decisions. Two base standards are aligned: content knowledge and critical thinking.

Box 5.8.   Task Alignment Example (Part I)

Base Standards: Knowledge of Subject Matter and Critical Thinking and Problem Solving

Actual Standards/Indicators Assessed:

INTASC Indicators:	1.1, 1.2, 1.8, 1.10 (Subject Matter) 4.1, 4.3, 4.7–4.10 (Critical Thinking)
ACEI Indicators:	2.1–2.4 (Subject Matter) 3.3 (Critical Thinking)
CEC Indicators:	4.0
Accomplished Practice Indicators:	8.1–8.4 (Subject Matter) 4.1, 4.2, 4.4, 4.5, 4.6 (Critical Thinking)
Florida Elementary Standards:	6, 12, 17, 25 (Subject Matter)

Part II of the alignment examples in Box 5.9 shows the backup for your alignment, the actual text of the standards and indicators aligned. Because it is lengthy, we will split the textboxes into two separate ones—one for each standard assessed.

Box 5.9.   Task Alignment Example (Part IIA): Content Knowledge

INTASC Principles

Principle #1: The teacher understands the central concepts, tools of inquiry, and structures of the discipline(s) s/he teaches and can create learning experiences that make these aspects of subject matter meaningful for students.

1. The teacher understands major concepts, assumptions, debates, processes of inquiry, and ways of knowing that are central to the discipline(s) s/he teaches.

2. The teacher understands how students' conceptual frameworks and their misconceptions for an area of knowledge can influence their learning.

8. The teacher effectively uses multiple representations and explanations of disciplinary concepts that capture key ideas and link them to students' prior understandings.

10. The teacher can evaluate teaching resources and curriculum materials for their comprehensiveness, accuracy, and usefulness for representing particular ideas and concepts.

ACEI Standards

Curriculum Standards

2.1 **English language arts**—Candidates demonstrate a high level of competence in use of English language arts and they know, understand, and use concepts from reading, language, and child development to teach reading, writing, speaking, viewing, listening, and thinking skills, and to help students successfully apply their developing skills to many different situations, materials, and ideas.

2.2 **Science**—Candidates know, understand, and use fundamental concepts in the subject matter of science—including physical, life, and earth and space sciences—as well as concepts in science and technology, science in personal and social perspectives, the history and nature of science, the unifying concepts of science, and the inquiry processes scientists use in discovery of new knowledge to build a base for scientific and technological literacy.

2.3 **Mathematics**—Candidates know, understand, and use the major concepts, procedures, and reasoning processes of mathematics that define number systems and number sense, geometry, measurement, statistics and probability, and algebra in order to foster student understanding and use of patterns, quantities, and spatial relationships that can represent phenomena, solve problems, and manage data.

2.4 **Social studies**—Candidates know, understand, and use the major concepts and modes of inquiry from the social studies—the integrated study of history, geography, the social sciences, and other related areas—to promote elementary students' abilities to make informed decisions as citizens of a culturally diverse democratic society and interdependent world.

Florida Standards

Florida Educator Accomplished Practice #8—
Knowledge of Subject Matter, Preprofessional Level:

The preprofessional teacher has a basic understanding of the subject field and is beginning to understand that the subject is linked to other disciplines and can be applied to real-world integrated settings. The teacher's repertoire of teaching skills includes a variety of means to assist student acquisition of new knowledge and skills using that knowledge.

8.1 Communicates knowledge of subject matter in a manner that enables students to learn.

8.2 Increases subject matter knowledge in order to integrate the learning activities.

8.3 Uses the materials and technologies of the subject field in developing learning activities.

8.4 Acquires currency in her/his subject field.

Florida Content Standards for Elementary Teachers

6.0 Knowledge and use of literacy assessment

12.0 Math: Knowledge of instruction and assessment

17.0 Social Science: Knowledge of instruction and assessment

25.0 Science: Knowledge of instruction and assessment

Box 5.10.   Task Alignment Example (Part IIB): Critical Thinking

INTASC Principles

Principle #4: The teacher understands and uses a variety of instructional strategies to encourage students' development of critical thinking, problem solving, and performance skills.

1. The teacher understands the cognitive processes associated with various kinds of learning (e.g., critical and creative thinking, problem structuring and problem solving, invention, memorization and recall) and how these processes can be stimulated.

3. The teacher knows how to enhance learning through the use of a wide variety of materials, as well as human and technological resources (e.g., computers, audio-visual technologies, videotapes and discs, local experts, primary documents and artifacts, texts, reference books, literature, and other print resources).

7. The teacher uses multiple teaching and learning strategies to engage students in active learning opportunities that promote the development of critical thinking, problem solving, and performance capabilities, and that help students assume responsibility for identifying and using learning resources.

8. The teacher constantly monitors and adjusts strategies in response to learner feedback.

9. The teacher varies his or her role in the instructional process (e.g., instructor, facilitator, coach, audience) in relation to the content and purposes of instruction and the needs of students.

10. The teacher develops a variety of clear, accurate presentations and representations of concepts, using alternative explanations to assist students' understanding, and presenting diverse perspectives to encourage critical thinking.

ACEI Standards

Instruction Standards

3.3 Development of critical thinking, problem solving, performance skills—Candidates understand and use a variety of teaching strategies that encourage elementary students' development of critical thinking, problem solving, and performance skills.

CEC Standards

4. Instructional Strategies.

Special educators posses a repertoire of evidence-based **instructional strategies to individualize instruction** for individuals with ELN. Special educators select, adapt, and use these instructional strategies to promote **positive learning results in general and special curricula** and to appropriately **modify learning environments** for individuals with ELN. They enhance the **learning of critical thinking, problem solving, and performance skills** of individuals with ELN, and increase their self-awareness, self-management, self-control, self-reliance, and self-esteem. Moreover, special educators emphasize the **development, maintenance, and generalization** of knowledge and skills across environments, settings, and the lifespan.

Beginning special educators demonstrate their mastery of this standard through the mastery of the CEC Common Core Knowledge and Skills, as well as through the appropriate CEC Specialty Area(s) Knowledge and Skills for which the program is preparing candidates.

Florida Standards

Florida Educator Accomplished Practice #4—
Critical Thinking, Preprofessional Level:

The preprofessional teacher is acquiring performance assessment techniques and strategies that measure higher-order thinking skills in students and is building a repertoire of realistic projects and problem-solving activities designed to assist all students in demonstrating their ability to think creatively.

4.1   Provides opportunities for students to learn higher-order thinking skills.

4.2   Identifies strategies, materials, and technologies which she/he will use to expand students' thinking abilities.

4.4   Varies their role in the instructional process (instructor, coach, mentor, facilitator, audience, critic, etc.) in relation to the purposes of instruction and the students' needs, including linguistic needs.

4.5   Demonstrates and models the use of higher-order thinking abilities.

4.6   Encourages students to develop open-ended projects and other activities that are creative and innovative.

3. **Select the scoring approach you want to use (hopefully analytic, but possibly with a holistic final decision). Samples of various types are included at the end of this step, Step 3B. Here are some pointers for making your selection:**

- Analytic scoring includes checklists and rating scales. Each criterion receives a separate decision, providing detailed feedback to the teacher. It is also easier for the rater to use, since decisions do not need to be made about a global score in cases where the teacher is successful on some criteria but not others. A common 3-point scale (e.g., 3, 2, 1 or 2, 1, 0 or target, acceptable, unacceptable) works well. The trick is to determine how many points on the scale you *really* need and can *really* see clearly in the teacher's work. Criteria should be very specific and easy to use—typically not more than five per standard to keep things under control!

- Holistic scoring is possible but not recommended by itself. In this approach, the teacher gets an overall rating in a single score with no feedback on the individual criteria, which are clustered in a lengthy description. It can be useful to combine the approaches as suggested in the next bullet.

- Analytic and holistic can be combined for decision-making purposes. A rating scale or checklist can be used to provide detailed evaluation and feedback with a holistic decision-making rubric used to make the

Analytical Scoring

When raters score analytically, they think about and rate each of the criteria in the rubric. The ratings are then summed or aggregated in some way, and the teachers have feedback on what they did correctly and what they did not do correctly.

Guiding Question: "Do I want to give my teachers feedback on what was right and what was wrong so they can fix it, or is a global single score adequate to the purpose?"

Holistic Scoring

Scoring guides that are holistic in nature lead to a single decision (e.g., a 6 or a "satisfactory"). While raters think about multiple criteria, they do so all at once and do not systematically rate each criterion. They make a single, global judgment instead—based on the criteria they keep track of informally or in their heads. This method provides no feedback for improvement to teachers unless comments are provided.

Guiding Question: "Do I want to give feedback for diagnostic purposes or is a summative single score adequate for the purpose?"

standards demonstration decision. It is also possible to collapse several related criteria into holistic judgments.

- We recommend an analytic rubric with a 3-point scale and a cut-score decision rule. An example of the decision rule is: "The standard is 'not demonstrated' if any criterion level decision is 'unacceptable.'"

4. Write directions for the teachers to use in completing the task. Here are some pointers:

Directions

Directions are the same as instructions. They tell teachers precisely what evaluators are looking for so that they can complete the task successfully.

Guiding Question: "What do I want teachers to do in this task?"

- Directions are a detailed, step-by-step list of everything you want your teachers to do to complete the task.
- Describe the length and scope of the response, making sure you include everything you are going to evaluate.
- Embed the language of the standards in the instructions to the extent feasible.

We now provide an example of task directions, again from the Portfolio of K–12 Student Work, in Box 5.11.

Box 5.11. Task Directions Example

Your students' work is the best evidence of your success as a candidate. If they have learned the content well from you, then there is clear evidence that you not only know your content but can teach it and you can teach students to use knowledge to problem solve and think critically. After all, the proof is in the pudding! For that reason, this task is one of the most important tasks in this assessment system. In this task, you will create a showcase portfolio of student work over the semester. Some students are so good that anyone could teach them. For that reason we are asking you to show us not just the best work from the best students but also some work that caused you to do a little extra with students who were not as easy to teach. You should do the following:

1. Select four assessments in which you made judgments about whether or not your students were thinking critically and creatively. If you are in elementary education, these assessments should span the subject areas you teach (e.g., language arts, mathematics, social studies, and science). The assessments should include at least one objective test and three alternative assessments.

2. Select eight samples of your students' work on these assessments as follows:
   a. All assessments should be aligned with the state grade level content standards.
   b. There should be two samples for each of the assessments.
   c. Each of the samples should show not only mastery of content but also the ability to think critically/creatively and/or solve problems.
   d. There should be two work samples in which the students exceeded your expectations, four in which they met your expectations on the first try, and two in which you had to provide extra assistance to the students to get them to achieve your learning objectives.

3. Write a reflection with each work sample that includes the following:
   a. Why you selected the piece
   b. How you prepared the students for the assessment, including the materials you used, explanations you provided, student misconceptions you anticipated or cleared up, as well as how you modeled critical thinking for your students
   c. How it demonstrates the student's ability to use knowledge and skills in the content area

d. The state content standards learned

e. How the work demonstrates the student's ability to think critically or creatively and to solve problems

f. How you linked the work to real-world experiences

g. Source materials you used to create the assignment or test, including the Internet, materials located through a search of a database such as ERIC, and/or materials from 20 or more professional content organizations (e.g., National Council of Teachers of Mathematics or International Reading Association) or others, and why you selected them (National Council for Accreditation of Teacher Education, 2006).

h. For those work samples selected for not meeting expectations initially, describe any **misconceptions** the student had and how you provided **multiple representations of content**, **modeled skills**, and **coached** the student to success.

4. For each work sample, include in your portfolio the assessment materials provided to the student, your scoring rubric(s) for that student, the student's work, and your reflection. If the work was scored once, resubmitted, and rescored, include all rubrics and feedback provided to the student. Be sure to address any misconceptions the students had and how you cleared those up.

Source: Adapted from Florida Department of Education (2002).

Note: Not all direction elements are created equal in terms of the standards alignment. Some indicators are more heavily "hit" than others. Take for example, direction #3h in Box 5.11. That single direction taps the indicators listed in Box 5.12. Note the boldfaced text in the direction #3h and its alignment with the boldfaced text in the indicators in Box 5.12.

Box 5.12.   Example of Alignment of Directions and Indicators: #3h

INTASC Principle #1

2. The teacher understands how students' conceptual frameworks and their **misconceptions** for an area of knowledge can influence their learning.

8. The teacher effectively uses **multiple representations and explanations** of disciplinary concepts that capture key ideas and link them to students' prior understandings.

INTASC Principle #4

9. The teacher varies his or her role in the instructional process (e.g., instructor, facilitator, **coach**, audience) in relation to the content and purposes of instruction and the needs of students.

10. The teacher develops a variety of clear, accurate presentations and **representations of concepts**, using alternative explanations to assist students' understanding and presenting diverse perspectives to encourage critical thinking.

Florida Educator Accomplished Practice (FEAP) #4

4.7. Varies her/his role in the instructional process (instructor, **coach,** mentor, facilitator, audience, critic, etc.) in relation to the purposes of instruction and the students' needs, including linguistic needs.

4.8. Demonstrates and **models** the use of higher-order thinking abilities.

5. Last but not least, create the scoring form. Again, here are some pointers:

- Typically, scoring forms include:
  - Demographic information (name, identification number, date, and so forth)
  - Criteria and scoring choices
  - Total score and/or decision
  - Comments or feedback

- Make sure the criteria are as clear as possible and, again, use the language of the standards wherever possible, and *keep each standard separate for decision-making purposes.*

- Do not include criteria that are irrelevant to the standards-based decision (e.g., neatness and organization). If the product is sloppy, return it unscored.

- Keep your style grammatically consistent. That means your criterion statements should all look alike—complete sentences, or phrases beginning with a verb, but not a mixture of the two. This makes your work look more professional, and models that value for your teachers.

- Make sure the criteria are directly observable and clearly defined, focused on important aspects of performance, sequenced appropriately for easy scoring, and manageable in number.

Figure 5.1 on the next two pages provides an example of a rubric for our sample task—the Portfolio of K–12 Student Work. Here, we demonstrate how to keep the criteria to a minimum, just three per standard.

Note that just as in the case with the directions, not all rubric criteria are created equal in terms of the standards alignment. Some indicators are more heavily "hit" than others. Take for example, the third point in the directions, the reflection component of the portfolio. It is assessed twice for the two standards—once in criterion #3 and again in criterion #6 of the rubric in the figure above. Criterion #6, where we look at the extent to which the candidate's reflections (the task component required in the directions) indicate mastery of the ability to teach critical thinking (the standard). That single criterion in the rubric taps the six indicators in Box 5.13 on page 153. Note the **boldfaced** text in the rubric criterion in Figure 5.1 and in the indicators in Box 5.13.

Rubric

A rubric is a set of scoring guidelines that facilitate the judgment-making process. They typically include a set of criteria and a mechanism (rating scale or checklist) to determine and record levels of quality.

Guiding Question: "How will I decide whether or not teachers performed the task well?"

We realize that there are many ways to write a rubric. We have demonstrated our favorite in the K–12 portfolio example. In the following section, "A Rose Is a Rose," we provide some examples of various rubric styles, using a different task—the unit exam. Ultimately, the decision about the style you select will be based not only on your personal preferences but also the decisions you need to make. When we review the requirements for cut-score setting in CAATS Step 4B (Chapters 6 and 8), this will become more obvious. For now, suffice it to say that the decision about "unacceptable"—or whatever you call it—has to be made with the greatest of care. The more detailed your rubric is, the easier it is to be consistent and accurate in making that decision. It is hard work to create the kind of rubric we demonstrated above, but, in the end, it is usually worth it. If your assessment system is not a high-stakes one (e.g., does not lead to a certification decision), then your opportunity to pick one of the easier rubric styles from the following section is greater.

Figure 5.1. Example of a Rubric—The Portfolio of K–12 Student Work

---

Portfolio of K–12 Student Work

Name: _____   Submission #: _____

Decision for INTASC 1 and AP 8 (Subject Matter) on this task (check one):

☐ Demonstrated: 2–3 ratings are target; none are unacceptable.

☐ Partially Demonstrated: 2–3 ratings are acceptable; none are unacceptable.

☐ Not Demonstrated: 1 or more ratings are unacceptable.

#	Target	Acceptable	Unacceptable
1	**Assessments:** The candidate has selected one test and three alternative assessments that reflect a grasp of key concepts, assumptions, debates, processes of inquiry, and ways of knowing in the disciplines. These assessments sample a variety of current content appropriate to the certification area and are aligned with state and national standards.	The work meets the essential characteristics of target except that the materials are limited to state standards.	The candidate fails to show an understanding of content and is teaching concepts that are not correct, current, or important, or are insufficient with regard to state content standards.
2	**Student work samples:** The candidate has communicated the subject matter in a way that helped students learn. All eight of the work samples provide direct evidence of the students' grasp of the knowledge and skills required in state grade-level content standards in language arts, math, science, social studies, physical education, and/or the arts.	Six students grasped the content well; however, the two who were selected as difficult to reach show limited, but not adequate, improvement.	One or more of the students demonstrated major misunderstandings of the content.
3	**Candidate reflections:** The candidate demonstrates knowledge of current content by evaluating and selecting current materials and assessments. It is clear that s/he understands, and continues to learn about, the disciplines and how they are articulated in state and national standards, can explain and re-explain content, as needed, and can resolve content acquisition problems, including misconceptions, among all students.	The work meets the essential characteristics of target except the candidate may not be using current materials or the candidate had missed minor problems, reducing the success of the one or two more challenging students.	The candidate does not know how to select materials that will assess content knowledge and skills and/or is unable to diagnose student learning problems.

(Continued)

Figure 5.1 (Continued)

Decision for INTASC 4 and AP 4 (Critical Thinking) on this task (check one):

☐ Demonstrated: 2–3 ratings are target; none are unacceptable.

☐ Partially Demonstrated: 2–3 ratings are acceptable; none are unacceptable.

☐ Not Demonstrated: 1 or more ratings are unacceptable.

#	Target	Acceptable	Unacceptable
4	**Assessments:** The candidate has selected one test and three open-ended (creative and innovative) alternative assessments that effectively diagnose students' ability to think critically and creatively. A wide variety of current and professional materials and learning strategies are used to stimulate students' thinking.	The work meets the essential characteristics of target except that the materials or strategies do not reflect a wide variety or may be limited in their creativity/ innovation, thereby limiting their potential to stimulate thinking in multiple contexts.	At least one of the assessments presented is limited to the knowledge level.
5	**Student work samples:** The work samples demonstrate the students' ability to think critically and creatively in both traditional test and open-ended project contexts. All eight of the work samples demonstrate the students' ability to think critically.	Six students demonstrated critical thinking; however, the two who were selected as difficult remained somewhat shallow in their work.	One or more of the students failed to reach a level of critical thinking.
6	**Candidate reflections:** The candidate can analyze effective teaching strategies, materials, and technologies in terms of his/her own modeling of thinking skills. The candidate understands the cognitive processes associated with critical thinking as they impact his/her strategies in responding and adjusting to individual needs, explaining, coaching, listening, and modeling.	The candidate has described the strategies, materials, and technologies used but may not have clearly articulated clearly their relationship to learning goals or how s/he made modifications that were targeted to individual students.	The candidate is unaware of teaching strategies, materials, or technologies needed to teach critical thinking, or is unable to connect his/her need to modify approaches with the needs of individuals for remediation.

Rubric Examples: A Rose Is a Rose

The examples of rubrics in Figures 5.2 through 5.7 are taken from a different task—creation of a unit exam. Each of these examples uses the same set of criteria, but they are assembled differently to model the different rubric writing styles from which you can chose. Worksheet #3.1 at the end of this chapter suggests that you write a rubric using your favorite format for a task of your choice.

In Figure 5.2, a holistic rubric is modeled. Notice how only one decision is made (target, weak, or unacceptable) with all criteria combined into that single proficiency level.

Figure 5.3 shows the simplest of the analytic rubrics—the checklist. Notice how the decisions about proficiencies are being made for each of the criteria individually. In the checklist, there is no middle ground, as in a rating scale. It's yes or no, present or not present, okay or not okay.

With Figure 5.4, we introduce the first of several rating scales. These scales allow us to have proficiency levels that come in between okay and not okay—a

Box 5.13. Example of Alignment of Rubric Indicators for Criterion

INTASC Principle #4

1. The teacher understands the **cognitive processes** associated with various kinds of learning (e.g., critical and creative thinking, problem structuring and problem solving, invention, memorization and recall) and how these processes can be stimulated.

8. The teacher constantly monitors and **adjusts** strategies in response to learner feedback.

9. The teacher varies his or her role in the instructional process (e.g., instructor, facilitator, **coac**h, audience) in relation to the content and purposes of instruction and the **needs** of students.

10. The teacher develops a variety of clear, accurate presentations and representations of concepts, using alternative **explanations** to assist students' understanding and presenting diverse perspectives to encourage critical thinking.

FEAP #4

4.2. Identifies strategies, materials, and technologies which she/he will use to **expand students' thinking** abilities.

4.4. **Varies her/his role** in the instructional process (instructor, coach, mentor, facilitator, audience, critic, etc.) in relation to the purposes of instruction and the students' needs, including linguistic needs.

Figure 5.2. Rubric Example #1: Holistic

Unit Exam Scoring Rubric

Name: _____   Date: _____

Target	Weak	Unacceptable
The exam is appropriate and comprehensive with a well formatted test map. Higher-order thinking is tested. Accommodations for special students, including both Exceptional Student Education (ESE) and Limited English Proficiency (LEP), are appropriate. Individual items are appropriate, well formatted, and address linguistic needs. Technology is effectively used.	The exam is generally appropriate although there may be some gaps in coverage of instructional content, item formatting, and scoring. Higher-order thinking is tested and accommodations for special students, including both ESE and LEP, are appropriate. The directions are essentially clear. Most individual items are well formatted and linguistically appropriate. Technology use was not maximized.	One or more of the following problems exist: The exam is not appropriate for the instructional content. The test map is not accurate and/or properly formatted. The test is limited to lower-order thinking. The directions are vague. Accommodations for special students, including both ESE and LEP, are inadequate. Items are not all matched to outcomes or formatted correctly or appropriate to all populations. The scoring key has errors. Technology was not used effectively.

Figure 5.3. Rubric Example #2: Checklist

Unit Exam Scoring Rubric

Name: _____   Date: _____

Acceptable		#	Criterion
Yes	No	1	Test is appropriate and comprehensive for instructional content.
Yes	No	2	Test map is accurate and properly formatted.
Yes	No	3	Items address knowledge/comprehension, application/analysis, and synthesis/evaluation.
Yes	No	4	Directions are clear.
Yes	No	5	Accommodations for special students, including both ESE and LEP, are appropriate.
Yes	No	6	Items are appropriate for instructional outcomes.
Yes	No	7	Items are appropriate for developmental and linguistic level of students.
Yes	No	8	Items are written at the specified taxonomic levels.
Yes	No	9	Items are clear, free from bias, and formatted correctly.
Yes	No	10	Key, rubric, or sample answers are correct.
Yes	No	11	Technology was used effectively in creating this test.

Figure 5.4. Rubric Example #3: Unweighted Rating Scale

Unit Exam Scoring Rubric

Name: _____   Date: _____
Rating Scale Key: T = target; A = acceptable; U = unacceptable
(Note: Rating scale could also be 2, 1, 0 or 3, 2, 1, with scores summed.)

#	Criterion	Rating
1	Test is appropriate and comprehensive for instructional content.	__ T __ A __ U
2	Test map is accurate and properly formatted.	__ T __ A __ U
3	Items address knowledge/comprehension, application/analysis, and synthesis/evaluation.	__ T __ A __ U
4	Directions are clear.	__ T __ A __ U
5	Accommodations for special students, including both ESE and LEP, are appropriate.	__ T __ A __ U
6	Items are appropriate for instructional outcomes.	__ T __ A __ U
7	Items are appropriate for developmental and linguistic level of students.	__ T __ A __ U
8	Items are written at the specified taxonomic levels.	__ T __ A __ U
9	Items are clear, free from bias, and formatted correctly.	__ T __ A __ U
10	Key, rubric, or sample answers are correct.	__ T __ A __ U
11	Technology was used effectively in creating this test.	__ T __ A __ U

middle ground. In this example, there is only one level in the middle, and all criteria in the scale contribute equally to the total score. The rating scale could use words (or abbreviations for words), as it does here, or numbers, such as 3, 2, 1.

In Figure 5.5, we add another midpoint and use numbers instead of words. We also allow for missing, with the addition of zero. Most important, we use weighting factors to show that some criteria are more important than others. For example, criterion #3 is three times as important as criterion #1.

Figure 5.5. Rubric Example #4: Weighted Rating Scale—Numeric

Unit Exam Scoring Rubric

Name: _____   Date: _____
Rating Scale Key: 4 = excellent; 3 = satisfactory; 2 = weak; 1 = unacceptable; 0 = missing

#	Criterion	Rating	Weighting Factor	Points
1	Test is appropriate and comprehensive for instructional content.	4 3 2 1 0	1	.
2	Test map is accurate and properly formatted.	4 3 2 1 0	2	
3	Items address knowledge/comprehension, application/analysis, and synthesis/evaluation.	4 3 2 1 0	3	
4	Directions are clear.	4 3 2 1 0	2	
5	Accommodations for special students, including both ESE and LEP, are appropriate.	4 3 2 1 0	3	
6	Items are appropriate for instructional outcomes.	4 3 2 1 0	2	
7	Items are appropriate for developmental and linguistic level of students.	4 3 2 1 0	3	
8	Items are written at the specified taxonomic levels.	4 3 2 1 0	3	
9	Items are clear, free from bias, and formatted correctly.	4 3 2 1 0	3	
10	Key, rubric, or sample answers are correct.	4 3 2 1 0	1	
11	Technology was used effectively in creating this test.	4 3 2 1 0	2	
Total Score:				

In Figure 5.6, we progress from a single word or number on the scale to a more complete description of what a proficiency level is. This format is what many people actually call a "rubric," although technically all of these examples are rubrics.

Figure 5.7 is the ultimate rubric—descriptions for each proficiency level and weighting factors. It requires the most work, but it can yield the most valid and reliable results.

Content Validity

Content validity is a form of validity evidence that ensures that the test measures the construct comprehensively and appropriately and does not measure another construct instead of, or in addition to, the construct of teacher performance on the job.

Guiding Question: "How do I know that the decisions I will make about teachers will be based on adequate coverage of the construct of teacher performance and nothing else?"

?

Figure 5.6. Rubric Example #5: Descriptive Rating Scale

Unit Exam Scoring Rubric

Name: _____   Date: _____

Element	Target	Acceptable/Marginal	Unacceptable
Overall exam	The test is appropriate and comprehensive for instructional content. The test map is accurate and properly formatted. The items address knowledge/comprehension, application/analysis, and synthesis/evaluation. The directions are clear. Accommodations for special students, including both ESE and LEP, are appropriate.	The exam is generally appropriate, although there may be some gaps in coverage of instructional content. The test map is accurate and properly formatted. There are at least two levels in Bloom's taxonomy, including one for higher-order thinking. The directions are essentially clear, although there may be some minor ambiguity. Accommodations for special students, including both ESE and LEP, are appropriate.	One or more of the following problems exist: The exam is not appropriate for the instructional content. The test map is not accurate and/or properly formatted. The test is limited to lower-order thinking. The directions are vague. Accommodations for special students, including both ESE and LEP, are inadequate.
Individual items	Individual items are appropriate for objectives. Items are appropriate for developmental and linguistic level of students. Items are written at the specified taxonomic levels. Items are clear, free from bias, and formatted correctly. The scoring key, rubric, or sample answers are correct.	Individual items are, for the most part, appropriate for instructional outcomes. Items are appropriate for developmental and linguistic level of students. Most items are written at the specified taxonomic levels. Most items are clear, free from bias, and formatted correctly. The scoring key, rubric, or sample answers are correct.	One or more of the following problems exist: Many individual items are not appropriate for instructional outcomes. Some items are not appropriate for developmental and linguistic level of students. Most items are not written at the specified taxonomic levels. Several items are unclear, biased, and/or formatted incorrectly. The scoring key, rubric, or sample answers contain errors.
Technology	Technology was used effectively in creating this exam.	Technology was used in creating this exam, although its potential use was not maximized.	Technology was not used or was used ineffectively in this exam.

Figure 5.7. Rubric Example #6: Another Descriptive Rating Scale

Unit Exam Scoring Rubric

Name: _____   Date: _____

INTASC #8 and FEAP #1: Assessment

Criterion	Target (3)	Marginal (2)	Unsatisfactory (1)	WF*	Score
1. Test is appropriate and comprehensive for instructional content.	Test is both appropriate and comprehensive.	Test is appropriate but not comprehensive.	Test is neither appropriate nor comprehensive.		
2. Test map is accurate and properly formatted.	Test map is both accurate and properly formatted.	Test map contains minor problems in accuracy.	Test map is neither accurate nor properly formatted.		
3. Items address knowledge/ comprehension, application/analysis, and synthesis/ evaluation.	Items cover the range of Bloom's taxonomy and include higher-order thinking questions in both the essay and in one or more other items on the test.	Knowledge/ comprehension items are included, but there is only one item at the application/analysis level, typically the essay.	Items are restricted to the knowledge/ comprehension level.		

Criterion	Target (3)	Marginal (2)	Unsatisfactory (1)	WF*	Score
4. Directions are clear.	Directions are clearly written for the grade level for each part of the test.	Directions are stated for all sections, but some are too vague or to complex to be helpful.	Directions are missing from one or more sections.		
5. Accommodations for special students, including both ESE and LEP, are appropriate.	Accommodations for both populations are well formulated.	Accommodations are provided for both ESE and LEP children, but there are minor problems in the accommodations for one of the populations.	Accommodations are provided but they are largely inappropriate for either ESE or LEP children.		
6. Items are appropriate for instructional outcomes.	All or most of the items (2/3 or more) match the instructional outcomes.	About 2/3 of the items match the instructional outcomes.	More than a third of the items fail to match the instructional outcomes as listed on the blueprint.		
7. Items are appropriate for developmental and linguistic levels of students.	The items are well developed for both the developmental and linguistic levels of the students.	There are minor errors in relating the items to either the developmental or linguistic levels of the students.	The items are not appropriate for either the developmental or linguistic levels of the students.		
8. Items are written at the specified taxonomic levels.	All items match their taxonomic levels on the blueprint.	Knowledge and application level items are appropriate, but analysis, synthesis, and evaluation are not.	Items do not match the taxonomic levels specified in the blueprint.		
9. Items are clear, free from bias, and formatted correctly.	Items are, for the most part, clearly written, without bias, and formatted correctly.	Minor problems exist in terms of clarity, bias, and/or formatting.	There are substantive problems in multiple items in terms of clarity, bias, and/or formatting.		
10. Key, rubric, or sample answers are correct.	The key is correct, and the essay scoring procedures are appropriate.	The key is correct, but there are minor problems in the essay scoring criteria.	While the key may be correct for most answers, the essay is scored inappropriately.		
FEAP #12: Technology					
11. Technology was used effectively in creating this test.	The test was formatted in a word processing or test authoring program, and it is well formatted, and technology was used to locate content.	The test was formatted in a word processing program, but it is not easy to follow or the content was weak because of a failure to do research on the Internet.	The test is sloppy and/or handwritten.		

*NOTE: WF is short for weighting factors.

AERA, APA, and NCME (1999) *Standards*
and CAATS Step 3B

Standard 3.14:

The *criteria used for scoring test takers' performance on extended-response items should be documented.* This documentation is especially important for performance assessments, such as scoreable portfolios and essays, where the criteria for scoring may not be obvious to the user.

    CAATS Steps Influenced: 3A, 3B

Standard 3.20:

The *instructions presented to test takers should contain sufficient detail* so that test takers can respond to a task in the manner that the test developer intended. When appropriate, sample material, practice or sample questions, criteria for scoring, and a representative item identified with each major area on the test's classification or domain should be provided to test takers prior to the administration of the test or included in the testing material as a part of the standard administration instructions.

    CAATS Steps Influenced: 3B, 3D

Standard 3.22:

Procedures for scoring and, if relevant, *scoring criteria* should be presented by the test developer *in sufficient detail and clarity as to maximize the accuracy of scoring.* Instructions for using rating scales or for deriving scores obtained by coding, scaling, or classifying constructed responses should be clear. This is especially critical if tests can be scored locally.

    CAATS Steps Influenced: 3B

Standard 5.9:

When test scoring involves human judgment, *scoring rubrics should specify criteria for scoring.* Adherence to established scoring criteria should be monitored and checked regularly. Monitoring procedures should be documented.

    CAATS Steps Influenced: 3A, 3B

Discussion

It is clear from the above standards that it is important to maximize the accuracy of decisions by creating clear and detailed instructions and scoring rubrics, and this is especially true for a performance-based or portfolio assessment system.

NOTE: Emphases added for clarity.

CAATS STEP 3C: CONDUCT FIRST VALIDITY STUDY

Evidence of content validity should be gathered to ensure that the tasks are representative of the construct and its conceptual framework, proportional, and in fact job related. Reviews of coverage of the standards, combined with surveys of (or focus groups with) experts, can help ensure that the tasks are representative and job related. This would constitute an important source of validity evidence. It is also a crucial component of your cut-score setting process, which will be discussed further in CAATS Step 4B and Chapter 8. We describe these sources of validity evidence in this step and provide two worksheets (Worksheets #3.3 and #3.4) to guide your planning in this area.

> ### Construct
> The concept or characteristic that a test or assessment system is designed to measure. In this work, we name it *teacher performance.*
>
> *Guiding Question: "What's the big picture idea of what we are assessing?"*

At this point, you have done at least six things that will have prepared you well for having a system that can yield valid results.

1. You based the structure on a defined purpose/use, propositions/principles, content, and context.

2. You aligned and synthesized the standards so you could use them.

3. You based your tasks on a job analysis that resulted from your visualization of the competent teacher performing in standards-based ways.

4. You used a common format for the task and for scoring so that data could be aggregated and decisions could be made.

> ### Common Format
> A common format is helpful for writing tasks and includes, at a minimum, detailed instructions and scoring rubrics written in the same style.
>
> *Guiding Question: "How can I provide adequate instructions to teachers and scoring rubrics for raters that will yield high quality and consistent data?"*

5. You stated your expectations clearly and specifically in the directions and rubrics.

6. You honestly aligned each task with standards and indicators, making sure that each indicator selected was truly visible somewhere in the task.

It is now time to think about how we can ensure content coverage and how we can avoid failing to ensure content coverage.

Ensuring Content Coverage

All of this hard work has led you in the direction of having representative coverage of the standards and ensuring that one source of irrelevancy has been omitted—wrong tasks for specific standards. The clear directions and rubric also helped you avoid reliability problems, another source of irrelevancy or error. Much inconsistency in ratings is due to raters looking for different things in substantially different products. Now, it is time to start doing some analysis of what you have created to see if you need to adjust any tasks already created or add any new ones to make sure you have sufficiently covered (sampled from) the domains (base standards) you are measuring.

If you have used software that allows you to record the selections of standards and indicators that you made, it is now time to print your first report. If you have not had this kind of technology available to you, then you can start creating some reports by hand. Although tedious, it is best to prepare this analysis at the indicator level to ensure that there is coverage of most important indicators. Table 5.1 provides an example of a report that uses the Florida standards and the critical-thinking tasks we described earlier:

Table 5.1. Sample Coverage Report for FEAP #4, Critical Thinking, Key Indicators, and Tasks

#	Criteria	Tasks
4.1	Provides opportunities for students to learn higher-order thinking skills.	4A, 4B, 4C, 8A, 8C, 8D
4.2	Identifies strategies, materials, and technologies which she/he will use to expand students' thinking abilities.	4A, 4B, 4C, 12A
4.3	Has strategies for utilizing discussions, group interactions, and writing to encourage student problem solving.	4A, 4B, 4C, 9B
4.4	Poses problems, dilemmas, and questions in lessons.	4A
4.5	Assists students in development and use of rules of evidence.	Not covered
4.6	Demonstrates and models the use of higher-order thinking abilities.	4A, 4B
4.7	Modifies and adapts lessons with increased attention to the learners' creative-thinking abilities.	4A, 4B, 10B
4.8	Encourages students to develop open-ended projects and other activities that are creative and innovative.	4A, 4B, 10A
4.9	Uses technology and other appropriate tools in the learning environment.	4C, 12B

CRITERIA SOURCE: Adapted from Florida Education Standards Commission (1996).

Note that the above report has task numbers in the 04 series (Critical-Thinking Base Standard), as well as tasks in the 8, 10, and 12 series. This means that we have aligned tasks with standards other than critical thinking—content knowledge, planning, and technology. We cannot overemphasize the importance of this being an iterative process. As you design tasks and align them with standards, it is always helpful to go back through the tasks and standards, looking for additional alignment possibilities that can make your tasks richer. This is an excellent way to take advantage of the complexity of the teaching role. As you identify these linkages, you can then go back to the tasks and update them, incorporating ideas from the newly discovered alignments. This will enrich the assessment experience for your candidates.

You should prepare a report for every set of standards that you are using in your assessment system and are really important to you. That may not be all of the sets! If your state standards form the basis of a certification exam, state standards are ones you certainly would not want to miss at this important stage of your design process. It is critically important that we ensure that we have adequately prepared teacher candidates for the exam they are going to take (another big validity issue)!

Once the reports are created, you need to analyze them. It is not enough to put them on paper and toss them in a drawer! The decision-making question is: Are we creating a system that is likely to yield valid decisions? The questions on Worksheet #3.3 and the ratings from Worksheet #3.4 will help you answer that fundamental question. They are designed around four critically important validity criteria that we need to apply:

1. Representativeness

2. Relevance

3. Proportionality

4. Job-relatedness

Below are the questions you will find on the worksheet. You can ask them of yourself, and you should ask them of your stakeholders, as well. This is the perfect place to get them heavily involved in your process, making sure it is job related in their eyes—not just because it looks good or is an accreditation requirement, but because it is the first step to cut-score setting and legal safety.

You may want to go through this process in two rounds (called an *iterative process*). First, answer the questions yourself and make necessary changes in your system. Then ask stakeholders and revise again. Within round #2, you may also want to go through the process more than once. If there is any way humanly possible to reach consensus, do it. It will pay off later—especially if you face a legal challenge from a teacher you do not certify. The number of stakeholders you use will be dependent on how high stakes the system is and how large your constituency is. If you are a small school district or university, one or two stakeholders may be enough. If you are a state agency, the rule of thumb is 10 to 15. Here are some questions you can check off:

✓ Are all the critical aspects of the standard assessed in the tasks at least once?

✓ Will these tasks help me to distinguish among teachers or other professional educators who are competent and not competent on those critical aspects?

✓ For any indicators not represented, are they important to me in my visualization of a competent professional, or am I comfortable that they can be omitted from my system? If I need to add something to address them, where should I add it?

✓ Have I overloaded any of the indicators? If so, is that what I think I need to determine competence (i.e., is it a really important indicator and therefore needs a higher proportion of tasks to assess it adequately or are these "freebees" because I need the task for another indicator)?

✓ As I look at these tasks one more time:
  o Are there any tasks that really are not relevant to the standard or not job related?
  o Do I have the right kind of (and enough) evidence for the decision about the standard?
  o Does each scoring instrument measure what it is supposed to measure?

In conducting this last look at the standard before moving on, a critical review of the set of tasks proposed for the system should include a review of each task individually for its relevance to the standard and the overall coverage of the depth and breadth of the standard. In the next section, we show some potential pitfalls that result in a failure to cover a standard adequately and some quick fixes for them.

Fixing Gaps in Content Coverage of Standards

Let us look at two examples for the Base Standard on Assessment (INTASC Principle #8) that requires teachers to know how to use a variety of assessment methods **to improve K-12 learning**. Both examples, in Boxes 5.14 and 5.15, would lead to a decision for which the validity is highly questionable. In the first example, we demonstrate an error at the standard level.

Box 5.14.   Coverage of INTASC Principle #8 on Assessment: Error at the Standard Level

Error: The teacher creates two objective tests and two alternative assessments. One of each must be used in a K–12 classroom.

Problem: Validity can be threatened **by lack of coverage** of the Standard in its entirety in a system. In this example, candidates are asked to create and use both traditional and alternative assessments, but there is no analysis of the results. There is a huge gap in coverage (representativeness) of this standard, even though there is direct evidence of competency in part of it. And, assessors will not have the most important piece of information needed to determine minimal competency—**use** of the resulting data.

The Fix: For this standard to be assessed adequately, among other things, the teacher needs to **use** assessment data from these two instruments for diagnosis of student strengths and weaknesses, feedback to individual students and the class, and instructional modifications where needed. An existing task needs to be modified accordingly.

In the second example, in Box 5.15, we demonstrate an error at the task level.

Box 5.15. Coverage of INTASC Principle #8 on Assessment: Error at the Task Level

Error: The teacher prepares a unit plan that includes reference to a post-test and an alternative assessment but there is no requirement that these instruments be developed or used.

Problem: In addition to obvious coverage issues at the standard level, validity is threatened by an **exaggeration** of the importance of a single aspect of a good task. A unit plan, which requires the identification of assessment methods, is used inappropriately as evidence of competence in assessment in this example. Remember that it is one thing to know to use a test or a quiz, even pre- and post-, but it is entirely another to be able to do it. For assessment, this is a good formative indicator of competency in the standard, but it is clearly not sufficient to serve as any summative evidence for the **assessment** standard.

The Fix: Use this task as evidence of planning but not assessment. It is good practice for demonstrating the assessment standard and, as such, is formative in nature not summative.

These two examples include some rather significant flaws. There are also minor flaws that are easily remedied. Chief among them is forgetting to include an important indicator. A simple example of a minor modification like this would be a Classroom Management Plan that targets INTASC Principle 5 but misses the opportunity to have students develop shared values and expectations. The Principle provides for students to do so in order to have them take individual and group responsibility for the classroom climate. The existing Classroom Management Plan can easily be modified to incorporate this skill through a simple addition to the directions and rubric. To summarize, there are three errors for which we need to be on guard:

1. A set of tasks that misses a major thrust of the standard.

2. A task that overemphasizes the importance of a minor component, using it as summative evidence rather than formative.

3. A gap in coverage of an important indicator.

Before leaving this topic, let's put the first two errors in a different, and more familiar, context. Let's think about airline pilots and whether or not we would want to fly with them.

- The pilot can take off well, but s/he may not be able to land the plane! (There are big gaps in the set of tasks assessed.)

- The pilot has only found the button to put down the landing gear and has spotted the runway. We can only hope that s/he knows how to land the plane! (There is an overemphasis of the significance of a task.)

AERA, APA, and NCME (1999) *Standards*

and CAATS Step 3C

Standard 3.1:

Tests and testing programs should be developed on a *sound scientific basis.* Test developers and publishers should *compile and document adequate evidence bearing on test development.*
    CAATS Steps Influenced: 1C, 2E, 3C

Standard 13.3:

When a test is used as an indicator of achievement in an instructional domain or with respect to specified curriculum standards, *evidence of the extent to which the test samples the range of knowledge and elicits the processes reflected in the target domain should be provided.* Both tested and target domains should be described in sufficient detail so their relationship can be evaluated. The analyses should *make explicit* those aspects of the target domain that the test represents as well as those aspects that it fails to represent.
    CAATS Steps Influenced: 2E, 3C

Standard 13.5:

When test results substantially contribute to making decisions about student promotion or graduation, there should be *evidence that the test adequately covers only the specific or generalized content and skills* that students have had an opportunity to learn.
    CAATS Steps Influenced: 3C

Standard 14.14:

The *content domain to be covered by a credentialing test should be defined clearly and justified* in terms of the importance of the content for credential-worthy performance in an occupation or profession. A rationale should be provided to support a claim that the knowledge of skills being assessed are required for credential-worthy performance in an occupation and are consistent with the purpose for which the licensing or certification program was instituted.
    CAATS Steps Influenced: 1C, 2E, 3C, 5A

Discussion

This first validity study helps to provide evidence that the test, or assessment system, does elicit all of the important aspects of the content standards and is, therefore, clearly defined and justified. This will enable us to set a well-founded cut score later.

NOTE: Emphases added for clarity.

CAATS STEP 3D: ALIGN TASKS WITH INSTRUCTION

Since the performance-based approach advocated here is designed to be conducted over time and to ensure comprehensive coverage of all of the critical functions of teaching, and since validity evidence is in part gathered based on fairness and opportunities to learn, it is fundamental to the development of this task-based system that instruction be well-aligned with the tasks. Evidence that adequate instruction, samples, and practice are provided for each task needs to be gathered so that teachers have the maximum opportunity possible to complete successfully the tasks. This has been called instructional validity, although it is not a technical term in the AERA, APA, and NCME *Standards* (1999).

One of the best ways to ensure that alignment is to sort formative from summative tasks, as was done in CAATS Step 2E and Worksheet #2.5. All of those tasks that were removed from the summative assessment component of the system can now be used to help prepare teachers for the summative assessments, but with far less rigor in their design and monitoring at a group level. We need to make sure there are enough formative tasks, in the right places, to help teachers succeed in the summative ones. In addition to formative assessment tasks, there is also, of course, a variety of instructional activities and readings that provides the necessary learning tools. For example, preparation for development of a classroom assessment plan could be development of a smaller unit assessment plan, practice activities with developing a grading plan for a marking period, experiences with developing formative and summative assessments, and so on. The last worksheet provides an opportunity to chart these early experiences that may be provided in the course or workshop during which the summative assessment is given, or they may span a longer time period.

Once formative and summative assessments are sorted and separated, it is important to add formative assessments (and probably additional instruction), as needed, to ensure that teachers have adequate opportunity to become familiar with the content and format of tasks. In some tests, particularly objective tests, it is possible to provide sample items right on the test. Clearly, that is difficult in a performance-based task system; however, such samples and examples may become a part of instruction.

AERA, APA, and NCME (1999) *Standards*

and CAATS Step 3D

Standard 3.20:

The instructions presented to test takers should contain sufficient detail so that test takers can respond to a task in the manner that the test developer intended. When appropriate, *sample material, practice or sample questions*, criteria for scoring, and a representative item identified with each major area on the test's classification or domain *should be provided to test takers* prior to the administration of the test or included in the testing material as a part of the standard administration instructions.

CAATS Steps Influenced: 3B, 3D

Discussion

The sorting of formative from summative assessments, accompanied by the creation or identification of additional formative assessments and instructional activities serves the purpose of providing sample items in the assessment process itself.

NOTE: Emphases added for clarity.

V WRAP-UP

In this chapter, we implemented the blueprint or sampling plan we created in CAATS Step 2. We began by developing a common format for tasks that would facilitate data aggregation. It included a task number, name, and brief description; standards alignment; directions; and a rubric. Existing tasks were modified using this format and new ones created. We carefully examined our coverage of the standards and indicators, reflecting on whether we had too much or too little coverage for important indicators, modifying our tasks based on those decisions. We used stakeholders to help us evaluate the extent to which our tasks were adequate for the decision about competency and certification, and we noted that this was a critical first step in cut-score setting. Finally, we aligned tasks with instruction so that all teachers have the necessary opportunities to learn.

Before moving on to CAATS Step 4, fill in the rows for CAATS Step 3 of the action plan in Chapter 2, and, if you have not already done so, complete the worksheets at the end of this chapter!

Story Starters

Starter #1:

Professor/Teacher Reedmyminde stomps into your office and says:

"I had all my students do those tasks you decided were important, but they all failed miserably. They're really pretty dumb and shouldn't be teachers if they can't figure out how to do this stuff themselves. Am I supposed to lead them by the nose?"

You say....

Starter #2:

Mr. Hartintheriteplace was absent the day they taught rubrics and is afraid to tell anyone. You figured it out when you saw some of the material he was giving to his students. Now, he chairs the School Advisory Committee and is actively involved in selecting mentors for new teachers. In fact, he is mentoring one himself. He is acknowledged by the staff as an excellent teacher leader, but you have had students tell you they don't know what he wants on the assignments he gives or where their grades are coming from. What will you do?

Starter #3:

Professors Reedmyminde and Hartintheriteplace bump into each other at the grocery store and commiserate about accountability requirements in their college/district. They found a copy of the Berk article (see Chapter 8) in the library and decide to write you a note telling you to leave them alone because there is no agreement in the field about how to do this stuff and Berk has the best advice of all—take antacids. So, they write the note making it clear that they believe that all this stuff is garbage. They don't need to select critical tasks and write good rubrics to achieve valid decisions and set useful cut scores. They buy you a bottle of antacid and leave the note on your desk.

What will you say?

CAATS STEP 3—WORKSHEET #3.1

Proficiency Level Descriptions

Explanation:

Use this worksheet to think through the proficiency levels you will use for all of the tasks in your system.

Individual Activity: Using the "Rose Is a Rose" models, select your favorite style. Think about what you would prefer to receive in terms of feedback from your teacher. Answer the following questions:

1. Am I satisfied with a numeric score, such as 3, 2, 1, or do I prefer a word, such as excellent, satisfactory, poor (e.g., Examples #3 and #4)?

2. Would I rather have a more detailed description of each category on the scale—a phrase or a sentence on each task rubric (e.g., Example #6)—or is the number or word enough?

3. How many levels of quality can I really define clearly? Two? Three? Four? Five?

4. Now take your favorite task from something you teach. Take three of the criteria you use to grade it, and write a description of each level of proficiency and see if you can make meaningful differences between the levels. If you cannot, reduce the number of scale points.

Group Activity: Report out and reach consensus on the following:

1. How many levels of proficiency will your unit use for each criterion on each task?

2. Will you use a numeric scale or a descriptive (word) scale?

3. Will you provide a detailed description to supplement the numbers/words?

4. Define the general levels of proficiency in your scale as we did for "target," "acceptable," and "not acceptable" that will be common to all tasks in the system.

Levels	Descriptions
Level 1 (lowest—poor)	
Level 2	
Level 3	
Etc.	

CAATS STEP 3—WORKSHEET #3.2

Task Design

Explanation:

Use this worksheet as a model for designing tasks. You may change it based on what you decided to use as a format. This is the one we used.

Task Name: _____

Task Number: _____

Standards Alignment: List standards or elements of conceptual framework/mission assessed in this task:

INTASC	State	Specialty Professional Association (SPA)	Local

Task Description: Write a brief description of the task:

The teacher will . . .

_____

_____

Directions: Write step-by-step directions for teachers to follow in completing the task:

1.	
2.	
3.	
4.	
5.	
6.	
Etc.	

Scoring Rubric: Write a detailed rubric for each standard assessed, starting with your decision-making structure.

Standard # _____ :

Decisions:

- Demonstration is defined as: _____
- Partial demonstration is defined as: _____
- Nondemonstration is defined as: _____

#	Criteria	Rating of ***	Rating of **	Rating of *
1				
2				
3				
Etc.				

*** Great
** Okay
* Unacceptable

Standard # _____ :

Decisions:

- Demonstration is defined as: _____
- Partial demonstration is defined as: _____
- Nondemonstration is defined as: _____

#	Criteria	Rating of ***	Rating of **	Rating of *
1				
2				
3				
Etc.				

*** Great
** Okay
* Unacceptable

CAATS WORKSHEETS

CAATS STEP 3—WORKSHEET #3.3

Standards and Indicators Coverage Report

Explanation:

Make a list of all of the indicators from the standards that are being assessed (e.g., INTASC). Then list the tasks you will be using to measure each indicator and answer the questions at the bottom of the worksheet.

Indicator #	Indicator Text (optional)	Tasks Measuring Indicator

Assessment:

Are all critical indicators addressed at least once?	Yes No
Does the set of tasks help differentiate competent from incompetent teachers?	Yes No
Is the set of tasks complete; does my visualization of the competent teacher remain complete without the missing indicators?	Yes No
Are any indicators overloaded such that I could eliminate a task (or are these "freebees" because I need the task for another indicator)?	Yes No
Are any indicators underrepresented such that I need to add or modify an existing task?	Yes No
Are there any tasks for which I could not make a strong linkage to at least one indicator? If so, should I eliminate or change that task?	Yes No

CAATS STEP 3—WORKSHEET #3.4

Individual Task Review for Job-Relatedness

Explanation:

Use this worksheet to develop a survey for stakeholders to evaluate your tasks. District personnel should be used for colleges, and college faculty might be used for districts.

For each task in the system, rate the task on the following job-relatedness scale:

Criticality (C): How important or critical are the knowledge, skills, and attitudes measured in the tasks? 3 = critically important; 2 = very important; 1 = somewhat important; 0 = not important at all. For ratings or 1 or 0, please share with us your concerns.

Authenticity (A): Determine if teachers really do the kind of work represented in the tasks (or are observed for these behaviors)—even if they do not typically put the results of their work in a neat folder or write a report/reflection about it. 3 = highly authentic; 2 = moderately authentic; 1 = slightly authentic; 0 = not authentic at all. For ratings of 1 or 0, please share your concerns.

Frequency (F): How frequently are the knowledge, skills, and attitudes measured in the tasks evidenced by good teachers in the classroom? How often should they display these skills? 3 = daily or weekly; 2 = monthly; 1 = once a semester; 0 = or not at all.

Task #	Task Name	Criticality			Authenticity			Frequency		
		3	2	1	3	2	1	3	2	1
		3	2	1	3	2	1	3	2	1
		3	2	1	3	2	1	3	2	1
		3	2	1	3	2	1	3	2	1
		3	2	1	3	2	1	3	2	1
		3	2	1	3	2	1	3	2	1
		3	2	1	3	2	1	3	2	1
		3	2	1	3	2	1	3	2	1
		3	2	1	3	2	1	3	2	1

CAATS STEP 3—WORKSHEET #3.5

Checklist for Reviewing Individual Tasks

Explanation:

After writing each task, use this checklist to self-assess the task.

Task Name: _____ Reviewer Name: _____

_____ The task name is short, to the point, and adequately descriptive.

_____ The task description provides an effective overview of the task so the reader can visualize the product or performance.

_____ The assessors will be able to "see" evidence of each standard and indicator aligned with this task in the actual work of the teacher.

_____ The instructions are clearly written and sufficiently detailed so teachers will know exactly what is expected.

_____ The scoring criteria are clearly stated, observable, and grammatically consistent.

_____ The scoring criteria use standards-based language wherever possible.

_____ Criteria are worded in such a way that credit is given for effective work. (Words such as "avoids" are used to make sure teachers get credit for doing the right thing!)

_____ The points on the scale can be clearly differentiated.

_____ A separate decision is made for each standard assessed.

_____ The form is easy to use.

CAATS STEP 3—WORKSHEET #3.6

Instructional Alignment

Explanation:

Use this worksheet to make sure that your teachers have adequate opportunity to practice and prepare for each summative task in the system. Opportunity to learn is a critical element of validity and fairness.

Task # and Name	*Preparatory Experiences, Activities, Readings, and Formative Assessments*

Where We Have Been So Far

To this point, we have drilled the need to build a lean and focused assessment system that includes only those instruments (tasks) that are truly important to make summative decisions about teacher competence based on standards and the assessment purpose(s) we want to achieve. We created tasks that aligned teachers' performances with standards and included clear directions and rubrics. We ensured that the tasks provided adequate and appropriate coverage of the standards. We also ensured that sufficient opportunities to learn the standards were provided. In preparation for CAATS Step 4, we encouraged you to reach consensus on a rubric format or at least a summative decision-making format at the task level so that data could be aggregated. We also advised that in a standards-driven approach to performance assessment, we need data on performance on standards—that means we need to know whether an individual (base) standard has or has not been demonstrated task by task.

Assuming you are okay on those core assumptions, let's take things one step further. There's nothing worse than collecting a bunch of data and then wondering what you are going to do with it. "Doing something with it" is the subject of CAATS Step 4. Well, on second thought, maybe there is something worse. If we don't know what the data are, then we really are in a pickle. The best tasks in the world are of little use if the results remain known by only an individual assessor and aren't stored somewhere. We need to be able to store and manage our data as a team so that we can use the data for whatever purpose(s) we identified in CAATS Step 1. That's really where we are headed in CAATS Step 4—sharing and using the data for the purpose(s) intended.

The advice provided in this step is contingent on three core assumptions: (1) common assessment tasks are used; (2) data are derived at the standards level; (3) you have stuck like glue to the concept of criticality—all tasks and all evaluation criteria are critical measures of teacher job performance. If any of these assumptions is not met, you may want to revisit your work in previous CAATS steps before moving on. Here we will propose a new cut-score setting methodology that relies heavily on these assumptions. You may want some background on where this methodology comes from. If so, please read Chapters 8 and 9. If anyone questions you about why you are implementing the model we will propose in this chapter, the answers are in Chapters 8 and 9.

6

CAATS Step 4

Decision Making and Data Management

If we take the view that decision making needs to be shared, all decision makers need access to a common core of data from which they can make their decisions collaboratively, taking into account all of the important data. When we talk about decisions here, we are speaking not only about the decisions about an individual teacher's performance on an individual task, but also about that teacher's performance on all tasks, and then all teachers' performance on each task and all tasks. It is only when we build a data aggregation system that starts with the teacher and task levels, that we can hope to obtain data that will be useful for decision making about teacher credentialing and pro-

> **CAATS Step 4: Design and implement data aggregation, tracking, and management systems.**

gram improvement. As we approach CAATS Step 4, that dual purpose—individual teacher and overall program—needs to be kept clearly in mind. It will have implications for how far we go in our cut-score setting approaches.

In this step, we will explore strategies for accumulating and managing data for decision making so that we can **aggregate** it. This will include **setting some quantitative standards for minimal (or advanced) competency**. **Tracking systems**, record keeping, and other procedural details, are necessary to do this. Consensus around the system needs to be built and supported. Reward systems could include anything that makes faculty or other assessors more amenable to the accountability requirements. A **maintenance program** is necessary and should be created to include training of assessors, collection of scored examples showing different levels of proficiency, orientation of teachers being assessed, alternative strategies or tasks for teachers who need them, advising materials (including due process), and an appeals process. Formal review times to update and improve the tasks and the system should be established in advance. Identifying people or committees responsible for data collection in a timely and regular fashion is also important for the valid implementation of the system.

As in previous chapters, we will use some terms for which we need to have a common understanding. New definitions and guiding questions for this step are found in the glossary terms throughout this chapter.

The substeps of Step 4 are rather obvious:

CAATS Step 4A: *Determine how data will be aggregated.*

CAATS Step 4B: *Set standards for minimal competency.*

CAATS Step 4C: *Select and develop a tracking system.*

CAATS Step 4D: *Develop implementation procedures and materials.*

P.S.: Don't forget to keep working on that action plan from Chapter 2!

Before Moving On . . .

1. Are the tasks you are planning to use in your assessment system aligned with individual teacher standards such that you can make decisions at the standards level (e.g., the teacher demonstrated Standard 1 and Standard 4 separately and distinctly in Task #01A? If not, why not? Do you want to go back and revisit?

2. Have you selected a computer program to aggregate data? If not, are you considering one? Will it help you make decisions at the standards level? If not, are you willing to supplement it with a little hand calculating?

3. Are you still comfortable with the way you visualized the competent (or advanced) teacher? Are you prepared to say no to some teachers? If not, what will you do with teachers who are not ready to move on?

4. Are you committed to due process? Is competency demonstration addressed in your procedures for due process? What do your graduation or promotion procedures say about the requirement to demonstrate competency? Do your written procedures provide information and protection for you and your teachers?

CAATS STEP 4A: DETERMINE HOW DATA WILL BE AGGREGATED

So What Is Data Aggregation?

Data aggregation is one of the greatest challenges currently being faced by teacher preparation programs seeking NCATE reaccredidation, even if they make it over the hurdle of a common task format in CAATS Step 3. Because faculty members tend to teach and assess within the confines of their own classrooms, sharing of information is typically rare, and NCATE Board of Examiners teams are writing many weaknesses about data aggregation in Standard 2. A parallel situation exists in district training and staff development programs. The results stay with the trainer "in the drawer," and summary information may only exist in the form of a "completion" record in the teacher's file.

Data aggregation simply means that we assemble the data in ways that will support our decision-making needs. If we need to make decisions about individual teachers, individual standards, individual programs, or the unit as a whole, then we need to aggregate the data in ways that will allow us to make decisions and create reports to meet each need. In fact, as we described in CAATS Step 3 in the previous chapter, we cannot tell much at all about a teacher if we have not reached consensus on task scoring formats. In this substep, we begin with the assumption that you have achieved consensus on a common format and scale for each task in the assessment system. If not, we again encourage you to do so by revisiting CAATS Step 3.

Data Aggregation

Data are compiled in ways to make different decisions. Decisions at a criterion level could be based on a rubric and then combined (or aggregated) to reach a task level score (e.g., raw percent or scale score) or a decision related to a standard (demonstrated/not demonstrated). Data continue to be aggregated for the standard across tasks and then for the certification decision itself. Data can be combined for individuals in this way and subsequently for programs as a whole.

Guiding Question: "How can I combine decisions throughout my system in a way that is useful for decision making?"

One thing that is often confusing is the transformation of data to some other form so that it can be aggregated, graphed, or statistically analyzed. A picture of the data can be worth 1,000 words! The most common example is changing raw scores to percentile ranks so that a person's place within the set of scores has some meaning. There are many such transformations that usually require a statistician armed with a computer and special software. You may have seen standard scores such as those reported on the SAT test. You may also have seen specialized measures such as

Measures

The scientifically determined amount of any predetermined construct expressed in equally defined units.

Guiding Question: "How well did I do? How much do I know?"

Lexiles (Stenner, 1996) that are reported on reading assessments. If you find that score transformation and analysis is important, you'll probably find a person who enjoys statistics to do the job anyway. You can help by being clear when you need transformed scores and what you need them to do for your system. Consider the questions in Box 6.1. If you answer yes to any of them, you may be headed in the direction of using transformed scores.

Box 6.1. Questions That May Indicate the Need for Transformed Scores

- Do you need to compare boys to girls, rich to poor, or ethnic backgrounds as official or legal evidence that will keep you from being challenged as unfair?
- Is it important to put growth or gains of the students into reports where you can defend how much progress they made on standards because of your program?
- Do you require a report of your data as statistically significant or scientifically based for a research presentation?

In our model, we have allowed for high-quality data to undergo later transformation and statistical analysis, and we will provide you with some options to take to your statisticians when we discuss validity and reliability in CAATS Step 5 in the next chapter. Supporting information on item response theory (IRT)—the rationale for using it, how it works, and what you can do with it—can be found in Chapter 9.

The Relationship of Data Aggregation (Step 4A), Cut Scores (Step 4B), and Data Tracking—Use and Reporting (Step 4C)

Once you have faculty and trainers "on the same page" about scoring (CAATS Step 3), the next big challenge is to get the data "out of the drawer," aggregate the data in a way that will yield useful decisions, establish a cut score for minimal competency (and other levels of proficiency, as needed), and track and report results. We will address cut-score setting and tracking and reporting in more detail in the next two substeps and in Chapter 8, but we need to introduce them here as part of the data aggregation function.

First, the cut score essentially asks the bottom line question: At what point will we say to a teacher, "you cannot obtain your teaching license or certificate because you do not have the minimum skills it takes to be a teacher in this state or in my school?" How do we put together the decisions at the individual criterion level to reach the big decision at the end of the process? The challenge is to set the cut score in such a way that it holds to a minimum the number of qualified people you keep out of the profession ("false negatives") and the number of unqualified people you let into the profession ("false positives"). While we recognize in advance that there will be some errors made—unqualified teachers certified and qualified teachers turned away—our challenge is to keep the number of mistakes as near zero as is humanly possible.

> **Cut Score**
>
> The cut score determines who passes and who fails. Teachers below the cut score are not allowed to continue in the program. It may be reported as a raw score, percent correct, or scaled score derived through classical or item response theory.
>
> *Guiding Question: "At what point is the total score so low that we are comfortable saying to a prospective teacher, 'You cannot be a teacher because you do not have the minimal skills required and you might harm children'?"*

Getting to a final score and then figuring out where you divide the final points on the scale between yes and no, okay and not okay, or certified and not certified is difficult with a traditional paper-and-pencil test taken in one sitting and made up of a predetermined set of items. We talked about this in Chapter 1. Aggregating scores and establishing the cut score on a set of tasks administered over a period of one to two years can be far more complex, and the literature does not provide us with an established methodology for this. So, we have created a simple one for you in CAATS Step 4B. It will work if you have been following the criticality aspects of this model.

In CAATS Step 4 in this chapter, we discuss one way of making the decisions on each task in such a way that each step in the decision-making process leads to the next step, and finally the ultimate credentialing decision is reached and all of the data can be reported and used at the individual teacher and program levels.

A quick reminder before we proceed. In a performance-based task system, the literature and the AERA, APA, and NCME 1999 *Standards* are all clear. There need to be criteria at the task level. We recommended earlier that a 3-point scale (or 5 at the most) be used for those criterion-level decisions. While many names are possible for the points on the scale, one that seems to be evolving as workable is *target, acceptable* (or *marginal*), and *unacceptable*. Another is *excellent, satisfactory,* and *unsatisfactory* (or *needs improvement*). Both allow for a midpoint that is above the cut score and a bottom point that defines how and where we say no.

An Approach to Decision Making Without Using Points and Percents

If we carefully write our tasks and ensure that all of the criteria are truly important, then it becomes acceptable to say that all criteria must be met at least at a minimal level of acceptability. If any single criterion is unacceptable, the work needs to be attempted again so that each criterion is at least at an acceptable level. The whole is equal to the sum of its parts in a different way. The pilot just has to be able to land the plane. Whoops! We just let the cat out of the bag. Our cut score is going to be 100%. Fasten your seat belts; we'll explain as we go.

By a similar logic, although somewhat less stringent, we could say that if several aspects, or criteria, are marginal, or just acceptable, then there are enough issues in the whole task to consider it at a marginally acceptable level or even overall competence to be marginally acceptable. It seems to us that such a statement has utility for growth at the next stages of the teacher's career.

Given that our decision needs to be about whether or not tasks show that the teacher has demonstrated standards, we can convert our language to *demonstrated, partially demonstrated,* and *not demonstrated.* Bumping this up just one more notch, any task that shows the standard was not demonstrated, even after multiple attempts at remediation, should mean that there is a critical flaw in the teacher's competence on that standard, and the teacher can be declared not competent on that standard.

This logic allows us to establish the following decision-making structure, represented in Figure 6.1, and the rubric, shown in Table 6.1. We developed these for the Florida Alternative Certification Program Assessment System; however, note that they have been updated over time and are, therefore, not current.

Figure 6.1. Four Levels of Decision Making in the Florida Alternative Certification Program Assessment System

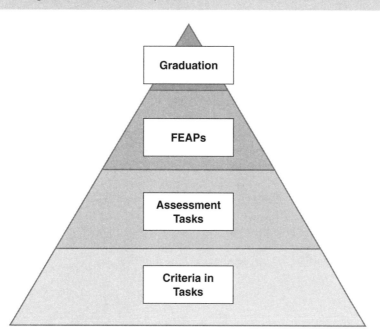

Table 6.1. Three Levels of Decision Making With Three Score Points Each Developed for the Florida Alternative Certification Program Assessment System

Criterion Decisions	Task Decisions	Practice (FEAP) Decisions*
Target (T): The teacher's work meets all expectations.	**Demonstrated (D)**: If all the criteria are rated at the "target" level or "acceptable" level, the teacher has demonstrated the Practice. **Up to** one-third of the criteria may be rated as just "acceptable." None of the criteria can be rated as "unacceptable."	**Accomplished**: The teacher has successfully demonstrated this Practice, consistently showing evidence of ability in the Practice. He or she is ready to assume full responsibility for teaching and continuing professional development with regard to this Practice. This level of achievement has been demonstrated by multiple ratings of "demonstrated" on the tasks in this system. The candidate has received not more than one rating of "partially demonstrated," and *no* ratings of "not demonstrated."
Acceptable (A): The teacher's work is essentially correct but has minor problems that can be addressed through counseling or advising. The assessor expects that the teacher will be able to self-correct without difficulty in subsequent attempts at similar tasks.	**Partially Demonstrated (PD)**: If **more than** one-third of the criteria were rated as just "acceptable," the teacher is rated as having partially demonstrated the standard. None of the criteria can be rated as "unacceptable."	**Competent**: The teacher has demonstrated this Practice adequately for certification. However, there are some gaps in performance that require continued monitoring, and there were two or more final decisions of "partially demonstrated" on the tasks for the Practice. These performance gaps need to be remediated over time through implementation of a professional development plan and should be monitored closely by the employing district.
Unacceptable (U): The teacher's work has a major problem that needs to be corrected and rechecked. The problem is serious enough to question whether or not the teacher can be effective and should be certified.	**Not Demonstrated (ND)**: One or more of the criteria were rated as "unacceptable." The teacher must fix whatever was unacceptable and earn a PD or D rating on the task to be certified.	**Not Competent**: The candidate has not demonstrated minimal competence on this Practice and, therefore, is not eligible for certification. The teacher has received a "not demonstrated" rating on one or more products or performances in the assessment system for this Practice, despite three opportunities provided for successful demonstration.

SOURCE: Adapted from Florida Department of Education (2002).

NOTE: In Florida, all Florida Educator Accomplished Practices (FEAPs) must be demonstrated; hence, for the final decision on certification, all 12 FEAPs must be at the accomplished or competent level. Note also that the original version of the system provided for the final decisions to be competent, minimally competent, and not competent. We preferred that as more realistic, but Florida decision makers noted that "minimally competent" and "highly qualified" did not go well together. Remember the conflicting paradigm we talked about in Chapter 2?

Worksheet #4.1 is designed to help you establish your own decision-making levels, the first of which you developed in CAATS Step 3. You may decide to modify that scale here as you think through the other decisions in your system. Here are some hints on how to do this:

1. *Missing or Not Missing a Standard (a.k.a. Failure):* Determine if your state allows some standards not to be demonstrated. This will influence the extent to which the "not competent" decision is required by failure at a single standard. If you find that the standards are critical from your own perspective, this, too, will influence the amount of leeway you will allow teachers in failing one. In our case, we would say that a teacher who cannot plan or assess or treat children equally should not be a teacher, so we are committed to a very high-stakes standard. You may feel differently or have an opportunity to set a lower standard if you have some standards in your state that you look at as "filler."

2. *Separate Decisions for Each Standard:* If decisions are being made on more than one standard in a single task, we will not have a valid measure unless the decision for each standard reflects that standard alone. This is one of the most difficult realizations for institutions and school districts attempting the model, and it was one of those core assumptions we noted at the beginning of this chapter. Most assessors want to combine multiple standards into a single task for two reasons: (1) they *falsely* believe it will reduce the amount of time spent assessing, and (2) they *falsely* believe it acknowledges the complexity of teaching and the overlapping nature of standards. We counsel strongly against the clustering of more than two or three standards in a single task at the initial certification level (except for classroom observations such as final internship). It becomes very difficult to keep track of evidence of each standard if too many standards are being evaluated. Even if there are just two standards being evaluated, it is imperative that separate decisions be reached for both standards; otherwise, it is not possible to determine from the demonstration score or decision if each standard was actually demonstrated adequately. So, for a task with two standards, two decisions are necessary. For a task with three standards, three decisions are necessary, and so forth. Otherwise, you may find yourself in the "pilot not landing the plane" scenario. In Box 6.2, we illustrate what happens when two areas of content are co-mingled with a familiar example from the K–12 classroom context.

3. *Consequences:* If the teacher preparation program results in a long-term certificate, the stakes are higher for children, so the stakes in the assessment system need to be higher. But the decisions need to be valid!

4. *Exceptions:* With a high-stakes model, there needs to be room for exceptions. We recommend the use of a committee charged with responsibility for determining whether a waiver or an alternative should be provided to a specific teacher. The occasions in which such exceptions are made should be both rare and well-documented.

With a process and scale established to combine scores at each level—criterion, task, standard, and final decision—we can now move to the next substep: determining how much is enough—the actual cut score.

> ### Box 6.2. A Familiar Example of Mixing Up Content
>
> Most of our readers may not be used to thinking about standards as needing to be assessed individually for decision-making purposes, so here is a K–12 example.
>
> *Scenario:* Suppose you ask your students to write an essay or report comparing the French and American Revolutions. One student, let's call her Susie, does a superlative job (i.e., an A) on the content, but she does not know her grammar at all (i.e., an F). We give her a C on the paper and record it in our grade book under Social Studies. What does that C mean? How do we interpret or use that C? Can we say that her understanding of history is just average? The more we mix content areas in our K–12 based grading, the less we know about what kids know and can do. The same is true in standards-based teacher assessment. A score of satisfactory on a task that measures both assessment and planning could mean satisfactory on both or excellent on one and unsatisfactory on the other. The validity of the decision is dead.
>
> Before leaving this example, let's toss in a criterion on neatness. ***Poor*** Susie does not do neat work. There are cross outs all over her paper, and she didn't type it. Low socio-economic status (SES), no computer at home; little baby brother ate her only eraser the night before the paper was due. Now she has a D. What does that mean about Susie's expertise in social studies?
>
> ———————————— ❖ ————————————
>
> **We need to think carefully about what our scores mean, how we will use them and what consequences they have on our decisions. Susie probably won't be a teacher even though she is smart and loves children—even her baby brother. We should have sent her for remedial work in English and given her another eraser. That is what we mean by a false negative.**

CAATS STEP 4B: SET STANDARDS FOR MINIMAL COMPETENCY

Different Strokes for Different Folks—Déjà Vu, or Purpose Revisited

There are a number of accepted methods of standard or cut-score setting in the literature, although none of these was created with the system we are developing in CAATS in mind. They were either for objective tests (typically multiple choice) or performance tests—with examinees taking the test in one sitting or submitting it for review in one package (portfolio). The system we have been creating is quite different in three respects.

1. Assessment tasks are completed over a one- to four-year period.

2. Assessment tasks may be repeated after remediation.

3. Assessment tasks are all critical, with each candidate completing the same set.

AERA, APA, and NCME (1999) *Standards*
and CAATS Step 4A

Standard 1.12:

When interpretation of subscores, score differences, or profiles is suggested, the rationale and relevant evidence in support of such interpretation should be provided. *Where composite scores are developed, the basis and rationale for arriving at the composites should be given.*
    CAATS Steps Influenced: 4A

Standard 4.9:

When raw score or derived score scales are designed for criterion-referenced interpretation, including the classification of examinees into separate categories, *their rationale for recommended score interpretations* should be clearly explained.
    CAATS Steps Influenced: 4A

Standard 14.13:

When decision makers integrate information from multiple tests or integrated test and nontest information, *the role played by each test in the decision process* should be clearly explicated, and the *use of each test or test composite* should be supported by validity evidence.
    CAATS Steps Influenced: 4A

Discussion

These standards establish the requirements to explain the rationale behind score aggregation and the expectation of using combined scores for the summative decision.

NOTE: Emphases added for clarity.

Nonetheless, there is much to be learned from existing models, and we will build a new one here in this CAATS step. We encourage our readers to prepare for this step by jumping ahead to Chapter 8, which tells you most everything you ever wanted to know but were afraid to ask about the history and techniques of cut-score setting. If you haven't read it yet, this would be a good time to take a break from the CAATS steps and do so. Actually, it's really just a short summary, but the references help you delve deeper if you so choose. The discussion and references in that chapter will also help you support the decision we are advising, should you decide to make it.

Based on past history (as described in Chapter 8) and our focus on the critical nature of tasks in an assessment system built using the CAATS model, we recommend an initial cut score of 100% passing (at least minimally acceptable performance) on all tasks. After all, if the tasks are really critical, how could we certify a teacher who cannot do them successfully after three attempts? Remember also that we allow for imperfection in our rating scales. Unlike multiple-choice tests where there is right/wrong answer, in performance tasks, some performance can be on the weak, but still satisfactory, side.

You probably saw our approach coming a long time ago, but we will bet that you didn't guess our name for it—the CYA approach. Lest that conjure up the image that we suspect you may be having (and hoped you would), we will use the acronym CYA here to spell out Critical Yardstick Approach. If you thought of a different (more anatomically based) acronym for CYA, you get extra credit! When you read Chapter 8, you will see references to the yardstick, for us, being criticality. By now, that should come as no surprise either! As a preview of coming attractions, you will see in bullet #14 below and in Chapter 8 that there is actually a measurement process that yields "rulers" of ability. Yardsticks are, after all, just bigger rulers.

Judges

Judges are experts or stakeholders who can render an important and useful opinion about your work or can help you make a decision such as how to set a cut score. Measurement people also talk about judges as the raters on performance tasks. They are not the folks sitting at the bench listening to lawyers and instructing the jury.

Guiding Question: "Who would be a good expert to help me decide or evaluate something?"

Fortunately, there is support for the 100% cut score in previous work (not just ours), as you also will see in Chapter 8. Amazingly, it was teachers serving as expert judges attempting to set cut scores the old-fashioned way who actually came up with that support. Measurement professionals just didn't get it and didn't listen to them. This is a no-nonsense, no statistics approach to setting the standard. We see this performance standard as what we need to protect the public from harm and maintain professional integrity.

If you are representing a college of education or a school district developing an alternative certification assessment system, you may be very comfortable stopping at the cut score of 100%. If you are working at a state level or if you are truly interested in using your data for purposes other than deciding who gets the certificate and who does not, you may want to kick things up a notch and make a second level cut. The second cut would be used for other levels of proficiency and to control for rater effect. It would require a little more statistical work and expertise. So, we are looking at a two-stage process, for those who want or need it. We implied that earlier in this chapter, now we explain it.

Cut-score setting can be an expensive endeavor. As you approach this step, remember that we are advocating for expending time and resources on the design of high-quality, critical assessment tasks and rubrics, and using judges to fix them rather than to argue over an artificial cut score. You have been doing that with your involvement of stakeholders in previous steps, although you may not have thought about it as part of your cut-score setting methodology.

If you have the resources to go to the second level, we recommend that you use the Rasch model of IRT to do so. Chapter 9 will tell you everything you were afraid to ask about that. Again, more information is available through the references, which will add to your knowledge and help you defend your decisions. Our rationale for using the Rasch model is provided in the beginning of that chapter, and we will not repeat all of its advantages here. Instead, we will focus on how you have already essentially established your first cut score by following the CAATS model, and a few additional details you need to complete that process. Let's talk about the 100% idea first.

Is 100% Really Reasonable?

Florida made it easy for us to say "yes." So did the teachers used as judges in our cut-score literature review in Chapter 8. In Florida, the first Continued Program Approval Standard is: "100% of teacher candidates will demonstrate all 12 Accomplished Practices." If you are having trouble swallowing this high standard and smiling because your state did not do that to you, then start visualizing the teacher who misses any one of the INTASC Principles and then is allowed through the school door.

The Florida Education Standards Commission set the bar high. They had the courage to say that this is what they think is critically important and everyone has to do it. The standard met with an immediate uproar in the state. However, when deans and faculty alike were faced with the question, "Which standards are optional? Ethics? Planning? Diversity?" and so forth down the list, no dean and no faculty member was ever willing to discard any standard. They accepted the 100% cut score. The yardstick they used was criticality.

The Criticality Yardstick Approach (CYA) to Cut-Score Setting in Complex Performance Assessments

As we noted above, the Criticality Yardstick Approach (CYA) requires the use of a 100% cut score as a starter, with the option of subsequently establishing multiple cut scores using the best of the other cut-score methodologies discussed in Chapter 8 in order to enhance decision-making capabilities. The implementation procedures that follow link the first cut to all of the previous steps of the CAATS model, then add a few more parts, and finally conclude with some basic remarks about the second cut. Here we also provide some additional advice on working with judges.

First Cut

1. Go back to Step 1A and revisit your purpose. If one purpose was certification, you will need to make a yes/no certification decision. If another purpose was diagnosis and improvement, you will need scores, but not necessarily to make the first cut on certification.

2. Go back to Step 1B and revisit your propositions. If you agreed to use the example statements or ones similar to them, and all you want to do is make a certification decision, the yes/no cut may be all you need to do—especially at the institutional or district level for initial certification.

3. Go back to Step 1D and see how much money you have. Determine if you can afford to bring together groups of judges to give you feedback on the criticality of the tasks *and* the cut score on two different occasions. You may need to do two things at one time.

4. Go back to Step 2B and visualize the minimally competent teacher. Hold that thought now that you know more about why you had to do it.

5. Go back to Step 2D and pat yourself on the back for moving noncritical tasks to the formative level. Reconsider any that troubled you the last time you thought about this.

6. Go back to Step 3A and celebrate if you decided to have a common format. Rethink that decision if you didn't.

7. Go back to Step 3B and celebrate if you limited your rubrics to three (maybe four) proficiency levels if you are going to do diagnosis. Rethink that decision if you didn't. The more proficiency levels you have, the more work you have to do now.

8. Go back to Step 3C (and Worksheets #3.1 and #3.5 in Chapter 5) and double check the rating scales on each task and the global ones to make sure the proficiency levels are clearly delineated, especially at the unacceptable level. Make sure unacceptable is equivalent to Berk's putrid in *every* case (see Chapter 8 for definition of *putrid*). Is it really the person you want to stop from teaching? It is the wannabee teacher who is clueless about content, clueless about how to select materials to teach, or clueless about how to recognize learning progress in a child of his/her choice. (Those were our criteria from the model task on the K–12 Portfolio—by the way.) Think *putrid*. The wannabee airline pilot who says—"Uh—Was *THAT* the runway?"

9. Stay on Step 3C for a little while longer and revisit your stakeholder survey (Worksheet #3.4 in our system). "Stakeholders" is another, more user-friendly term for "expert judges." Look at those scores again. Think about fixing or eliminating (or moving to formative) any tasks that were not highly rated when you convened the panel of experts or sent them the survey by mail. At this point, you could calculate means and establish a cut score for task inclusion. If a task had a mean rating below a 2.5, for example, on the 3-point criticality scale, there would be a high proportion of judges who were not convinced that it was truly critical, and it should be reviewed or excluded from the system.

10. Go back to Step 3D and revisit the opportunities to learn. In a high-stakes model like this, candidates must have adequate instruction to succeed. These opportunities to learn, combined with multiple opportunities to remediate and succeed (the three tries idea), moderate the high cut score and provide teachers with an opportunity to learn while being assessed.

11. Go back to Step 4A and revisit your decision rules one more time. You may be getting tired of this, but this is your cut score. It has to represent your best thinking. We suggested the labels "unacceptable," "not demonstrated," and "not competent" for our three levels of decision making. You may have called them something else or have more of them. Rethink your decisions and definitions and make sure you have defined "putrid."

12. Now we're caught up. If you are comfortable with everything you have done so far, it is time to convene your panel of judges with your stakeholder survey (Step 3C, Worksheet #3.4 results) and rubrics in hand. You could do this at the same time, if you prefer to do it all at once. We will use Berk's work as a baseline for what to do at this stage. You're not going to ask them to play guessing games with numbers, as is the case in traditional cut-score setting methodologies. You're going to ask them to fix your mistakes and make

better tasks and decisions. The cut score is already set. In whatever words you chose, it is 100% okay or better, and no putrids. We talk more about what to do with the judges in the next section.

13. Evaluate (validate) your results after adequate data are accumulated to determine if the cut score is working to eliminate the teachers who are not acceptable and help the ones who are. Too many tries or too few? Use a confirmatory analysis or an empirical approach (see CAATS Step 5 in Chapter 7) to do this. For the confirmatory analysis, several options are available:

    - Keep careful count of the number of tries per task, the pattern of response of students who leave the program, and the tasks that appear to be unusually easy or difficult.

    - Collect data on eligibility for rehire rates of newly hired teachers. If a troublesome number of teachers (e.g., 10% or more) are found inadequate and fired within a specified time period (e.g., within one or two years) or sent for remediation, the cut score is probably too low or your process is too weak (e.g., too many tries, missing critical tasks, weak judges making too many acceptable ratings).

    - Collect information through interviews and/or surveys of principals to determine if unqualified practitioners are coming into the system but being provided additional support to help them succeed, or just kept because of the teacher shortage. Again, this would mean your process was too weak.

    - Determine if teachers rejected from the program are hired under a different certification route and rehired one or two years later. This would mean that your criteria were too stringent—the opposite of the problems in the point above.

14. Begin to build your library of tasks or bank of items by adding to the base or anchor core of assessments. Once you establish the minimum competency set of assessments, you can start building two other types of performance tasks: (1) equivalent ways to assess the same standard using alternate forms, and (2) upward extensions of assessments to more complex skills, advanced expectations, and higher performance. The upward extensions are necessary to build a "ladder or ruler" of assessment scores that can be calibrated into measures that have qualities allowing the setting of advanced program targets.

> ——— **Ruler (Logistic Ruler)** ———
>
> A construct of imaginary but defined equal units or intervals. Physically, the unit may be inches or centimeters. With teacher performance measures, the unit is generically called a logit.
>
> *Guiding Question: "How can I determine the level of teacher knowledge and ability in a scientific way?"*

> **Parting Words on the First Cut**
>
> The numbers are a means, not an end. Don't let any statistician tell you otherwise. Use the KISS approach—keep it statistically simple. That is sufficient to cover your "anatomy"—CYA.

Second Cut

15. We have suggested that the second cut be used to sort levels of proficiency higher than minimal competency. Prerequisite to the second cut is a common scoring format with criteria the same on all tasks and for the standards themselves, so that we can count and add raw scores. Previously in the CAATS

model, and the example proficiency levels we provided, we made the cut from "minimally competent" to "competent" at the standard level by setting an arbitrary cut score of one-third. We said that if one-third or more of the tasks were scored as "partially demonstrated" (less than two-thirds demonstrated), then the standard rating was minimally competent. If less than one-third were rated "partially demonstrated" (more than two-thirds demonstrated), this generated a competent decision for the standard. Similarly, at the task level, we used the one-third cut to differentiate between "partially demonstrated" and "demonstrated." The system was cumulative, with one-third always serving as the cut. Here we provide an opportunity to change that through classical or item response theory.

- The classical cut-score approaches would allow us to establish a total score for each task, and these could be summed for each standard. Judges would establish the cut score between proficiency levels based on that total score. Judges might say that one standard (e.g., critical thinking) was more difficult or important than another (e.g., collegiality), and could set the cut score for movement between proficiencies higher or lower accordingly—allowing for more-or-less acceptable ratings. Procedures, such as Angoff or Dominant Profile, could be used, and these are all described in Chapter 8.

- The Rasch model of IRT could be applied to accomplish the same target of defining levels of competency above minimum. In addition to the advantages noted in Chapter 9, you would use the computer to calculate accurate and precise scores on an interval scale and then assemble judges to draw a line between proficiency levels—somewhat like the bookmark approach—but based on scores that were scientifically calculated. The objective standard setting (OSS) model described in Chapter 8 could be used.

16. With the second cut-score setting methodology implemented, you are now ready to perform some serious analyses of individual and item performances, conduct reliability studies, and do some research. See Chapter 9 and CAATS Step 5 in Chapter 7 for details.

NOTE: If points 14 through 16 sounded like Greek to you, you probably did not read Chapter 8.

Scores (Raw Scores)

The count of items correct or rating of judges on items in tests or assessments.

Guiding Question: "How many did I get right?"

Using judges well remains the only topic we have not adequately addressed thus far in this step (and in Chapter 8) on cut scores or standard setting. We turn there now.

Working With Judges

Proper use of judges will be important as you develop surveys and/or focus groups to solicit their opinions on the quality of your tasks and cut scores. In Table 6.2, we provide Berk's Top Ten Picks for the Judgmental Standard-Setting Process (Berk, 1995, pp. 23–24) and the uses we see for the CAATS model of critical tasks and working with judges.

	Table 6.2. Berk's Top Ten Picks and the CAATS CYA Application	
#	*Berk*	*CAATS CYA Application*
10	Select a broad-based sample of the most qualified and credible judges you can find.	*Same:* Also include Berk's suggestion of including both broad-based and specialized groups, asking the broad-based group to look at the system as a whole—proficiency level descriptions and list of tasks. Ask the specialists to look at the criteria based on their field of expertise (e.g., a special educator to look at diversity, an educational psychologist to look at child development and assessment). Aim for a panel of 15 to 20 judges.
9	Train these judges to perform the standard-setting tasks to minimize "instrumentation effect" and maximize intrajudge consistency.	*Same:* Note, most judges will have prior experience with the same or similar tasks if they are truly critical tasks. Your training will focus most heavily on the directions and examples you provide.
8	Use a multistage iterative process whereby judges are given one or two opportunities to review/refine their original decisions based on new information to maximize interjudge consistency.	*Same:* These judges should include, at a minimum, the judges used in the validity study conducted in CAATS Step 3C. In fact, you may do these two things at the same time. Then talk, edit, and rescore when there are disagreements or improvement suggestions.
7	Require judges to provide explicit behavioral descriptions for each achievement level with corresponding anchor items.	*Modified:* The rubrics are provided in draft form for the judges to verify or modify. It would be too time-consuming to have them start from scratch.
6	Determine the judges' decision policy based on the objectives or dimensions measured.	*Different:* The decision policy (100% success criterion) is predetermined and verified. Here decide how many judges have to agree—80%? If you are using classical test theory (CTT), you could have the judges select a cut score for other proficiency levels at this point—the cut between minimally competent and competent, for example.
5	Provide judges with feedback on their individual and panel's decisions.	*Same:* Share ratings and rationales.
4	Supply judges with meaningful performance data on a representative sample or appropriate subsample of examinees to "reality-base" the ratings.	*Same:* Note that the judges could include judges who have experience with pilot test versions of the tasks. No matter what, the panel should be reconvened when there are sufficient results to determine if the system is working as intended.

(Continued)

(Continued)

#	*Berk*	*CAATS CYA Application*
3	Allow judges the opportunity to discuss their decisions and pertinent data without pressure to reach consensus.	*Same*. Note that the 80% agreement target will help.
2	Allow judges' content-related decisions about achievement levels via consensus, but all item and test score decisions via independent ratings, to avoid pressuring "outlier judges" into alignment of the influence of "dominant judges."	*Same:* The 80% rule may help avoid dominance.
1	Compute the cut score(s) from the mean/median item or test scores based on the judges' ratings.	*Different/Same:* The cut score is predetermined at 100%. No more fuzzy numbers. Here we do final edits of the tasks and criteria. Use Berk's advice for the second cut.

SOURCE: Adapted from Berk (1996).

An Example of What to Say to the Judges

The primary job of your judges is to verify that you have defined well the points on the scale—both the generic ones (like target, acceptable, and unacceptable; not competent, minimally competent, and competent), and the specific ones (the ones in the cells for each task (e.g., the K–12 Portfolio example in CAATS Step 3). Have you pinpointed the points of no return—the unacceptable—the no-license decision? The panel will need to look at each criterion one by one. You might offer your judges an explanation like the one modeled in Box 6.3, which uses the K–12 Portfolio example we used in Chapter 5, Step 3. A similar set of instructions could be written for each task in the system.

Box 6.3. Directions to Judges on Establishing Behavioral Anchors

You will be reviewing the *unacceptable* rating for a task in which the teacher candidate has to select 10 examples of student work that show his or her ability to teach critical thinking in the content area. The teacher candidate has had an entire semester to collect this work and has had support from the supervising teacher and/or mentor. The teacher candidate can repeat this task three times to succeed. Your job is to determine if, after three times, and with support from other professionals, this teacher should be certified if an unacceptable rating is earned on the third try. If you think the number of tries is too high or too low, we need to know that, too.

Remember that this rubric does not require that the teacher reach every child; we are not looking for consistency of performance (although we would certainly like to have it).

It only requires that the teacher has been able to reach some children once, can recognize them, and then can select and describe their work. Ask yourself this question:

"If the teacher cannot meet this criterion even one time, and with help, should this teacher be licensed?"

If the answer to the question is yes, then the criterion stands. If the answer is no, then you will be asked to explain your answer and make suggestions on your worksheet.

Example: Criterion #1, unacceptable rating: The candidate fails to show an understanding of content and is teaching concepts that are not correct, current, or important, or are insufficient with regard to state content standards.

Decisions:

1a. Yes—This decision (meaning the teacher *should not* be certified with a rating of unacceptable) means that you agree that the teacher cannot make bad mistakes in the content area and still be certifiable.

or

1b. No—This decision (meaning the teacher *should* be certified even if the rating is unacceptable) would be tantamount to saying that it is okay for a teacher to exhibit gross misunderstandings of content even when the teacher has selected evidence that he or she believes is just fine.

and

2. Tries—I agree/disagree with three tries on this. For a disagree decision, what number would you use and why?

Worksheet #4.1 provides a sample recording form for judges. Don't forget that you will need to keep an eye on consistency during this process. Check the consistency of ratings from your judges, using one of the techniques described in CAATS Step 5—Cohen's kappa (Cohen, 1960)—if you are using classical test theory or the judge parameter in the Rasch model.

AERA, APA, and NCME (1999) *Standards*

and CAATS Step 4B

Standard 4.19:

When proposed score interpretations involve one or more cut scores, the *rationale and procedures used for establishing cut scores* should be clearly documented.
    CAATS Steps Influenced: 4B

(Continued)

(Continued)

Standard 4.20:

When feasible, cut scores defining categories with *distinct substantive interpretations* should be established on the basis of *sound empirical data* concerning the relationship of test performance to relevant criteria.

    CAATS Steps Influenced: 4B

Standard 4.21:

When cut scores defining pass-fail or proficiency categories are based on direct judgments about the adequacy of item or test performances or performance levels, the *judgmental process should be designed so that judges can bring their knowledge and experience to bear in a reasonable way.*

    CAATS Steps Influenced: 4B, 5A

Discussion

In this step we have defined the procedures for establishing cut scores, using a new approach designed specifically for a high-stakes, task-based performance assessment system that has defined the content sampled as all critically important to the job and provides for opportunities to remediate. The knowledge judges bring to the process is used to verify the criticality of each task and suggestions for improvement of rubrics rather than calculating a percentage of teachers who should do the work correctly.

NOTE: Emphases added for clarity.

CAATS STEP 4C: SELECT AND DEVELOP A TRACKING SYSTEM

Sharing Information for Decision Making: The Big Challenge

If we are to overcome the tendency of assessors to store data themselves for their own personal use, we need to have some form of tracking system that serves as a container for storing and retrieving data about their decisions. You may remember that we presented this as one of our greatest challenges when we introduced Step 4A. Some faculty and trainers will want to bury their decisions in a course grade or personnel folder; others will be willing to share a final decision or score on a task; others will be willing to provide the detailed feedback available at the criterion level. Much will depend on their acceptance of the need for accountability and shared decision making. The challenge to leadership is to help them see the need for both of these.

In the next four sections, we will present four typical options for data storage: course grades or records of participation/attendance, student folders, portfolios, and electronic databases. We will include a basic description of each, followed by a discussion of pros, cons, and pitfalls. Our last option will be the electronic database, which is typically the best option for programs with more than 20 teachers to track. We then move on to the reporting aspects of data aggregation.

> **Management or Tracking System**
>
> The management or tracking system is the process used to keep track of scores in the system so that reports can be generated for decision making. It may be kept by hand or on a computer.
>
> *Guiding Question: "What procedures and materials do I need to have in place to retrieve data?"*

Data Storage Option #1: Course Grades or Records of Participation/Attendance

In this option, faculty or trainers include the standards decision in the course grade or record. The only way this can be done is to require teachers to complete the task successfully, demonstrating at whatever level of competency is predetermined, that the work is of sufficiently high caliber on the task (and standard) to complete the course or training. This is by far the simplest method of storing data, but it has at least two major shortcomings:

- *Appropriateness of the Failing Grade:*

    Faculty have to be willing to fail or give an incomplete to a teacher who does not successfully complete the task or the component of the task reflecting the standard. This includes failures and incompletes based on a partially unsuccessful task if more than one standard is assessed in the task, as well as failures and incompletes for tasks that may be critical to standards demonstration but not for the course or training itself. While on the surface this method appears to increase academic freedom for college faculty, it more likely decreases it by restricting what we will assess and count. It is also virtually impossible in staff development contexts. In Box 6.4 we provide an example of the conflict generated when using course grades that reflect decisions on multiple standards in a single task.

Box 6.4.   Sample Problem With Course Grading Approach

One of our Florida standards requires competence in using technology for the management of instruction. It is conceivable that an undergraduate measurement course might include a small assignment on creating a grade book or a portion of a project on test development requiring use of item-writing or analysis software. In the grand scheme of things in a basic measurement course, entering data into grading software and using item writing or analysis software are far less important than writing good tests and knowing how to interpret the results. In the course grade approach to data storage, however, a student unable to manipulate item-writing software well but able to write good items in word processing software could fail the course.

- *Data Aggregation Issue:*

    Even if the task importance/course completion dilemma is resolved and only critical tasks are included in the assessment system with each counting for a single standard, records of course grades or attendance provide no data useful for aggregation. The unit is unable to answer questions about which aspects of a task were difficult for large numbers of students. The unit is also unable to include any kind of quantitative data in the levels of decision making other than percent pass rates by task. All the rest remains buried in the faculty member or trainer's office desk drawer or computer. If the course grading option is selected, it will be important to have the raw data (instructors' completed rubrics) available for analysis.

Data Storage Option #2: Teacher Folders

In this approach, the administration, possibly the student advising office or personnel office, keeps a folder on each teacher with records showing successful completion of each required task. These could easily be copies of completed scoring forms for each task. There is typically a checklist at the front of the folder indicating that each piece has been filed. The data can then be aggregated across teachers to identify strengths and weaknesses in the program, but this has to be done for the most part by hand. The folder approach is a good method for handling data aggregation requirements with very limited populations across programs or schools—possibly a few secondary programs with less than 20 teachers each. In programs of this size, it does not pay to set up an electronic system. It is easy enough to keep two copies of every form—one in the teacher folder and one in the task folder, so the data can be aggregated by teacher or by task for decision making about teacher progression and program quality.

Data Storage Option #3: Portfolios

There are two types of portfolios used in accountability systems, as we noted earlier in this book: one that works well for accountability, and one that works well for showcasing, continuing growth, and other purposes. We discussed these in more detail in Chapter 2; however, in this chapter we note that the accountability portfolio is an expansion of the teacher folder and contains not only the completed scoring rubrics but also the teacher's actual work. The portfolio here is a container of required work, and there is no additional assessment of the portfolio needed—other than a completion checklist. Other assessments, such as the quality of reflection, have other purposes beyond the establishment of minimal competency. In cases where the purpose includes reflective practice, then reflection must be evaluated in and of itself either in the portfolio or elsewhere.

The value of the portfolio in this context is the ability of the institution to select samples of teacher work—both effective and ineffective—for studies of reliability and for presentation to accrediting groups. If the folder option is used, such samples could be collected from individual faculty or trainers on a regular basis. With the portfolio option, teachers need to be asked to provide duplicates of their portfolios, which is easy for electronic portfolios and difficult for paper portfolios.

Data Storage Option #4: Electronic Data Management System

The electronic storage system is by far the most advisable, especially if there are more than 20 or so teachers in the program. Once data are in a database, manipulation becomes an easy task, and this is the key to decision making. There are many options available for how an electronic database can be set up, but the most important concept is to be able to differentiate between electronic data management systems and electronic portfolios. In an electronic data management system, only the decisions are stored—not the actual work, although a data management system can be combined with a system that stores original work. ***The important thing is not to substitute a storage system of work products with a storage system of decisions about those work samples.***

The data management system can be developed as a stand-alone system that includes all the work produced by the teacher for meeting standards, or it can combine all of the records the institution or district needs to keep on the teacher (e.g., admissions or employment data, certification test scores, demographics). This is a decision that relates to practicality and utility. As long as information about demographics can be retrieved to collect validity evidence related to fairness and information about test scores and other relevant factors for completing the decision-making process about credentialing, the extent of the database coverage is not a critical issue. What is important is that the data about standards be as extensive as possible. So, for example, if teachers are assessed using a rubric on a specific task, all the scores for that task need to be included in the database.

Once data are entered by teacher by criterion by task, if the tasks are properly coded to standards, a wealth of information for decision making is available through the reporting functions of the database software. A second advantage of using a database that has information at the criterion level is the potential to export data to other software packages useful for summing scores and statistical analysis. This will be important in conducting empirical validity and reliability studies and in researching a variety of topics of interest to the faculty and to the unit. We mentioned a few of them back in Step 4A. We now turn our attention to reporting aggregated data.

Reporting Aggregated Data

In CAATS Step 4A we discussed ways to make decisions for data aggregation purposes after faculty and trainers have agreed on a common format (CAATS Step 3). We focused predominantly on establishing levels of decision making by criterion, task, standard, and a cut score for making the final decision about progression. Here we discuss the formatting and reporting of those decisions—after they are recorded in folders, portfolios, or databases. In this section, we will provide six examples of the kinds of reports that can be easily generated from a database, or by hand for a small number of students:

1. Results of an individual task for an individual teacher

2. Results for a group of teachers on an individual task

3. Results for an individual teacher for a given standard

4. Results for an individual teacher on all standards

5. Results for a group of teachers on a given standard

6. Results for a group of teachers on all standards

Clearly, each of these reports can be useful in analyzing results for an individual teacher candidate, an individual task, an individual standard, or some combination of any of these. These analyses can then lead to valid decisions about teachers' competence, instruction on tasks and standards, and overall program quality. The database should be versatile enough to provide for such decision-making flexibility. Of course, if you have not established any of these as purposes for your system, then they can be omitted. If, for example, you are not expecting to improve your programs, you can skip reports 2, 5, and 6—the group reports.

As programmers or assessors set up reports, the general format (for a 3-point scale) provided in Table 6.3 can be helpful.

	Highest Proficiency Level		Mid-Range Proficiency Level		Lowest Proficiency Level	
Table 6.3. General Format for Aggregating Data on a 3-Point Scale						
Criteria	#	%	#	%	#	%
Criterion or Task or Standard 1						
Criterion or Task or Standard 2						
Criterion or Task or Standard 3						
Criterion or Task or Standard 4						
Etc.						

Using this general format, we provide examples for each of the above six reports in Tables 6.4 through 6.9. We also include examples of how faculty might interpret the results.

Table 6.4. Example 1: Results for an Individual Task for an Individual Teacher Candidate

Sarah Smith's Feedback for Unit Exam			
Criteria	*Target*	*Acceptable*	*Unacceptable*
Test is appropriate and comprehensive for instructional content.	X		
Test map is accurate and properly formatted.	X		
Items address knowledge/ comprehension, application/ analysis, and synthesis/evaluation.	X		
Accommodations for special students, including both ESE and LEP, are appropriate.			X
Etc.			

Interpretation: Sarah knows how to write a test for the general population but needs to rework her accommodations.

Table 6.5. Example 2: Results for a Group of Teacher Candidates on an Individual Task

N = 30

Criteria	Target		Acceptable		Unacceptable	
	#	%	#	%	#	%
Test is appropriate and comprehensive for instructional content.	25	83	5	17	0	0
Test map is accurate and properly formatted.	30	100	0	0	0	0
Items address knowledge/comprehension, application/analysis, and synthesis/evaluation.	15	50	10	33	5	17
Accommodations for special students, including both ESE and LEP, are appropriate.	25	83	4	13	1	3
Etc.						

Interpretation: Students in Professor Jones's class are successful in writing the test but have trouble with Bloom's taxonomy. Instruction needs to be reinforced in writing objectives for this group and/or for subsequent classes. Professor Jones may want to do this in his measurement class or ask methods faculty to work more on this in their classes. With this many unacceptable ratings, the modification should probably be applied next semester with information about the deficit passed along to clinical faculty or school-based mentors. Sarah still has to fix her accommodations.

Table 6.6. Example 3: Results for an Individual Teacher for a Given Standard

All INTASC Principle #8 Tasks for Mary

Key: Demo'd = demonstrated

INTASC Principle #8 Tasks	Demo'd	Partially Demo'd	Not Demo'd
Unit Test	X		
Alternative Assessment	X		
Case Study of an Individual Child	X		
Analysis of Learning of a Class		X	
Etc.			

Interpretation: Mary has a good handle on assessment, especially when working with individual children. She needs a little more assistance in interpreting data for a class, but this should not prevent her from being certified.

Table 6.7. Example 4: Results for an Individual Teacher Candidate for All Standards

John's Results on All Instruments

Criteria	Demonstrated		Partially Demonstrated		Not Demonstrated	
	#	%	#	%	#	%
INTASC 1	3	100	0	0	0	0
INTASC 2	2	50	2	50	0	0
INTASC 3	4	100	0	0	0	0
INTASC 4	3	67	1	33	0	0
Etc.						

Interpretation: John is a good teacher, and he should be certified. His most immediate need for continuing staff development services (or for assistance during his internship) is in the area of learning and development, with a secondary need in teaching critical thinking and problem solving. He is comfortable with his content expertise and works well with diverse groups of children.

Table 6.8. Example 5: Results for a Group of Teachers on an Individual Standard

All Science Teachers on INTASC Principle #8

N = 40

INTASC Principle #8 Tasks	Demo'd		Part. Demo'd		Not Demo'd	
	#	%	#	%	#	%
Unit Test	30	75	10	25	0	0
Alternative Assessment	40	100	0	0	0	0
Case Study of an Individual Child	20	50	10	25	10	25
Analysis of Learning of a Class	30	75	10	25	0	0
Etc.						

Interpretation: This group of science teachers is competent in assessment in general; however, some teachers have trouble showing progress with individual students needing special assistance. Staff development (or additional work in a course) needs to be provided to help them overcome this deficit.

Table 6.9.	Example 6: Results for a Group of Teachers on All Standards					
All Science Teachers on All INTASC Principles						
N = 40						
Principles	_Target_		_Acceptable_		_Unacceptable_	
	#	%	#	%	#	%
INTASC 1	40	100	0	0	0	0
INTASC 2	20	50	20	50	0	0
INTASC 3	40	100	0	0	0	0
INTASC 4	30	75	10	25	0	0
Etc.						

Interpretation: This group of science teachers is competent in all of the standards; however, some teachers have trouble with learning and development and with teaching critical thinking. The college should review courses to see if instruction can be improved or the district should implement a staff development series to assist teachers needing help in these two areas.

We said earlier that frequency counts and percents at the criterion level will suffice, but something more sophisticated is available if you want to actually measure teacher performance and have scores that can be mathematically combined and used for research and evaluation purposes, including empirical analyses of validity, reliability, and fairness. It will also help you to overcome some of the problems in data analysis. We are talking about an item analysis technique called item response theory (IRT) that can radically improve the utility of the data for decision making (Baker & Kim, 2004). In our case, we have chosen a particular method of IRT called the Rasch model. Your measurement or statistics person may choose a different method, like in other aspects of the CAATS model. We prefer this method because our experience with it has demonstrated effective results with a minimal level of complexity. We describe it Chapter 9, but, before moving on, let us conclude the discussion of this set of examples with three general warnings.

— Data Analysis —

The analysis of data often starts with a philosophy that dictates a technical choice of a statistical technique.

Guiding Question: "What kind of data analysis, item analysis, or statistical reports do I need?"

1. _No means and standard deviations:_ We repeat this from above, because it is such a major problem. Most of the software manufacturers specializing in portfolio-based data collection and aggregation systems proudly boast their capability to provide statistics at every step of the way. Means and standard deviations abound for rubrics used in the system. We remind our readers of that oft-forgotten tidbit from statistics classes taken long ago: ordinal data do not meet the requirements for mathematical operations. It takes interval level data to add, subtract, multiply, and divide in meaningful ways. More important, we saw in our earlier example that a percent or point-based score means nothing if something important was missed. In fact, it is deceptive and

potentially dangerous. You can use the Rasch model to convert ordinal scores to interval level data if you do want to calculate means and standard deviations, but if all you want to know is at the ordinal level (rating scales), then leave it at that. Frequency counts and percentages are all you need, and all you should use to get to that first cut score for minimal competency. Pie charts and bar charts are also a nice addition. You may need to take the raw counts from the e-portfolio programs and do a little hand work with Excel.

2. *No holistic scales by themselves:* If the software you are looking at only allows you to define proficiency levels globally for each task—three descriptions of what good, mediocre, and bad are—or something like that, don't use it. You'll soon find that everyone is fine and nothing or no one can be improved, and you will have defeated your program improvement purpose and have no data to help your teachers improve. Remember that measurement requires variability. If that doesn't help, remember some bad teachers who passed through a system where they were all rated as "just fine." If that doesn't help, we will try one more: "Since we all acknowledge that nobody is perfect, then we have to agree that everybody just can't be perfect."

3. *Potentially bad decisions based on bad items:* We made some conclusions about what individual teachers and groups of teachers were and were not able to do based on the assumption that all of the criteria were well defined and working well. This may not be a valid assumption. If we are truly interested in making good judgments, we need to perform an item analysis, using either classical test theory or IRT to see if the criteria are functioning properly. These two measurement methods help us to determine if the scores make sense empirically. Both are based on the theory that students (or teachers) who tend to do well on a complete test, also tend to do well on each item. Or at least they do better than the students (or teachers) who did not do well at all. We explain more about this in Chapter 9.

> HINT! KISS—Keep it statistically simple!

AERA, APA, and NCME (1999) *Standards*
and CAATS Step 4C

Standard 3.9:

When a test developer evaluates the psychometric properties of items, *the classical or item response theory (IRT) model used for evaluating the psychometric properties of items should be documented.* The sample used for estimating item properties should be described and should be of adequate size and diversity for the procedure. The process by which items are selected and the data used for item selection, such as item difficulty, item discrimination, and/or item information, should also be documented. When IRT is used to estimate item parameters in test development, the item response model, estimation procedures, and evidence of model fit should be documented.

CAATS Steps Influenced: 4C, 5A (Element #6)

Discussion

In this section we have identified the two measurement models (CTT and IRT). You can explore that in more depth in Chapter 9 and create a worksheet to help you select your preferred model. The procedures used to collect evidence of validity and reliability in Step 5A will make use of both models. What is important is to carefully select one or both models to meet institutional needs.

NOTE: Emphasis added for clarity.

CAATS STEP 4D: DEVELOP IMPLEMENTATION PROCEDURES AND MATERIALS

In this step, we look at management issues, such as advising and due process, scoring of tasks, and general implementation issues.

Advising and Due Process

Once a decision is made about how the data will be used for making difficult decisions and for providing support to teachers, then the institution, school, or district needs to create advising/counseling structures and due process procedures for teachers exhibiting competency-based problems. Written explanations and procedures need to be in place, stating the unit's policies and procedures and the opportunities teachers have to remediate and/or appeal any adverse decisions or reports entered into their files. Sample policy statements for universities and school districts are provided in Boxes 6.5 and 6.6 on page 204.

> **Warning**
>
> We are not lawyers. Your general counsel may have many changes to suggest on these draft policy statements. Use these as a starting point for discussion, and go with his or her advice.

Teachers need to know what is expected of them. This should be first discussed at the time of admission or hire, with feedback provided regularly and in a timely way (not more than two weeks after completion of each task). Advisors or human resource personnel should provide updates to teachers on their progress during the appropriate phases of program completion or career development. Any failed tasks should be discussed with the teacher as soon as possible, with all efforts to remediate recorded and filed. If counseling is necessary for remediation purposes, a record of such counseling should be kept on file, with a copy provided to the teacher. This record should include the following information:

- Name of teacher or candidate
- Date of the meeting

Box 6.5.   Sample University Monitoring and Due Process Policy Statement

_____ University requires that all teacher candidates demonstrate the competencies (knowledge and skills) required of effective teachers in order to maximize the opportunities for all children to learn. University faculty will monitor and assess the acquisition of these competencies through a variety of assessment tasks embedded in courses and field experiences, and students will receive copies of all results in a timely fashion. Faculty members are required to advise candidates of any identified deficiencies and to provide counseling and opportunities to remediate. When teacher candidates fail to demonstrate a standard in any of the critical tasks in the university's assessment system, the teacher candidate will have two additional opportunities to complete the task successfully after adequate time to learn the material has elapsed, but not more than two months after each failed attempt. Upon failure to adequately demonstrate the standard after three attempts, the candidate will be dropped from the program. Exceptions to this policy will only be made if the candidate is a non–native speaker of English or has a documented learning disability. The candidate may appeal the decision to the dean, who will convene a committee of two faculty members (excluding the faculty member responsible for the failed task) and one high-achieving candidate to review the candidate's appeal. The decision of the committee will be binding.

Approved: _____   _____
                              University General Counsel   date

---

Box 6.6.   Sample Monitoring and School District Due Process Policy Statement

_____ County Schools require that all teachers demonstrate the competencies (knowledge and skills) required of effective teachers in order to maximize the opportunities for all children to learn. District administrators monitor and assess the competencies of teachers through a variety of assessment tasks completed on the job and under the supervision of a mentor teacher. Mentors and site-based administrators are required to advise teachers of any identified deficiencies and to provide counseling and opportunities to remediate. Each teacher will have a maximum of three opportunities to demonstrate each task, and feedback on task completion will be provided in a timely way to the teacher. When ___ or more pieces of evidence of competency-based deficits are identified, a district personnel committee is convened to determine if the teacher will be terminated or nonrenewed.

Approved: _____   _____
                              School Board General Counsel   date

- Personnel present
- Summary of meeting
- Action plan, including a schedule for second meeting, if any
- Results noted or follow-up required

All procedures should be in writing and made available to the teachers when they begin their program or job. Included in these materials should be the following:

- Candidates' or teachers' rights and responsibilities
- A description of the task-based system
- Scoring procedures including data aggregation procedures
- Rubrics and scales to be used and how scores will be interpreted
- Procedures and timelines for receiving feedback, remediation, and repeating tasks
- Policy on cheating
- Appeals and due process procedures
- Policy on confidentiality of records and record retention

Universities and districts should also consider having the teachers sign a form approved by legal counsel that explains the institution's or district's expectations with regard to program completion and removal from the program.

Scoring Procedures

Faculty and administrators often need guidance in how to score analytic instruments. It can help to outline a set of steps for them, such as the instructions modeled in Box 6.7.

Box 6.7. Sample Instructions to Raters

Before rating the tasks, read through the scoring rubric in its entirety. Analyze any anchor examples available to get an overall sense of how the scoring process is intended to work and how we differentiate between points on the scale. Then begin scoring. It helps to follow this sequence:

1. Work on one section at a time for all candidates.
2. Read the scoring guidelines and examples for that item one more time.
3. Score each candidate.
4. Go back and rescore candidates if you think your scoring shifted during the process.
5. Go to the next section and repeat steps 1 through 4.

Remember that some sections may be harder than others. It is okay for some sections to have high ratings and some to have low ratings on any individual task.

It can also help to lay out expectations to prevent ceiling effects. In our work, we have found that faculty members and teacher mentors tend to be humanistic; they always want to say that the rating is target—even if it is not.

Implementation

Once the system is determined and moving along in the implementation stage, a plan to manage and revise it needs to be developed. Included in this plan should be an assignment of responsibilities and a timeline, as well as a formal maintenance plan. The following are some elements of the plan to be developed, and Worksheet #4.4 provides a format:

1. *Oversight:* Responsibilities for oversight of the tasks should be delegated to a small group of faculty or district administrators with representation from certification areas, generalists (e.g., foundations faculty or human resource personnel), and at least one measurement specialist or educational psychologist. This committee should be charged with ensuring that the assessments are working as intended and revised as needed. Of particular importance is a constant review of changes in the standards and scorer drift toward more lenient or harsh ratings. Revisions should not be made by individual faculty or administrative personnel without some level of central coordination to ensure that the intent of the assessments, as it relates to validity and reliability issues, is not hurt.

2. *Training:* All those individuals responsible for assessing must understand the assessments and the scoring rubrics. This is particularly true for adjuncts in the universities and mentor teachers in the districts. Discussions on how to use each score point, with examples provided at each level, need to be provided and practiced to improve reliability. These sessions can be short but they must be conducted. In a university context, this is relatively straightforward, since full-time faculty will assess as part of their regular course load. In district-based programs, however, decisions need to be made about who will assess—mentor teachers, university collaborators, building administrators, district personnel, or some combination of these. Some alternative certification models provide for a single assessor or assessment team for all tasks; others provide for specialization within the content domains. This, too, needs to be carefully decided and planned. Training should be provided to all assessors with rubrics explained and samples provided. Much of this will need to be developed over time as assessors and assessment designers identify examples of acceptable and unacceptable work. Records should be kept of the qualifications and training of all scorers unless they are faculty who have been credentialed to teach courses in which the tasks are embedded. The records should include the following:

   a. Name of rater
   b. Highest degree
   c. Special experience or expertise with regard to the task(s)
   d. Training materials used

It can help to have a rater monitoring process. Worksheet #4.5 helps set that up.

3. *Maintenance:* It is just so easy to start a system and hope it will run by itself and need no changes. Formal review times need to be built into the system so that problems can be discussed and fixed. This could be just once a year, but it needs to be organized and accomplished.

> ── Maintenance System ──
>
> The maintenance system is the set of procedures and plans used to keep the system going and to make updates and changes as needed.
>
> *Guiding Question: "How will I know what needs to be changed, when, and by whom?"*

4. *Programmatic Improvement:* Since much of the need for performance-based certification is the result of the public outcry for increased accountability, it is important to document improvements as they are made. This will serve as a public statement that the institution or district is committed to the same level of continuous improvement that it expects its teachers to value. Running records of improvement are a useful strategy and can be built into the management system database, linked to individual tasks. Other records can be kept of improvements to program maintenance issues.

5. *Rewards:* Administrators also need to assume responsibility for monitoring task implementation by full-time and adjunct faculty and ensuring that the work is completed with integrity. Just as in any good classroom management plan, there need to be rewards and consequences for cooperation. Children respond to various sorts of praise, smiley faces, and M&Ms. Perhaps the key to getting faculty to respond is to find those rewards that are meaningful to them—room assignments with more space or a window, annual review criteria that support use of performance data as a measure of teaching accomplishment, course load, summer salary, travel money, supplies and equipment, graduate students, even M&Ms and smiley faces, if that will work. Your next faculty meeting might include something like our statement in in Box 6.8.

Box 6.8. Sample Feedback to Supportive Faculty

"I like the way Dr. Weeluvu is turning in his task data. He has taken this job seriously, and there has been consistent variability in the scores he has assigned. His students have shown improvement on Principle #4. Congratulations, Dr. Weeluvu! You get an extra course assignment this summer in that new computer lab we just finished! Aren't you due for a sabbatical soon? How about some new software or a printer? And your own key to the photocopying machine, which we just moved to the room next to your new office—the one with the big window and new furniture."

While the above example is more than a little facetious (like those Story Starters!), we hope we have made the relevant point. Somehow, cooperation needs to have its rewards. Faculty who support the integrity of the unit and contribute to the improvement of the profession through meeting the public outcry for accountability should be supported and rewarded.

AERA, APA, and NCME (1999) *Standards*
and CAATS Step 4D

Standard 1.7:

When a validation rests in part on the opinions or decisions of expert judges, observers or raters, *procedures for selecting such experts and for eliciting judgments or ratings* should be fully described. The *qualifications, and experience, of the judges* should be presented. The description of procedures should include any training and instructions provided, should indicate whether participants reached their decisions independently, and should report the level of agreement reached. If participants interacted with one another or exchanged information, the procedures through which they may have influenced one another should be set forth.

CAATS Steps Influenced: 4D

Standard 3.23:

The *process for selecting, training, and qualifying scorers should be documented by the test developer.* The training materials, such as the scoring rubrics and examples of test takers' responses that illustrate the levels on the score scale, and the procedures for training scorers should result in a degree of agreement among scorers that allows for the scores to be interpreted as originally intended by the test developer. Scorer reliability and potential drift over time in raters' scoring standards should be evaluated and reported by the person(s) responsible for conducting the training session.

CAATS Steps Influenced: 4D, 5A

Standard 3.25:

A *test should be amended or revised when new research data, significant changes in the domain represented, or newly recommended conditions of test use* may lower the validity of test score interpretations. Although a test that remains useful need not be withdrawn or revised simply because of the passage of time, test developers and test publishers are *responsible for monitoring* changing conditions and for *amending, revising, or withdrawing* the test as indicated.

CAATS Steps Influenced: 4D

Standard 5.10:

When test score information is released to students, parents, legal representatives, teachers, clients, or the media, those responsible for testing programs should provide appropriate interpretations. *The interpretations should describe in simple language what the test covers, what scores mean, the precision of the scores, common misinterpretations of test scores, and how scores will be used.*

CAATS Steps Influenced: 4D

Standard 5.16:

Organizations that maintain test scores on individuals in data files or in an individual's records should develop a clear set of *policy guidelines on the duration of retention of an individual's records, and on the availability, and use* over time, of such data.
CAATS Steps Influenced: 4D

Standard 7.12:

The test or assessment process should be carried out so that *test takers receive comparable and equitable treatment during all phases* of the testing or assessment process.
CAATS Steps Influenced: 4D, 5A

Standard 8.2:

Where appropriate, *test takers should be provided, in advance, as much information* about the test, the testing process, the intended use, test scoring criteria, testing policy, and confidentiality protection as is consistent with obtaining valid responses.
CAATS Steps Influenced: 4D

Standard 8.6:

Test data maintained in data files should be adequately protected from improper disclosure. Use of facsimile transmission, computer networks, data banks, and other electronic data processing or transmittal systems should be restricted to situations in which *confidentiality can be reasonably assured.*
CAATS Steps Influenced: 4D

Standard 8.7:

Test takers should be made aware that having someone else take the test for them, disclosing confidential test material, or any other form of *cheating is inappropriate* and that such behavior may result in sanctions.
CAATS Steps Influenced: 4D

Standard 8.9:

When test scores are used to make decisions about a test taker or to make recommendations to at test taker or a third party, the *test taker or the legal representative is entitled to obtain a copy of any report of test scores or test interpretation,* unless that right has been waived or is prohibited by law or court order.
CAATS Steps Influenced: 4D

Standard 8.13:

In educational testing programs and in licensing and certification applications, test takers are entitled to *fair consideration and reasonable process, as appropriate to the particular circumstances, in resolving disputes* about testing. Test takers are entitled to be informed of any available means of recourse.
CAATS Steps Influenced: 4D

(Continued)

(Continued)

Standard 13.6:

Students who must demonstrate mastery of certain skills or knowledge before being promoted or granted a diploma should have a reasonable number of opportunities to succeed on equivalent forms of the test or be provided with construct–equivalent testing alternatives of equal difficulty to demonstrate the skills or knowledge. In most circumstances, when students are provided with *multiple opportunities to demonstrate mastery, the time interval between the opportunities should allow for students to have the opportunity to obtain the relevant instructional experiences.*

CAATS Steps Influenced: 4D

Standard 14.16:

Rules and procedures used to combine scores on multiple assessments to determine the overall outcome of a credentialing test should be *reported to test takers*, preferably before the test is administered.

CAATS Steps Influenced: 4D

Discussion

Each of the above standards has been embedded in this step to ensure that candidates or teachers have every chance to succeed, and institutions and districts are reasonably well protected in the event of legal challenges. We have not provided specific examples of each of the requirements in these *Standards* in our discussion. In this step of the model, we suggest that our readers look closely at the above *Standards* and use them as a planning tool to check their existing policies, such as giving proper notice to teachers about the use of scores, records retention, confidentiality, cheating policies, and other common policies used in schools.

NOTE: Emphases added for clarity.

⩔ WRAP-UP

In this chapter, we discussed the establishment of levels of decision making and cut-score setting to define minimal competency. We shared a variety of strategies that can be used to track teacher progression and program quality in paper-based or electronic systems. Samples of the types of reports that should be generated have been modeled, and we focused on some of the important steps needed to implement and then manage the assessment system, noting the probability that once it is up and running (and no one is looking for awhile), slippage is likely to occur. We also reminded readers to double check on some typical existing policies, such as cheating.

Story Starters

Starter #1:

Professor/Teacher Stuckinarutt stomps into your office and says:

"I have been using my own rubrics for years, and I am not going to rewrite them to cover all of this standards-based stuff. Besides, my grades are private between me and my students. You can use my course grade for accountability. You have my syllabus, and that tells you what my grade means in terms of your standards. I have tenure, and you can't make me."

You say.....

Note: You may be getting tired of this person by now, but the correct answer is not, "Take a hike." Sorry!

Starter #2:

Mrs. Kidsaretutuff has completed every workshop you offered, and the trainers filed their check-sheets with you. They did not offer anything related to collegiality per se, but teachers are complaining that she is aloof and won't plan with them or discuss remediation needs of individual children. You had a workshop in which lessons were planned and included collaborative work and feedback, and the trainer says she did okay on that one—about average for the group. Now what do you do?

Starter #3:

Mr. Wecandoitall, chief sales rep for Portfolios United (PU) Corporation, tells you their software does everything you need to make standards-based decisions about teacher competency. You ask him if you can retrieve separate decisions for each standard assessed in a single task. He tells you that you don't need to do that for NCATE or your state; the PU system is better because it will give you statistics.

You say...

CAATS STEP 4—WORKSHEET #4.1
Cut-Score Decisions

Directions:

Read the *unacceptable* rating for each of the criteria for this task, and ask yourself the following question: **"If the teacher cannot meet this criterion even one time, and with help, should this teacher be licensed?"** A "yes" decision will keep the criterion the same. A "no" decision requires that you explain your answer and suggest a modification, if appropriate. Then accept or reject the number of tries and suggest a change if you reject it.

Task Number and Name: _____

#	Criterion at the Unacceptable Level	Is an unacceptable rating cause for denying certification?		Should the teacher be allowed three tries to succeed?	
		Yes	No	Yes	No

Explanations for not using criterion (your decision was a "no") as cause for denying certification:

_____

_____

_____

Explanations for no decisions on three-try rule and suggested number of tries: _____

_____

Suggestions for improvement of criteria: _____

_____

_____

CAATS STEP 4—WORKSHEET #4.2
Sample Format for Candidate/Teacher Tracking Form

Teacher's Name: _____

Teacher's ID: _____

Instrument #1

   Instrument Name: _____

   Date Administered: _____

   Score/Results: _____

   Counseling (if any): _____

      Personnel: _____

      Date: _____

      Action Plan: _____

      Follow-Up (if any): _____

      Comments:_____

      _____

      _____

Instrument #2, etc.

Final Decision

_____ Graduate   OR   _____ Rehire

_____ Deny Graduation   _____ Terminate

CAATS WORKSHEETS

CAATS WORKSHEETS

CAATS STEP 4—WORKSHEET #4.3
Format for Data Aggregation

Criteria	Level 3 (high)		Level 2 (medium)		Level 1 (low)	
	#	%	#	%	#	%

CAATS STEP 4—WORKSHEET #4.4
Management Plan

Oversight

Person(s) Responsible	Committee Charge	Meeting Schedule	Revisions Procedures
Measurement Professional			

Training

Persons to Be Trained	Schedule	Plan and Materials

Maintenance

Date	Item to Be Reviewed	Personnel Responsible

Programmatic Improvement Log

Date	Problem to Be Addressed	Improvement Made

CAATS STEP 4—WORKSHEET #4.5

Rater Monitoring Record

Rater Name: _____

E-mail/Phone Contact Information: _____

Highest Degree: _____

Special Expertise (if applicable and no terminal degree): _____

_____

_____

_____

Tasks Assigned for Assessment if Outside of Regular Courses/Workshops: _____

_____

_____

_____

Date Training Completed: _____

Training Materials Used: _____

_____

_____

_____

_____

CAATS WORKSHEETS

Where We Have Been So Far

Throughout this book, beginning with CAATS Step 1, we have been applying the theories and standards that guide the process of gathering evidence of psychometric integrity or credibility. We have learned that the most important of these is the latest set of standards published in 1999 by a joint committee of the American Educational Research Association (AERA), the American Psychological Association (APA), and the National Council of Measurement in Education (NCME), called the *Standards for Educational and Psychological Testing*. They establish the requirements for determining psychometric integrity and are the foundation for this chapter and much of what we have done in the previous four steps of the CAATS model. So, the good news here is that we have been building a process, which has most of what we needed from the *Standards* already built in, and we have documented that by including selected AERA *Standards* at the end of each substep. This will be helpful to colleges and districts or states that want to demonstrate that their assessment system has been designed with psychometric integrity in mind.

Many, many years ago, Judy went on a class field trip to Washington, DC, from New Jersey. The teacher, Mr. P., was plagued for five hours with teenagers asking how much further it was. He answered consistently (that would be reliably), "We're almost exactly halfway there." Although the answer was not accurate (that would be validity), it is where we are now in this journey of competency-based assessment. We are more than halfway there. Just one more step to go, and that step will require some fine-tuning or revisiting and a few more pieces of the puzzle, as we continue to apply the *Standards for Educational and Psychological Testing* to ensure the credibility of the data we produce and use for decisions about teacher competence.

7

CAATS Step 5

Credible Data

*W*hile federal and state legislators and NCATE accreditation agents say that they require evidence of credibility, technically known as psychometric integrity, this is an issue that college faculty, school administrators, and state department of education personnel, like Scarlet O'Hara, say they will think about tomorrow. If they do acknowledge the need to ensure any aspect of psychometrics, it tends to be a study of rater agreement with little or no attention to validity or fairness other than possibly some due process procedures (which are a different matter altogether!).

The **rater agreement study** is often based on a weakly designed rubric, frequently holistic unless it is the teacher observation form used in internships or performance appraisals. Typically, the data show that everyone is the same or almost the same, rated at the highest rating on the scale. The mid-point and lower ratings are rarely, if ever, used in the reported results. Then, remarkably, everyone is consistent in providing the same rating for every teacher, and we obtain a reliability coefficient of near 1.0.

> **CAATS Step 5: Ensure credibility and utility of data.**

We have what could be called face reliability. On the surface of it, it looks reliable, but, in actuality, it is simply failing to measure the differences among people and, therefore, is somewhat dishonest. This problem is exacerbated in performance assessment systems that make use of holistic scoring. There simply is not enough **variability** to have measurement meaning. Everybody is fine, and no deficiencies can be traced because the data are in chunks that are just too large for fine tuning. So, all opportunities for systematic improvement are lost.

In this chapter, we will think about what it takes to achieve more credible information about the **validity, reliability, and fairness** of scores so that we have data that are both credible and useful. Prior to delving into the details, we will provide some background information on what psychometric integrity is and why it is important. We will then move on to Step 5 of the CAATS model and its two sub-steps. As we progress through this chapter, readers should find that if they paid close attention to the processes outlined in CAATS Steps 1 through 4, they have already completed much of what they need to do for solid **psychometrics**, and we will carefully document those successes in this step.

In CAATS Step 5A we depart somewhat from our previous format of including the AERA, APA, and NCME Standards at the end of the substep. Instead we propose a planning process within a planning process. We have been planning an assessment system and now move on to the plan for **credibility** of data that is embedded in the overall process in CAATS Step 5A. That plan will have eight elements, and we will align our AERA, APA, and NCME Standards with each of the eight elements.

As in our previous chapters, we provide terms and definitions throughout. The two substeps of CAATS Step 5 are:

CAATS Step 5A: *Create a plan to provide evidence of validity, reliability, and fairness.*

CAATS Step 5B: *Implement the plan conscientiously.*

P.S.: Don't forget to finish (and implement) that action plan from Chapter 2! If you have not yet read Chapter 9 on the Rasch model, now is the time to do so.

Before Moving On . . .

1. Before reading this book, did you spend much time thinking about validity? How do you feel about it now? What about reliability? Which do you think is more important? Why?

2. Is there variability in your current performance assessments, or are most ratings near perfect? Do you live in Lake Wobegon where everyone is "above average"? Do your results seem consistent with your personal and professional experiences with teachers in the schools?

3. Have you detected informally or formally any differences in performance among protected populations? If so, what is causing it and what have you done about it?

4. Have you ever written a plan that died on the paper on which it was written?

WHAT IS PSYCHOMETRIC INTEGRITY AND WHY DO WE HAVE TO WORRY ABOUT IT?

When we make an important decision in any aspect of life, we want to have confidence that we are making the right decision. That is what psychometric integrity is really all about. *Psychometric* simply means we are trying to measure some function that involves thinking and/or feeling, and *psychometric integrity* means that we are doing it honestly.

There are three cornerstones to psychometric integrity—validity, reliability, and fairness—with fairness being a more recent addition to the long-standing issues of validity and reliability. We also add to that the notion of utility. Why collect great data if they are not going to be useful for decision making? So, if our measurement process does not help us identify the really good and the really bad, what good is our measurement process other than to pat ourselves on the back about the great job we did and hide our heads in the sand when the bad teachers are found out? Kids and parents can tell, and legislators who are often parents, too, try to force the issue. That is precisely what is happening with those inter-rater reliability coefficients of 1.0 based on all raters saying all teachers are great.

If we think of validity as truthfulness (being accurate so that we can be honest about what we are measuring) and reliability as trustworthiness (doing it consistently), then the terms may be a little less intimidating. Fairness simply means that no one group is treated favorably or unfavorably because of the measurement process and that everyone's rights are conscientiously observed. So, perhaps if we look at psychometric integrity as just plain doing what's right, we can better see that this is an ethical issue and moral imperative that we face as education professionals. If we do it wrong, someone gets hurt, and that someone could be the children in the schools or the teacher who wants to teach them. At a gut level, this is motherhood and apple pie.

Unfortunately, integrity often has a price. To do the right thing, we often have to make difficult decisions that take careful thought. Such is the case with psychometric integrity. There is substantial analytical work involved in ensuring that no one is hurt by design rather than by accident. Typically, when faced with a difficult decision, the analytic thinker gathers evidence to support the decision-making process, and this is precisely how we make decisions about the truthfulness and trustworthiness of data in the world of social science measurement.

By this time, it should come as no surprise that the CAATS model has a heavy focus on planning, and, as might be expected, we advocate for a plan to ensure credibility so that the process is systematically designed and implemented. Here we present yet another blueprint, this time for psychometrics.

Psychometric

Psychometric is a big word that refers to the measurement of aspects of people such as knowledge, skills, abilities, or personality.

Guiding Question: "What do the data tell me about validity, reliability, and fairness in this test?"

Psychometric Integrity

Psychometric integrity, like other forms of integrity, is about doing what is right—in this case when we assess teachers. It is making sure people (children and teachers) don't get hurt by design rather than by accident.

Guiding Question: "Will I be able to sleep at night if I make these decisions?"

Utility

Utility of data refers to usefulness. There's no point in collecting a bunch of stuff to fill a filing cabinet if you have no expectation of using it.

Guiding Question: "Will the data I collect give me useful information so I can have better teachers and programs?"

CAATS STEP 5A: CREATE A PLAN TO PROVIDE EVIDENCE OF VALIDITY, RELIABILITY, FAIRNESS, AND UTILITY

Elements of a Plan

It is *not* typically necessary to have a formal written psychometric plan unless this is a high-stakes process in a large-scale program (large school district or state), but we will provide some elements of the planning process that can help with competency assessments, and, as we are now accustomed, we will use worksheets.

We are also providing a set of examples to help illustrate the statistics we are proposing. Embedded in a couple of them are some opportunities to practice the techniques with a calculator or an online statistics link, because they are very simple to do and provide good evidence of the credibility of your assessments.

We also remind our readers at this point that much of what we have seen in the AERA, APA, and NCME *Standards* points to the need to keep records of how we put together and monitor our assessment system. This is not unlike what NCATE requires in the accreditation context.

Based on our review of the AERA, APA, and NCME (1999) *Standards*, we recommend the inclusion of eight elements in the planning process for credibility and utility. Most of them are already complete, if you have been following the CAATS model, although we will use some fancier names here. We discuss each in some detail, providing examples from our previous work and referencing you back to what you have already done in the worksheets from previous steps in Chapters 3–6. We will note where necessary the work that remains to be completed.

Here in Box 7.1 are the eight elements of the planning process for credibility and utility of cognitive (and dispositional) data (Lang & Wilkerson, 2005).

Credibility

Believability. Used as a user-friendly synonym for the triad of validity, reliability, and fairness.

Guiding Question: "Is there any evidence that this stuff is right?"

> **Box 7.1.   Elements of a Psychometric Plan: A Plan for Credibility and Utility**
>
> 1. Purpose and use
> 2. Construct measured
> 3. Interpretation and reporting of scores
> 4. Assessment specifications and content map
> 5. Assessor/rater selection and training procedures
> 6. Analysis methodology
> 7. External review personnel and methodology
> 8. Evidence of validity, reliability, and fairness

Element #1: Purpose and Use

Purpose drives every aspect of the design and implementation process. We spent much time in CAATS Step 1 talking about that. The AERA, APA, and NCME *Standards* make the decision about purpose easy in our context. As an assessment system that leads to a credentialing decision, the purpose is essentially predefined by the *Standards* as protection of the public. The *Standards* tell us the following:

Licensing requirements are imposed by state and local governments to ensure that those licensed possess knowledge and skills in sufficient degree to perform important occupational activities safely and effectively. Certification plays a similar role in many occupations ... Certification has also become widely used to indicate that a person has certain specific skills (e.g., operation of specialized auto repair equipment) or knowledge (e.g., estate planning), which may be only a part of their occupational duties ... Tests used in credentialing are intended to provide the public, including employers and government agencies, with a dependable mechanism for identifying practitioners who have met particular standards. The standards are strict, but not so stringent as to unduly restrain the right of qualified individuals to offer their services to the public. *Credentialing also serves to protect the profession by excluding persons who are deemed to be not qualified to do the work of the occupation.* (p. 156, emphasis added)

In Box 7.2 we provide a sample statement of purpose.

Box 7.2. Sample Statement of Purpose

To protect the public from unqualified practitioners by determining whether the teachers assessed have demonstrated the essential competencies, as defined in the standards of _____. These competencies are necessary for safe and appropriate practice and certification in the State of _____.

We have identified some other potential purposes—diagnosis and remediation of individual teachers and program improvement being among the most important. Additional statements of purpose would need to be written for those purposes, and additional evidence of validity for those purposes would need to be collected.

We also talked about use in CAATS Step 1, noting that assessment results could be used for both low-stakes (e.g., advising) and high-stakes (e.g., firing or not certifying) decisions. The more high stakes the decision, the more we need to focus on the elements of the plan described in this step. In Box 7.3 we provide a sample statement on use.

Box 7.3. Sample Statement of Use

Scores or aggregated data are used to determine, in part, if teachers are eligible to graduate and/or to receive the state certificate or license (or to continue employment in the district). Additional licensure requirements required for the licensure decision include a grade point average of ___ (or a bachelor's degree in___), a passing score on the state certification exam, and a background clearance check conducted by the state Department of Law Enforcement.

If you thoroughly attended to purpose and use in Step 1 of this process, you are done with the first element of your psychometric plan. At this point, you may want to review your work on Worksheet #1.2 for CAATS Step 1.

AERA, APA, and NCME (1999) *Standards*
and CAATS Step 5A, Element 1

Standard 3.2:

The *purpose(s) of the test*, definition of the domain, and the test specifications *should be stated clearly* so that judgments can be made about the appropriateness of the defined domain for the stated purpose(s) of the test and about the relation of items to the dimensions of the domain they are intended to represent.
   CAATS Steps Influenced: 1A, 1C, 2E, 5A (Element #1)

Standard 13.1:

When educational testing programs are mandated by school, district, state, or other authorities, the *ways in which test results are intended to be used should be clearly described.* It is the responsibility of those who mandate the use of tests to monitor their impact and to identify and minimize potential negative consequences. Consequences resulting from the uses of the test, both intended and unintended, should also be examined by the test user.
   CAATS Steps Influenced: 1A, 5A (Element #1)

Discussion

This standard establishes the need to identify the purpose and use of the test; the quote from page 156 of the *Standards* in the text above helps to focus on a specific purpose relevant to credentialing teachers.

NOTE: Emphases added for clarity.

Element #2: Construct Measured

   The AERA, APA, and NCME *Standards* help us define the construct in this assessment system. It can be as simply stated as *teacher performance.* In Chapter 1 on page 9 of the *Standards* (after the introductory materials), the following examples of constructs are provided: performance as a computer technician, mathematics achievement and depression, and self-esteem. The leap to teacher performance is not difficult, given the first example.

   The important thing about a construct is that it be unique or different and capable of being operationally defined. This simply means that we hypothetically visualize a set of characteristics and describe them meaningfully. The INTASC Principles and all of the other teacher standards for knowledge and skills do precisely that for us. So, these standards, plus our own beliefs about what is important for teachers to know and be able to do, operationally define the construct, forming the content, or conceptual framework, we are expecting to measure.

In this model, we have used a standards-based process to define the construct, and we stay with that definition throughout the process, including the collection of evidence about credibility. The analyses conducted in this part of the process do not go backwards and attempt to redefine the construct using factor analysis or other statistical procedures. We do not recommend rewriting the standards and saying that it all boils down to four factors! We repeatedly advise you in this chapter and others to keep it statistically simple (the KISS approach). Our view of a construct is based on the standards assessed as organized by a logical framework or taxonomy. So, once again, the good news is, we are done with another element. In Box 7.4 we provide a sample statement of construct, and in Box 7.5, we provide a sample statement of the conceptual framework.

Box 7.4. Sample Statement of the Construct: Teacher Performance

In our psychometric planning process, we can also include a statement about the content or conceptual framework that defines the construct in more detail. Here is the place to identify the specific sets of standards, incorporating your own, that are used.

Box 7.5. Sample Statement of Conceptual Framework

All the relevant standards, including _____ State/District Standards, INTASC Principles, and all standards of specialty professional associations. Additional local standards (or mission/values, etc.) include: _____.

Element #3: Interpretation and Reporting of Scores

Useless data need not be collected. Knowing how we will use the data has a significant influence on what data we collect and when and how we collect it. The AERA, APA, and NCME *Standards* remind us on the first page that the most important thing we do to help ensure that we are making valid decisions is to determine how we will interpret the scores or data we obtain. If the interpretation is wrong, we are in trouble. Examples of bad interpretations would be to say that (1) teachers have the necessary competencies when they may harm children (a false positive) or (2) teachers are harmful if they will be just fine (a false negative). Part of what we need to do is to think about how to minimize these bad decisions and the direction in which we want to err when we do err. As humans, we certainly will do that.

Interpretation provides meaning to a score. It is how we differentiate between good and bad in either a quantitative or qualitative scale, or how we make an important decision based on the data. It determines what we will call acceptable and unacceptable. The interpretation in this system is of minimal competence for beginning practice.

AERA, APA, and NCME (1999) *Standards*
and CAATS Step 5A Element 2

Standard 14.4:

When empirical evidence of predictor-criterion relationships is part of the pattern of evidence used to support test use, the criterion measure(s) used should reflect the *criterion construct domain* of interest to the organization. All criteria should represent *important work behaviors or work outputs, on the job or in job-relevant training,* as indicated by an appropriate review of information about the job.

CAATS Steps Influenced: 1C, 2B, 5A (Element #2)

Standard 14.14:

The *content domain* to be covered by a credentialing test should be defined clearly and justified in terms of the *importance of the content for credential-worthy performance in an occupation or profession.* A rationale should be provided to support a claim that the knowledge of skills being assessed are required for credential-worthy performance in an occupation and are consistent with the purpose for which the licensing or certification program was instituted.

CAATS Steps Influenced: 1C, 2E, 3C, 5A (Element #2)

Discussion

These standards again make the link between job performance and the construct measured—teacher performance. The construct is defined, then, in operational terms through the content domain – on our case, the standards.

NOTE: Emphases added for clarity.

If you use the CAATS CYA approach, the statement of interpretation is straight forward and you only need to talk only about the 100% requirement. Even though some tasks or items may be more difficult than others, all must be passed or rated acceptable. Setting an artificial standard, such as 80%, simply does not work with critical tasks. If you add additional cut scores where scores are summed and even transformed or calibrated to measure different levels of proficiency, then this should be discussed as well. Remember that we use the term *scores* for raw scores in the original data and *measures* for scores translated into an interval Rasch scale. In Box 7.6, we provide an example of how you can write about the interpretation of scores.

> **Box 7.6. Sample Statement About Interpretation of Scores**
>
> Teachers are determined to have the competencies necessary to teach, or they are determined not to have those competencies. Having the competencies means that there have been no major performance gaps, and all (100%) required, job-related performance tasks have been completed satisfactorily. Teachers are considered, therefore, "safe to practice," having achieved no *unacceptable* ratings in the system.
>
> In addition to the 100% requirement, scores are calibrated on a Rasch logistic ruler for diagnostic and improvement purposes and to determine differences in proficiency levels, including *acceptable* and *exemplary*.

In CAATS Step 4, we talked about developing scoring rubrics, data aggregation, and cut scores (Steps 4A to 4C). These aspects of system implementation help us focus on how to interpret scores in valid and reliable ways that reduce error. We also talked about advising and due process procedures under Step 4D, and there we noted that it is important to establish routines to keep teachers informed of their progress or lack thereof—score reporting.

In a high-stakes test, examinees have the right to know as soon as possible what their scores are. They also have the right to privacy, with the exception of those individuals who have a stronger right to know about the quality of their performance (e.g., faculty and supervisors). Score reporting ensures that scores are maintained, reported, and secured. We established procedures for managing these aspects in CAATS Step 4D, and in Box 7.7 we provide a public statement for our psychometric plan.

> **Box 7.7. Sample Statement of Score Reporting**
>
> Reports of scores will be given to teachers on an ongoing basis as tasks are completed. Reports and scores will be stored in a database that can be accessed by university or school system administrators, faculty or mentor teachers, and assessors. Security provisions restrict access to those personnel directly responsible for individual teachers' evaluation and performance.

So, once again, the news is positive. Review your work on Worksheets #4.1 and #4.4 in CAATS Step 4 for this element. Three down, five to go. As Mr. P. said on that infamous bus ride to Washington, "We're almost exactly halfway there."

Element #4: Assessment Specifications and Content Map

Assessment specifications and content maps provide us with a blueprint or a plan for assessment design. The *Standards* provide guidance on how these should be

---

AERA, APA, and NCME (1999) *Standards*
and CAATS Step 5A, Element 3

Standard 14.17:

The *level of performance required for passing a credentialing test should depend on the knowledge and skills necessary* for acceptable performance in the occupation or professional, and should not be adjusted or regulated for the number or proportion of persons passing the test.
   CAATS Steps Influenced: 5A (Element #3)

Discussion

This *Standard* reminds us that the score interpretation, particularly the cut score, should not be based on meeting the need for teachers, but rather on ensuring the quality of teachers admitted to the profession. Criticality is the yardstick. From that perspective, it provides strong support for the 100% cut score on critical tasks. Adjusting downward would fail to protect children from harm in order to meet critical shortage needs for teachers.

NOTE: Emphases added for clarity.

---

organized, including the content, format and scoring procedures. Readers should feel comfortable with these specifications, since they summarize much of what was already developed in the earlier steps of the model. Here, they merely establish that there was a plan! If you decide to write this up as a formal plan, Worksheet #5.1 for this step is provided for that purpose, with a sample provided below. We believe this is an often overlooked step. In fact, most assessment planners simply make lists of existing measures or arbitrarily decide that three to five assessments seem about enough. Boxes 7.8 to 7.10 provide samples for how to write the specifications.

Box 7.8.   Sample Test Specifications: Content

- Tasks are measures composed of related items, expectations, behavioral indicators, or trials, which relate to the INTASC Principles and can be demonstrated both judgmentally and empirically to measure the associated Principle. In accordance with the AERA, APA, and NCME *Standards* (1999), they will be developed based on a job analysis and will be limited to those tasks deemed to be critical for teacher performance.

- The set of tasks will be organized around the 10 INTASC Principles. The assessment system will ensure that most indicators from the **P**rinciples are measured at least one time. Locally defined standards and other state and national standards identified by the assessment designers will be integrated into the tasks as appropriate.

- Tasks will use a variety of formats, including products and observed performances, as appropriate to the knowledge or skill being measured.

- Assessments will also have a focus on impact on K–12 learning wherever possible. Impact on students can be measured as a skill of the teacher.

- Dispositions represent a different construct and are measured using a different process.

- Each Principle will be measured at multiple points in order to have confidence through depth and breadth of the system. Each Principle will be proportionally represented in the overall system. There will typically be three to five tasks per Principle and five to 10 indicators per task to demonstrate traditional reliability, although some tasks may be used for more than one Principle.

- A content map will be developed to assure adequate construct representation for each Principle.

Box 7.9. Sample Test Specifications: Format

- No task will assess more than three Principles. More often, one Principle is measured.

- All tasks will include a brief description, standards alignment, comprehensive directions, and an analytic rating scale composed of criterion statements linked directly to the directions and using language from the principles or other standards wherever possible. **A decision rule will be included in each task.**

- The scale will use three decision points **at the criterion level**—target, acceptable, and unacceptable.

Box 7.10. Sample Test Specifications: Scoring Procedures (Criterion Referenced)

- Scoring procedures—Criterion referenced

- Composite scores/decision rules:
  - Decision points (ratings) on individual criteria within tasks will be converted to a demonstrated, partially demonstrated, or not-demonstrated decision for the Principle assessed.
  - Any unacceptable rating at the criterion level results in a not-demonstrated rating at the task or Principle level.
  - Up to one-third of the criterion ratings may be acceptable to achieve the demonstrated rating at the task or Principle level, until such time as a logistic cut score can be set for this proficiency level.
  - Between one-third and all ratings of acceptable result in a partially demonstrated rating on the task or Principle, until such time as a logistic cut score can be set for this proficiency level.
  - Decisions are again aggregated at the principle level for all tasks used. The decisions at the Principle level are competent, minimally competent, or not competent.
  - One not-demonstrated decision on a task results in a not-competent rating on the Principle.

(Continued)

(Continued)

- More than one partially demonstrated decision at the task level results in a minimally competent rating on the Principle, until such time as a logistic cut score can be set for this proficiency level.
- The affirmative credentialing decision (graduation leading to certification) is made with any combination of competent and minimally competent ratings. Credentialing is denied with any decision of not competent on any Principle.

- College faculty or district personnel are the assessors, with assessments made during regular teaching or training assignments. Assessors provide feedback on criteria that are rated as less than target.

- Teachers will be required to redo tasks for any criteria rated as unacceptable. The maximum number of attempts is three, unless otherwise specified by judges during the panel cut-score review process.

- Scores will be entered into the electronic database.

- Examples and training will be provided to support accurate decision making. Scored tasks will be sampled for expert review.

- Scores will be examined (and adjusted) for rater effects.

In the above specifications, the content was determined in CAATS Step 1, the formats and commitment to multiple measures to increase confidence in CAATS Step 2. The need for rubrics was determined in CAATS Step 3, along with all of the scoring procedures in CAATS Step 4. Here we just summarize for a public statement about the system.

The *content map* is typically a chart or matrix that shows how items come together in two dimensions. In a standards-based system, the standards drive the mapping process; one of those dimensions in the map can clearly be standards themselves. The other is the assessment instruments. Such maps, or frameworks, were created in CAATS Step 2E and the associated worksheets. To ensure that there is adequate evidence of construct representativeness in the content validity study, it is helpful to map even further at the indicator level if standards lend to that level of planning. We also did that in Step 3C with our first validity study and Worksheet #3.3, the Standards and Indicators Coverage Report.

In CAATS Step 2, you created a map using Worksheet #2.9 based on a model that looked like the following chart. You also saw a sample framework in the text that we repeat below. While the chart in CAATS Step 2 was used as a planning tool to make sure you had good coverage, the end product translates nicely into your final content map. So, again, if you did your work well in earlier steps, this step is done. Table 7.1 provides a sample content map.

So for Element #4, we have already considered all of the aspects of the assessment specifications, even though they were not practiced before, and the content map was already completed. Sometimes, well-written state and national standards already have sample indicators and expected evidence to meet the standard. This makes the content map a breeze for your program by simply choosing the frameworks that apply to your situation and planning your assessment. If the first column is not defined, you have

Table 7.1. Sample Content Map

INTASC Principle				
#	Key Words	Knowledge and Skills	Impact	Disposition
1	Content Knowledge	Test Lesson and/or Unit Plan	K–12 Work Portfolio	Observation Checklist K–12 Focus Group Teacher Questionnaire
2	Learning and Development	Test Lesson and/or Unit Plan and/or IEP	Test Score Comparisons with Same Age/Develop.	Teacher Belief Scale Teacher Questionnaire
3	Diverse Learners	Individual Educational Plan	IEP Results	Observation Checklist K–12 Focus Group
4	Critical Thinking	Lesson and/or Unit Plan	K–12 Work Portfolio	Teacher Questionnaire K–12 Focus Group
5	Motivation and Learning Environment	K–12 Attitude Scale	Use of K–12 Attitude Scale and Results	K–12 Focus Group Observation Checklist
6	Communication	Folder of Communications Interaction Observation	Real-Time Monitoring	Focus Group Observation Checklist
7	Planning	Lesson and/or Unit Plan	Readiness Test in Next Grade	Teacher Questionnaire K–12 Focus Group
8	Assessment	Objective Test Alternative Assessment	TWSM Remediation Plans and Results	Teacher Belief Scale K–12 Focus Group
9	Reflection and Professionalism	Ethics Test Lesson and/or Unit Plan	Results of Modified Lesson	Scenario Interview
10	Collegiality	Record of Work on School Improvement Team	Interviews with Coteachers	Teacher Belief Scale Principal Interview

some work to do. One example of a set of standards with performance indicators and visualized expectations organized by position titles is the *Technology Standards for School Administrators* (TSSA Collaborative, 2001). Unfortunately, the state and national standards you use may require you to create sample indicators.

There is one more element of specifications and mapping we need to address before moving on. When choices are available for tasks to be completed, there is a need for a discussion of how that will occur. In objective test situations, we refer to this as an *item pool* or *item bank*. Test writers draw from the bank to construct individually configured tests. Similarly in performance-based assessment, more than one task may measure the same set of competencies and could be used on an equivalent basis. If choices are going to be provided, the plan needs to address how assessors will make these choices and determine the equivalency of results from different tasks. It is unlikely that alternative tasks will be a part of the initial system, but early planning for incorporating them can be of great help later. Sometimes alternatives are necessary for various formats of the same overall task. Think, for example, of the many versions of a lesson plan used in most colleges.

If alternative tasks or alternative versions of the tasks are incorporated into a system, then it will be important to ensure that procedural checks are in place to maintain construct representativeness, relevance, proportionality, and job-relatedness. This helps prevent the kind of slippage that can occur in the decision-making process when multiweek units become one-day lesson plans, or classroom management plans that are developed and implemented are reduced to plans that are developed only.

In order to maintain validity, all students within a content area or program should be assessed on a core or anchor set of tasks within the task bank that can be used to assure a baseline. Alternatives and specialized tasks would be best for tasks outside of the common core. Alternative versions of tasks should at least use the same scoring rubric to ensure consistency of results. Extensive use of alternatives may also lead to a need for considering a study of parallel forms reliability or an equating study in order to ensure that decisions made using the alternative forms are consistent and do not introduce error into the decision. If the college or district expects to provide alternatives and create a pool of tasks, or item pool, a sample statement can be included in the psychometric plan (see Box 7.11).

Box 7.11.   Sample Statement of Item Pool

Alternative tasks and variations on existing tasks will be developed so that users have choices of tasks for use in their systems. Each alternative or variation will be verified for standards alignment, and each set of tasks will be studied for construct representativeness. Alternative versions of tasks will be equated and will use a common scoring rubric.

Element #5: Assessor/Rater Selection and Training Procedures

Procedures need to be established for assessor or rater selection and training, and we settled on these procedures in Step 4D (Chapter 6) under implementation, working through the details in Worksheets #4.4 and #4.5, the Management Plan and the Rater Monitoring Form. In a university context, this is relatively straightforward, since faculty will assess as part of their regular course load.

AERA, APA, and NCME (1999) *Standards*

and CAATS Step 5A, Element 4

Standard 3.2:

The purpose(s) of the test, *definition of the domain, and the test specifications* should be stated clearly so that *judgments can be made about* the appropriateness of the defined domain for the stated purpose(s) of the test and about *the relation of items to the dimensions of the domain they are intended to represent.*
CAATS Steps Influenced: 1A, 1C, 2E, 5A (Element #4)

Standard 3.3:

The test specifications should be documented, along with their rationale and the process by which they were developed. The test specifications should define the *content of the test, the proposed number of items, the item formats,* the desired psychometric properties of the items, and the item and section arrangement. They should also specify the amount of time for testing, *directions* to the test takers, procedures to be used for test administration and *scoring,* and other relevant information.
CAATS Steps Influenced: 2E, 5A (Element #4)

Discussion

These standards reinforce the need for the kind of planning we did in CAATS Steps 2E and 3C and formalize here. *Test specifications* is a broader term than *framework,* but it encompasses some of the other design aspects that have been practiced to date (e.g., task formatting and scoring).

NOTE: Emphases added for clarity.

In district-based programs, however, decisions need to be made about who will assess—mentor teachers, university collaborators, building administrators, district personnel, or some combination of these. Some alternative certification models provide for a single assessor or assessment team for all tasks; others provide for specialization within the content domains. This, too, needs to be carefully decided and planned. Training should be provided to all assessors with rubrics explained and samples provided. The selection and provision of sample results is one of the most useful things one can do to ensure reliability, as we discuss in more detail under Element #8. These samples should include examples that clearly demonstrate the various levels of proficiency in the rubrics. Much of this will need to be developed over time as assessors and assessment designers identify examples of acceptable and unacceptable work. Sample statements related to assessor or rater selection and training procedures for universities and for districts are provided in Boxes 7.12 and 7.13.

Box 7.12.   Sample Statement of Assessor/Rater Selection and Training Procedures (University Model)

Faculty will assess candidates as part of their regular teaching assignments. Training sessions will be provided in conjunction with faculty meetings. Adjuncts will attend special training sessions at the beginning of each semester. Training will be four hours in duration and will include explanations of the rubrics, examples of acceptable and unacceptable work, and practice activities on individual tasks. Assessment decisions will be sampled, with feedback to assessors provided.

Box 7.13.   Sample Statement of Assessor/Rater Selection and Training Procedures (District Model)

Staff development personnel, curriculum specialists, school-based administrators, and mentor/NBPTS-certified teachers will serve as assessors. Training sessions will be required and will be four hours in duration. These sessions will include explanations of the rubrics, examples of acceptable and unacceptable work, and practice activities on individual tasks. Assessment decisions will be sampled, with feedback to assessors provided.

AERA, APA, and NCME (1999) *Standards*
and CAATS Step 5A, Element 5

Standard 3.23:

The process for *selecting, training, and qualifying scorers* should be documented by the test developer. The *training materials, such as the scoring rubrics and examples of test takers' responses that illustrate the levels on the score scale, and the procedures for training scorers* should result in a degree of agreement among scorers that allows for the scores to be interpreted as originally intended by the test developer. Scorer reliability and potential drift over time in raters' scoring standards should be evaluated and reported by the person(s) responsible for conducting the training session.

CAATS Steps Influenced: 4D, 5A (Element #5), Because Step 5B just says do what you said you were going to do.

Discussion

The sample statements we provided in Boxes 7.12 and 7.13 lay out most of the elements required in the Standard. As training programs are developed and implemented, an eye toward record keeping will be important.

NOTE: Emphases added for clarity.

Element #6: Analysis Methodology

The test analysis methodology specifies the measurement model that will be used to conduct item analysis, validity, and reliability studies, and why it has been selected. This sets the stage for Element #8 of the plan. We present our rationale for preferring the Rasch model of item response theory in Chapter 9 and provide a worksheet for you to use in making your selection of a measurement method in that chapter. Unless we have some degree of confidence that our items (or criteria on our rubrics) are working the way we intended, we cannot be sure that the results (our scores) are credible. Analysis methodologies are useful for more than quality assurance. In this part of the plan, you will write about the methodology or combination of methodologies you have selected for your assessment system. Use the information and worksheet in Chapter 9 to make that decision.

AERA, APA, and NCME (1999) *Standards*
and CAATS Step 5A, Element 6

Standard 3.9:

When a test developer evaluates the psychometric properties of items, the *classical or item response theory (IRT) model used for evaluating the psychometric properties of items should be documented.* The sample used for estimating item properties should be described and should be of adequate size and diversity for the procedure. The process by which items are selected and the data used for item section, such as item difficulty, item discrimination, and/or item information, should also be documented. When IRT is used to estimate item parameters in test development, the item response model, estimation procedures, and evidence of model fit should be documented.

CAATS Steps Influenced: 4C, 5A (Element #6)

Discussion

Most assessors will use some classical test theory; others will add to that item response theory. Element #8 will show you where and when those two models apply. In all likelihood, the item analysis procedures, whether CTT or IRT is used, will be limited to item difficulty and not include discrimination or guessing factors.

NOTE: Emphasis added for clarity.

Element #7: External Review Personnel and Methodology

It is important that assessment designers not work in isolation. They should receive feedback on the test and methodology from external reviewers. In CAATS Step 3, we encouraged the use of stakeholders in reviewing materials, so you may now wish to review the work you did on Worksheet #3.4 of that chapter. We provide a sample statement for this section in Box 7.14.

Box 7.14. Sample Statement of Task Review Personnel and Methodology

Ongoing review by practitioner experts in the districts (stakeholders) will be conducted to ensure practicality and utility. Practitioners will be used as expert panels to ensure the criticality of tasks, the quality of rubrics, and cut-score setting procedures.

Methodological and theoretical review will be conducted by measurement experts and through peer-reviewed outlets.

AERA, APA, and NCME (1999) *Standards*
and CAATS Step 5A, Element 7

Standard 3.5:

When appropriate, *relevant experts external to the testing program should review the test specifications.* The purpose of the review, the process by which the review is conducted, and the results of the review should be documented. The qualifications, relevant experiences, and demographic characteristics of expert judges should also be documented.

CAATS Steps Influenced: 5A (Element #7)

Discussion

Here again the *Standards* establish not only the need to do something but also the need to keep careful records of the process and the results. Many assessors forget this critical step, keeping their work "in-house." This flaw in the process is contrary to both the NCATE and AERA, APA, and NCME *Standards.*

NOTE: Emphases added for clarity.

Element #8: Evidence of Validity, Reliability, and Fairness (VRF)

The above design elements and much of the work already done in the CAATS model helped to prepare the assessment developer at the institutional, district, or even state levels to provide evidence of validity, reliability, and fairness. In this element, we review our previous work in the section below (Psychometric Evidence Collected Already) and include a chart that shows how a number of the worksheets completed as part of the CAATS model have started the process of collecting evidence of validity, reliability, and fairness. We continue with the next steps (Next Steps in Collecting Evidence of Validity, Reliability, and Fairness—VRF), asking and answering three basic VRF questions and providing four examples of what the studies might look like. We end with a look toward the future (Future Studies) where more evidence of validity and additional research is on the horizon. That section includes another five examples of what the studies might look like if you move to the highest level of analysis. Not everyone will want to go the highest level, but the option is out there for those who chose to do so.

We provide you with some sample reports to demonstrate what you can do with the data you have collected. Such reports could be used for internal or external accountability or for accreditation purposes first and then combine the newly collected evidence into a second example report.

Psychometric Evidence Collected Already

In this section, we identify the work you have already undertaken that can be used in a report of evidence of psychometric integrity. It is a good idea to have a formal report in case your decisions are ever challenged, even if you did not write a formal psychometric plan for the previous seven elements. (See Chapter 10 for a discussion of possible legal challenges.) The report is also useful for accreditation purposes. In your report, you might want to attach the worksheets as documentation, describing the process you used to complete them in a brief narrative. Actually, an updated action plan—the one you started in Chapter 2—could contribute greatly to that function. References to meetings and minutes are always helpful, and meeting minutes should be kept in back-up files.

> **Judgmental Evidence**
>
> Judgmental evidence relies on expert opinion rather than numbers.
>
> *Guiding Question:* *"What do the experts say?"*

Some of the worksheets you already completed are direct evidence of your efforts at validity, reliability, and fairness considerations, and we note those in the following table. As you read this table, start thinking about the kinds of mini-studies you could do to keep the worksheets current. Every time you check on one, it's another round of evidence of validity and/or fairness confirmation. For example, updating your critical task list (CAATS Step 2, Worksheet #2.4) is another job analysis. Similarly, if you have a process by which you check to see if the formative tasks are adequate to achieve the summa-

> **Empirical Evidence**
>
> Evidence based on numbers and scores that the assessment is credible.
>
> *Guiding Question: "What do the numbers tell us about credibility?"*

tive results you want (CAATS Step 2, Worksheet #2.5), then you are gathering evidence of opportunity to learn. You can construct many studies like this that help build your collection of evidence, and that is your main goal—continuing to collect evidence of validity, reliability, and fairness. Some will be judgmental, like these two examples; other evidence will be empirical or statistical. While you need both, do not underestimate the importance of the judgmental process. Most people don't even think about it and miss many opportunities to showcase the credibility of their decisions.

In Table 7.2 we align the worksheets you have already created with our three cornerstones of psychometric credibility: validity, reliability, and fairness.

Table 7.2. Alignment of CAATS Worksheets With Psychometrics—Summary of Initial Credibility Studies

Step	Worksheet	Validity	Reliability	Fairness
1	#2: Purpose, Use, Content	Construct		Decisions based on purpose (and not on anything else!)
	#3: Propositions	Conceptual Framework		
2	#1: Organizing for Alignment	Construct—domain specification		Decisions made based on professional, national, and state inputs
	#2: Our Critical Skills	Construct—domain specification		
	#3: Visualizing the Competent Teacher	Construct—job analysis		
	#4: Critical Task List	Construct—job analysis	Generalizability— same data used for decision making	
	#5: Sorting Formative and Summative Tasks	Instructional		Opportunity to learn
	#8: List of Summative Assessments by Points in Time			Opportunity to learn
	#9: Matrix of Standards by Competency Type	Content— representative		Decisions based on both knowledge and skills
3	#1: Proficiency Level Descriptions	Construct— minimal competence defined	Rater Consistency— anticipatory set	Decision points known in advance by assessors and assesses—due process
	#2: Task Design	Content— alignment	Rater Consistency— anticipatory set	Opportunity to learn and remediate
	#3: Standards and Indicators Coverage Report	Content— representative, relevant, and proportional	Rater Consistency— anticipatory set	

Step	Worksheet	Validity	Reliability	Fairness
	#4: Individual Task Review for Job-Relatedness	Content—criticality	Internal consistency—same thing measured	Decisions based on authentic criteria
	#5: Checklist for Reviewing Individual Tasks	Content—representative and relevant		Opportunity to demonstrate enhanced by thorough review of tasks
	#6: Instructional Alignment	Instructional		Opportunity to learn and remediate
4	#1: Cut-Score Decisions	Construct and social consequences		Decisions based on authentic criteria
	#2: Sample Format for Candidate/Teacher Tracking Form			Fair monitoring ensured—due process
	#3: Format for Data Aggregation			Opportunities to learn improved through identification of program weaknesses
	#4: Management Plan	Content validity through system updates	Checks for rater drift	Fair monitoring and due process ensured
	#5: Rater Monitoring Record	Ensures expert judgments	Assists with consistency	Decreased risk of unfair decisions

We noted above that you could use these worksheets in a report. In Box 7.15 we create a sample of how you might write such a report.

Box 7.15   Sample Report of Initial Credibility Studies

During the developmental phase of our assessment system, we followed an action plan (Appendix A) that included the completion of a large number of worksheets (Appendix B) that helped us design a credible system. In this report, we summarize some of the psychometric aspects to which we were attending throughout our design process. We refer to worksheets by the steps in the CAATS model that we used and the worksheet numbers within those steps. For example, 2.8 would be CAATS Step 2, Worksheet #2.8.

(Continued)

(Continued)

Validity: After defining our construct as teacher performance, we agreed upon the purpose, uses, and content of our system to ensure construct validity (Worksheet #1.2). We further fleshed out our conceptual framework, including the propositions concerning what we believe and value about the assessment system, an alignment of all of the standards we will use, and lists of critical skills and tasks to serve as operational definitions of the construct (Worksheets #1.3, 2.1, 2.2, 2.3, and 2.4). To ensure content validity, we developed frameworks to analyze the extent to which our tasks were representative, relevant, and proportional of the construct, covering adequately our content (Worksheets #2.8, 2.9, and 3.3). We validated these through internal and external reviews focusing on coverage of the standards, clarity of the directions and rubrics, the criticality of the tasks to measuring job performance, and appropriateness of the proficiency levels to determining minimal competency (Worksheets #2.9, 3.1, 3.2, 3.3, 3.4, and 3.5.). We ensured instructional validity by sorting formative from summative tasks and reviewing the alignment of instruction and assessment (Worksheets #2.5, 3.5, and 3.6). We worked toward construct validity and consequential validity by reviewing our cut-score decisions (Worksheet #4.1). We developed procedures for aggregating data so that future studies can be conducted of improvement (one of our purposes) as well as monitoring the validity of our decisions for each teacher (Worksheet #4.3). We planned for the collection of continuing evidence in the management plan (Worksheets #4.4).

Reliability: By selecting a common set of critical tasks (Worksheet #2.4), we will have generalizable results. The development of consistent and carefully constructed proficiency level descriptions and task descriptions (Worksheets #3.1, 3.2) allows for rater consistency. Similarly, the coverage report of standards and indicators, along with the listing of standards on task information and the task review process, establishes an anticipatory set for judges that should bring consistency to the process (Worksheets #3.2, 3.3, and 3.4). The management plan and rater monitoring record (Worksheets #4.4 and 4.5) provide for the avoidance of rater drift.

Fairness: Our predominant focus has been on the assurance of opportunities to learn and remediate (Worksheets #2.5, 2.8, 3.1, 3.4, 3.5, and 4.1) with the inclusion of adequate formative assessments, clear directions and rubrics, and decisions based on authentic and critical tasks. We have also focused on providing information to teachers on decisions in a timely way and throughout programs (Worksheet #2.9), and we provided for multiple opportunities to succeed (Worksheet #3.1). We are monitoring raters actively to decrease the risk of unfair decisions (Worksheet #4.5).

Next Steps in Collecting Evidence of Validity, Reliability, and Fairness

We now turn to your continuing collection of evidence of validity, reliability and fairness. You already have a great head start, as the sample report above demonstrated, especially in the area of validity and fairness, and we will make those connections below as well. One useful approach to collecting such evidence is to ask and answer a series of questions, just as one would do in a research study. For the two examples of continuing your previous work above, we could ask these two questions:

- Is my job analysis current and adequate?

- Do my teachers continue to have an adequate opportunity to learn?

A sample report on these continued efforts might look like the one you find in Box 7.16.

Box 7.16. Sample Report on Continuing Assessment Process Review

Two years after the implementation of our system, we conducted a follow-up job analysis to ensure that our original work remained current and adequate. We found that most tasks met that criterion. We removed the task on "journaling" and added a task on "improvement ideas for next year."

We surveyed our teachers to ensure that they believe they have adequate opportunities to learn. Of the 200 teachers who responded, 180 (90%) said that they did. Several teachers suggested the addition of more instruction in the area of critical thinking. We have added an additional component to the unit plan on critical thinking strategies and a new formative assessment on writing higher order objectives.

We have developed the following series of additional questions and methodologies as a sample of the kinds of questions that could be asked to obtain evidence on a performance-based assessment system. For these questions, it is useful to use a combination of two response strategies— one logical or judgmental (qualitative) and the other empirical (quantitative). We begin with three basic questions, noted in Box 7.17, and then expand to some more specific ones matched to the methodologies. With this level of expansion, we will show you four examples (Examples #1 to #4) at the end of the chapter to demonstrate how each process works. We expect that most of our readers will complete the judgmental processes outlined and a few of the empirical ones, depending on their needs and their choice of measurement model (classical or item response theories).

Tables 7.3-7.5 provide more specific questions and analysis techniques for each of the three cornerstones of credibility—validity, reliability, and fairness. Note that we have included both judgmental and empirical studies that can work with competency-based, as well as dispositional, data. In our tables, we refer you to several worksheets and examples at the end of the chapter. We also repeat our user-friendly definitions and guiding questions for validity, reliability, and fairness to help keep our focus.

> **Fairness**
>
> Fairness ensures that rights are protected and that test takers are not penalized because they are a member of a protected group, or because they don't have adequate opportunities to learn and succeed, or because the criteria and tasks have language or contexts that are offensive to them, or because their rights to due process were violated.
>
> *Guiding Question: "Do all teachers have an equal opportunity to complete the tasks successfully, regardless of gender, ethnicity, or handicapping condition, and is there an appeals process in place?"*

Box 7.17. Three Basic VRF Questions

Validity: Does the assessment system provide adequate coverage of the standards?

Reliability: Are scorers consistent in their ratings?

Fairness: Do all teachers have an equal opportunity to complete the tasks successfully, regardless of gender, ethnicity, or handicapping condition?

Table 7.3. Questions and Methods for Collecting Validity Evidence

Psychometric Question	Judgmental Methods	Empirical Methods
1. Does the assessment system provide adequate coverage of the standards? (content validity)	Alignment charts showing coverage of each indicator across instruments (CAATS Step 3, Worksheet #3.3)	*IRT Method:* Logistic ruler showing gaps in coverage, if any; concept map (Example #1)
2. Are the tasks an adequate representation of the job? Critical to job performance, authentic, and frequent? (content validity)	Stakeholder survey (CAATS Step 3, Worksheet #3.4)	*Classical Method:* Content validity ratio CVR (Example #2)
3. Are any teachers being denied a diploma or dropping out who would be good teachers? (consequential)	Analysis of appropriateness of reasons for teacher failures. (Worksheets #5.2 and #5.3)	*Classical Method:* Disparate impact analysis (Example #3)
4. Are program completers acquiring improved knowledge and skills over time? (Note, this question only applies if continuous improvement is a stated purpose of the system.)	Analysis of improvement results (Worksheet #5.4)	*IRT Method:* Increasing mean measures over time on a ruler

In a process such as this, the majority of validity evidence can be judgmental. The best news here is that you have already completed much of what you needed to do in earlier steps of the CAATS model. We add to the judgmental process reviews of the reasons for failure and the results of improvement efforts, if improvement was one of the purposes of the system. We consider these all critical to complete.

On the empirical side, there is room for evidence in the early stages of the process, but it is not as critical as it is for reliability. Analyzing the difficulty of tasks in comparison to your expectations about them (concept map) is an easy product of the Rasch model. If you have not yet read Chapter 9, the example will not be helpful. The Content Validity Ratio (CVR) is easy to calculate, and the example will show you how. Disparate impact is also easy to calculate with free software on line, so please refer to that example. At a minimum, this study should be completed. If you are serious about program improvement, a quick comparison of mean scores using the Rasch model is your best bet—if your teachers are learning more, the program is probably improving! Other validity studies are possible in the future, and we deal with that in our last section of Element #8 (*Future Studies*).

> ### Validity
>
> Validity is the extent to which assessment measures are truthful about what they say they measure, or the degree to which evidence and theory support the interpretations and use of a test or assessment process.
>
> *Guiding Question: "Does this test really measure what it says it measures? Does the assessment system provide adequate coverage of the standards?"*

Table 7.4. Questions and Methods for Collecting Reliability Evidence		
Psychometric Question	*Judgmental Methods*	*Empirical Methods*
1. Are scorers consistent in their ratings? (rater agreement)— conducted on a regular basis (e.g., every three years)	Expert rescoring of instruments (Worksheet #5.5)	*Classical Method:* Cohen's kappa (Example #4) *OR* *IRT Method:* Rater effects and category probability analysis (see Chapter 9)
2. Are scores obtained on teachers sufficiently precise as to create confidence that they could be replicated under different or new conditions or administrations? (internal consistency and measurement error)	Insertion of artificial cases (blind) analysis (described below)	*IRT Method:* Fit analysis of persons (see Chapter 9) *OR* *Classical Method:* Cronbach's alpha and standard error (see note below)

Reliability is a tougher nut to crack judgmentally, so the empirical side of this chart overrides the judgmental one. In your early work, you were able to establish a context in which reliability was likely to be present, but you were unable to actually examine it as you were with content validity. In choosing your method of determining reliability, you might want to consider what is most important to your assessments: consensus of ratings, consistency over time, or fair correction of rater errors.

Consensus is likely best approached with a traditional Cohen's kappa statistic (Cohen, 1960) and rubric review. We have provided a worksheet example of the computation of Cohen's kappa. This is a traditional check for inter-rater reliability. Expert rescoring allows you to compare ratings by different raters, and an example with some opportunity to practice is provided for you to use for that study. The computations are very simple. The blind review process in the table would allow you to select (or create) some anchor tasks that well represent each of the proficiency levels and give them to raters along with new assessment tasks to score. If the raters score as you expected them to score, they are on track; if not, you have something to talk about. Here you would keep a record of whether they are consistent and advise accordingly. If you want a modern discussion of methods to estimate inter-rater reliability, Stemler (2004) provides a readable overview and ends with a statement reflective of our view: "The appropriate approach to estimating inter-rater reliability will always depend upon the purpose at hand" (Summary and Conclusions, ¶ 4).

Reliability

Reliability is the degree to which test scores are consistent over repeated applications of the process and are, therefore, dependable or trustworthy.

Guiding Question: "If students took the same test again under the same conditions (or a similar version of the test), would they score the same scores?"

Inter-Rater Reliability

Inter-rater reliability is an index of consistency across raters calculated using correlations. Raters' scores should consistently go up or down across students. When one rater rates a student high, the other rater should rate him/her high. Low ratings should also be consistent across raters. If some raters score students high and the other raters score the same students as low, then the ratings are not consistent or reliable.

Guiding Question:
"Are scorers consistent in their ratings?"

❓— Differential Item Functioning (DIF) —

DIF is a statistical process that seeks to determine if there are meaningful differences in the way subgroups perform, particularly groups that are classified as protected—women and minorities. It is okay for the performance to be different, as long as it is not because of problems in the construction or administration of the assessment itself.

Guiding Question: "Are minorities and women doing worse on the assessments because they are minorities and women?"

We have done much in earlier steps to ensure that the construct is well defined, so we are not likely to have other typical problems associated with reliability. Rater error (leniency or harshness) will be our biggest challenge. With regard to other forms of reliability evidence, clearly we are limited by the nature of the system. The test-retest approach to reliability would not work here because we cannot ask teachers to repeat their performances. Alternate or parallel forms are difficult to create because we have carefully selected and constructed our assessment tasks—all of which are critical to the job. That leaves us with internal consistency.

For those who really want a reliability index (internal consistency), we note that one of the advantages of the Rasch model is that it automatically produces a traditional reliability coefficient that is similar to Cronbach's alpha but is called separation reliability. We provide an example of how that works and what it looks like in Chapter 9. An even more important advantage of the Rasch model is that computer software called FACETS (Linacre, 1994) allows us to actually estimate the amount of rater error present and adjust for it with a minimal number of repeated ratings. This is a very intriguing possibility, but you would need some software training to perform the analysis. Again, see Chapter 9 for a few more details on this.

Table 7.5. Questions and Methods for Collecting Fairness Evidence		
Psychometric Question	*Judgmental Methods*	*Empirical Methods*
1. Do all teachers have an equal opportunity to complete the tasks successfully, regardless of gender, ethnicity, or handicapping condition? (nonbiased materials and processes)	Representative teachers' and assessors' examination of items for offensiveness (Worksheet #5.6)	*IRT Method:* Differential item and differential person fit analysis (Example #9) OR *Classical Method:* Disparate impact analysis (Example #3)
2. Are procedures in place to ensure that all teachers know the requirements and have adequate opportunity to learn the content and remediate when completion of tasks is not initially successful? (Equal Opportunity and nondiscriminatory practices)	Analysis of reasons for noncompletion and remediation efforts and EO impact (Worksheet #5.7, which may be completed based on results of survey of noncompleters)	*IRT Method:* Differential item and differential person functioning and fit analysis (Example #9) OR *Classical Method:* Descriptive statistics on patterns by group

The question of fairness or absence of bias in an assessment system is important in today's world. For the most part, judgmental studies are adequate, although we highly recommend some simple descriptive statistics for the second question— nothing more than numbers and percents. Our method suggested above to answer Question #1 is purely judgmental, common practice, and should be practical for most institutions or school districts looking for evidence. Question 2 is also reasonably easy to provide, and many reports include descriptive statistics divided by demographics or logical comparisons.

There is only one issue that confronts the assessment systems today that is not addressed easily by judgmental and classical methods: that is the power to detect subtle bias in individual items or assessment tasks that add up to *disparate impact* despite the best intentions. There is likely no easy way to obtain this information without the use of advanced *differential item* and *differential person analysis* provided by the Rasch model IRT. We are not going to detail the statistical models here, but we would suggest that those interested consider the excellent illustration of techniques to detect item bias provided by Richard Smith (2004) for scored items and Elder, McNamara, and Congdon (2004) for performance items in the text *Introduction to Rasch Measurement* (Smith & Smith, 2004). We have provided an example of this (Example #9) at the very end of this chapter as well.

Future Studies

Over time, you may want to conduct some additional research studies for both evidence of validity and for general research purposes. We have provided examples of where the Rasch model can help you with validity, reliability, and fairness studies in the previous sections. Here we provide examples of how the Rasch model, and to a lesser extent the classical approach, can provide many opportunities for continuing research. This is largely due to the fact that the Rasch model converts ordinal data (what you always have with rating scales) into interval data.

You may remember from your statistics training that some statistical computations are not supposed to be performed on ordinal data. You may also remember that most statistical tests, at least the parametric kind, require a normal distribution as one of their important assumptions. Most performance assessment systems end up having a high degree of negative skew—otherwise known as mastery learning. After all, that is our purpose in this system. We can try hard to convince raters not to use the high point on our rating scales, but often that simply is not a realistic expectation.

Rasch does not presume a normal distribution and works with interval level data. You may have noticed in our Cohen's kappa example at the end of this chapter that we had a bit of a problem with our raters in differentiating between acceptable and exemplary. While we may try our darnedest to get past that, in all likelihood we will never succeed. So, you may see inadequate Cohen's kappas for eternity. With Rasch, you can simply make the correction, focus on the cut score (which was okay in the example), and let it go.

The amount of research you can do with good data is virtually endless. We suggest a few studies here to give you a flavor of "coming attractions." Some will add to your store of validity evidence. Others may add to your store of contributions to the knowledge base within your own system (evaluation) or generalizable (research) to the world at large, depending on how you design your studies and what other questions you ask. As in the previous section, we use the question approach. We suggest a possible or likely analysis and process. There are too many options to be complete and too many questions that can be asked, so please view these only as illustrations.

You will see from the outset that you can do much with descriptive statistics, graphs, and simple correlations. They are powerful and easy to produce, and you can easily do

> **Differential Person Functioning (DPF)**
>
> DPF is a statistical process that seeks to determine if there are meaningful differences in the way item subsets perform, particularly patterns that are classified as a certain type—representing a subconstruct. It is okay for the performance to be different, as long as it is not because of *problems in the persons* such as anxiety, cheating, guessing, or test strategy.
>
> *Guiding Question: "Are any item patterns demonstrating a person's score needs individual interpretation?"*

all of this yourself, just as you can do Cohen's kappa and the content validity ratio yourself. You may also wish to progress to some more sophisticated techniques, such as regression analyses and significance tests, which may also be within your comfort zone. We are specifically not discussing SEM, HLM, MANOVA, 2PL, 3PL (Structural Equation Modeling, Hierarchical Linear Modeling, Multiple Analysis of Variance, Two-Parameter Logistic Model, Three-Parameter Logistic Model), discriminant analysis, canonical analysis, factor analysis, or all the "third tier" statistics. These, like the Rasch model, may call for a statistician if you are not inclined to do much with statistics on your own.

Here are five questions to get our continuing analysis started. For each question, we provide a suggested design that includes your assessment scores (sometimes both raw scores and Rasch interval level scores), other evidence, the type of analysis, and some brief comments (Tables 7.6–7.10). We also point out the uses of these questions in terms of validity and other research.

Question #1: Is there a relationship between unit assessment results and other current assessment(s) such as national or state certification tests (e.g., Praxis, GPA, and the like)?

This is an excellent source of ***concurrent validity***. (See Examples #5 and #6.)

Table 7.6. Suggested Design for Question #1		
Your Assessment System Scores	*Other Unit Evidence or Outcomes*	*Type of Analysis*
Total rating scale raw scores across all tasks	GPA or Praxis percentile rank	Spearman Rho Correlation Coefficient
Rasch or IRT measures or standard scores	Praxis standard scores	Pearson Correlation Coefficient
Comments: This is likely to be one of your best statistical studies of validity because the evidence of outcomes is readily available to you. Note that it will not work if everyone has a perfect rating and 4.0 GPA!		

Question #2: Is there a relationship between assessment results and future external assessments (e.g., hiring success, rehire rates, and placement surveys).

This is an excellent source of ***predictive validity***. (No new calculation examples provided; see Examples #5 and #6 for examples of correlations.)

Table 7.7. Suggested Design for Question #2		
Your Assessment System Scores	*Other Unit Evidence or Outcomes*	*Type of Analysis*
Total rating scale raw scores across all tasks	Principals' total or overall satisfaction ratings from survey	Spearman Rho Correlation Coefficient
Total rating scale raw scores across all tasks	Hire/rehire status if available from your state or districts	Point Biserial Correlation Coefficient
Comments: While predictive validity is very desirable, do not be surprised if there is not as much relationship as you expected. The biggest challenge you face with predictive validity studies is that you do not have data on folks who failed the tasks but were certified and are teaching, since they did not graduate. So you only have half of the data you really need! Following graduates for up to five years is useful.		

Question #3: Do tasks from specific standards or organizing structures contribute *similar* information about overall pedagogical skill or content knowledge?

This is an excellent source of ***convergent validity***. (No new calculation examples provided; see Examples #5 and #6 for examples of correlations.)

Table 7.8. Suggested Design for Question #3		
Your Assessment System Scores	*Other Unit Evidence or Outcomes*	*Type of Analysis*
Summed scores of tasks from selected standards, thematic portfolio scores, or individual task scores	A second set of scores that *should* correlate, plus intercorrelations between your tasks	Spearman Rho Correlation Matrix and SPLOM (scatter plot matrices)
Rasch or IRT measures or standard scores	A second set of scores that *should* correlate, plus intercorrelations between your tasks	Pearson Correlation Matrix and SPLOM (scatter plot matrices)
Comments: You will have to hypothesize logical expected relationships. For example, you might expect high correlations between diversity and human development, critical thinking and content knowledge, knowledge and skill, skill and impact. Also see comments for divergent validity in Table 7.9.		

Question #4: Do assessments contribute *different* information about knowledge, skills, dispositions, and impact?

This is an excellent source of ***discriminant validity***. (See Example #7 for a knowledge, skills, dispositions, and impact set of correlations.)

Table 7.9. Suggested Design for Question #4		
Your Assessment System Scores	*Other Unit Evidence or Outcomes*	*Type of Analysis*
Measures from the assessments produced by the Rasch model	Aggregations of related tasks that *should* correlate or that *should not* correlate	Pearson Correlation Matrix and SPLOM (scatter plot matrices)
Rating scale raw score data	Aggregations of related tasks that *should* correlate or that *should not* correlate	Spearman Rho Correlation Matrix and SPLOM (scatter plot matrices)
Comments: If we use a summed score on individual instruments, we are likely to see high correlations within the taxonomic level. For example, we might see high correlations between a belief scale and a questionnaire or a lesson plan and an accommodations plan. We might also see high correlations between a total score on dispositions and a total score on impact, but we might see a low correlation between a total score on dispositions and a total score on knowledge. This low correlation is evidence of discriminant validity while the high correlation is evidence of convergent validity.		

Question #5: How do teachers completing the elementary program compare to teachers completing the secondary program (or traditional vs. alternative certification, or 2 + 2 vs. 4-year graduates, or teachers from New Jersey vs. teachers from South Carolina)?

This is an example of program *improvement data*. (See Example #8 for a *t*-test.)

Table 7.10. Suggested Design for Question #5		
Your Assessment System Scores	*Other Unit Evidence or Outcomes*	*Type of Analysis*
Rasch or IRT measures or standard scores by type of assessment	Results from pairs of programs with the same or linked tasks and items	Descriptive statistics, bar graphs, *t*-tests, and differential item functioning (DIF) to compare programs
Comments: A comparison across programs is a useful diagnostic tool to find and improve areas that vary based on content or facilitator.		

That brings us near the end. We note here that we have provided one more example at the end of the chapter to demonstrate differential item functioning (DIF). It is Example #9. In this example, we show how the Rasch model can be used to identify bias in items, but we also note that the DIF analysis can be used to identify differences in programs.

Before leaving the psychometric planning process, it may be useful to have a vision for where these types of studies can take us and what kind of reports you should be able to write. Below is a sample report, based on fictitious data that show the type of conclusions you could reach if you addressed most or all of the questions we have identified under CAATS Step 5A, Element #8. Some of the data are taken from the worksheets and examples at the end of this chapter; other data are even more fictitious and written to aid in this example. In Box 7.18 we present the sample report for validity.

Box 7.18. Sample Report of Psychometric Studies—Validity

We conducted a wide range of validity studies, detailed results of which are included in the appendix. We used a combination of judgmental and empirical methodologies and classical and item response theories. Our conclusions follow:

- The assessment system provides adequate coverage of the standards and, therefore, has evidence of content validity. We created an alignment chart of standards and tasks, and no standards had less than three tasks used to assess them. A logistic ruler showed that we had no gaps in coverage either and that tasks were ordered logically in terms of difficulty. For example, we expected Task #1 to be the most difficult and Tasks #4, #5, and #7 to be the easiest, and the measures calculated confirmed our expectations.

- The assessment system shows evidence of construct validity based on the results of a stakeholder survey during our developmental phase. We had responses from 75 principals and school system personnel, who were asked to evaluate each item for criticality, frequency, and authenticity. We dropped three tasks from the system based on this survey because their mean criticality ratings were less than 2.5 All other tasks ranged from 2.5 to 3.0, with 3 representing critical, 2 useful, and 1 not useful. We subsequently used the same scale with a panel of 10 expert judges and computed a Lawshe (1975) content validity ratio for all tasks in the system. All tasks were in the .50 to .80 range, meeting the criterion of .50.

- The assessment system shows evidence of concurrent validity; we correlated GPA and Praxis scores with the scores from the system, finding a Pearson's $r = .81$ and .88 respectively. We used the Pearson correlation coefficient because of the Rasch scores, which are interval, as are GPA and Praxis.

- The assessment system shows evidence of predictive validity; we correlated overall satisfaction ratings from principals and program completers for the 2005 year, finding a Spearman's rho correlation on these ordinal data of .93.

- The assessment systems has evidence of convergent and divergent validity based on correlations of sets of tasks representative of knowledge, skills, dispositions, and impact on K–12 learning. We found a Pearson's product moment correlation of .88 between knowledge and skills, and a Pearson's product moment correlation of .95 between impact and disposition. Task subtotals for knowledge are not well correlated with either impact or dispositions, with Pearson's product moment correlations of .13 and .23 respectively.

- Consistent with our program improvement purpose, we analyzed the mean ratings for all criteria and found that only 10 criteria fell below a mean rating of 2.0 on a 3-point scale. We initiated improvement efforts related to instruction for all 10 criteria, and we will monitor results in analyses next year. We also used a Rasch analysis to determine that teachers' mean scores increased over a three-year period from 75 to 82. Finally, we performed a series of t-tests comparing results in various programs, finding only that there were significant differences between mathematics and science, with mathematics teachers performing better than science teachers by 4.8 points. We expect to determine if these differences are related to instruction or differences in tasks.

In Box 7.19 we present the sample report for reliability.

Box 7.19. Sample Report of Psychometric Studies—Reliability

We conducted four reliability studies, detailed results of which are included in the appendix. We used a combination of judgmental and empirical methodologies and classical and item response theories. Two studies focused on scorer consistency and two on internal consistency. Our conclusions follow:

- The assessment system showed scorer consistency through a study of expert rescoring. In this study, we had three judges rescore the selected tasks and compared their ratings. While we found five differences between acceptable and target ratings for two judges, there were no discrepancies on the unacceptable rating. We also computed a Cohen's kappa, obtaining a .51 correlation coefficient, below our .70 expectation. We were pleased, however, to note that we had 100% agreement on the unacceptable ratings; hence, we are comfortable that our cut score is reliable. The difficulty is in separating acceptable and exemplary ratings. We will repeat both studies next year, and we are reviewing rubrics and training materials to determine areas of potential lack of clarity and other causes for the rating problem.

- The assessment system showed internal consistency through the Rasch approach. The reliability coefficient was .81, and we had no misfitting scores (MNSQ >2.0) for any of our teachers.

In Box 7.20 we present the sample report for fairness.

Box 7.20. Sample Report of Psychometric Studies—Fairness

We conducted four fairness studies, detailed results of which are included in the appendix. We used a combination of judgmental and empirical methodologies and classical and item response theories. Our conclusions follow:

- Experts reviewed each task to ensure that none of the tasks were potentially biased against protected populations. They looked specifically for cultural bias, finding none. We do have some Creole students, and we found through the differential item functioning (DIF) analysis (Rasch model) some statistically significant differences for our French-speaking population. We will review the translated items accordingly. The DIF analyses revealed no other gender or ethnic bias in the tasks.

- A disparate impact analysis, as referenced under validity, showed that minorities were having difficulty in passing, and we will explore the reasons for these failures in our study next year. These findings are inconsistent with the DIF analysis and may be attributable to factors other than the quality of the rubrics and rater judgments.

- We documented and reviewed remediation efforts for all members of protected populations who were failing. There were only two minorities and one disabled person in this group, and we determined that all three had received extensive support but were unable to complete the tasks satisfactorily with a level of quality consistent with other passing teachers.

At this point you may be wondering if you will have to do all of these studies and generate reports such as the ones modeled in Boxes 7.18–7.20. The answer to that question is a resounding "NO!" Our goal here has been to show you the possibilities, give you a menu of options, and share with you a vision of a target at which to aim. You may pick and chose from the menu and create your own new recipes and selections. Some are easier than others. Your "meal" will be what you want it to be and what you need it to be for your own definition of a healthy assessment system that hits the target you choose.

Before closing the narrative portion of CAATS Step 5 and moving into worksheets and examples, we go back to one of our starting points from Chapter 1 as you reflect on your menu and target. There we wrote that the National Commission on Teaching and America's Future (NCTAF, 1996) advocated that all teachers should be licensed on the basis of demonstrated performance, including the teaching skills that reflect the core competencies of a highly qualified beginning teacher. The Commission concluded that more must be done if licensure is to gain the respect it holds in other professions:

> Most states test prospective teachers, but many are still not using true performance-based assessments that provide valid measures of teaching competence. . . . States have raised teaching standards substantially in the past decade; now they need to improve the measures of teaching competence that make standards credible. (p. 23)

AERA, APA, and NCME (1999) *Standards*
and CAATS Step 5A

Standard 3.6:

The type of items, the response formats, scoring procedures, and test administration procedures should be selected based on the purposes of the test, the domain to be measured, and the intended test takers. To the extent possible, test content should be chosen to ensure that intended inferences from test scores are equally valid for members of different groups of test takers. *The test review process should include empirical analyses and, when appropriate, the use of expert judges to review items and response formats.* The qualifications, relevant experiences, and demographic characteristics of expert judges should also be documented.

CAATS Steps Influenced: 5A (Element #8—Validity and Fairness)

Standard 13.2:

In educational settings, when a test is designed or used to serve multiple purposes, *evidence of the test's technical quality should be provided for each purpose.*

CAATS Steps Influenced: 5A (Element #8—Validity)

(Continued)

(Continued)

Standard 3.23:

The process for selecting, training, and qualifying scorers should be documented by the test developer. The training materials, such as the scoring rubrics and examples of test takers' responses that illustrate the levels on the score scale, and the procedures for training scorers should result in *a degree of agreement among scorers that allows for the scores to be interpreted as originally intended* by the test developer. Scorer reliability and potential drift over time in raters' scoring standards should be evaluated and reported by the person(s) responsible for conducting the training session.

CAATS Steps Influenced: 4D, 5A (Element #8—Reliability)

Standard 2.10:

When subjective judgment enters into test scoring, evidence should be provided on both *interrater consistency in scoring and within-examinee consistency over repeated measurements*. A clear distinction should be made among reliability data based on (a) independent panels of raters scoring the same performance or procedures, (b) a single panel scoring successive performances or new products, and (c) independent panels scoring successive performances or new products.

CAATS Steps Influenced: 5A (Element #8—Reliability)

Standard 2.15:

When a test or combination of measures is used to make categorical decisions, *estimates should be provided of the percentage of examinees who would be classified in the same way* on two applications of the procedure, using the same form or alternate forms of the instrument.

CAATS Steps Influenced: 5A (Element #8—Reliability)

Standard 14.15:

Estimates of the reliability of test-base credentialing decisions should be provided.

CAATS Steps Influenced: 5A (Element 8—Reliability)

Standard 7.3:

When credible research reports that *differential item functioning exists across age, gender, racial/ethnic, cultural, disability, and/or linguistic groups* in the population of test takers in the content domain measured by the test, test developers should *conduct appropriate studies* when feasible. Such research should seek to detect and eliminate aspects of test design, content, and format that might bias test scores for particular groups.

CAATS Steps Influenced: 5A (Element #8—Fairness)

Standard 7.4:

Test developers should strive to *identify and eliminate language, symbols, words, phrases, and content that are generally regarded as offensive* by members of racial, ethnic, gender, or other groups, except when judged to be necessary for adequate representation of the domain.

CAATS Steps Influenced: 5A (Element #8—Fairness)

Standard 7.10:

When the use of a test results in outcomes that affect the life chances or educational opportunities of examinees, *evidence of mean test score differences* between relevant subgroups of examinees should, where feasible, be examined for subgroups for which credible research reports mean differences for similar tests. Where mean differences are found, an investigation should be undertaken to *determine that such differences are not attributable to source of construct underrepresentation or construct-irrelevant variance*. While initially the responsibility of the test developer, the test user bears responsibility for uses which groups other than those specified by the developer.

CAATS Steps Influenced: 5A (Element #8—Fairness)

Standard 9.1:

Testing practice should be designed to reduce threats to the reliability and validity of test score inferences that may arise from *language differences*.

CAATS Steps Influenced: 5A (Element #8—Fairness)

Standard 10.1:

In testing individuals with *disabilities*, test developers, test administrators, and test users should take steps to ensure that the test score inferences accurately reflect the intended construct rather than any disabilities and their associated characteristics extraneous to the intent of the measurement.

CAATS Steps Influenced: 5A (Element #8—Fairness)

Discussion

The standards reinforce the need for both judgmental and empirical studies. The validity studies proposed focus on content validity and the job-relatedness criterion, as well as the utility of the data for program improvement—two different purposes of the system. Provision is made not only to check rater consistency for reliability but also to do so at regular intervals (e.g., every three years). Provision to check for biased items includes both expert review by representatives of protected populations and for differential item functioning analysis.

NOTE: Emphases added for clarity.

CAATS STEP 5B: IMPLEMENT THE PLAN CONSCIENTIOUSLY

Like all good planning processes, it is important to think about who will do what, when, where, and how. So it is advisable to develop an action plan that helps keep the psychometrics on track. At least one measurement person should be involved from the start. While we do not need to see a dozen statisticians biting at the heels of teacher education faculty, it is a good idea to have one practical-minded measurement person to help with the nitty-gritty details and make sure you do not miss something that later could be embarrassing. In our fairness example, it would likely be a statistician who found the problem for Creole students. While the tail should not wag the dog, the dog should have a tail. Teamwork helps.

Make a sign to post over your door that says: Keep it Statistically Simple. KISS. Point to it whenever you are confused by something being discussed. Even if you understand, point to it on occasion just to keep everyone honest!

Box 7.21.   Double Secret Advice From an Anti–Tail Wagger

Have you seen the movie *Born Yesterday*? If not, rent it. Focus on the scene where Melanie Griffith memorizes a few standard phrases that dazzle the politicos at a Washington party. Then memorize a few of the AERA, APA, and NCME *Standards* and sprinkle them into your conversations with measurement folks. Then tell them that you are going to use the Rasch model because you want to put the people back into the measurement process by using the fit statistic while reducing rater effect at the same time.

That may work even better than pointing to your KISS sign.

P.S.: Don't let them see Chapter 9. Make them work harder. Refer them to Bond and Fox (2001) or Mark Wilson (2005) if they don't know the model. It will be our little secret. The happy faces on the ruler might not work for everyone!

⋁ WRAP-UP

In this chapter we discussed the reasons why it is important to have data that are credible and useful, noting that there are standards for psychometrics just as there are standards for teacher competencies and dispositions. We used the *Standards* from AERA, APA, and NCME as the basis for developing a plan for credibility and utility with eight elements in it: (1) purpose and use; (2) construct measured; (3) interpretation and reporting of scores; (4) assessment specifications and content map; (5) assessor/rater selection and training procedures; (6) analysis methodology; (7) external review personnel and methodology; and (8) evidence of validity, reliability, and fairness.

We found that because we had done careful planning throughout the first four steps of the CAATS model, we were well on the way to ensuring credibility and utility of our data. In this step, we reviewed our earlier work, placing it in the credibility (validity, reliability, and fairness) context. Then we needed only to add a few more pieces to complete the task, most of which can be handled with relative ease.

Story Starters

Starter #1:

Professor/Teacher Leevmeealon stomps into your office and says:

"We all know what we do is important and how to score teachers' work, so we don't need to check on any of this validity/reliability junk. That's just a bunch of statisticians being a pain in the butt. Nobody is going to challenge my decisions, much the less take me to court over a grade. If I think it is necessary to drop a student out of the program, then I have the academic freedom to do so. I expect my students to do poorly on some of the parts of my assignments. It builds character. They need to learn to deal with imperfection, as you do. After all, I'm the expert, and that's why I have the PhD and the student doesn't. And you don't know anything about what I teach. Obviously I can tell the difference between unacceptable, acceptable, and exemplary work. Can't everybody?

You say.....

Starter #2:

Professor Dr. Neelbeformee, wearing a Harris Tweed jacket, scratches his beard and takes a drag from his pipe. There are funny looking charts and graphs and pictures of the normal curve all over his office. He looks at you with a frown and says, "Let's try some factor analysis and hierarchical linear modeling. I will tell you what you are measuring. It may or may not be all of these standards."

You say, "Gee Doc, we have developed a specific assessment plan. Here's our checklist of the *exact analyses* we need, the *reports* we want, and an example of the way the results are *tabled and graphed*. Let's save the fancy stuff for the doctoral students."

And then,...

CAATS WORKSHEETS

CAATS STEP 5—WORKSHEET #5.1
Assessment Specifications

Explanation:

Fill in the cells based on the guidance in the chapter.

Content	Standards assessed:	
	Instrument types:	
	Use of multiple measures for decisions:	
Format	Components of each instrument:	
	Decision points/scale:	
Scoring	Computer or rater:	
	Personnel:	
	Exemplars and training:	

CAATS STEP 5—WORKSHEET #5.2

Analysis of Appropriateness of Decisions for Teacher Failures

Explanation:

Identify all of the teachers who were counseled out of the program or simply failed. Summarize the results of their assessments and confirm that an appropriate decision was made to counsel them out of the program. Calculate the percentage of each protected population that was counseled out and determine if it was more than 80% of the members of that population enrolled in your institution or district.

Year: _____

Name	Gender	Ethnicity	Handicapping Condition	Cumulative Data Summary	Correct Decision
					Yes No
					Yes No
					Yes No
					Yes No
					Yes No
					Yes No
					Yes No
					Yes No
					Yes No

Females: ____ Total enrolled   ____ % Failed   ____ yes ____ no 80% rule problem

Minorities: ____ Total enrolled   ____ % Failed   ____ yes ____ no 80% rule problem

Disabled: ____ Total enrolled   ____ % Failed   ____ yes ____ no 80% rule problem

CAATS WORKSHEETS

CAATS STEP 5—WORKSHEET #5.3
Analysis of Rehire Data

Explanation:

Identify all of the teachers who were not eligible for rehire. This includes those teachers who left for reasons other than personal reasons (moved, changed careers, had a family). The reason in this case is typically "fired" but districts often cannot reveal the reasons. Calculate the percentage of teachers in each certification area (or by whatever categories you need) who are not eligible for rehire.

Year: _____

Teacher Name	Certification Area	District of Employment*	Eligible for Rehire
			Yes No
			Yes No
			Yes No
			Yes No
			Yes No
			Yes No
			Yes No
			Yes No
			Yes No

*Districts might want to substitute in-state/out-of-state, alternative/college-based certificate, graduating institution, or any other useful data.

CAATS WORKSHEETS

CAATS STEP 5—WORKSHEET #5.4
Program Improvement Record

Explanation:

Record the mean rating for each criterion and make a determination about whether or not improvement is needed. Keep a running record of those improvements, noting the reason why improvements were not made if such is the case.

Criterion	Mean Rating	Improvement Needed	Improvement Made/Date
		Yes No	
		Yes No	
		Yes No	
		Yes No	
		Yes No	
		Yes No	
		Yes No	
		Yes No	
		Yes No	

CAATS WORKSHEETS

CAATS STEP 5—WORKSHEET #5.5
Expert Rescoring

Explanation:

Record each rater's score, noting differences. If any raters are markedly different from their colleagues, discuss these differences with the rater, attempting to bring him or her into line with the others.

Instrument Name: _____

Criterion	Rater 1	Rater 2	Rater 3	Analysis of Differences

Conference Report

Date: _____

Rater: _____

Counselor: _____

Summary of Conversation: _____

_____

CAATS STEP 5—WORKSHEET #5.6
Fairness Review

Explanation:

Each reviewer should complete a worksheet for each task.

Instrument: _____

Reviewer Name: _____

If the criterion or item is found to be offensive, please suggest modifications in the third column.

Criterion or Item	Offensive	Suggested Modification
	Yes No	
	Yes No	
	Yes No	
	Yes No	
	Yes No	
	Yes No	
	Yes No	
	Yes No	
	Yes No	

CAATS WORKSHEETS

CAATS STEP 5—WORKSHEET #5.7

Analysis of Remediation Efforts and EO Impact

Explanation:

For each teacher from a protected population who required assistance, record the results of the remediation efforts. Then make a judgment about whether improved remedial opportunities are needed.

Name	Gender/ Ethnicity	Handicapping Condition	Date	Problem and Remediation Efforts	Failed
					Yes No
					Yes No
					Yes No
					Yes No
					Yes No
					Yes No
					Yes No

Remediation Efforts Sufficient?   ____ yes ____ no

Improvements Suggested:

Completer Name and Signature: _____

CAATS STEP 5—WORKSHEET #5.8
Psychometric Plan Format

Explanation:

Complete each cell based on the readings in the chapter.

Purpose of System	
Use of Data	
Construct Measured	Teacher Performance
Conceptual Framework	
Interpretation and Reporting of Scores	

Assessment Specifications
    Content Map
    Format
    Scoring Procedures	

Assessor/Rater Selection and Training Procedures	
Analysis Methodology	
External Review Personnel and Methodology	
Evidence of Validity, Reliability, and Fairness	

CAATS WORKSHEETS

CAATS STEP 5—EXAMPLE #1
Logistic Ruler for Content Validity

Since most tasks do not have the same number of criteria in each rubric, it would be difficult to rank order the tasks in terms of difficulty based on teachers' total scores. A Rasch ruler, however, takes care of that, if one has an advance conceptualization of what to expect in terms of difficulty. The concept-mapping process provides a powerful tool to facilitate such a process. Mark Wilson (2005) describes it well, highlighting that it provides "a coherent and substantive definition for the content" (p. 28) by creating a continuum for measuring both items and people.

In this example, we have listed tasks in order of expected difficulty or complexity, with the most difficult on top. Note that the tasks are clustered in categories. In the two example rulers that follow, the map on the right is aligned with the ordering and shows good coverage of the concept—no big gaps. It provides good evidence of validity. The map on the left shows gaps in coverage and problems with the ordering. Assessment designers need to rethink the map or look for problems causing some tasks to be easier than expected and others to be harder. For example, are there problems in the directions, rubrics, or judges' ratings?

Task 1	difficult
Tasks 2, 10	moderately difficult
Tasks 3, 6, 8, 9	moderately easy
Tasks 4, 5, 7	easy

(Continued)

```
TABLE 12.2 Sample Test for Rasch Demonstation ZOU855ws.txt Apr 16 15:17 2006

INPUT: 10 persons, 10 items MEASURED: 10 persons, 10 items, 2 CATS 3.57.2
```

Item Logistic Ruler with a Gap in a Critical Region of Measurement	Item Logistic Ruler with No Gap in a Critical Region of Measurement

```
   persons MAP OF TASKs              persons MAP OF TASKs
        <more>|<rare>                     <more>|<rare>
    71          + TASK2            68          +T TASK1
    70          +                  67      XX  +
    69      XX  +                  66          +
    68          +                  65          +
    67          +                  64          +
    66          +                  63          +
    65          +                  62          +
    64          +                  61          + TASK10
    63          S+                 60          +
    62      X   +S                 59          S+S
    61          +                  58          +
    60          + TASK1 TASK3 TASK5  57        +
    59          +                  56      X   + TASK2
    58          +                  55          +
    57      X   +                  54          +
    56          +                  53          +
    55          +                  52          + TASK9
    54          +                  51          +
    53          +                  50      X   M+M
    52      XX  M+                 49          + TASK3 TASK6
    51          +                  48          +
    50          +M                 47          +
    49          +                  46      XX  + TASK8
    48          +                  45          +
    47          +                  44          +
    46          +                  43      XXX + TASK4 TASK7
    45          +                  42          +
    44          +                  41          S+S
    43          + TASK6 I0010      40      X   +
    42      XX  +                  39          +
    41      S+                     38          +
    40          +                  37          +
    39          + TASK7 TASK9      36          +
    38      XX  +S                 35          + TASK5
    37          +                       <less>|<frequ>
    36          +
    35          +
    34          + TASK4 TASK8
        <less>|<frequ>
```

> Tasks 3 and 5 are supposed to be easy!?! This is the hard end of the ruler.

> In this important center region of the ruler, this set has **no tasks!** This means that the error for scores on people in the center region will be large— a problem for both validity and reliability.

> This set has a dispersion of tasks in the center area of person difficulty which greatly improves the accuracy and precision of reported scores. It also validates the concept mapping, since the tasks are in the order predicted.

> These items are too easy to be useful in terms of scaling, but they do help with certification.

CAATS EXAMPLES

CAATS STEP 5—EXAMPLE #2

Computation of the Lawshe (1975) Content Validity Ratio

The content validity ratio (CVR) can be used to quantify the extent to which a panel of expert judges thinks each task is critically important. In this example, 10 judges (a mixture of NBPTS teachers, school district supervisory personnel, and university faculty) were given a performance task being considered for inclusion on a teacher certification performance assessment. They were asked to rate the task as follows:

- Essential job function
- Useful but not essential job function
- Not necessary for the job

Results in this example: Our experts rated the task: 8 essential, 2 useful, 0 not necessary

Here's how to calculate the CVR for this task: *ne=number of essential ratings.*

$$CVR = \frac{ne - (N/2)}{(N/2)} = \frac{8 - (10/2)}{10/2} = (8 - 5)/5 = .6$$

Conclusion: Since a CVR that is greater than .50 is considered acceptable and the CVR on this task was .60, we can be comfortable using this task as one that is critical in our assessment system.

Examples to Try

Here are some examples for you to practice computing. What would your decision be about the criticality of each task?

N (Number of experts)	ne (Number of essential ratings)	Number of useful ratings	Number of not necessary ratings	CVR*
11	7	3	1	
20	18	1	1	
14	10	2	2	
10	7	0	3	
15	11	4	0	

*CVR answers = .27, .8, .42, .4, .53

CAATS STEP 5—EXAMPLE #3
Disparate Impact Analysis

Checking for disparate impact is relatively simple using a variety of free online calculators. It helps to use these calculators because the calculation is not as straightforward as it appears, and a statistical test of significance is helpful in decision making. The decision rule is based on what is called the 80% rule, which requires that protected populations succeed at a rate that is at least 80% of the success rate of the majority population. So, we have percents of percents.

Protected populations include women, minorities, and disabled persons. In this example, we use an online calculator that is designed for employment selection, but the process works the same way for certification decisions. So that you can see behind the scenes the "percent of percent" calculations, we will work the numbers for you first in our own tables, and then show you the computer-generated output that does the chi-square analysis report for you. To help you find the percent on which the 80% rule is to be calculated, we put it in bold italics.

We entered data for 111 teachers for the year 2005–2006 based on our definition of program completers/noncompleters as follows:

- Completers included all of those teachers for whom an affirmative certification decision was made.
- Noncompleters included all of those prospective teachers who were denied certification or dropped out of the program.

Gender

	Total		Completer		Noncompleter	
	#	%	#	%	#	%
Male	19	17	18	**95**	1	5
Female	92	83	87	95	5	5
Total	111		105		6	

Decision Rule: Males have a 95% certification rate; females should have 80% of that rate or a 76% rate. Since 95% of the females were certified, the 80% rule was upheld.

(Continued)

(Continued)

CAATS EXAMPLES

Ethnicity

	Total		Completer		Noncompleter	
	#	%	#	%	#	%
Majority	99	89	99	**100**	0	0
Minority	12	11	6	50	6	50
Total	111		105		6	

Decision Rule: The majority population has a 100% certification rate; minorities should have 80% of that rate—still 80%. Since only 50% were certified, the 80% rule was *not* upheld.

Disability

	Total		Completer		Noncompleter	
	#	%	#	%	#	%
Nondisabled	109	98	103	**95**	6	5
Disabled	2	2	2	100	0	0
Total	111		105		6	

Decision Rule: The nondisabled population has a 95% certification rate; disabled should have 80% of that or 76%—same as for gender. The certification rate is 100%, so the 80% rule is upheld.

Conclusion: Out of 111 teachers, 6 teachers were not certified, and all were minorities. This indicates a disparate impact that needs to be addressed. A chi-square statistical analysis confirms that the minority disparity is statistically significant. The analysis is on the opposite page.

Chi-Square Report

Observed Expected	Selected	Not Selected	Row Totals
Males	18 17.973	1 1.027	19
Females	87 87.027	5 4.973	92
Column Total	105	6	111

Chi-square = 0.0009
The value of the statistic is less than 3.841. This indicates that there is a 95% chance that these results have been obtained absent any form of bias. Therefore, you may conclude that *these results fall within normal random variations and are not the result of bias.*

Observed Expected	Selected	Not Selected	Row Totals
Nonminorities	99 93.6486	0 5.3514	99
Minorities	6 11.3514	6 0.6486	12
Column Total	105	6	111

Chi-square = 52.3286
The value of the statistic is greater than 6.635. This indicates that there is a less than 1% chance that these results would have been obtained absent any form of bias. Therefore, *you may conclude that these results may have been the result of bias.*

Observed Expected	Selected	Not Selected	Row Totals
Nondisabled	103 103.1081	6 5.8919	109
Disabled	2 1.8919	0 0.1081	2
Column Total	105	6	111

Chi-square = 0.1164
The value of the statistic is less than 3.841. This indicates that there is a 95% chance that these results have been obtained absent any form of bias. Therefore, *you may conclude that these results fall within normal random variations and are not the result of bias.*

The URL is in the public domain, and you can use it for your computations as well. We have reproduced the results from this URL: http://www.hr-software.net/EmploymentStatistics/DisparateImpact.htm.

CAATS EXAMPLES

CAATS EXAMPLES

CAATS STEP 5—EXAMPLE #4

Computation of Cohen's Kappa (1960) for Inter-Rater Reliability

Kappa is a statistic that can be used as a measure of inter-rater reliability. It ranges from 0 to 1.0, like all correlations. The usual expectation is that a kappa > .70 is desired for adequate reliability. In this example, two judges each rated 36 teacher performance tasks on a three-category rating scale (exemplary, acceptable, and unacceptable). Here are the steps we go through to calculate kappa:

Step 1: Enter the raw data into a table by placing a tally mark into the cell that corresponds to the two judges' ratings. In the example, we tally the ratings for nine examples only, skipping tasks 8 to 34. After you finish placing all of the tally marks in the cell, count them and enter them into the table in Step 2.

Task Number:	1	2	3	4	5	6	7	(Tasks 8 to 34)	35	36
Rater # 1:	E	E	U	U	E	E	E	(Scores)	A	U
Rater # 2:	E	A	U	U	E	A	A	(Scores)	A	U

Rater #1 Across > Rater # 2 Down $\bigvee$	Exemplary	Acceptable	Unacceptable
Exemplary	‖		
Acceptable	⫴		
Unacceptable			⫴

Step 2: Fill in the total counts per cell plus the row totals **(RT)** and column totals **(CT)**:

Rater #1 Across > Rater # 2 Down $\bigvee$	Exemplary	Acceptable	Unacceptable	Row Totals (RT) $\bigvee$
Exemplary	13 **(8.97)**	4	0	17
Acceptable	6	10 **(6.22)**	0	16
Unacceptable	0	0	3 **(.25)**	3
Column Totals (CT) >	19	14	3	*36* *Grand Total (GT)*

Step 3: Compute total number of rater agreements by summing the diagonal cells: 13 + 10 + 3 = 26

Step 4: Compute the expected frequencies (Ef) for each diagonal cell.

$$\text{Ef(cell 11)} = \frac{RT * CT}{GT} = \frac{17 * 19}{36} = 8.97$$

$$\text{Ef(cell 22)} = \frac{RT * CT}{GT} = \frac{16 * 14}{36} = 6.22$$

$$\text{Ef(cell 33)} = \frac{RT * CT}{GT} = \frac{3 * 3}{36} = .25$$

Step 5: Sum the expected frequencies (Ef): 8.97 + 6.22 + .25 = 15.44

Step 6: Compute kappa: $\kappa = \dfrac{\sum diagonal - \sum ef}{N - \sum ef} = \dfrac{26 - 15.44}{36 - 15.44} = .51$

Step 7: Since the obtained K is less than .70, we decide that the inter-rater reliability is *not* good.

Conclusion: The news is not all bad, though! Our judges are in agreement about what constitutes unacceptable work, so we are comfortable with our cut score since it is based on that decision. In fact, we have 100% agreement (K=1.0) for the decision of certify/do not certify. Where we have a problem is in differentiating between acceptable and exemplary. Note that we have an equal amount of agreement and disagreement about the acceptable rating (10 the same and 10 different). This inconsistency is reflected in the kappa and calls for improvement in either the rater training or rubric refinement at the exemplary and acceptable levels.

Examples to Try

Here's a table of data filled in. You can calculate the kappa yourself and then reach some conclusions about your results:

Rater #1 Across > Rater # 2 Down VVV	Exemplary	Acceptable	Unacceptable	Row Totals (RT) VVV
Exemplary	44	5	1	
Acceptable	7	20	3	
Unacceptable	9	5	6	
Column Totals (CT) >>>				Grand Total (GT)
Categories = 3, N = 100				

You can go to http://faculty.vassar.edu/lowry/kappa.html and find a kappa calculator.

CAATS EXAMPLES

CAATS STEP 5—EXAMPLE #5

Spearman Correlation Coefficient and Scatterplot: System Scores and GPA

Suppose we had 10 students who were scored on a 3-point scale: Unacceptable = 1, Acceptable = 2, and Exemplary = 3. There were 12 tasks in the assessment system. The total number of points would range from 12 to 36. Because the data are ordinal level, we use the Spearman rank-order correlation (rho). In this example, we see a correlation that is good, $r = .81$, which provides convergent validity evidence for our assessment system.

Student	Total Ratings Points	GPA
Jane	35	4.0
Joe	30	3.8
Sam	22	3.5
George	29	3.3
Scarlett	29	3.1
Daryl	18	2.1
Anne	31	4.0
Mike	30	4.0
Bill	28	3.1
Tom	32	3.6

Spearman correlation matrix

	RATING	*GPA*
RATING	1.000	
GPA	0.808	1.000

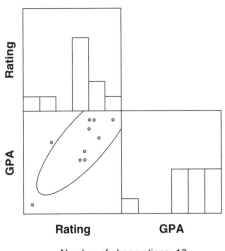

Number of observations: 10
Created with Systat Software

CAATS STEP 5—EXAMPLE #6

Pearson Correlation Coefficient and Scatterplot: System Scores and Praxis

Suppose we had 10 students who were measured on a Rasch ruler scaled from 0 to 100. They also took a Praxis test in elementary content. Because the data are interval level, we use the Pearson product moment correlation. In this example, we see a correlation that is good, $r = .88$, which provides convergent validity evidence for our assessment system.

Student	Rasch Ruler Measure	Praxis Score
Jane	76	190
Joe	41	170
Sam	54	176
George	77	188
Scarlett	60	189
Daryl	50	175
Anne	51	170
Mike	56	172
Bill	39	160
Tom	66	180

Pearson correlation matrix

	MEASURE	PRAXIS
MEASURE	1.000	
PRAXIS	0.883	1.000

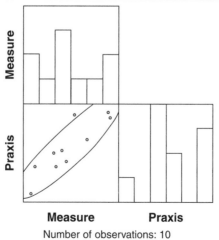

Number of observations: 10

Figure created with Systat Software

CAATS EXAMPLES

CAATS STEP 5—EXAMPLE #7

Correlation Matrix and Scatterplots: Knowledge, Impact, Dispositions, Skills (KIDS)

Suppose we had 30 teachers who were scored on a series of assessments in a framework. Scores are reported here on a fictitious Rasch ruler, but they could also be summed raw scores. The framework is the INTASC Principles, where each task is organized by the type of evidence (we changed the traditional order to make a statement—but it is knowledge, skills, dispositions, and impact). A correlation matrix and set of scatterplots reveal relationships.

Name	Knowledge (Certification Test)	Skills (All Tasks)	Impact (TWSM)	Dispositions (Behavior Checklist)
Cathy	74.6	70.8	56.1	55.1
Debbie	75.6	74.6	88.9	83.0
Don	75.7	75.6	75.5	79.6
Ed	81.0	97.5	92.3	99.8
Fred	80	81.0	97.1	96.5
George	74.9	72.9	88.4	88.3
Henry	66.1	64.0	73.5	68.5
Ike	65.0	66.4	111	123.4
Jan	123.4	123.4	97.1	96.7
Karen	70.2	67.4	54.3	57.0
Lacey	64.6	64.4	74.9	76.5
Mike	100.5	102.4	80.9	81.5
Margaret	81.6	84.5	77.5	71.5
Nancy	95.8	89.5	66.1	64.8
Oprah	91.5	95.8	81.5	88.9
Paul	57.0	95.8	75.6	71.5
Quincy	84.5	89.5	66.1	60.5
Rita	81.5	95.8	74.0	71.1
Steve	123.4	115.7	57.0	63.5
Tom	81.5	89.5	80.1	81.5
Ulysses	111.6	123.4	96.5	97.6
Valarie	123.1	123.4	92.2	97.6
William	74.6	70.8	56.1	55.1
Xenia	75.6	74.6	88.9	83.0
Yianni	75.7	75.6	75.5	79.6

Name	Knowledge (Certification Test)	Skills (All Tasks)	Impact (TWSM)	Dispositions (Behavior Checklist)
Zach	81.0	97.5	92.3	99.8
Cathy	80.5	81.0	97.1	96.5
Debbie	74.9	72.9	88.4	88.3
Don	66.1	64.7	73.5	68.5
Ed	65.3	66.4	111.3	123.4
Fred	123.4	123.4	97.1	96.7

Pearson correlation matrix

	KNOWLEDGE	SKILLS	IMPACT	DISPOSITIONS
KNOWLEDGE	1.000			
SKILLS	0.876	1.000		
IMPACT	0.131	0.207	1.000	
DISPOSITIONS	0.177	0.230	0.948	1.000

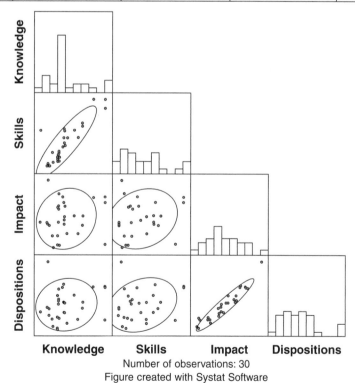

Number of observations: 30
Figure created with Systat Software

Knowledge is correlated with skills, and dispositions are correlated with impact. This is revealed in the correlation coefficients in the table, as well as in the scatterplots.

CAATS STEP 5—EXAMPLE #8

t-Test Comparing Mathematics and Science Teachers Performance

Suppose we had 150 teachers, 75 in mathematics and 75 in science, who were scored on a series of assessments in a framework. Here we want to see if there is a significant difference in their overall performance, based on their mean scores. Group 1, the math teachers, has a higher mean score than Group 2, the science teachers, by approximately five points. The difference is significant at the .015 level. We can conclude, therefore, that math teachers are performing better than science teachers, and we can review instructional strategies and differences in assessment tasks to determine if that accounts for the difference in performance results.

```
Two-sample t-test on MEASURE grouped by GROUP against Alternative =
'not equal'
```

Group	N	Mean	SD
1	75	92.361	13.909
2	75	87.534	9.595

```
Separate variance:
Difference in means = 4.828
95.00% CI = 0.968 to 8.687
t = 2.474
df = 131.4
p-value = 0.015
Pooled variance:
Difference in means = 4.828
95.00% CI = 0.972 to 8.683
t = 2.474
df = 148
p-value = 0.014
```

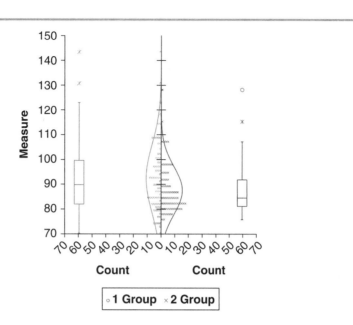

Figure created with Systat Software

Here are the item measures correlated from the first administration to the second, indicating stability on the ruler despite the different sample of people.

	ITEM1	ITEM2
ITEM1	1.000	
ITEM2	0.805	1.000

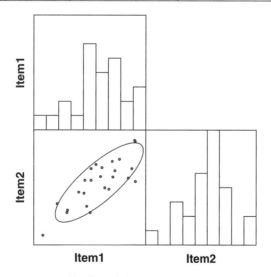

Number of observations: 25

Figure created with Systat Software

CAATS STEP 5—EXAMPLE #9

An Example of DIF and Detection of Bias in Item Responses Using the Rasch Model

Differential item functioning, or DIF, is a statistical process that seeks to determine if there are meaningful differences in the way *subgroups* perform, particularly groups that are classified as protected—women and minorities. It is okay for the performance to be different, as long as it is not because of *problems in the construction or administration* of the assessment itself. Smith (2004) describes the independent sample *t*-test method as a well-documented approach to detecting item bias.

In this example, we look at the results of a DIF analysis on a preschool readiness test of 52 items given to 470 children. The test is performance based and the test taker has to point, draw, answer verbally, or demonstrate knowledge and skills. A test administrator gives the test and scores the responses by observation. The test is provided in three languages: English, Spanish, and French.

We present a total of three tables or analyses, each one looking at the mean results for different populations. In this first analysis, we look for difference caused by translation. The second looks at different ethnic backgrounds; the third looks at both genders.

Each table is organized the same way, so we will explain the tables only one time and then give only the results for the second and third tables.

A complete DIF analysis would look at every item on the test or task in the system; we are only looking at a small sample here.

```
TABLE 30.1 Lollipop Test Analysis Three Languages ZOU355ws.txt Apr 25 22:59 2006

INPUT: 478 persons, 104 items MEASURED: 470 persons, 52 items, 42 CATS 3.57.2
```

DIF class specification is: DIF=$S12W1; **Analysis of LANGUAGE BIAS in TEST TRANSLATION**

person CLASS	DIF MEASURE	DIF S.E.	person CLASS	DIF MEASURE	DIF S.E.	DIF CONTRAST	JOINT S.E.	t	d.f.	item Prob.	Number	Name
E	29.31	3.33	F	33.52	2.77	-4.21	4.33	-.97	426	.3311	1	Item 1
E	29.31	3.33	S	46.08	4.18	-16.77	5.34	-3.14	239	*.0019*	1	**Item 1**
F	33.52	2.77	S	46.08	4.18	-12.55	5.02	-2.50	269	*.0129*	1	**Item 1**

Item 1 is compared by all possible pairs of languages of the test taker in the person CLASS: E = English, F = French, S = Spanish. The items are identical except for language. Here, the Spanish version of the item appears to be significantly more difficult than the English and French, which were not significantly different.

Bias Analysis #1—Language: p < .05

- Columns 1 and 4—Person Class provides the language of the test—the test taker's native language. Coding is English (E), French (F), or Spanish (S).

- Columns 2 and 5—DIF Measure provides the mean (average) scale score of Item 1 in each of three languages; English = 29.31, French = 33.52, Spanish = 46.08. Higher is harder.

- Columns 3 and 6—DIF S.E. are the standard error of the measures found in columns 2 and 5. We can add and subtract one S.E. from a child's obtained measure to estimate the score s/he would earn if retested.

- Column 7—DIF contrast is the difference between the means of the different language scale measures in paired comparisons; English-French, English-Spanish, French-Spanish.

- Columns 9 and 11—The *t* statistic of significance is a unit normal deviate. A value (*p*) less than .05 is the traditional level of statistical significance. In this case, a probability of .0019 (which is less than .05) indicates that the contrast between English and Spanish of −16.77 is statistically significant. The contrast between French and Spanish of −12.55 is also statistically significant. Typically, we only investigate contrasts that are statistically significant although Smith (2005) warns against the strict use of preset cutoffs due to Type I error.

- Column 10 (*df*) are the degrees of freedom used for the statistical analysis.

- The last two columns simply give the item number and name, which in this case is "Item 1."

Conclusion: Item 1 may be culturally loaded and needs to be reconsidered as potentially biased with Spanish-speaking children, since the difficulty should be the same for both populations. A revision or replacement item may be necessary.

```
DIF class specification is: DIF=$S13W1; Analysis of ETHNIC ORIGIN BIAS of TEST TAKER
```

person CLASS	DIF MEASURE	DIF S.E.	person CLASS	DIF MEASURE	DIF S.E.	DIF CONTRAST	JOINT S.E.	t	d.f.	item Prob.	Number	Name
B	30.24	6.19	H	39.06	3.09	−8.82	6.92	−1.27	153	.2045	5	Item 3
B	30.24	6.19	O	39.36	7.17	−9.12	9.47	−.96	64	.3392	5	Item 3
B	30.24	6.19	W	42.84	1.78	−12.60	6.44	−1.95	343	*.0515*	5	*Item 3*
H	39.06	3.09	O	39.36	7.17	−.30	7.81	−.04	123	.9695	5	Item 3
H	39.06	3.09	W	42.84	1.78	−3.77	3.57	−1.06	402	.2912	5	Item 3
O	39.36	7.17	W	42.84	1.78	−3.47	7.38	−.47	313	.6384	5	Item 3

Item 3 is compared by all possible pairs of Ethnic Origin of the test taker in the person CLASS: B = Black, H = Hispanic, W = White, O = Oriental.

(Continued)

(Continued)

Bias Analysis #2—Ethic Origin Bias: p< .05

Here is the second analysis for the test. In this analysis, we look for differences that can be attributed to ethnic loading on Item 3. The ethnicity of test takers is coded as: B = Black, H = Hispanic, W = White, and O = Oriental. In this analysis, we note that the only statistically significant result is the comparison between Blacks and Whites ($p = .0515$) and about 13 scale points. The other contrasts are much less in terms of the scale points (not more than 3 points) and are, therefore, not statistically significant.

Conclusion: The cultural loading for Item 3 needs to be reconsidered as potentially biased for Blacks. A revision or replacement item may be necessary.

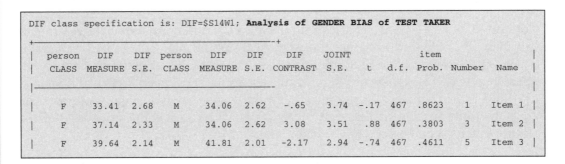

```
DIF class specification is: DIF=$S14W1; Analysis of GENDER BIAS of TEST TAKER

+                          -+
| person   DIF    DIF  person   DIF    DIF    DIF    JOINT              item              |
| CLASS  MEASURE  S.E.  CLASS  MEASURE  S.E.  CONTRAST  S.E.   t   d.f. Prob. Number  Name |
|                                                                                         |
|   F     33.41   2.68    M    34.06   2.62   -.65    3.74  -.17  467  .8623    1   Item 1 |
|   F     37.14   2.33    M    34.06   2.62   3.08    3.51   .88  467  .3803    3   Item 2 |
|   F     39.64   2.14    M    41.81   2.01  -2.17    2.94  -.74  467  .4611    5   Item 3 |
```

Bias Analysis #3—Gender Bias: p< .05

This is the final analysis, and no cultural loading for gender was found; there are no statistically significant results for Items 1, 2, or 3 as examined by gender contrast.

Conclusion: Items 1, 2, and 3 do not appear to be gender biased, and no revisions are suggested by the analysis.

8

The Trouble With Tribbles

Standard Setting for Professional Certification

$\mathcal{T}$here is probably no aspect of the assessment system design process that makes state-level testing and certification personnel more nervous than the need to establish the line that separates those who are allowed to move forward from those who are denied. It is an oft-forgotten aspect of the assessment system design process for university-level personnel. So, we devote an entire chapter to it—where we have been to date and why we will propose a new methodology as part of the CAATS model. If you want to understand standard setting and cut scores, consider taking your meds and read the entire chapter. This chapter should prove to be an eye-opener for you.

Cut-score setting occurs in every high-stakes testing situation, whether it is traditional (objective) paper-and-pencil tests or performance-based tests. Certification exams and K–12 NCLB tests are examples of the standardized objective type. Authentic assessment by products and observation in the professions are examples of performance assessments. Much has been written about how to set standards, or cut scores, probably more than you want or need to know. Berk (1995) concludes there are nearly 50 standard-setting methods documented in the literature. In fact, there are numerous studies and meta-analyses of cut-score setting that are described along with a variety of modifications of each method (Berk, 1986, 1995; Bontempo, et al., 1998; Livingston & Zieky, 1982; Marks, & Karabatsos, Hambleton, Jaeger, Plake, & Mills, 2000).

Our chapter title alludes to the famous Star Trek (Gerrold, 1973) television show episode, where the starship Enterprise is overwhelmed by seemingly innocent and adorable little tribbles. The crew eventually learns that their uncontrolled breeding becomes a threat to the very existence of the crew. Berk (1995) sets the stage well for a review of cut-score setting methodologies that reminds of us this episode. He wrote the following:

> Truckloads of articles, pamphlets, and book chapters have been published on the topic of standard setting. When charged with the task of executing a particular standard-setting method, executors throughout the land have exhibited high blood pressure, high anxiety, ulcers, and, in one case, even hairballs.

> Due to these possible physiological effects of standard setting, it has been suggested that some professionals who are involved in the standard-setting process seriously consider taking the new medication STANDARDSET® (generic name is CUTSCOR) (Berk, 1995, p. 11).

Despite the "truckloads" of advice, some would say that there is no easy answer about how to do this. Take heart, though; we have established the ambitious goal of creating one for our readers. We will propose a rather radical, but very simple, approach that is logically and intuitively appropriate. Before doing so, however, we need to provide as simple an explanation of the state of the art as we can so our readers can make an informed decision about whether or not they are comfortable in trying our method. We begin with some basic explanations and examples of the existing methodologies and continue with some quotes from the best of the literature that provide support for something new and easier. Should we pique your curiosity about some of the methods we describe, the reference section at the end of the book shows you where to go to read more. We will attempt to show that what appears easy can quickly get out of hand and often results in undesirable decisions after following all the traditional rules precisely. As such, a new beginning is appropriate.

AN OVERVIEW OF CURRENT CUT-SCORE SETTING

In a world of standards, standardized tests, and accountability, there is an expectation that students and teachers meet some standard of proficiency. Tests are written to measure the level of proficiency. Once established, as tradition would have it, a standard is translated into a cut score in order to separate examinees that meet the standard, or have mastered it or are proficient at it, from those who do not (Ricker, 2003).

From Norm-Referenced Objective Tests to Criterion-Referenced Subjective Tasks

Historically, the standard-setting or cut-score process has its roots in a method proposed by Nedelsky in 1954, and subsequently modified by Angoff (1971) and Ebel (1972). This family of models, and all of its variations, is now collectively called the Angoff model. We describe it below. We note from the outset that in 1954 and for about 40 years, testing was primarily accomplished with paper-and-pencil instruments, also called objective tests, usually of the multiple-choice format. Sampling of specific demographics representing a particular population was important, and answers were scored right or wrong (dichotomous scoring). Normative, rather than criterion-referenced, scoring was the goal.

In the early 1990s, things starting changing. Performance assessment became the rage, along with accountability and new kinds of standards. The creation of a national certification process for accomplished teachers by the National Board of Professional Teaching Standards (NBPTS) and their performance-based portfolio process called for a new kind of cut-score setting methodology in a criterion-referenced environment. We will attempt to briefly take you through this evolution. First, there are three contextual factors we need to describe that influence all cut-score setting methodologies and their use: controlling human judgment, difficulty vs. importance, and social consequences of raising the bar.

Controlling Human Judgment

As we begin the history lesson, it is critical to understand that there is no argument in the literature countering the fact that all cut-score setting methods are based on human judgment. Every article we reference in this section confirms that. All methods require the convening of a panel of expert judges who render decisions about the relationship between test content and examinee expected or observed performance. All analysts concur that the selection and training of the judges is the most critical aspect of establishing valid and reliable cut scores. At least we have agreement on one thing! In fact, until 1999, the only standard established in the *Standards of Educational Psychological Testing* related to judge selection and training. Now there are three standards dedicated to this important activity. (See the *Standards* referenced at the end of the Chapter 6 section on CAATS Step 4B.) Analyses of the models by Livingston and Ziesky (1982) and Hambleton (1998) indicate that the critical elements of the judgmental process are:

- Selection of competent judges

- Training the judges

- Collecting the judgments

- Combining the judgments to derive a cut score

In each method of cut-score setting proposed in the literature, including ours, judges are asked to visualize the minimally competent test taker. This concept is so fundamental to the process that we are asked by those creating the newest methodologies for NBPTS to visualize the "just barely competent" "accomplished teacher." We have separated these two phrases, since they are separated in the articles we have collected for you. There's even an acronym out there for the first part of it— JBC. We ask you now only to pause for a minute before we start throwing these models at you and reflect on what that pair of phrases means in less jargonistic terms—would that be "minimally excellent"? Read the phrases one more time before moving on: "just barely competent" "accomplished teacher." You are now thinking like the judges who set the cut scores. You may be ready for your first dose of the medicine Berk called STANDARDSET®?

Difficulty vs. Importance

There is another piece we need to add to your frame of reference as you read through the various methodologies. All methods have at their core a fundamental belief that the more difficult the item or task, the higher the degree of competency needed to get it right. We call it *item difficulty* (symbolized p). It is simply the proportion of folks answering correctly, often just a raw count. Theoretically speaking, the more competent the person is, the better s/he should do on the test or task, and vice versa. Highly competent people have a better chance of getting a difficult item or task correct. The less competent they are, the less likely they are to do it right. You may be pausing now, thinking to yourself, "That's just common sense." You are correct.

In terms of cut-score setting, judges are asked about the *proportion* of minimally competent examinees that *should* get an item right. Difficulty trumps everything else, based on the concept that a test should be too difficult for the examinee that should not pass. Judges are asked, "How hard is the item?" not "How important is it?" As you progressed through this book, you saw that our focus is on criticality (or importance) not difficulty, so obviously, we present you with a somewhat biased rendition of cut-score setting theory.

We want teacher candidates to learn and get things right, because we want good teachers who are competent on the critical tasks of teaching—not hurdle jumpers. In the end, you will need to decide for yourself based on your educational philosophy. You will have to ask yourself: Which comes first—the chicken or the egg—difficulty or criticality? Clearly, now that you have read our focus on selecting only critical tasks for your assessment system, you can see how that is a major concern for us. We believe that criticality is more important than item difficulty.

As you think through that question, be aware that the construct of difficulty contains much room for error in making decisions about competency and cut scores. (Psychometricians don't like to admit that.) We will illustrate with an example that shows how difficulty is not just a function of content or examinee skill, but is also a function of item construction. Specifically, the item writer's quality of distracters clearly impacts who gets the item correct and who does not. In Table 8.1, we provide an example of how we can change the difficulty of an item by changing the distracters.

In the item analysis shown in Table 8.1, we see p values (the difficulty index or the proportion of folks who got it correct) varying from 1.0 to .75 to .50. The closer the distracters are to the correct answer, the harder the item. Same question, different results. Clearly the first set of responses makes the question much easier than the second set and then the third set. More people got the question correct, but this is not because they are more competent in history. Of course, the responses we chose exaggerate the issue, but the point should be clear. In standardized testing contexts, psychometricians would find and fix the distracters that no one selected. How many times have you tossed in a distracter just to fill up space on a test and because you couldn't think of anything else. Frequently, poor distracters creep their way into items and change the difficulty level of the item, even when psychometricians (who are mere mortals) work on the tests.

So, as you can see from the example shown in Table 8.1, the difficulty of the item or task (and the likelihood that a person will get it correct) is influenced by how well it is written and how competent the item writer is in anticipating wrong answers. You don't have to be smart to know that queens, popes, and cartoon characters are

Table 8.1. Sample Items With the Same Content but Different Levels of Difficulty		
The Question: Who was the northern President of the United States during the Civil War? *(Answer: Abraham Lincoln)*		
Response Options with Percent Correct in Parentheses after Each Response		
Donald Duck (0%) Queen Elizabeth (0%) Pope John Paul (0%) Abraham Lincoln (100%)	George Washington (25%) Queen Elizabeth (0%) Pope John Paul (0%) Abraham Lincoln (75%)	Jefferson Davis (12%) Ulysses S. Grant (13%) George Washington (25%) Abraham Lincoln (50%)
Item Analysis: $p = 1.0$	Item Analysis: $p = .75$	Item Analysis: $p = .50$
Conclusion: Version 1 is very easy; version 2 is moderately easy; version 3 is moderately difficult, based on the proportion (p) of people responding correctly.		

not presidents. You do have to know a little history to write an item about the Civil War that includes Jefferson Davis, Ulysses S. Grant, and George Washington. It's not just about whether the examinees should know the answer and how smart they are. It's about how smart the item writer is.

Now toss into this mix the need for norm-referenced scores. When a standardized test is being developed, test writers, based on field test results, may find the need to change the distribution of examinee scores. One way to do this is to select items that are more or less difficult. Another way is to rewrite some items to make them more or less difficult. Difficulty, and scores, can be controlled by item writers.

Social Consequences

We leave you with one more lens through which to filter these methodologies—a set of conclusions about cut-score setting in traditional teacher certification based on item difficulty reached by Berk in 1996 (p. 224):

1. Higher standards on tests for admission to teacher education programs would probably produce higher-quality teachers.

2. Higher standards on licensure tests would probably produce higher-quality teachers.

3. Higher standards on certification tests would probably produce higher-quality teachers.

4. Executing conclusions (1), (2), and (3) in every state would significantly curtail the supply of potential teachers and the gender and ethnic diversity of the teacher workforce.

Berk makes it pretty clear. Raising standards, based on difficulty, could have some dire social consequences. If your state and district are overloaded with qualified teachers already, then don't worry about it.

In Box 8.1, we leave you with three tidbits to remember about cut-score setting before delving into the details of how various approaches work.

Box 8.1. Tidbits to Remember About Cut-Score Setting Methods

To summarize, there are three points to remember as you read through the methods:

1. All cut-score setting is dependent on the subjective decisions of a panel of human judges. There's a lot of guessing and estimating in the process. If the judges cannot reach agreement or consensus, the cut score does not mean a whole lot.

2. All cut-score setting is based on the concept that difficulty and ability are related, but the process can be unduly influenced by how smart the item writers are.

3. Traditional methodologies for cut-score setting, which include setting the bar based on difficulty (and raising it), may produce fewer teachers.

CUT-SCORE SETTING IN TRADITIONAL, OBJECTIVE TESTS

Walter and Kapes (2003) provide a useful summary of the approaches and methods of cut-score setting for objective tests. They categorize the methodologies into three approaches and over 30 different methods. We summarize their work and add our own concerns and examples for each method in the next subsections to help you see how the traditional models work.

Holistic Impressions: Method One

This first method uses a panel of subject matter experts (at least 15 to 20 judges) who individually review the entire test and provide an estimate of what proportion of items overall should be answered correctly by the minimally competent person. The cut score is the mean proportion of all judges. In Box 8.2, we show you how the holistic impressions model works with a calculation.

Box 8.2. Example of Holistic Impressions Cut-Score Setting

Judge 1: 72%
Judge 2: 90%
Judge 3: 85%
Judge 4: 90%
Judge 5: 98%

Mean proportion or cut score: 85%

From our perspective , this methodology benefits and suffers from all of the same attributes as any holistic decision-making process. It yields an overall impression without the details to back it up. There's just a lot to keep in one's head. The primary issue is clear; the validity of most assessment decisions rests in the details.

Item Content: Method Two

A second method is designed for multiple-choice tests. There are typically four possible answers, with one correct and the others as distracters. This process can be split into three approaches, each of which has variations in practice, and all of which continue the focus on minimal competency:

Nedelsky (1954): A panel of judges reviews each item, crossing out the distracters that the minimally competent person should be able to eliminate (e.g., Donald Duck and Queen Elizabeth from our example). For each item, the reciprocal of the number of remaining responses becomes the basis for estimating item difficulty leading to an expected cut score. For example, if the minimally competent person would *not* pick one of the four choices, three remain, and the reciprocal is 1/3 or .33. In the Donald Duck example, the numbers would be 1/1 or 1.0—the *p*-value we obtained. All the reciprocals are added and the mean is calculated. Box 8.3 shows you an example of how the Nedelsky approach works.

Box 8.3. Example of Nedelsky Cut-Score Setting Approach

Judge 1 on a Five-Item Test with Four Response Options Only

Item 1: .33
Item 2: .75
Item 3: .50
Item 4: .50
Item 5: .67

Mean or cut score for Judge 1: .55 or 55%

From our viewpoint, this method requires quite a bit of work, which is probably why it was replaced with less labor-intensive versions. A test of 100 items in which each item had four response options would require 400 decisions—a lot to ask! And a whole lot of room for rater inconsistency.

Angoff (1971) provides a variation on Nedelsky's procedure. He suggested that each judge estimate the proportion of minimally competent individuals who would answer each item correctly. The resulting probabilities (*p*-values) are summed over each item for all judges with means calculated and then all items for the cut score. This is the most common approach currently used for cut-score setting in multiple-choice tests. Box 8.4 shows you an example of how the Angoff approach works.

Box 8.4. Example of Angoff Cut-Score Setting Approach

Test population: Second graders

Test decision: Progression to third grade

First Test Item: $2 + 3 = $ ___.

Judge 1: 89%
Judge 2: 90%
Judge 3: 100%
Judge 4: 95%
Judge 5: 80%
Average cut score for item: 91%

Second Test Item: $5 + 15 = $ ___.

Judge 1: 75%
Judge 2: 90%
Judge 3: 80%
Judge 4: 60%
Judge 5: 85%
Average cut score for item: 78%

Third Test Item: $98 + 12 = $ ___.

Judge 1: 45%
Judge 2: 50%
Judge 3: 35%
Judge 4: 40%
Judge 5: 35%
Average cut score for item: 41%

The test cut score (unscaled) for this three-item test is the average of 91%, 78%, and 41%, which comes to 70%.

In our view, which is widely shared in the literature, the chief difficulty here is envisioning 100 barely competent yet different teachers or other examinees, but this method does remove the difficulties of placing too much emphasis on the distracters. It became the foundation of all subsequent cut-score setting methods. So, Nedelsky started the trend toward thinking about "item difficulty" as the focal point; Angoff made it more realistic. Ebel, who developed the next variation, recognized that lack of focus on *importance or criticality,* and we turn to him next.

Ebel (1972) used a two-dimensional grid with each judge categorizing items two ways: essential, important, acceptable, and questionable in one dimension and easy, medium, and difficult in the other dimension. After all test items were categorized into their appropriate cell in the 12 grid categories, each judge estimates what proportion of items within each category a minimally competent person could answer. The average proportion over all items and judges would be the cut score. In Tables 8.2—8.4, we provide an example of Ebel's Cut-Score Setting Approach. In the first table, we show how one judge, Judge #1, classifies the 100 items on a test.

Next, in Table 8.3, we continue the Ebel approach by showing the calculations used to determine the cut-score for Judge #1.

In the last step of the Ebel process, we show in Box 8.5 the final cut-score calculation across all three judges.

Table 8.2. Example of Ebel's Cut-Score Setting Approach (Part I): Classification of Items by Judge #1

Number of items expected to be answered correctly on a 100-item test:

	Essential	Important	Acceptable	Questionable
Easy	20	15	10	2
Medium	10	15	5	2
Hard	5	10	5	1
Total = 100	35	40	20	5

Table 8.3. Example of Ebel's Cut-Score Setting Approach (Part II): Calculation of Cut Score for Judge #1

	Essential	Important	Acceptable	Questionable
Easy	$20 \times .90 = 18$	$15 \times .85 = 12.75$	$10 \times .60 = 6$	$2 \times .3 = .6$
Medium	$10 \times .75 = 7.5$	$15 \times .70 = 10.5$	$5 \times .40 = 2$	$2 \times .2 = .4$
Hard	$5 \times .50 = 2.5$	$10 \times .35 = 3.5$	$5 \times .25 = 1.25$	$1 \times .1 = .1$

$18 + 7.5 + 2.5 + 12.75 + 10.5 + 3.5 + 6 + 2 + 1.25 + .6 + .4 + .1 = 65.1$

Cut score for Judge #1 = 65.1

> ### Box 8.5. Example of Ebel's Cut-Score Setting Approach (Part III): Calculation of Final Cut Score for All Judges
>
> Judge 1: 65.1
> Judge 2: 67.8
> Judge 3: 75.3
> Cut Score: 69.4*
>
> *There should really be 10 to 20 judges, but you get the point!

Ebel was the first to introduce criticality into the approaches, but he introduced a level of complexity that did not take hold by attempting to scale the level of criticality on a 4-point scale. Another problem of concern to us is the failure to acknowledge that items of questionable importance should just be removed from the test—not weighted low. Why keep them at all? Finally, you would have to have 10 or more judges complete the above process. Whew!

Performance of Examinees: Method Three

This form of cut-score setting results from the consideration that subjective judgments using the previously described methods may result in unrealistic expectations—usually too high. The alternative suggested is to obtain actual performance data (Hambleton, 1998; Livingston & Zieky, 1982). Subject matter experts select individuals based on "known" levels of competency. There are two basic methods and one complex performance method:

Contrasting groups: One group of qualified and one group of unqualified individuals take the test, and scores are plotted on a continuum. The cut score is the point that produces the fewest misclassifications. The most obvious problem with this methodology is that it is hard to find a group of not qualified individuals to use. Would they be those teachers who were just fired for incompetence or the ones just counseled out of the program? So, this method is heavily sample dependent and a tad unrealistic in terms of implementation, so we don't even attempt an example here. If you are wondering how this example can work in practice, note that the work of Hambleton in 1998 was based on National Board Certification—where there really are folks teaching who did not make it but are still practicing in the profession. We do not have that "luxury" in initial certification.

Borderline groups: This method is a variation on contrasting groups. A single group of individuals is tested. This group falls into the "borderline" classification on competencies. The cut score is the median for the group. The same issue applies here—the lowest group is gone in initial certification. We also wonder about obtaining groups to test in low-incident classifications, such as French teachers or physics teachers. Institutions and districts are not likely to have enough teachers to use the model, although states might.

Decision theory: This method is a statistical variation similar to the above performance approaches even though it uses entirely different mathematics. The goal of decision theory is to make classification of new test takers accurate and efficient, assuming you have available the prior results from one of the previous approaches (which is not likely, given the above constraints of not having examinees who failed during the initial certification test). Here's a summary by Rudner (2002):

From pilot testing, one estimates:

1. The proportion of masters and nonmasters in the population, and

2. The conditional probabilities of examinees in each mastery state responding correctly to each item.

After the test is administered, one computes (based on the examinee's responses and the pilot data):

1. The likelihood of an examinee's response pattern for masters and nonmasters

2. The probabilities that the examinee is a master and the probability that the examinee is a nonmaster

Rudner (2002) explains that this technique is accurate in classifying examinees into categories such as master and nonmaster based on a small sample of pilot-tested candidates. The method is math intensive and still requires *a priori* determination of what constitutes a person considered competent, or the items correctly answered necessary to be competent. Again, we have a circular argument that depends on the original judgment.

Combination Approach: Method Four

Jaeger (1982) proposed a combination method, taking into account all three of the previous standard setting methods (holistic, item content, and examinee performance). His method uses the following steps:

1. Each item is rated as yes or no in terms of whether a competent person would select the correct response. "Yes" is counted as a 1 and "no" as a 0.

2. The number of yes or 1 responses is summed for all judges to establish a item difficulty or *p*-value for each item. For example, if 7 out of 10 judges say yes, the *p*-value is .70.

3. The test is then administered to a heterogeneous group (competent and not-competent), with actual *p*-values calculated (proportion of test takers getting each item correct). (Again, we have the problem of finding some not-competent teachers.)

4. Judges are asked if they want to reconsider their yes/no decision and the third *p*-value is calculated.

5. The cut score is the median *p*-value for all judges over all items.

In Table 8.4 we show the calculations for cut-score setting using Jaeger's approach.

Table 8.4. Example of Jaeger's Cut-Score Setting Approach		
Item #	*Number of yes decisions for all judges on their second rating*	*p-value*
1	7	.70
2	7	.70
3	7	.70
4	8	.80
5	8	.80
6	8	.80
7	8	.80
8	9	.90
9	9	.90
10	10	1.0
The cut score is the median value, or .80.		

We see two major contributions here from Jaeger. He introduced the opportunity for judges to talk to each other to make difficult decisions, and, even more important, he reduced the decision making to a yes/no process. The problem of having incompetent folks as a viable sample, though, remains troublesome for us.

Suffice it to say that, even with this limited review, there is a variety of methods, but all have some issues that make them less than useful given the time and resources necessary to implement them.

CUT-SCORE SETTING IN PERFORMANCE TESTS FOR PROFESSIONALS: IS IT THE SAME AS MULTIPLE CHOICE?

Quotes (or Tribbles) to Remember

With the advent of NBPTS performance assessments, the measurement community was challenged to find new ways to establish cut scores. Attempts were made and reported by Hambleton and Plake (1995), Plake, Hambleton, and Jaeger (1997), and Hambleton, Jaeger, Plake, and Mills (2000). Prior to describing the new methodologies, we begin this discussion with some quotes from the last of these references (Hambleton, et al., 2000), a recent and very influential arrival, to set our stage. We have numbered the quotes for ease of reference, and we see our conclusions along the side.

1. "Performance assessments have become popular in education and credentialing, and performance standards are common for interpreting and reporting scores. However, because of the unique characteristics of these assessments compared to multiple-choice tests. . . . , new and valid standard-setting methods are needed." (p. 355)

2. "Although the trend toward PA [performance assessment] use is increasing, much of the available methodology for assessing psychometric quality of measurement instruments was developed for P&P [paper-and-pencil] tests. The applicability of these methods to PA measures is limited, questionable, or untested." (p. 355)

3. "It is common to have three performance standards for classifying examinees; at times, however, two, four, and even five performance standards are set . . . In the credentialing field, one performance standard is always required for sorting examinees into two performance categories, "certifiable" or "not certifiable." Sometimes additional performance standards are set for diagnostic purposes." (p. 356)

4. "Different SSM [standard-setting methods] produce different results; different panels, using the same SSM, will produce noncomparable results. Therefore, results from an SSM would be strengthened by running simultaneous panels using the same method and by employing a combination of standard-setting approaches . . . The use of multiple methods in standard setting is an area that should be studied." (p. 365)

> **CONCLUSION #1**
>
> Don't use any of the cut-score methodologies we just described. Do something different aimed specifically at performance-based assessment.

> **CONCLUSION #2**
>
> It is the yes/no decision that really matters in certification. The rest is for a different purpose—diagnosis—and can be handled differently.

> **CONCLUSION #3**
>
> If 10 folks cannot agree, is it not better to have 20 to 50 folks who still disagree? The averaging of flawed data does not make accurate data.

Now let's look at the methodologies developed for NBPTS. While you are reading this, remember NBPTS is looking for that "minimally excellent" teacher, a.k.a., in the psychometricians' terminology: the "just barely competent" (JBC) accomplished teacher. They are not deciding minimal competence in the traditional sense of readiness to teach and "do no harm." We will discuss the three approaches developed to date: Extended Angoff, Judgment Policy Capturing (JPC) approach, and the Dominant Profile Judgment (DPJ) approach.

The Extended Angoff Procedure for Performance Assessment

Hambleton and Plake (1995) proposed an Angoff-type approach for tasks rated on a scale (a.k.a, polytomously scored items). Panelists are asked to estimate the typical score that a borderline examinee would earn on a question. The average of the panelists' performance estimates for each question is determined. The performance standards on the total score scale are then calculated as per-question averages. The averages are then added to set the standard for the assessment or weighted by estimates of an individual question's importance/value or some other weighting factor.

The literature uses the term *question*, but it also could mean task. Either way, the results are of concern. We just noted that these methods do not work for performance tasks, and these same authors wrote that just two years later (Plake, et al., 1997), learning from their own research with NBPTS. Why do we even include it? Like tribbles, the method reappears in 2002 in Berk's work. Before the demonstration, though, we will review the actual conclusions of Hambleton and Plake (1995):

> In the absence of any established standard-setting procedures for use with performance assessments, it seemed reasonable, therefore, to explore the utility of the Angoff standard-setting procedure, or at least a modification of it, as a first step in a program of research concerning standard setting on complex performance assessments, such as the National Board for Professional Teaching Standards. (p. 1)

When all was said and done, and the cut scores were set, the researchers surveyed their panelists about the process. Here is what they found. We italicize a few things we want you to note in particular.

1. Ten of the 12 panelists indicated they felt there were certain exercises a candidate should have to pass to be certified, but the Angoff procedure does not allow for that because it is what is called a compensatory process—*examinees can do really well on one part and really poorly on the other and they still pass because the good compensates for the bad.*

2. All 12 panelists said that two of the NBPTS exercises—student learning and planning and teaching—should be passed for board certification. Ten of the 12 said that they would require that *all of the exercises be passed* for certification.

3. *None* of the panelists supported the use of *an overall test score* as the standard for cut-score setting.

CONCLUSION #4:

If you don't get the results you want, don't blame the panelists for not understanding. Maybe they have something important to say! In this case, they advocated for critical tasks and no total score. Compensatory scoring is not appropriate for certification.

That sure sounds like critical tasks to us! By the way, the panelists were all teachers. Hambleton and Plake (1995) concluded that there was "at least one troublesome finding" in the study that called into question the validity of the resulting standard—the compensatory policy. What was their final conclusion?

> There is nothing necessarily wrong with that result. . . . The clear implication is that the panelists did not fully understand the implications of the extended Angoff procedure that they had implemented. Had they fully understood the procedure, they most likely would not have so strongly endorsed the procedure or the standard they set. (p. 10)

Berk (2002) inadvertently provides a useful example of why compensatory scoring does not work (although he did not intend to do so—it was his recommended process). We note that this research was published eight years *after* Hambleton and Plake (1995) released their findings. Berk establishes a recommended template for what we would call data aggregation in the accountability world, and he then supplies some sample data based on the portfolio of one student (Bucko Berk) scored by two judges (p. 51). We replicate that table in our Table 8.5.

Note the lack of consistency (rater reliability) in the example. Judges agree only twice! And where do the weights come from? Why 10 vs. 8? Numbers out of a hat? We rework the Bucko example in our own version of the data, using a fictitious cousin—Bingo, in Table 8.6.

Note here that the raters are in total agreement. Having achieved the nearly impossible—inter-rater reliability of 1.0, we now turn to the validity question. Bingo cannot produce acceptable student work samples or evidence of professional growth; yet, he still passes. In the Hambleton and Plake (1995) study, the necessity of the student work samples was unanimously supported by the teacher/panelists, and it is at the core of the current accountability movement and NCATE standards. If the teacher cannot provide evidence of impact on student learning, then there is a critical flaw in the teacher's competency. Or at least, so one would hope to conclude. In CAATS Step 5, we talked about how validity trumps reliability. Here we have an example of how that can happen in practice. Raters agree, but the process is so flawed that we make the wrong decision anyway.

> **CONCLUSION #5:**
> Summing and weighting does not compensate for missing out on critical tasks.
>
> You can't escape criticality, even if you try. Compensatory scoring does not work for certification. Conjunctive scoring is necessary for the first cut—certify or not certify.

Table 8.5. Berk's Example of Sample Scoring for Bucko

Element	Outs. 3	Accept. 2	Min. Acc. 1	Unaccept. 0	Average Scores	Weight	Weighted Score
Videotape I	3/3				3	10	30
Videotape II	3	2			2.5	10	25
Lesson Plan	3	2			2.5	8	20
Student Work Samples		2	1		1.5	8	12
Prof'l Growth			1/1		1	5	5

Judges only agreed twice!

Score Range: 0–123
Cut Score (Pass): 82 or higher
Adjusted Pass: 88 (takes into account SEM of 6)
Decision for Bucko: passes with a score of 92

Outs. = Outstanding = 3
Accept. = Acceptable = 2
Min. Acc. = Minimally Acceptable = 1
Unaccept. = Unacceptable = 0

SOURCE: Redrawn from Berk, 2002.

Table 8.6. Wilkerson and Lang's Example of Berk's Model for Bingo

Element	Outs. 3	Accept. 2	Min. Acc. 1	Unaccept. 0	Average Scores	Weight	Weighted Score
Videotape I	3/3				3	10	30
Videotape II	3/3	Even though two tasks are **unacceptable,** the student passes!			3	10	30
Lesson Plan	3/3				3	8	24
Student Work Samples				0/0	0	8	0
Prof'l Growth				0/0	0	5	0

Score Range: 0–123	Outs. = Outstanding = 3
Cut Score (Pass): 82 or higher	Accept. = Acceptable = 2
Adjusted Pass: 88 (takes into account SEM of 6)	Min. Acc. = Minimally Acceptable = 1
Decision for Bingo: passes with a score of 84	Unaccept. = Unacceptable = 0

SOURCE: Adapted from Berk (2002).

The Judgmental Policy Capturing Approach for Performance Assessment

A year after Hambleton and Plake (1995), Jaeger (1995) introduced a new approach that allowed a combination of compensatory (what we had in the Extended Angoff Approach—a.k.a."good makes up for bad") and conjunctive (critical tasks—a.k.a."do or die") scoring. Panelists had to specify a minimum level of performance on some of the exercises in the assessment package, the most important ones, as a requirement for passing the assessment. Panelists sorted hypothetical profiles of candidates' scores into performance categories, and mathematical models were used to fit the panelist's categorization of those profiles to infer a standard-setting policy for each panelist. There are several iterations (they have to keep doing it until they get it right—a.k.a.,"enhanced consistency.") At the end, they reach consistency on conjunctive or compensatory scoring. The problem researchers found was that it was an indirect approach and was not well suited to a combination of compensatory and conjunctive (Plake, et al., 1997) scoring. They wrote the following before moving on to the next approach:

CONCLUSION #6:

If something doesn't work, making it part of a more complicated process results in something longer and more costly that still doesn't work.

Finally, there remain two troubling aspects of this approach to setting standards. First, there does not appear to be a way of ensuring that a final standard-setting policy will result . . . This is a fundamental difference among panelists that may never be resolved. . . . A second problem is the effect of conjunctive standard-setting policies on measurement reliability. (p. 409)

Clearly, more research on this type of standard-setting procedure is needed. (p. 410)

The Dominant Profile Judgment for Performance Assessment

Plake, et al. (1997) developed a modified approach to JPC that they called the dominate profile judgment (DPJ)—more acronyms. You may need to be ready to hunt for some of Berk's STANDARDSET® in the medicine cabinet if you've developed indigestion. In this project, panelists had to develop their policy statements and again attempt to reach consensus—this time through three rounds, ending with a mailed follow-up questionnaire.

This is getting very costly and time consuming. Let's take a break and make a pretend budget for the result we are about to get—just for fun. Note that it excludes *your* time! Our budget is in Table 8.7 for 15 panelists. No costs for antacids are included either.

Table 8.7. Pretend Budget for DPJ Cut-Score Method	
15 panelists for five days	
Consulting Fees for Panelists: $500/day (approx. NSF rate)	$37,500
Per Diem: $200/day	$15,000
Airfare: $300 each	$4,500
Coffee and Donuts (Be nice if you're not on a state budget!)	$2,000
Photocopying and Other Expenses	$1,000
Statistician	$10,000
Room Rentals in Meeting Hotel	$2,500
Total	$72,500

Here are the actual results of Round 2 (Plake, et al., 1997). The researchers generated three "synthesis policies" to represent the combined views of all 20 panelists:

Policy 1 (Synthesis of 15 Panelists):

- Minimum score of 3 on the teaching and learning exercise (Exercise 2).
- No scores of 1 on any of the exercises.
- No more than two scores of 2 on any of the other exercises.
- Sum of scores across the six exercises must be 18 or higher.

Policy 2 (Synthesis of 3 Panelists):

- Minimum score of 3 on the teaching and learning exercise (Exercise 2).
- Minimum score of 3 on the analyzing your lesson exercise (Exercise 3).
- No scores of 1 on any of the exercises.
- No more than two scores of 2 on any of the other exercises.
- Sum of scores across the six exercises must be 18 or higher.

Policy 3 (Synthesis of 2 Panelists):

- Minimum score of 3 on the teaching and learning exercise (Exercise 2).
- Minimum score of 3 on professional development and service exercise (Exercise 1).
- No scores of 1 on any of the exercises.
- No more than two scores of 2 on any of the other exercises.
- Sum of scores across the six exercises must be 18 or higher.

In looking at the results, it is clear that the panelists agreed that *no exercise could be eliminated or scored as a 1.* Their point of contention was on the weighting or importance of individual exercises. In Round 3, the mailed survey, 16 of the 20 voted for Policy #1 (one person moved positions). In the end, the researchers reported that the panelists were confident about the process they had used and liked it, believing it would be credible. After spending all that time and energy, who would want to say they wasted their time? At this point, the tribbles have taken over, and the *Enterprise* is doomed!

Troubling aspects identified by the researchers at the end were the lack of consensus and the lack of reliability potentially inherent in the conjunctive process, which could generate a "fail" decision based on one component of the system. For the second time, the researchers disagreed about the one common finding of their expert teacher/judges. They concluded the following about the process:

It has the advantage of allowing panelists to specify complex performance standards. Disadvantages include the possibility of the method coming to a conclusion without a clearly articulated policy for making a pass-fail (or certify/do not certify) decision. Further, the opportunity to set conjunctive policies may lead to unacceptably low assessment reliability. (p. 410)

CONCLUSION #7:

Throwing good money after bad doesn't give you better value.

So, where does this leave us? The panelists had the opportunity to set complex performance standards, but even after days of working and reworking, they never reached consensus on how much is enough task by task, only that each task had to be okay—the conjunctive decision of "do or die." The researchers concluded that setting complex standards was a good thing, even if consensus was not reached, and they disagreed with the call for a conjunctive process because of potential reliability issues—*again!* We conclude our history lesson on classical approaches with one final quote from Stone (2004):

Traditional standard setting does not work. The volume of evidence in support of this observation is overwhelming. The models fail to meet goals of judge agreement, fail to produce acceptable standards, and fail to produce reproducible standards. (p. 446)

STANDARD SETTING USING ITEM RESPONSE THEORY

There remains one family of measurement models that we have not yet talked about. All of the above were developed with classical test theory approaches focused on traditional reliability, and we have provided some specific details on how to use them. The more modern approach is called item response theory (IRT). We devote the next chapter to some simple explanations of how one of the models, the Rasch model, can help with a second level of cut-score setting, as well as validity, reliability, fairness, rater consistency/adjustment, continuous improvement, evidence of growth, and research studies. Because the numbers require a computer, and because the concepts are a bit more complex, we defer most of our discussion of the model to that chapter. Here we do little more than mention the primary Rasch cut-score setting methodology, but we caution you that it may not make much sense until you read the next chapter. This model, like the classical ones, also sorts the competent from the noncompetent examinee on a dichotomous (typically multiple choice) testing environment, so many of the problems we noted above carry forward into this cut-score setting approach.

The Rasch cut-score setting approach is called objective standard setting (OSS) and consists of four steps that are completed after there are sufficient data on test results to calibrate the items by difficulty onto a ruler or scale (Stone, 2004). Again the standard-setting process is completed by expert judges, but here they determine whether items are "essential to qualify"—something we have been advocating for in the strongest of terms. Stone (2004) compared OSS results from a longitudinal study with the Angoff methods as follows:

> Testing relationships consist of three parts: the test taker, the test, and the standard. Within this relationship, ability of the test taker and difficulty of the test change. However, using Rasch equating models, both ability and difficulty can be controlled. When these factors are controlled the result should be stabilization over time . . . OSS produced a stable passing rate across time and therefore meets the requirement of stability. Conversely, the traditional [Angoff] standard produces a passing rate considerably less than stable. If the passing rate changes even after ability and difficulty are controlled, it suggests that the criterion itself shifts and is lacking in clearly defined meaning. (pp. 453–454)

Reading the next chapter will help make the above citation more clear, but for now, think back to our multiple-choice example about Abraham Lincoln being President of the United States during the Civil War. There we demonstrated the impact of not looking at ability and difficulty at the same time. We saw that the easier the choices were, the more examinees we had who could answer the item correctly. Everyone knew that Queen Elizabeth was never an American President! A Rasch equating model would identify the difficulty on our measurement ruler of the three multiple-choice items we presented in that example, so we would not be dependent on just the proportion of test takers who got the item right—the Angoff and classical approach. The inability of the Angoff methods to compensate for the differences in our Honest Abe example is what makes the cut-score results unstable. We would depend instead on how each test taker performed on each item to estimate the probability of test takers answering correctly—no matter what the response choices were! Mathematically this is complex, but the logic should be clear. Read all about it in Chapter 9!

Also, as discussed all through this chapter, performance assessment is very appropriate for professional assessment of complex skills, but it is fraught with problems of inconsistent judges; yet expert opinion is the basis for performance systems.

These issues appear unresolved by the methods described so far. Again, we turn to a modern measurement application of the Rasch model that is described by Myford and Wolfe (2004):

> While ratings are often rich sources of data to inform decisions, they are unfortunately subject to various sources of bias and error.... Our purpose in writing this paper is to introduce researchers to the many-facet Rasch measurement (MFRM) approach for detecting and measuring rater effects. (p. 461)

In this chapter we mention the possibility of controlling for rater effect. In Chapter 9, we show you how it works. Suffice it to say, though, that if you are concerned that your judges are making inconsistent decisions, a Rasch approach can help you overcome this problem.

WHAT'S REALLY WRONG WITH CURRENT APPROACHES TO CUT-SCORE SETTING, AND HOW DOES THAT LEAD US TO A NEW APPROACH?

Let's take a few minutes to summarize where we have been and where we are in analyzing the status quo. We will summarize the issues before moving on to some concrete suggestions.

1. A distinction between making a certification decision (yes/no) and making diagnostic decisions has been envisioned but not operationalized. Validity standards call for different evidence for different purposes, but this is not happening. **We need to start with the necessary professional bottom-line high-stakes decision: certification, graduation, or licensing, which is a yes/no decision. A different process and purpose is needed for diagnosis of problems, differentiating between levels of proficiency beyond the minimum, and measurement of growth of professionals who are advancing or in-service. Cut scores are set at each level of proficiency in performance-based approaches, and there is no apparent reason why two different methods cannot be used for different decisions and different levels.**

2. Nobody is asking the teachers for their input on the scoring rubrics (or item distracters) that define acceptable performance task by task. The measurement community is only asking them to make cuts on quality criteria that they did not define or have an opportunity to fix. If panelists were asked to repair the descriptions of unacceptable performances, consensus might be easier to achieve about the floor. **We need a method that allows expert judges to edit the assessments, along with deciding what is critical to the certification decision.**

3. Current approaches to cut-score setting are labor and cost intensive, and the results remain mixed. The models are so complex that consensus is sought but not achieved. **We need a method that is simple and doable that takes the best of various approaches and configures them in a new way.**

4. There is consensus in the literature that the fundamental flaw in the methods designed for multiple-choice test cut scores is that they require judges to perform a nearly impossible cognitive task (i.e., estimating the probability that hypothetical examinees at the borderline of each achievement level will answer each item correctly). The estimates are confounded by test items that are of different difficulties. For performance tasks, the situation is not much different—borderline performance is still profiled in terms of capacity and difficulty, not criticality. **We need to start with a plan that reduces the confusion introduced by item difficulty, while also controlling for judge effects. That means Rasch.**

5. These models do not take into account a situation where data are collected over time with opportunities to redo work permitted. Assessment for learning is not in the picture. **Professional performance is complex. Sometimes a beginner requires several opportunities to try but eventually gets it right. Our method must not confound this issue with setting minimal standards of performance. The number of reasonable tries allowed is a decision based on utility and patience—but that's a different decision.**

6. Teacher/panelists have sent a clear message: conjunctive approaches—critical tasks—make sense. Total scores do not help; unacceptable performance on a single critical task is enough to make the certification decision. Measurement folks are afraid of this because of the potential for reliability problems. Reliability is trumping validity; the tail is wagging the dog, and we're not listening to the teachers. But there is no substitute for defining critical tasks and sticking by them. The pilot has to be able to land the plane. The teacher has to be able to write a lesson plan and impact children's learning. *Criticality is the yardstick* **that we need to allow our judges to use with a simple, first-level decision: all professionals are required to do it or else they should not be endorsed. Records of participation, grades, and hoping and praying are not substitutes for empirical evidence that job-related critical tasks were completed successfully.**

7. Measurement professionals have sent a clear message that a compensatory approach is necessary for reliability. **There is no apparent reason that would prohibit use of a combined approach, first establishing the competency decision based on a conjunctive approach—100% pass rate—and the second (and even third, fourth, and so on) cuts between higher proficiency levels being based on a scaled score. That means two scores: (1) good enough and (2) how good.**

Let's go back to pilot school for a minute. No one (in their right mind) would argue that the pilot has to be able to land the plane safely, even if they can do everything else except land the plane! The trick is to define *safely*, not whether the task is important. How bumpy can the landing be and under what circumstances? Those are the questions (criteria and proficiency levels) that need to be defined. If we decided that in extreme windy conditions, it was okay for two people to bruise their arms, then that is one decision-point for the landing task. Our expert judges are the best ones to decide criteria and proficiency levels, yet they are often given untenable choices among items and tasks that they didn't write. Once we decide a teacher has to write a lesson plan, and the judges need to help make that decision, we then need to decide what a good lesson plan must contain. We often call that *rubric writing*. Berk (1996) calls it *behavioral anchoring*. That's where we go next.

BERK'S SUGGESTIONS AND COMMENTARIES OVER THE YEARS

The need to write high-quality rubrics is no secret in the assessment world. We cite Berk (1996), here, because he is the only author we have found in the cut-score setting literature who talks about the importance of well-defined rubrics. He notes that with performance-based methods, one typically includes ratings for the level of quality or proficiency (e.g., advanced, proficient, and basic—you knew that!) With these levels of quality, he says that multiple cut points are needed to distinguish between advanced and proficient and proficient and basic—a different way of phrasing what we have already thought about. Berk recommends the development of "behavioral anchors" for each achievement level and provides a tongue-in-cheek example, which we provide below to demonstrate that he is talking about the same thing. He also provides us with a much needed moment of comic relief. In Box 8.6, we reprint Berk's examples, and later in this book we will continue to cite his definition of the really low score—"putrid."

Box 8.6. Berk's (1996) Examples of High- and Low-Achievement Levels and Their Behavioral Anchors

Ultra-Stupendous (Gold Medal)

- Leaps tall buildings in a single bound.
- Is more powerful than a locomotive.
- Is faster than a speeding bullet.

Kinda Better Than Ordinary (Silver Medal)

- Leaps short buildings in two or more bounds, maybe.
- Can draw a picture of a locomotive.
- Is about as fast as a speeding BB.

Middling Garden-Variety (Bronze Medal)

- Leaps short buildings with a running start and a strong tailwind.
- Can pick out the locomotive in an HO train set.
- Tries to catch speeding BBs in teeth.

Putrid (Pet Rock)

- Barely leaps over a Port-O-Potty.
- Says, "Look at the choo-choo!"
- Wets self while shooting a water pistol. (p. 21)

SOURCE: Quoted from Berk (1996).

THE CRITICALITY YARDSTICK APPROACH

In Chapter 6, CAATS Step 4B, you read our conclusions from this analysis. We concluded that item writers and external judges have one goal for their efforts: all performance tasks must be completed at an acceptable level as scored by competent judges on an appropriate rating. Reliability is focused on the judge and rubric issue, but the cut score is simply the entire set of items, all of which are essential and none of which can be rated as unacceptable. We call this the criticality yardstick approach (CYA). We do so because we know that all critical tasks are not likely to be equally difficult. There are easy tasks that are critically important and cannot be ignored in our decision-making process about certification. The fact that the task was visualized as critical implied validity for our purpose of certification.

We suggest that all performance task difficulties be calibrated on a ruler using the Rasch model, which allows difficulty and rater effects to be measured and controlled, so that we can then make accurate decisions about how good a teacher is. This decision is vastly different from whether or not the teacher is good enough to practice safely. If we do so well with our assessment system, then we are covering what we need to cover—CYA.

V WRAP-UP

In this chapter we laid the foundation for making the big decision at the end of a program—certify or do not certify a teacher. We talked about various cut-score setting methodologies to help prepare you for using or creating your own methodology, or using the one we suggest in CAATS Step 4B. We described the problems in current approaches and pointed toward a very simple approach that is, in essence, all or nothing for the certification decision but can be expanded to a scale for the definition of other levels of competency. The target in this book has been to help you think through what it means to be a competent teacher, how you know one when you see one in the early stages, and how to make a decision using data on critical tasks.

CAATS CHAPTER 8—ACTIVITY #1
Change the Difficulty of an Item

Explanation:

Most faculty are unaware of their ability to change the difficulty of an item (and the results on a test) by the simple technique practiced in this first activity. This activity may result in some helpful revelations about how standardized tests are written and some increased concern about their exclusive use in certification decisions. You may want to do this activity on your own or use it as a group learning experience with your faculty.

1. Select a test that can be administered to two different groups—either two halves of the same class or two class sections. This may be two classes you are teaching or two classes taught by teachers or faculty with whom you are working, or it may be a single class divided in half.

2. Select two items in the multiple-choice section of the test and change the response options to make one item more difficult and one item easier.

3. Administer the test and compare the results from the two groups on the two items.

4. Were you able to control the difficulty of the items?

CAATS CHAPTER 8—ACTIVITY #2
Replicate a Cut-Score Setting Process

Explanation:

That 100% CYA cut score is a tough one to think about. We are well indoctrinated into accepting the cut-score setting methodologies prevalent in this country because they sound sophisticated and mysterious. So, try this group activity and see if you change your mind. When you and your faculty are done with this activity, talk about fuzzy numbers vs. 100% based on criticality. How do you feel about fuzzy numbers?

1. Get the sample questions from a traditional, multiple-choice standardized test. (A sample or old test version from your state's teacher certification test would be a good choice.)

2. Pretend you are the judges.

3. Set the performance standard for the test using Nedelsky's, Angoff's, or Ebel's method.

4. Reflect on what you felt during the process. How hard was it for you to come up with the numbers? Did you feel like you were guessing? Did everyone agree? If not, how do you feel about making the high-stakes decision in this test based on your experience?

5. Remember that in many of the approaches we reviewed in this book, the teacher/judges called for the 100% cut score. What makes you more comfortable now—setting a traditional cut score or tweaking the tasks and weeding out the criteria and the tasks that are not critical so you can use the 100% CYA approach?

CAATS ACTIVITIES

CAATS CHAPTER 8—ACTIVITY #3
Change the Criticality of a Task

Explanation:

Most educators are reluctant to say that someone's work is really bad. It goes against that humanistic grain that brought us into this profession. Nonetheless, sometimes we have to bite the bullet and do so to protect the profession and the children we teach. In this activity, you and your faculty come to grips with the big "NO," using the images you had when reading about Berk and his use of the proficiency level, "putrid." Try this with all of your faculty. It, like the first activity, can be a real eye-opener. When you are done, please remind them that the use of "putrid" was just for us! Let's not let it creep visibly into our work.

1. Select a performance task that is assessed using a rubric—checklist or rating scale— from your class or the class of someone who works in your department/district. Make sure it is a task that you think is extremely important and can be linked to a specific objective, learning target, or standard.

2. Review the criteria in the rubric (the things you are scoring or checking off) and determine which ones are critical to the objective, learning target, or standard being measured. Set aside any that are *not* critical.

3. If you are reviewing a rating scale that has a description of proficiency levels on it (e.g., a chart with words in the cells for each rating), read the lowest level and see if it fits Berk's idea of "putrid." If not, rewrite it as putrid. If you are reviewing a checklist, describe what putrid would be. (No cheating, please—putrid has to be one level above missing. Think of it as attempted but really wrong.)

4. Review your conceptualization set of putrid ratings and determine if you would want to say that any of your students had met the objective, learning target, or standard if they received any putrid ratings on your revised scale.

5. Determine if it would be mathematically possible for a teacher candidate to score a "passing score" on the instrument (following its original directions) even with a "putrid" rating on your revised version. Do you think anyone who passed with this "putrid" rating should have passed?

CAATS CHAPTER 8—ACTIVITY #4
Take Your Choice

Explanation:

That 100% CYA cut score is a tough one to think about. We are well indoctrinated into accepting the cut-score setting methodologies prevalent in this country because they sound sophisticated and mysterious. This is yet another activity to help you and your faculty think about your preferences. In this activity, faculty practice both approaches—cut-score setting and CYA. This activity can be a group assignment. Select a group leader for each group of four, and ask that person to read the chapter before convening the group.

Part I:

1. Get three friends who teach the same specialization area you do.
2. Pick a major test for your area.
3. Visualize the population that will take the test.
4. Select a cut-score methodology from the chapter.
5. Set a cut score.

Part II:

6. Continue with the same specialization area, now thinking about skills to be performed in that area.
7. Visualize the competent person.
8. Write a performance task that the competent person must be able to do successfully to be considered competent.
9. Define unacceptable performance for a set of criteria for the task. Make sure you only include important ones.
10. Decide if you would give a passing grade to this person if s/he did not correctly complete the task or any of the criteria.
11. If you think the failing task score would not be warranted for a failed criterion, decide if you would change the rubric or change the task to warrant the failing score on the task. Where do YOU draw the line? Stay on this step until you find that point of failure.
12. Give your task and rubric to three colleagues. See if they agree with your decisions. If not, see if you can reach consensus on the criticality of the criteria and the task.
13. You probably now have four critical tasks. Can you identify some tasks that are important for learning but not critical to the job?

Part III:

14. Discuss with your friends which method you prefer—traditional cut-score setting methodology or CYA approach.

CAATS ACTIVITIES

9

Using Teacher Scores for Continuous Improvement

*I*f you are really serious about using the data to make good decisions about individual teachers, individual criteria on your rubrics, and program quality, then this chapter is written for you. Here, we hope to provide you with the background you need to decide if you want to use a modern measurement model to go beyond the 100% cut-score process for certifying teachers. This chapter prepares you to look at levels of proficiency beyond minimal competency and to do more extensive research on your results.

In this chapter, we write about our preferred method of analysis, called the Rasch model of item response theory (IRT). The Rasch model is named for its developer, Georg Rasch (1960), a mathematician from the Danish Institute for Educational Research. It is the simplest of the IRT models and works well with small samples. IRT is a relatively new technique that differs greatly from classical test theory (CTT) or true score theory. Most classical measurement is based on samples of data (called norms) that are used to generate distributional statistics such as the mean, standard deviation, percentile rank, and standard scores such as SATs, IQs, and NCEs. Rasch is not sample dependent, does not rely on a normal distribution, and creates an interval scale better suited to statistical analysis.

We recommend that those using the CAATS model choose the Rasch model for item analysis, reporting scores, and detecting rater effects because it provides powerful statistics that are relatively simple to understand (if not to compute). Our motto is KISS (keep it statistically simple).

Our purpose in this book is to help you make some informed choices, even if you do not want to do the computations yourself. We do not attempt to teach you everything you need to know to run the statistical software packages or read all of the printouts. Instead, our goals are (1) to help you understand what the model can do for you so that you can make informed choices, (2) to help you understand and use the results, and (3) to tell you what you can say to the statisticians about what you want (and don't want), if you want someone else to crunch the numbers.

Even if you are not interested in terms of measuring teacher competencies, you may find this chapter useful when you deal with all those standardized tests that are now scored using IRT models. If you are a principal, your school is graded on a standardized test that almost assuredly is developed using one of the IRT models. We even use some of the examples in this chapter to teach undergraduate students about modern measurement.

We start with a demonstration of classical item analysis, so that you have the tools you need to stay with the classical approach if you choose to do so. We continue with a list of seven reasons to use the Rasch model in this context. Next, we have a "getting started" section that tells you a little bit more about how the chapter is organized and begins to prepare you for working with—or would that be arguing with—your local statistician, if you need to use one to implement Rasch techniques. We continue with a simple, but technical, discussion of how the model works and what it will do for you.

REASONS WHY WE USE THE RASCH MODEL

Here are seven reasons we can cite here for using the Rasch model. If they sound like what you want to do, we think you will find this chapter intriguing.

1. *Valid Decisions About Individuals.* With Rasch, we can fine-tune the data to such an extent that we can be more confident in our decisions for an individual teacher than we can with classical models. Analyses conducted using Rasch tell us when the prediction is not valid or reliable for an individual person—not just the whole group. *Stop and reread that sentence, please.* It does this through individual calculations of error and something called *fit*, which replaces the standard error of measurement (SEM) in classical test theory. SEM works for the whole group but ignores individual *people* problems. If the teacher's answers are erratic or unpredictable, we know something is wrong with the way s/he answered or was rated. Armed with that knowledge, we can do something about it. So, if you are interested in the individual, then this model is unparalleled in its power to help you. It is, for us, tops on the list. We like to say that *"Rasch puts the people back in the measurement process."*

2. *Predictions and Diagnostics About Individuals.* Rasch is robust in cases of missing data (Bayley, 2001). That means we can have some data that are less

than perfect and still make valid decisions. So, we can make *early* predictions, from a subset of our items or instruments, about whether a teacher is likely to be high or low on the competency scale. This is not possible with CTT, which requires complete or relatively complete data. Rasch, therefore, gives us an early celebration (or warning) system. Again, if the individual teacher is of importance to you, the Rasch model is unparalleled.

3. *Finding and Controlling Rater Effect.* We can determine the harshness or leniency of raters so that we can *adjust scores to make them more fair* and avoid excessive use of multiple raters to calculate inter-rater reliability statistics—which takes a lot of time. The need for multiple ratings is vastly reduced. Rasch helps you make *better decisions while spending less time and money.* Analyses conducted using the multifaceted Rasch model (MFRM) of IRT are sensitive to differences among individuals—not just the teachers assessed, but also the judges doing the ratings (Myford & Wolfe, 2004). You can identify the raters who are too harsh or too lenient, along with other rater inconsistencies. This helps you have more confidence in the cut score—we are certifying people who should be certified and denying certification to those who shouldn't, without being unduly influenced by rater issues. It also helps you give the benefit of the doubt (or the opposite) when judge's ratings are too high or too low. You can estimate corrections to misjudged items on the computer, based on calculated rater error.

4. *Item Analysis and Sensitivity.* Analyses conducted using the Rasch model of IRT are sensitive to differences in items, making the job of identifying tasks or criteria that do not work well in practice easily identifiable for *replacement or editing* (Andrich & Wright, 1994).

5. *Using All the Data—Even Drop-Outs.* Since analyses conducted using the Rasch model are robust in cases of missing data, in case where teachers do not complete all tasks and drop out of the program, we have good numbers for comparison purposes. You could ask questions like, "Did the low ability teachers drop out or am I losing the winners for some reason I need to fix?" This may be the most important information you can get for *predictive validity* studies down the road.

6. *Research and Improvement.* The Rasch model creates an interval score (Wright & Linacre, 1989). That helps not only with the decision-making process for individuals and groups, but also for conducting other studies. We have a way of investigating important questions (e.g., the relationship between competency and teacher retention). If we ever hope to do a *predictive validity study or anything longitudinal,* then this capacity is critically important. If you want to do any research on the quality of the program, you need to have measurement quality in the results that will help you do that. Some studies can be done with CTT scores; more and better studies can be done with Rasch measures.

7. *Cost Effectiveness.* A single study using the Rasch model of IRT includes data that can *replace multiple complex statistical studies* when CTT is used as the approach. Because the Rasch model is not sample dependent, it is not necessary to obtain normal distributions representing multiple demographics, which often take lots of time and effort. Analyses conducted using the Rasch model of IRT provide evidence of both validity (construct unidimensionality) and reliability (precision).

THE CLASSICAL APPROACH

In both classical and modern approaches, item analysis procedures provide an empirical analysis of how difficult individual items were for the folks who took the test or completed the assessment. We can compare the empirical results with our expectations of how difficult the item or criterion should have been and make decisions about improvement in areas where they do not match in either model. In CTT, we base our decision about difficulty using sample-dependent proportions; in IRT, we use sample independent conjoint probabilities. Conjoint measurement means that both the difficulty of the item and the person's ability jointly contribute to the outcome. We show the proportions approach here.

Let's start with a simple example for two criteria in Box 9.1, using a simple scale (checklist approach) of "correct" or "incorrect" and only addressing two criteria from a larger set of criteria.

Box 9.1.   Case Study for a Classroom Management Plan: What an Item Analysis Can Tell You

Criterion #1: Teachers establish rules for student behavior in the classroom.

Criterion #2: Teachers involve students in planning the rules and consequences applied in the classroom.

Expectations: Criterion #1 is easier than Criterion #2.

Results: The p-values (proportion of satisfactory ratings) for Criteria #1 and #2 were .75 and .85 respectively, indicating that 75% were scored satisfactory on Criterion #1, and 85% on Criterion #2.

Conclusions: Overall, there were more satisfactory scores for Criterion #2 than for Criterion #1, showing that the second criterion was easier for teachers than the first criterion. This is the reverse of what we expected.

Decision: Something is wrong and we need to find out what because we might be making a bad decision about what teachers can do. Validity is threatened, and we could make a decision that hurts teachers or children.

To analyze difficulty if you have used a scale, as we recommended, you will need to be a little more creative in the CTT model. The easiest thing to do is to rank order the results, making sure that the criterion with the most unacceptable ratings is the hardest (at the bottom) and the criterion with the most high scores is easiest (at the top). You could reverse this order also. It really doesn't matter which direction you go, but your analysis should logically explain why the items are ordered the way they are. Below is the example we provided in Step 4, renumbered here as Table 9.1. Here, though, we would not look at Professor Jones's class but rather all sections over a period of time, say one year. In the original example, we had an interpretation about data aggregation, which still holds. Here we write the analysis and recommendations in terms of an item analysis. These are the same data, but they result in different interpretations and uses.

Table 9.1. Classical Difficulty Analysis of Criteria on the Unit Exam

N = 30						
	Target		Acceptable		Unacceptable	
Criteria	#	%	#	%	#	%
1. Test is appropriate and comprehensive for instructional content.	25	83	5	17	0	0
2. Test map is accurate and properly formatted.	30	100	0	0	0	0
3. Items address knowledge/comprehension, application/analysis, and synthesis/evaluation.	15	50	10	33	5	17
4. Accommodations for special students, including both ESE and LEP, are appropriate.	25	83	4	13	1	3
Etc.						

Analysis and Recommendations: The difficulty of items in rank order, beginning with the easiest criterion and ending with the most difficult, is: 2, 1, 4, 3. Item 3 typically represents the most difficult skill for teachers because it requires a high level of creative and critical thinking. Item 2 requires that they use a format that is easy to learn. The results are ordered in a predictable way, and no improvements are suggested.

If you are in a small department with minimal expectations regarding continued analysis and research, the process modeled above using CTT should work well for you.

A QUICK OVERVIEW OF WHERE RASCH FITS INTO THE GRAND SCHEME OF IRT MODELS

Know from the outset that IRT is a relatively recent development in measurement theory, getting started in the 1960s and taking more serious hold in the measurement community in the 1980s. All major test publishers now use IRT instead of (or in combination with) CTT, so if you have seen an SAT, GRE, ACT, or SAT-9 score recently, you have seen an IRT-based score. Even the states are moving in this direction for K–12 assessments. If nothing else, look at these next few pages as a professional development opportunity.

There are three major IRT models. The models calculate, and are identified by, the number of item parameters (statistics) that are estimated. All models estimate difficulty, and it is not counted in the number of parameters in the model-naming conventions. In its simplest form, the one parameter (1PL) model estimates the ability of people taking the test, in addition to the difficulty of test items. The 2PL model adds a discrimination parameter, and the 3PL model adds a guessing parameter. Explaining the differences, pros, and cons, is way beyond the scope of this book! Different people use different models, depending on their needs and preferences. For example, most major test publishers write multiple-choice tests designed to sort people into normally distributed categories. They tend to prefer the 3PL model. States, like Florida, have also selected this model for K–12 testing. The 3PL model requires a sample size of at least 1,000, eliminating it from consideration for most of our readers no matter what your in-house statisticians tell you. It also helps the test publishers avoid finding out about people problems (as Rasch does) and having to deal with them.

Other states prefer the 1PL model, or a version of it called the Rasch model, because they are less concerned about discrimination and guessing and want more stable estimates of ability and difficulty. The more parameters you add in, the fuzzier these numbers get. Texas has used the Rasch model for its K–12 tests (Texas Education Agency, 2005), as do the public schools for their classroom tests in Portland, Oregon (Ingebo, 1997), and the South Carolina High School Assessment Program (Wolfe & Mapuranga, 2004). It is also widely used outside the field of education in various human sciences (Bezruczko, 2005). This has become a bit technical, so we summarize key points in Box 9.2.

Box 9.2.   What You Need to Know So Far—Round 1

IRT is the current state of the art in measurement. It has three models. The Rasch model is the simplest. It is widely used and growing rapidly. Classical test theory is used less and less in the modern measurement world. Rasch is highly useful if you want to know about individuals as individuals—and not as members of a group—and if you are worried about raters and future research studies. Rasch is also useful for measuring performance along a predicted set of standards.

RASCH: THE BASICS

Here is the basic idea—the ability of individuals and the difficulty of items influence each other and are related. IRT models envision a continuum of knowledge or skills that can be placed on a ruler that measures people's ability, along with item difficulty, without regard to a particular sampling. The units of measurement of difficulty and ability are called *logits* (Barnard, 2001), just like the units of length on the other kind of ruler are called *inches*.

With the Rasch model of IRT, we answer questions like, can a person lift a stone because the stone is light or the person is strong? Obviously the person's strength (or ability) and the weight of the stone (or difficulty) are related and influence each other. A weak person will be unable to lift a heavy stone (Wright & Stone, 2004), and a strong person will do so easily. What is easy for one person is difficult for another, so talking about a stone's weight by itself does not tell you who will be able to lift it. The Rasch model works because we put both ability and difficulty on the same interval scale, so we can make predictions about one from the other. This is called *conjoint measurement*. The conceptual appeal is so clear that we have to pause to ask why it took us so long to figure this out. The answer to that question is that it took a very creative mathematician in Denmark to make it work.

If you are familiar with Lexiles (Stenner, 1996), a scale for reading, then you have heard of this model. When we estimate the ability of a reader and the difficulty of a reading passage using Lexiles, we acknowledge that the ***probability*** of a reader understanding what he or she has read is dependent on two things—how good a reader he or she is and how hard the passage is. The two work together, which is really common sense. It stands to reason that your assessment system will have some tasks that are more difficult and some teachers who are less talented, just as some people are stronger and lift heavier stones and others are better readers and can read more difficult passages. Rasch addresses the fundamental question: "What are the odds (probability) that this person can read this passage or this teacher can do this task well?"

The description of the model from the Rasch Unidimensional Measurement Model (RUMM, 2003) Laboratory Web site is useful:

> Rasch analysis can be applied to assessments in a wide range of disciplines, including health studies, education, psychology, marketing, economics and social sciences. . . . The Rasch model is the only item response theory (IRT) model in which the total score across items characterizes a person totally. . . . The aim of a Rasch analysis is analogous to helping construct a ruler, but with the data of a test or questionnaire. [http://www.rummlab.com.au/]

Again we have had a somewhat technical discussion, so we summarize in Box 9.3.

Box 9.3. What You Need to Know So Far—Round 2

Ability and difficulty are related, and that relationship can be used to measure both together. What is easy for one person might be difficult for another. Rasch puts ability and difficulty on the same scale, making the relationship between the two explicit. The method creates a "ruler" of abilities and difficulties. People and items are placed on the ruler based on probabilities or odds of success. This psychometric ruler will have measurement units on it (called *logits*), just like a wooden ruler has inches on it.

Now that you're armed and ready for meeting and greeting your friendly local statistician (just kidding), you might want to know just a little so you can teach him or her a thing or two. You can expect some arguments. Most statisticians and measurement folks will try to sway you toward classical test theory because that is what they studied in graduate school. They will often suggest exploratory methods like "factor analysis" or advanced statistics like structural equations. If they are familiar with IRT, they will probably try to push you toward the 2PL or 3PL models, because that, too, is what they studied. Remember these things about Rasch to end the debate:

1. Rasch is the model of choice for fit statistics about people (not just items); the others address fit statistics for items only and don't put the people back into the measurement process.

2. Rasch is the only IRT model that allows you to look systematically at rater effect.

3. Rasch is not sample dependent, does not require a large sample of people, and does not make assumptions about the normality of the distribution. It also works really well with missing data.

4. Rasch is easier to compute and understand, which will reduce your future dependency and debating time.

Here's your start. Take the statement in Box 9.4 and read it to the statistician (with conviction!):

Box 9.4.   Gaining Control of the Local Statistician: What You Say

I have selected the Rasch model because I am implementing a performance assessment system targeted at measuring critical skills. My expectation is that eventually almost all teachers will successfully complete all tasks and be certified. I only have 100 teachers in my program, so my sample size will be small. They will not be normally distributed; I will have data that have extreme negative skew—with most teachers mastering the skills even though it may take several tries. I am not interested in measuring the utility of my system in discriminating between high and low performers in a traditional single assessment, and guessing is not a factor. I am very interested, though, in locating and helping teachers who have scores with unexplained or unusual anomalies (misfitting scores) and identifying and correcting for rater effect. I also want to make use of data on noncompleters, so I need a model that is powerful with missing data. I am interested in building a ruler of progress on the standards and placing both people and items on the ruler. Rasch is the only measurement model that provides the fit statistic I need for diagnostic purposes and allows me to estimate and correct for rater effect. I want to use the Rasch model for those reasons. Thank you very much for expressing your concerns. I will be happy to help you obtain some of the references I have read about and purchase some software for you. [End of discussion]

GETTING STARTED

Do you remember your first statistics course? We would wager that at some point during the course, the professor said to you something like the following:

> In this course, you are going to do some statistical analysis that will generate some tables (probably in SPSS or SAS). You will not understand every number on every table. Don't worry about it. I'll tell you what you need to know.

If your statistics professor didn't tell you that, it may be too late to ask for your money back, but you should have done so at the time. Approach this chapter with that caveat about not needing to understand everything in mind. You will see some tables with lots of numbers on them because the best way to learn about this method is to read a little about it and then look at some actual output from some fake data sets. That is what we will do here. (Actually, we'll ease into one real one from the Educational Testing Service at the end, but get your antacids ready.) You may not understand every number, and that is fine. At a minimum, you will be able to converse intelligently about the model and what it can do for you. We will guide you through what you need to know to make an informed decision about whether this is something worth doing in your department. Skip the rest.

We note one more thing. For demonstration purposes, in the examples that follow, we use data based on a correct/incorrect response set—often the result of a multiple choice test or a task-based checklist. We add in scales later, just as we did in the classical example, to keep it statistically simple. Everything we present in the beginning is equally relevant to rating scales and performance assessments. The numbers are a bit easier to follow with dichotomous (right/wrong) data, though.

We get the ball rolling with a very big hurdle that we have to jump over. It is the differences that item writers can make. Like test takers, some are skilled, and some are not. The way the item is written influences how difficult it is.

DIFFERENCES THAT ITEM WRITERS MAKE

Now imagine Jo. Jo is smart and caring, and she would be a good teacher. She takes a 10-item test. (We know, that's too short, but it is easy to draw on a figure in a book, see Figure 9.1). If we have a cut score of 50%, as set by our judges (see the previous chapter), she has to get a score of five to be certified. Her score, though, can be influenced by the difficulty of the test.

Now let's imagine two sets of item writers—the tough group and the easy group. Think back to our Abraham Lincoln test item in Chapter 8. The tough group went to item-writing school with the ones who included Ulysses S. Grant, Jefferson Davis, and George Washington as distracters on the question about who was U.S. President during the Civil War. The easy group went to item-writing school with the group that gave response options that included the cartoon character, the Pope, and the Queen. If Jo takes the test from the tough group, she only gets a score of 2. If she takes the test from the easy group, she gets a score of 8. With the first test, she is denied certification; with the second, she is certified.

Remember now, Jo is Jo—same person, just a different test. Only the people who wrote the items were different. Her ability is a constant; the item writers' abilities vary. Now look at Figure 9.1, which shows where Jo would be placed on the test without taking into account the difficulty of the test items (and the skill/brains of the writers). Note also that we have symbolized her answers with ones and zeroes:

Figure 9.1. Jo's Test Score—A Moving Target

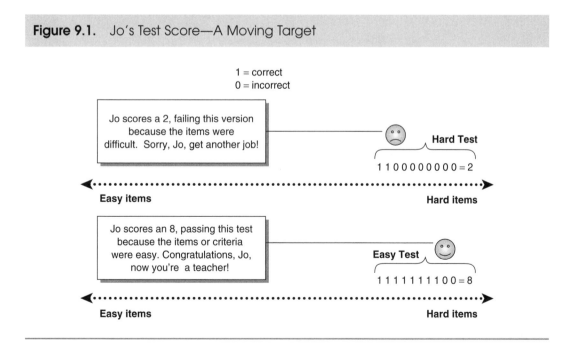

Assessment will always be misleading with sample-dependent scores. Counting the number of items right is not measuring, but measurement occurs when you know where the items and people both lie on the ruler (Wright & Stone, 1979).

GUTTMAN SCALING

We just looked at Jo's scores on two different tests, noting which items she had correct and which ones she had wrong, using ones and zeroes. A theoretical model exists (Guttman, 1944) that says people have a certain ability level and they will get items correct (on a perfect test) until their ability level falls off. Then they start getting items wrong when items become too difficult for them. Of course, there is no such thing as a perfect test, but we can use this theory to establish some expectations, or probabilities, that people will get certain items right and certain items wrong, based on their ability, and we can figure out where they are likely to make the transition to "not able." If a test works well, we can see a pattern of ones up to the point that their ability trails off, then we see zeroes. Usually, there is a mix of ones and zeroes in between. Remembering that there is no perfect test and no perfect testing situation for an individual, we allow for deviations in the pattern. This pattern is at the core of the Rasch model because it looks at the ability of the people and the difficulty of the items together.

The Guttman Scalogram in Figure 9.2 shows the results for 10 people taking a 10-item test. Remember that 1 stands for correct and 0 stands for incorrect. These are our first computer-generated data. We are using a software program called Winsteps (Linacre, 2003).

Figure 9.2. Example Guttman Scalogram of Responses to a 10-Item Test

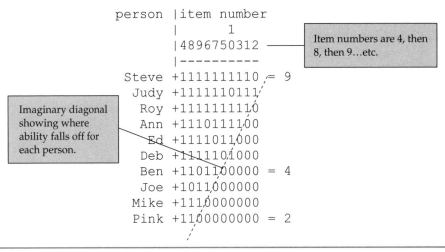

```
GUTTMAN SCALOGRAM OF RESPONSES:

person |item number
       |     1
       |4896750312
       |----------
 Steve +1111111110  = 9
  Judy +1111110111
   Roy +1111111110
   Ann +1110111100
    Ed +1111011000
   Deb +1111101000
   Ben +1101100000  = 4
   Joe +1011000000
  Mike +1110000000
  Pink +1100000000  = 2
```

Item numbers are 4, then 8, then 9…etc.

Imaginary diagonal showing where ability falls off for each person.

The items are in order from easiest to hardest. The item numbers are at the top (third and fourth row), beginning with Item 4 and ending with Item 2. Item 10 takes two rows to print. Item 4 (first column; read down) is the easiest because all 10 persons taking the test got the item correct (all ones). Item 2 is the hardest (last column), and only one student got it right. Putting items and people in the same analysis is called *conjoint measurement*, which is a special characteristic of the Rasch model. Notice also that there is a diagonal that runs through the data from top to bottom–most of the ones are to the left, and most of the zeroes are to the right of the diagonal.

You can also see that Steve, Roy, and Judy had the highest scores with nine correct. Pink was the lowest with two correct. Pink is at the bottom. Let's talk about Steve and

Judy first. Steve has a perfect Guttman pattern (as does Roy). He would; he wrote most of this chapter. Judy on the other hand is a bit weird, according to her scalogram, of course. She got #10 wrong and was the only person to get #2 right. If she had an ideal Guttman pattern, she would have answered #10 correctly, too, but then she might conclude that she was smarter than Steve, and he did create the data in this chapter!

There are other deviations from the Guttman pattern in the test, but it is not really about being "Guttman perfect." We said already that the pattern is theoretical, just like the normal curve. Ben and Jo, for example, also have an item wrong in the "right" zone, but we're all human and the test items are not perfect. We will revisit these later and see if they are something to worry about. For now, let's focus on the fact that the data are pretty close to a perfect Guttman Scale. We're ready to see how they would look on a Rasch ruler.

A SAMPLE RASCH RULER

In Figure 9.3, we show a Rasch ruler that places our items and people on the same scale. You can see that Item 4, our easiest item, is to the far left and Item 2, our most difficult item, is to the far right. For simplicity's sake, we did not put all 10 people on the ruler, just three—Steve, who was at the top of our Guttman scale, Pink, who was the bottom, and Ben, who was in the bottom half. Notice that the distance between the items is not equal. That is because the difference in difficulty between the items is not the same. That's a sure sign that we are converting to interval data, not ordinal data. The same would be true with the people—different distances because of differing abilities. Item 4 is a lot easier than Item 8, but Item 5 has less difference in difficulty than Item #3. The process of calculating the amount of difficulty in these items is called *calibration*.

Figure 9.3. Sample Logistic Ruler of 10 Test Items Calibrated on a Ruler—User-Friendly Version

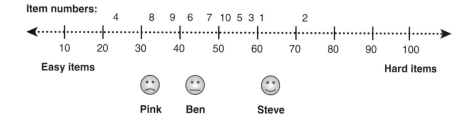

We write items that we believe represent the construct and *calibrate* them where they fall on the ruler. In CTT, item difficulty is based on the **proportion** of people who answer correctly. In IRT, difficulty is based on the **probability** that people will get the item correct. Some pretty basic and logical expectations follow:

1. At your ability level, you have a 50% chance of getting items with the same score (logit value) as you correct! In practical terms, because Guttman scaling is not precise—no perfect people and no perfect tests—there is a gray area of items

where people get some right and some wrong, but this is where your ability starts to fall off, so it makes sense that you only have a 50–50 chance of being right. It's the "coin toss zone."

2. When items are higher on the difficulty scale than the person is on the ability scale, the person is less likely to get the items correct. The items are too hard for the person. The more difficult they are (higher up on the scale), the less likely the person is to answer them correctly. It's all about the person and the item's relative position on the same scale.

3. When items are lower on the difficulty scale than the person is on the ability scale, the person is more likely to get them correct because the items are easy for that person. The less difficult they are, the more likely the person is to answer them correctly.

4. The more frequently you correctly answer questions that are too hard for you and/or you are wrong for items that are easier than your ability level, the more peculiar your total score is. You are not responding based on the mathematical odds. When this happens, if it happens just to you—most everybody else is responding as expected in terms of the odds—then we know that something went wrong for you! Were you really nervous?

5. This is what we meant by "putting the people back into the measurement process." We look at the score for each person as an individual and see if s/he responded according to the odds.

Let's go back to our example. Probabilistically speaking, Pink should get items easier than her ability correct (in this case, Items 4 and 8). Ben should get 4, 8, and 9 correct, but not 1, 2, or 3.

FROM PICTURES TO NUMBERS

If we are presenting a report to someone over the age of 10, we probably should lose the smiley faces. In this section we provide some real computer printouts for our fake data. Remember the warning we gave you at the beginning—you don't have to understand all of the numbers!

From the raw scores, the measure of each person and item can be calculated. Although it is a scale score, we use the term *measure* in Rasch because there are many types of scale scores. The measure is described in logits, which are the psychometric version of inches. We can label the scale to any set of values we want, so you will see logistic rulers that have positive and negative numbers, range from 0 to 100, from 0 to 10, or from 200 to 1,600. The default is –3.0 to 3.0, with a mean of 0 and a logit of 1. Our sample ruler has a mean of 50 and a logit of 10. The mean and standard deviation are indicated by *M* and *S*.

In the charts and tables that follow, we first convert the smiley faces to a graph generated again from the Winsteps (Linacre, 2003) software. We call it *The Ruler*; some folks, including Linacre, call it the *variable map*. It is the same thing. In Figure 9.4, we provide a ruler or map with our explanations of the ruler in the boxes on the side.

Figure 9.4. Sample Logistic Ruler of 10 Survey Items Calibrated on a Ruler—Grown-Up Version

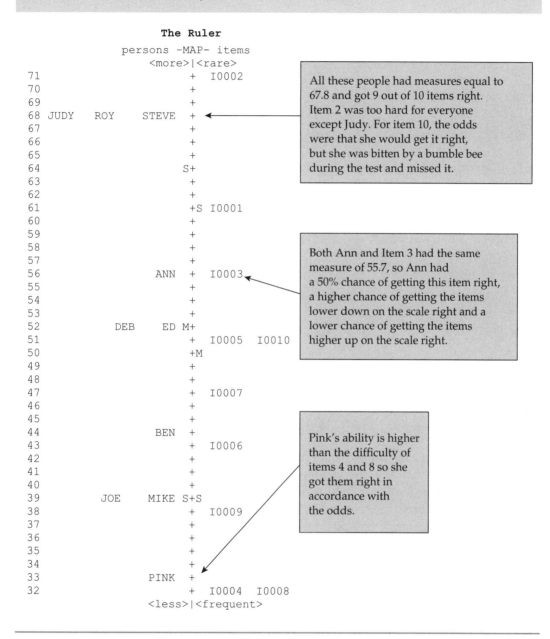

```
                    The Ruler
              persons -MAP- items
                   <more>|<rare>
   71                     +  I0002
   70                     +
   69                     +
   68 JUDY   ROY   STEVE  +  ◄─────
   67                     +
   66                     +
   65                     +
   64                 S+
   63                     +
   62                     +
   61                   +S I0001
   60                     +
   59                     +
   58                     +
   57                     +
   56           ANN       +  I0003 ◄
   55                     +
   54                     +
   53                     +
   52       DEB    ED M+
   51                     +  I0005   I0010
   50                   +M
   49                     +
   48                     +
   47                     +  I0007
   46                     +
   45                     +
   44           BEN       +
   43                     +  I0006
   42                     +
   41                     +
   40                     +
   39      JOE    MIKE S+S
   38                     +  I0009
   37                     +
   36                     +
   35                     +
   34                     +
   33           PINK      +
   32                     +  I0004   I0008
                   <less>|<frequent>
```

All these people had measures equal to 67.8 and got 9 out of 10 items right. Item 2 was too hard for everyone except Judy. For item 10, the odds were that she would get it right, but she was bitten by a bumble bee during the test and missed it.

Both Ann and Item 3 had the same measure of 55.7, so Ann had a 50% chance of getting this item right, a higher chance of getting the items lower down on the scale right and a lower chance of getting the items higher up on the scale right.

Pink's ability is higher than the difficulty of items 4 and 8 so she got them right in accordance with the odds.

Now let's look at a pair of tables from the Winsteps output that provides the data for the people (Figures 9.5 and 9.6). The first figure (Winsteps table) presents the information for each person, and the second figure (another Winsteps table) provides summary statistics. There will be the same kind of tables for items (Figures 9.7 and 9.8). This makes sense because Rasch is using conjoint measurement to measure people and items at the same time on the same scale. So, two pairs of tables are needed—one for people and one for items. First—the people, of course! Let's start with the table of measures (or scores) for the people (Figure 9.5).

Figure 9.5. Rasch Output for Sample Data—People

```
+---------------------------------------------------------------------------+
|ENTRY    RAW                     MODEL|   INFIT   |  OUTFIT  |PTMEA|        |
|NUMBER   SCORE  COUNT  MEASURE   S.E. |MNSQ  ZSTD|MNSQ  ZSTD|CORR.| PERSON|
|---------------------------------------------------------------------------|
|   4      8      9      67.8     6.8| .28   -.9| .10   1.3| .61| Steve |
|   5      8      9      67.8     6.8|2.64   1.6|3.33   1.9| .10| JUDY  |
|   7      8      9      67.8     6.8| .28   -.9| .10   1.3| .61| Roy   |
|   3      6      9      55.7     4.7|1.23    .6|1.80    .9| .54| Ann   |
|   2      5      9      51.6     4.5| .89   -.1| .59    .0| .70| Ed    |
|  10      5      9      51.6     4.5| .57  -1.1| .36   -.3| .77| Deb   |
|   8      3      9      43.6     4.7|1.12    .4| .72    .5| .68| Ben   |
|   1      2      9      39.0     5.1|1.37    .8| .79   1.0| .62| Joe   |
|   9      2      9      39.0     5.1| .41  -1.2| .22    .7| .79| Mike  |
|   6      1      9      32.9     6.1| .47   -.8| .17   1.7| .73| Pink  |
|---------------------------------------------------------------------------|
| MEAN    4.8    9.0    51.7     5.5| .93   -.2| .82    .9|     |        |
| S.D.    2.6     .0    12.4     1.0| .68       | .97    .7|     |        |
+---------------------------------------------------------------------------+
```

We can get output ordered in different ways. In this table, it is ordered based on ability, with the high-scoring people on top. We could have had the output in other orders: problems or misfits, order of data entry, or another useful order. The table presented in Figure 9.5 is divided into eight columns, as follows:

1. **Entry number** is the number assigned to the person as the data were entered into the computer. The first person, Steve (whose name is in the last column) was the fourth person in the pile of score sheets.

2. **Raw score** is the number of items correct. When calculating the score (or measure), Rasch eliminates all of the items that everyone got right or wrong, because they do not contribute to the calculation. That's a bitter pill to swallow, but we are looking for variability, so it works. Item 4 was excluded from this analysis, because everyone got it right. In Steve's case (first row), his score is 8.

3. **Count** tells you how many items Steve answered. Since Item 4 was eliminated, there were only nine items used to calibrate this test.

4. **Measure**, which we have bold-faced in the table, is the set of scores on the logistic ruler. Steve's score is 67.8 in our scale. Remember that we chose to label 50 as our midpoint.

5. **Model S.E.** is the standard error for Steve's score. We could be off by 6.8 logits, so if Steve were retested, he would probably score between a 61 and a 74.6. Notice that the error is different for everyone who took the test. This is a major difference from classical test theory where we do not differentiate for any individual. Scores are more precise (less error) for people in the middle, like Ed, for whom the standard error is only 4.5.

6. **Infit** is in the next column, and it is divided into two subcolumns. The first, mean square (MNSQ) tells us how accurate the measure is for Steve. Remember Guttman and the idea that no test or person is perfect? The fit statistic tells us how far off of the pattern we are—how well the odds worked for each person. We expect (and want) some difference, typically between .5 and 2.0. If the fit

statistic is less than .5, the odds were just too perfectly met. More than 2.0, we're not so sure what we've got—we call it a lot of "noise." The person did not respond as expected based on the probabilities. In these data, only Judy was in that range. Remember she got one wrong that she wasn't expected to get wrong. It's tough to make big decisions about fit with small numbers of people and items, but that is basically how it works. The standardized z (standardized numbers is a common technique that doesn't need an explanation) score is a significance test for the value of the MNSQ, and typically we look for values over 2.0 as indicating suspicious scores, but the sample size and the possibility of Type I error mean that we don't automatically assume anything until we investigate.

7. **Outfit** works a lot like infit except it takes into account whether the items that were not answered as predicted were on the high or low end of the scale. Infit focuses more on the mid-range. In practice, infit is sensitive to organized misfits like marking everything as answer Bs. Outfit is more sensitive to random misfits like test anxiety than an observer would notice from a raw score on a typical measure.

8. **PTMEA COR** is the point-biserial correlation. In classical test theory, you might recognize this as a measure of item discrimination. It's a little hard to think of what this means in terms of people, but we could say that it means that the people's scores are helping to differentiate between easy and hard items. Talk about role reversal!

9. People are people and they took the test—you probably guessed that one.

Next, in Figure 9.6, we show the Winsteps table output for the descriptive statistics for the people tested.

Figure 9.6. Rasch Output for Summary Statistics on the 10 Persons Measured

```
+-------------------------------------------------------------------+
|             RAW                      MODEL     INFIT     OUTFIT    |
|           SCORE     COUNT   MEASURE  ERROR   MNSQ  ZSTD  MNSQ  ZSTD |
|-------------------------------------------------------------------|
| MEAN       4.8       9.0     51.68    5.50    .93  -.2   .82    .9 |
| S.D.       2.6        .0     12.39     .96    .68   .9   .97    .7 |
| MAX.       8.0       9.0     67.81    6.80   2.64  1.6  3.33   1.9 |
| MIN.       1.0       9.0     32.91    4.46    .28 -1.2   .10   -.3 |
|-------------------------------------------------------------------|
| REAL RMSE   6.36  ADJ.SD  10.64  SEPARATION  1.67  person RELIABILITY  .74 |
|MODEL RMSE   5.58  ADJ.SD  11.07  SEPARATION  1.98  person RELIABILITY  .80 |
| S.E. OF person MEAN = 4.13                                         |
+-------------------------------------------------------------------+
           person RAW SCORE-TO-MEASURE CORRELATION = 1.00
     CRONBACH ALPHA (KR-20) person RAW SCORE RELIABILITY = .82
```

The Rasch model gives estimates of reliability of the test items and the persons taking the test at the same time.

As you can see, means and standard deviations are reported. Yes, they are what you think they are. The most important new number is the mean for INFIT ZSTD, which is expected to be 0.0 with a SD of 1.0. INFIT ZSTD is a standardized, unweighted statistical test of the disturbances in the data, as reflected in the fit of the data to the Guttman Scalogram.

Note that Figure 9.6 repeats the last two rows of Figure 9.5, making it a bit redundant. We only include the table because of the bottom part. Remember that we said earlier that a perk of using Rasch is that you get reliability as a bonus. Well, here is where you get it. For 10 items and 10 people, a Cronbach's alpha of .82 is pretty respectable!

Now it is time to turn to the items, and again we provide two Winsteps output tables in Figures 9.7 and 9.8.

Figure 9.7. Rasch Output for Sample Data—Items

```
                         ITEM STATISTICS:  MEASURE ORDER
+---------------------------------------------------------------------------+
|ENTRY    RAW                     MODEL|  INFIT   | OUTFIT   |PTMEA|        |
|NUMBER  SCORE   COUNT  MEASURE   S.E. |MNSQ  ZSTD|MNSQ  ZSTD|CORR.| ITEM   |
|-------------------------------------+----------+----------+-----+--------|
|    2       1      10    71.4    5.8| .90    .0| .31   1.9| .43| I0002|
|    1       3      10    60.6    5.1| .23  -1.5| .15    .0| .85| I0001|
|    3       4      10    55.7    4.9| .44  -1.1| .23   -.4| .86| I0003|
|    5       5      10    51.2    4.7| .56   -.9| .29   -.5| .84| I0005|
|   10       5      10    51.2    4.7|1.36    .8|3.03   1.5| .58| I0010|
|    7       6      10    46.9    4.7| .98    .1| .56    .1| .73| I0007|
|    6       7      10    42.6    4.7|1.50   1.0|1.76   1.0| .48| I0006|
|    9       8      10    38.0    4.9|1.03    .2| .53   1.0| .54| I0009|
|    8       9      10    32.3    5.9|1.25    .6| .51   2.0| .34| I0008|
|    4      10      10    24.9    9.4| MINIMUM ESTIMATED MEASURE | I0004|
|-------------------------------------+----------+----------+-----+--------|
| MEAN     5.8    10.0    47.5    5.5| .92   -.1| .82    .7|     |        |
| S.D.     2.6      .0    13.0    1.4| .41    .8| .90    .9|     |        |
+---------------------------------------------------------------------------+
```

The table provided in Figure 9.7 works the same way exactly as the one in Figure 9.5, just switching our attention to the individual items, consistent with our thinking that items and people influence each other. Think back about the concept of Lexile scores. Reading a passage is influenced by the ability of the child and the difficulty of the passage combined.

Here is where you see Item 4 (labeled I0004) being dropped out of the analysis. We mentioned it earlier in the people table. Rasch is labeling it "minimum estimated measure." If everyone got it wrong (and it was dropped), it would have been "maximum estimated measure." Either way, it does not contribute to the variability of scores.

All of the columns work the same way. You can see what Judy did to Item 10—the one she was likely to get right until the bumblebee stung her. Outfit was 3.03, which is above our ceiling of 2.0. It is showing up as outfit, because she was a top-scoring person, not a middle-range person. Again, though, we would need more people and items to be very worried about this. We probably would take a look at it, though, as part of our validation and evaluation efforts, and then put an ice cube on it in this case.

In Rasch, we make every effort to fix items rather than tossing them if they are problematic, because we found the item critical when we put it on the assessment. We start with a reason for putting each item on the test, so we need to salvage them.

Items and people are measured together and stay together. This is the measurement version of the Equal Rights Amendment. This is a different philosophy than the classical or traditional approach in which items are randomly representative of a domain of skills and a bit more expendable. We can't just toss out items in conjoint measurement, or we would have to shoot some people, too. The Rasch model is a conceptual approach to measurement as much as it is a statistical method.

Figure 9.8. Rasch Output for Summary Statistics on the 10 Items Measured

```
             SUMMARY OF 10 MEASURED (EXTREME AND NON-EXTREME) ITEMS
+----------------------------------------------------------------------------+
|            RAW                           MODEL      INFIT        OUTFIT     |
|            SCORE     COUNT    MEASURE     ERROR   MNSQ   ZSTD   MNSQ   ZSTD  |
|----------------------------------------------------------------------------|
| MEAN       5.8       10.0     47.49       5.48                              |
| S.D.       2.6        .0      13.00       1.38                              |
| MAX.      10.0       10.0     71.41       9.42                              |
| MIN.       1.0       10.0     24.92       4.69                              |
|----------------------------------------------------------------------------|
| REAL RMSE  5.90   ADJ.SD  11.58  SEPARATION 1.96  item   RELIABILITY  .79  |
|MODEL RMSE  5.66   ADJ.SD  11.71  SEPARATION 2.07  item   RELIABILITY  .81  |
| S.E. OF item MEAN = 4.33                                                    |
+----------------------------------------------------------------------------+
```

As in Figure 9.6, Figure 9.8 provides a repeat of the descriptive statistics. The Winsteps *person reliability* is equivalent to the traditional test reliability. Low values indicate a narrow range of person measures or a small number of items. To increase person reliability, test persons with more extreme abilities (high and low) or lengthen the test. Improving the test targeting may help slightly. The Winsteps *item reliability* has no traditional equivalent. Low values indicate a narrow range of item measures, or a small sample. To increase item reliability, test more people (Linacre, 2003).

THE FIT STATISTIC

In our example above, we noticed how the score for Judy had a potential problem called *misfit* because she answered one question incorrectly when the probability was that she would be correct on that question. We also noted that we do not make too big a deal out of one item, and we gave her an ice cube to cure the sting. Let's see what happens when the response pattern is really fouled up.

In the following example, we will change the results and have Ann doing some really bizarre things. In fact, her responses are all backwards; she gets wrong what she should get right (easy stuff) and right what she should get wrong (hard stuff). The Guttman scalogram is repeated below in Figure 9.9 with the data for Ann changed. We follow that with our people table in Figure 9.10.

Ann's score (7) is the same; but we've caused Ann to miss some easy items while getting some hard items correct. Remember that we said we could print out the tables in various orders. The following table is printed in misfit order—not measure order. A helpful feature of this process is that we can find the people who are not accurately measured very quickly by just changing the order in which the table is printed.

Figure 9.9. Guttman Scalogram With Ann's Data Manipulated for Misfit Demonstration

```
GUTTMAN SCALOGRAM OF RESPONSES:

            person |item number
                   |      1
                   |4896750312
                   |----------
            Steve +1111111110
             Judy +1111110111
              Roy +1111111110
              Ann +0010111111  (instead of 1110111100)
               Ed +1111011000
              Deb +1111101000
              Ben +1101100000
              Joe +1011000000
             Mike +1110000000
             Pink +1100000000
                   Easy    Hard
```

Figure 9.10. Rasch Output in Misfit Order Showing Ann on Top With the Most Misfitting Score (Not Reliable and Not Valid)

```
PERSON STATISTICS:  MISFIT ORDER
```

ENTRY NUMBER	RAW SCORE	COUNT	MEASURE	MODEL S.E.	INFIT MNSQ	INFIT ZSTD	OUTFIT MNSQ	OUTFIT ZSTD	PTMEA CORR.	PERSON
3	7	10	57.4	4.7	1.34	.8	8.53	2.5	A .39	ANN
5	9	10	69.5	6.8	2.60	1.6	2.86	1.9	B .09	JUDY
8	4	10	45.5	4.5	.93	.0	.59	.3	C .69	BEN
1	3	10	41.5	4.5	.93	.0	.59	.7	D .62	JOE
2	6	10	53.3	4.5	.88	-.1	.51	-.1	E .73	ED
10	6	10	53.3	4.5	.57	-1.0	.33	-.4	e .80	DEB
9	3	10	41.5	4.5	.54	-1.0	.31	.5	d .72	MIKE
6	2	10	37.3	4.7	.51	-1.3	.26	1.0	c .63	PINK
4	9	10	69.5	6.8	.28	-.9	.09	1.4	b .66	STEVE
7	9	10	69.5	6.8	.28	-.9	.09	1.4	a .66	ROY
MEAN	5.8	10.0	53.8	5.2	.89	-.3	1.42	.9		
S.D.	2.6	.0	11.8	1.0	.65	.9	2.49	.9		

Now Ann is at the top of this list. Her outfit is much higher than the normal value we expect (MNSQ > 2), so we need to look at Ann's test and responses carefully to see what's going on. This type of analysis is very sensitive to unusual patterns in students and can be used to detect carelessness, guessing, cheating, anxiety, clerical errors, response sets, and bias. There are reports in the Winsteps output to do that, but we will not present those here (Linacre, 2003).

GAIN SCORES—REAL OR IMAGINED?

One of the biggest advantages of using the Rasch model and calibrating items and people on the same interval scale is that we can make mathematical statements that make sense. We can talk about an item being twice as hard as another item or a person being twice as able in a scientific way. That allows us to measure growth accurately. In the data we have just fabricated, we could make the following mathematical computations and conclusions:

Steve (67.8) − Ben (43.6) = 24.3

Ben (43.6) − Pink (32.9) = 10.7

"Steve is twice as far ahead of Ben as Ben is ahead of Pink."

We can make this statement because we have scientifically based data on the difficulty of the items. One of the most common problems in using gain scores in the classroom context, such as the teacher work sample methodology, is that we reach conclusions about what students learned or did not learn based on tests that have items of different difficulty that have not been calibrated scientifically. While we could use CTT to calculate difficulty in one sense (the proportion of students responding correctly), that is dependent on the sample we happen to be working with, so the difficulty of the items is still not calibrated correctly. This makes faking possible. Here's an example:

The teacher administers a pretest of items that are pretty tough. He wants to show gains to graduate, and he does it by design.

The teacher teaches the unit and then gives an easier test. All students do better, but they may not have grown.

Let's illustrate this with the two test items that we used in Chapter 8 on cut scores. It's the same one we talked about for item-writing school above. This time we use it in the context of a pretest and a posttest:

Table 9.2. Pretest and Posttest Item Sample—Gain Scores Through Varying Level of Difficulty	
The Question: Who was the northern U.S. President during the Civil War? (Answer: Abraham Lincoln)	
Pretest Question Response Options and Percent of Students Selecting the Option	**Posttest** Question Response Options and Percent of Students Selecting the Option
a. Jefferson Davis (12%) b. Ulysses S. Grant (13%) c. George Washington (25%) d. Abraham Lincoln (50%)	a. Donald Duck (0%) b. Queen Elizabeth (0%) c. Pope John Paul (0%) d. Abraham Lincoln (100%)
Conclusion: Only half of the children knew who was president before instruction was provided; the remaining half learned as a result of the teacher's excellent teaching!	

If we had calibrated these two items on the same Rasch scale (sometimes called *test equating*), we would have produced person measures that showed no growth. Without such calibrations, we can make bar charts for the rest of time, but we do not have confidence that they are meaningful indications of growth.

RATINGS AND RATERS

One of the biggest challenges faced in performance assessment is ensuring that ratings are valid and reliable. We dedicated much attention in this book to the creation of good rating scales, including the definition of proficiency levels for each criterion rated. With Rasch, we have the opportunity to obtain empirical evidence of whether the ratings are working as we intended. Given the certification context, we expect that there will be very few unacceptable ratings. Depending on how we define upper levels of competency—acceptable and beyond—we need to know if our raters are using the scales in meaningful ways. Rasch output helps us make these judgments. Two examples follow in Figures 9.11 and 9.12. Both examples use three rating categories: high, medium, and low (so we don't argue about the descriptors!) As in all analysis, we need to compare our results with our expectations.

In the first example, provided in Figure 9.11, where rating categories are 0, 1, and 2, we see a clear distinction of categories in our ratings.

Figure 9.11. Sample Logistic Ruler of 10 Test Items Calibrated on a Ruler—User-Friendly Version

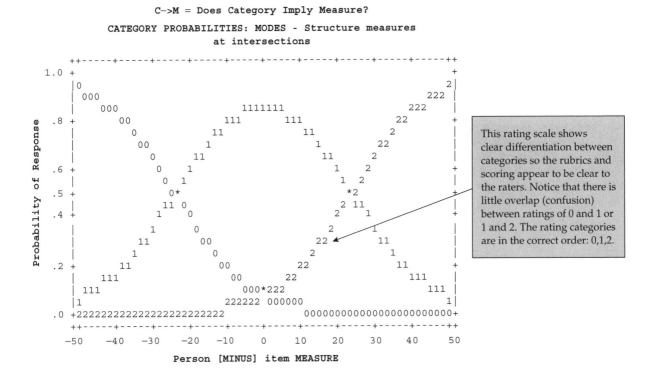

In the second example, provided in Figure 9.12, we see a problem. If we expect our raters to use the rating of 2—the middle ground—we see that they are not doing so. This can be a useful diagnostic tool. We see this when categories or rubrics are not clear (i.e., 1 = bridging, 2 = emerging, 3 = improving):

Figure 9.12. Rasch Output Showing Distinct Rating Categories

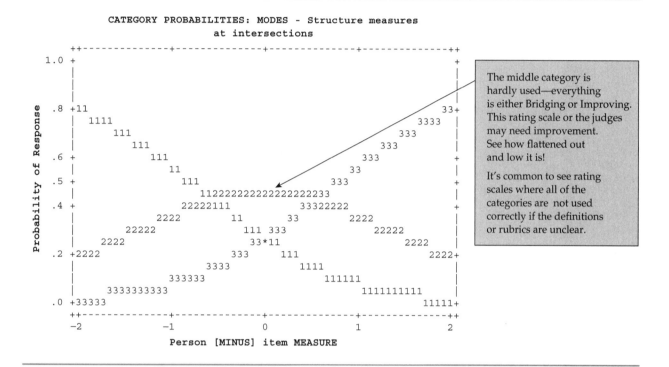

You may be thinking that you can obtain that information just from looking at the frequency counts of ratings, and this is partially correct. There are two major problems with that logic. First, we have already suggested that sometimes rating categories are unclear or misjudged. Second, ratings are not equal intervals; the distance from 1 to 2 is not always the same as the distance from 2 to 3. The Rasch model reveals category confusion and also puts the ratings on an equal interval ruler.

A final example is shown in Figure 9.13 on page 330. Sometimes rating scales have too many categories and folks get confused determining the difference between a score of 2 or 3 or 4. In this example, the rating scale has seven categories in the original items.

You can see that some categories aren't used and others are confused where there is a mixture of 5, 6, and 7 ratings. There are several solutions for this, but many people never realize the problem with their rating categories so they simply report misleading results.

Probably one of your greatest concerns, though, is the extent to which you can count on the raters to rate consistently. Everybody loves a good inter-rater reliability study! A special case of the Rasch model called the multifaceted Rasch model (MFRM) is useful at detecting rater errors such as leniency/severity, central tendency, randomness, halo, restriction of range effects (Myford & Wolfe, 2004). MFRM

Figure 9.13. Rasch Output Showing Rater Confusion—Too Many Categories

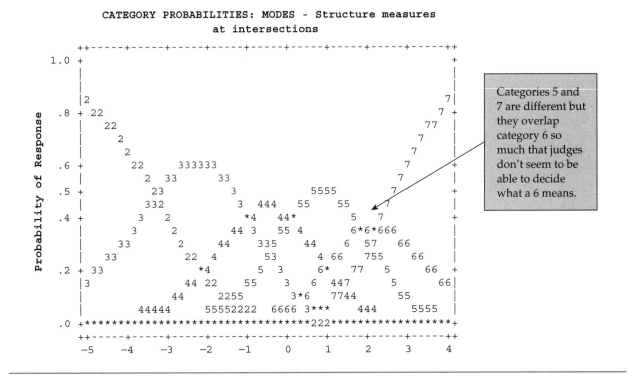

allows us to put judges on a ruler, just like items and respondents. We can see who is the harshest, who is the most lenient, and whether we should adjust teacher scores to report a fair measure.

All of our analyses thus far have used the Winsteps software. We now turn to another software package, FACETS, also from Linacre (1994), to demonstrate how to analyze rater effect. This time we also show you something real. Our example (see Figure 9.14) is from a study Braun (1988) did for the Educational Testing Service on the ratings of essays on the Advanced Placement English test. To this point, we have put two things on the same ruler—item difficulty and person ability. We now add the raters, whom we often refer to as judges. They are the "readers" in this study. The session is also calibrated on the same ruler. We can add other things, too, depending on our need, with this tool.

The first column is labeled *Measr* for measure. It is the logit value we use to create our ruler. In this case, the ruler is labeled from −2 to 1.

The second column is the students who wrote essays in response to one of three prompts. Each student, or examinee, is represented by an *. Better-rated essays are at the top and lower-rated essays are at the bottom. These tables are not produced here.

In the third column, each essay question is calibrated. This tells us that the essay questions are of approximately the same difficulty. B is slightly harder than A, which is slightly harder than C on the rulers. By examining the tabled values below, it looks like B is .15 logits harder than A, which is −.9 logits harder than C.

Figure 9.14. FACETS (MFRM) Output for Rater Consistency Analysis

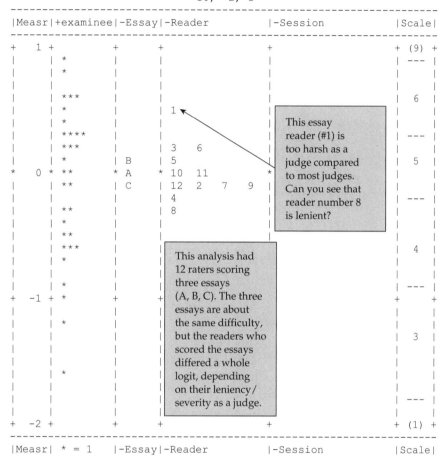

```
        AP English Essays (College Board/ETS)  04-10-2006 22:46:48
            Table 6.0  All Facet Vertical "Rulers". (Braun, 1988)

  Vertical = (1*, 2A, 3A, 4A) Yardstick (columns, lines, low, high)= 0,
                            10, -2, 1
  ------------------------------------------------------------------------
  |Measr|+examinee|-Essay|-Reader           |-Session           |Scale|
  ------------------------------------------------------------------------
  +  1 +         +       +                   +                   +  (9) +
  |    |   *     |       |                   |                   |  --- |
  |    |   *     |       |                   |                   |      |
  |    |         |       |                   |                   |   6  |
  |    |  * * *  |       |                   |                   |      |
  |    |   *     |       |  1                |                   |      |
  |    |   *     |       |                   |                   |      |
  |    | * * * * |       |                   |                   |  --- |
  |    |  * * *  |       |  3    6           |                   |      |
  |    |   *     |   B   |  5                |                   |   5  |
  *  0 *  * *    * A   * 10   11           * |                   |      |
  |    |  * *    |   C   | 12    2    7    9 |                   |      |
  |    |         |       |  4                |                   |  --- |
  |    |  * *    |       |  8                |                   |      |
  |    |   *     |       |                   |                   |      |
  |    |  * *    |       |                   |                   |      |
  |    | * * *   |       |                   |                   |   4  |
  |    |   *     |       |                   |                   |      |
  |    |         |       |                   |                   |      |
  |    |   *     |       |                   |                   |  --- |
  + -1 +   *     +       +                   +                   +      +
  |    |         |       |                   |                   |      |
  |    |   *     |       |                   |                   |   3  |
  |    |         |       |                   |                   |      |
  |    |         |       |                   |                   |      |
  |    |         |       |                   |                   |      |
  |    |   *     |       |                   |                   |  --- |
  |    |         |       |                   |                   |      |
  |    |         |       |                   |                   |      |
  + -2 +         +       +                   +                   +  (1) +
  ------------------------------------------------------------------------
  |Measr|  * = 1   |-Essay|-Reader           |-Session           |Scale|
```

> This essay reader (#1) is too harsh as a judge compared to most judges. Can you see that reader number 8 is lenient?

> This analysis had 12 raters scoring three essays (A, B, C). The three essays are about the same difficulty, but the readers who scored the essays differed a whole logit, depending on their leniency/severity as a judge.

In the fourth column is the rating of the readers by harshness/leniency. You can see that some readers are different from others on the rulers. The Session column could be used to determine if a particular time or day influenced the scores, but it's not used here. The Scale column is the raw rating scale for the essays, which could be scored from 1 to 9 (with higher being better) now aligned with the ruler.

Next we show a couple of tables from the computer output used to generate the rulers shown above. In these tables (our Figures 9.15 and 9.16), we show how the calibrations are used to adjust the scores to make them more fair. Figure 9.15 shows the adjustment for the essay scores—what would have been fair had there been less rater effect.

Figure 9.15. FACETS (MFRM) Output for Adjusting Scores to Make Them Fair—Essay Adjusted Average Score

```
AP English Essays (College Board/ETS)   04-14-2006 23:48:07
Table 7.2.1  Essay Measurement Report   (arranged by mN).
------------------------------------------------------------------------------
| Obsvd Obsvd Obsvd Fair-M|         Model | Infit      Outfit     |Estim.|
| Score Count Average Avrage|Measure S.E. | MnSq ZStd  MnSq ZStd|Discrm| N Essay
------------------------------------------------------------------------------
|  1762   384    4.6   4.51|   .13   .04 |  .98  -.2   .99  -.1| 1.03 | 2 B
|  1854   384    4.8   4.76|  -.02   .04 |  .80 -3.0   .79 -3.3| 1.21 | 1 A
|  1913   384    5.0   4.92|  -.11   .04 | 1.20  2.7  1.18  2.5|  .76 | 3 C
------------------------------------------------------------------------------
|  1843.0 384.0  4.8   4.73|   .00   .04 | 1.00  -.2   .99  -.3|      | Mean (Count:3
|    62.1    .0   .2    .17|   .10   .00 |  .16  2.4   .16  2.4|      | S.D.
------------------------------------------------------------------------------
RMSE (Model)  .04 Adj S.D.   .09 Separation  2.28 Separation Reliability  .84
Fixed (all same) chi-square: 18.5  d.f.: 2  significance (probability): .00
Random (normal) chi-square: 2.0   d.f.: 1  significance (probability): .16
------------------------------------------------------------------------------
```

Now let's look at how the raters' decisions can be adjusted based on their lenience or harshness in Figure 9.16.

If you look at the tabled values, you can see the differences. You can see that each judge scored 96 essays with Reader 1 awarding 392 points total while Reader 8 awarded 508 points. Reader 1 was too harsh by almost half a logit (.45); Reader 8 was too lenient by about one third of a logit (−.30), and Reader 10 was in the middle (0.0). FACETS can be used to provide a fair average to correct for this, but we won't do that here.

Well, why not? That's probably your big question now. Why take us this far? The reason is simple. This technique is used frequently in high-stakes testing to adjust examinee's scores when they fall just below the cut score. With the CYA approach, we do not need to do that. What we do need to do, though, is keep track of the degree to which our raters are scoring differently, yielding big differences in our decisions. Remember that in the data shared above, these are highly trained raters on a very high-stakes test. Being a little off is a dangerous thing.

In our work in teacher education, we may be doing less training and monitoring than ETS, but we may be in more danger of over- or under-rating. An analysis such as this can help us make mid-course corrections, with a gentle prompt to our raters to be tougher or harsher in their decisions! And that is only fair to our teachers and their students.

If this is something you feel the need to do, it may be far less expensive in the long run to hire your friendly statistician to run the numbers than to do lots of Cohen's kappas and retraining of all of your faculty.

LEARNING MORE ABOUT RASCH

If you want to know more, here is a list of useful texts These are ordered from beginning to advanced:

- *Applying the Rasch Model* by Bond and Fox (2001): This is a good beginner's book for anyone interested in learning the Rasch model.

Figure 9.16. FACETS (MFRM) Output for Adjusting Scores to Make Them Fair—Rater Adjusted Average Score

```
AP English Essays (College Board/ETS)   04-14-2006 23:48:07
Table 7.3.1  Reader Measurement Report   (arranged by mN).
```

Obsvd Score	Obsvd Count	Obsvd Average	Fair-M Avrage	Measure	Model S.E.	Infit MnSq	ZStd	Outfit MnSq	ZStd	Estim. Discrm	Exact Agree. Obs %	Exp %	Nu Reader	
392	**96**	4.1	4.00	.45	.08	.79	-1.5	.79	-1.5	1.23	19.7	19.8	1	1
433	96	4.5	4.43	.18	.08	1.06	.4	1.03	.2	.99	27.8	21.8	3	3
434	96	4.5	4.44	.17	.08	1.04	.3	1.06	.4	.93	38.9	21.9	6	6
444	96	4.6	4.55	.11	.08	.85	-1.1	.84	-1.1	1.14	36.1	22.0	5	5
461	96	4.8	4.73	.00	.08	.71	-2.3	.71	-2.2	1.31	42.4	21.9	10	10
466	96	4.9	4.79	-.04	.08	1.14	.9	1.11	.8	.81	30.6	21.9	11	11
470	96	4.9	4.83	-.06	.08	1.40	2.6	1.37	2.4	.63	27.8	22.0	12	12
473	96	4.9	4.86	-.08	.08	1.06	.5	1.06	.4	.93	20.8	21.7	2	2
479	96	5.0	4.93	-.12	.08	1.13	.9	1.13	.9	.83	28.8	21.7	7	7
484	96	5.0	4.99	-.15	.08	1.02	.1	1.01	.0	.97	24.1	21.6	9	9
485	96	5.1	5.00	-.16	.08	.52	-4.2	.53	-4.1	1.48	21.2	21.7	4	4
508	96	5.3	5.26	-.30	.08	1.23	1.6	1.21	1.4	.75	20.8	20.4	8	**8**
460.8	96.0	4.8	4.73	.00	.08	1.00	-.1	.99	-.2				Mean (Count: 12)	
29.5	.0	.3	.32	.19	.00	.23	1.8	.22	1.7				S.D.	

```
RMSE (Model)  .08 Adj S.D.  .17 Separation  2.17 Separation (not inter-rater) Reliability  .82
      Fixed (all same) chi-square: 66.2 d.f.: 11 significance (probability): .00
      Random (normal) chi-square: 10.9 d.f.: 10 significance (probability): .36
Rater agreement opportunities: 384  Exact agreements: 108 = 28.1% Expected: 82.6 = 21.5%
```

- *Rating Scale Analysis Rasch Measurement* by Wright and Masters (1982): An excellent early explanation of rating scale development.

- *Constructing Measures* by Mark Wilson (2005): This is a step-by-step process and explanation for creating a test with the Rasch model. Contains a CD.

- *Making Measures* by Wright and Stone (2004): A short and easy-to-read explanation of major Rasch concepts.

- *Probability in the Measure of Achievement* by Ingebo (1997): This work is from the Portland, Oregon, schools and describes their experience building tests.

- *Introduction to Rasch Measurement* by Smith and Smith (2004): A set of overview articles and applications for the Rasch model.

- *Best Test Design* by Wright and Stone (1979): This is a classic text, but it has excellent explanations, and basic statistical concepts are illustrated.

- *Item Response Theory for Psychologists* by Embretson and Reise (2000): A good overview of IRT, including the Rasch model along with others.

- *Item Response Theory* (2d Ed.), by Baker and Kim (2004): A serious mathematical explanation of IRT models, including Rasch. Contains a CD.

- *Rasch Measurement in Health Sciences* by Bezruczko (2005): A collection of application articles of the Rasch model.

- *Rasch vs. Two- and Three-Parameter Logistic Models From the Perspective of Conjoint Measurement Theory* by Karabatsos (1999): An article explaining the logic of different IRT models.

The online issues of *Rasch Measurement Transactions* (RMT) are also useful and readily available at the www.rmt.org Web site. A recommended journal is the *Journal of Applied Measurement*. A worksheet to help you sort out the pros and cons of IRT and CTT is provided at the end of this chapter.

V WRAP-UP

Classical test theory is viable, but it is limited in how far you can take it in terms of analyzing items and scores and conducting research. Rasch is a powerful technique that works well with small groups and has many advantages. The software is a little cumbersome, so you may need the help of a statistician if this is not something you enjoy doing. It is our method of choice if you:

- Want to find and fix teachers who were not tested accurately

- Want to find and adjust for rater error

- Want one analysis that gives you lots of information, including empirical evidence of validity and reliability

- Expect to do statistics to look for gain scores or longitudinal growth

- Need to report validity, reliability, or fairness of your assessments

You can use other methods, but here is our last comparison of the alternatives that are available to you:

- If you want a competitive test to determine the best teacher(s), some classical statistics work better.
- If you want to search for constructs such as personality, the 2PL or 3PL IRT methods work well, too.
- If you want to assess standards-based, complex performance with rating scales, Rasch is the best.

Parting Words of Wisdom: KISS—Keep it statistically simple!

CAATS CHAPTER 9—ACTIVITY #1

A Decision-Making Tool for Measurement Methods

List the pros and cons of both measurement theories. Then, select the one you prefer to use for each analysis you need to make.

Classical Test Theory		*Item Response Theory (Rasch Model)*	
Pros	*Cons*	*Pros*	*Cons*

10

Legal Integrity

They wrote the story on a column,
And on the great church-window painted
The same, to make the world acquainted
How their children were stolen away,
And there it stands to this very day.

—Robert Browning

In this chapter, as in Chapter 2, we reprint portions of an article titled "Portfolios, The Pied Piper of Teacher Certification: Legal and Psychometric Issues" (Wilkerson and Lang, 2003).[1]

When we wrote this article, even the title was controversial. Why the Pied Piper analogy reviewers asked us? We were thinking about the manner in which portfolios have been viewed as a kind of panacea to the assessment problem faced by institutions and districts seeking to provide educational programs leading to the credentialing of teachers. We also thought about the story of Hamlin, where panacea turned into Pandora's Box, and we used that piece of our work in Chapter 2. Now, we will talk about why.

For those who may not remember the fable well, it is the story of the small town of Hamlin, which was plagued by rats. The mayor hired the famed Pied Piper, renowned for his ability to charm animals into following him by tune of his magic flute. The mayor made an agreement with the piper to pay him a certain amount of money for ridding the town of the rats. The piper worked his magic, leading the rats to a bridge and causing them to all jump into the water and drown. On his return to the town to collect the debt owed him, he learned that the mayor had decided to renege on his bargain and would not pay him. In retribution, the piper again played his flute, but this time, he led all the children of the town away, never to be seen again.

The unstated (albeit morbid) analogy we were drawing in our article was that for those who hope to manage the requirements imposed by the accountability movement with portfolios, or any performance assessment device or devices, there is a need to pay the piper—the piper who plays the flute called psychometric integrity. If we fail to pay this piper, he, too may lead all the children (our teacher candidates) away through loss of program approval or accreditation or, worse, terribly costly litigation from the disgruntled teacher who was denied graduation and/or credentialing.

In the previous chapter, we concluded our discussion of how to collect evidence of validity, reliability, and fairness. To this point, we have attempted to convince our readers of the moral imperative of doing it right. Here, in this chapter, we introduce some of the potential legal consequences of not doing it right, drawing heavily on our EPAA article. There, we outlined the following scenarios of what could happen if an institution failed to do the necessary work in collecting evidence of validity, reliability, and fairness and is then sued by a disgruntled student or teacher. In Box 10.1, we summarize the Pied Piper story as it relates to our model.

Box 10.1. The Message of the Pied Piper

The unstated (albeit morbid) analogy we were drawing was that for those who hope to manage the requirements imposed by the accountability movement with portfolios or any other assessment devices, there is a need to pay the piper – the piper who plays the flute called psychometric integrity. If we fail to pay this piper, he, too may lead all the children (our teacher candidates) away through loss of program approval or accreditation or, worse, terribly costly litigation from the disgruntled teacher who was denied graduation and/or credentialing.

WHAT IF? A LEGAL SCENARIO

In this section, we reprint the story of Mary Beth JoAnne, a fictitious student suing a fictitious university because she was denied graduation after failing her portfolio. We present three scenarios, based on our understanding of the legal precedents. She prevails each time. We begin with the facts of the case.

Fictitious Case Facts

Mary Beth JoAnne, nicknamed MBJ, is a fictitious student who attends XYZ University, which is located in Florida where teacher education programs must certify that their graduates have demonstrated all 12 of the Florida Educator Accomplished Practices (FEAPs). The FEAPs are very similar to the INTASC

Principles. Florida has added two Practices, one on ethics and one on technology, which are embedded within the INTASC Principles. XYZ University requires candidates to successfully complete an electronic portfolio showcasing their work on the FEAPs. Here are the "facts" about MBJ and XYZ:

- Mary Beth JoAnne is 35 years old, is a single mother of three, works 20 hours a week at TarMart, and has typically enrolled in 15 to 18 credit hours per semester. She wants to get her teaching degree as quickly as possible so she can leave TarMart. She has the required grade point average (GPA) with a 3.0, has passed the certification exam, and has successfully completed all requirements of the internship except the portfolio requirement. Mary Beth JoAnne meets with the program coordinator, Jack, to challenge the result, since she has been given a U (unsatisfactory) in internship. The grade of U will prevent her from graduating and receiving her professional teaching certificate. Jack upholds his decision. There is no further appeals process.

- XYZ candidates must have the required GPA, pass the state teacher certification exam, and successfully complete the portfolio and the final internship to graduate. If they successfully pass the state's background check, they are awarded a five-year professional certificate, renewable every five years thereafter.

- XYZ's electronic portfolio includes 12 sections, one for each FEAP. At least three to five pieces of evidence are required for each practice. The same evidence may be used for multiple practices. These requirements are properly documented in the XYZ portfolio materials, the catalog, and an advising sheet provided to students on admission to the program.

- For each piece of evidence, candidates reflect on their work, linking it to the appropriate FEAP. The burden of proof, therefore, begins with the candidates; faculty either concur or do not concur with the student's reflection decisions, based on their re-evaluation of the work. Discussion about the FEAPs and strategies to write reflection are integrated into the curriculum.

- MBJ has attempted to complete the portfolio, but it was found to be unsatisfactory on two separate occasions in two sections. She failed to demonstrate the state's practice on critical thinking (FEAP #4) because she was unable to provide any examples of elementary student work showing that they had learned to think critically in her classroom. She also failed to demonstrate the adequate use of technology (FEAP #12) in the portfolio itself.

- There are orientations for students at the beginning of each semester to train them in the creation of their portfolios. The requirements are distributed or redistributed at that time. Faculty also trained on scoring the portfolios. Faculty advisors help candidates select their materials and sometimes provide candidates with the opportunity to fix their errors. Course syllabi provide advice on evidence that may be used in the portfolio, linking tasks to standards.

- The portfolios are reviewed prior to internship and at the end of internship. XYZ uses a scoring rubric for the portfolios that asks faculty to determine if the candidates have demonstrated each of the FEAPs and selected indicators for those FEAPs. Inter-rater reliability has been established.

- A fully equipped computer and materials lab is available Monday through Friday, 8 a.m. to 5 p.m.

In the following three sections, we invent scenarios to show what might happen if Mary Beth JoAnne decides to sue XYZ. Of course, there are many variables that remain unknown (e.g., testimony and dispositions, expertise and predispositions of lawyers and judges). These scenarios are intended as food for thought.

Scenario #1:

MBJ is Hispanic; her father is from Cuba, and her last name is Gonzalez.

She files a claim under Titles VI and VII of the 1964 Civil Rights Act. The results follow and are outlined in the steps used by the courts in such cases:

- Step 1: XYZ analyzes the results of the portfolio evaluations, and a smaller percentage of Hispanics (70%) passed than non-Hispanic Caucasians (95%). The court determines that there is disparate impact on minorities (biased results) with this test.

- Step 2: The burden of proof shifts to XYZ. MBJ claims that the portfolio could not provide valid evidence of her potential to perform in the classroom (i.e., to be certified). XYZ claims that the evidence is valid because the portfolio requirements were developed in direct response to the state's requirements, and it was organized around the state's FEAPs. The court finds as follows:

  - The court upholds XYZ on the decision about critical thinking, because the task is found to be job related. The judge's opinion notes that the state places a heavy emphasis on teachers' ability to impact K–12 learning, and this is documented in both state statute and State Board of Education Rule. The K–12 students' work is found to be one of the best measures of effective teaching within an internship context. There is an appropriate relationship between the requirement and the purpose, thereby establishing some evidence of validity.

  - The court finds that XYZ does not meet its burden of proof, however, for several other reasons. The most significant of these is that XYZ cannot show the relationship between the creation of a teaching portfolio and what teachers actually do in the classroom, thereby failing to establish adequate evidence of validity. While research indicates that portfolios are used as appropriate vehicles for self-improvement and showcasing, and MBJ may eventually need to create a portfolio for national level certification through NBPTS, this is not a task she would do in her K–12 classroom to help children learn. In fact, many schools in Florida do not have computers. More important, the standard on technology requires that teachers use the technology within the context of instruction and the management of instruction. Therefore, this test does not meet the standards of representativeness or relevance for the 12th Accomplished Practice on Technology. It is not an authentic representation of the work to be performed by MBJ in the classroom and is, therefore, not job related. The "business necessity" requirement for validity is not met.

  - The court also finds that the entire portfolio is not valid because the use of three to five pieces of evidence has not been validated for representativeness or relevance, nor was there any attempt on the part of the institution to look at issues of proportionality. Some evidence, and some practices, may be more important than others. Some may require more or less evidence to cover the depth and importance of the practice. Furthermore, XYZ has no procedures in place to ensure that the evidence selected by each candidate will meet the requirements of representativeness, relevance, and proportionality (validity). The court finds that the inconsistency in the specific contents of the portfolios makes the validation of the test virtually impossible.

– The court also finds that the institution has not used any research-based techniques to determine the cut score on the portfolio evaluation that could be reasonably used to differentiate between the potentially competent and incompetent teachers. There is no rational support for equally weighting the items used in each practice, and there could be no such support since the items vary from candidate to candidate.

– The court finds that instructional validity is also limited, since the preponderance of work on the portfolio was extracurricular. MBJ did not have adequate opportunity to learn the skills needed to prepare a portfolio, and she was given inadequate opportunity to remediate. These are also issues related to fairness and due process. The fact that she was able to document lack of support for, and experience in, the technological issues for building the portfolio adds weight to this claim. Finally, the court determines that it is not reasonable to require MBJ to use university labs that are only available during weekdays when she is a working adult. This impedes her opportunity to learn and succeed.

– The court finds that the use of different pieces of evidence by different candidates makes it impossible for adequate reliability studies to be conducted.

• Step 3: Not applicable, since MBJ prevails at Step 2. Step 3 addresses MBJ's rights to alternatives, and it is addressed below in Scenario #2. We summarize the reasons for MBJ's victory in Box 10.2.

Box 10.2.   Why MBJ Wins in Scenario #1

- Job-relatedness (construct validity)
- Lack of representativeness and proportionality (content validity)
- Invalid cut-score setting process (validity)
- No opportunity to learn and remediate (fairness and instructional validity)
- Lack of generalizability because of inconsistent evidence (reliability)

Scenario #2:

All of the contextual elements are the same; however, MBJ does not have very good lawyers, and there is no solid evidence brought forward on the psychometric integrity of the system. They do not make an effective case on all the aspects related to validity. Consequently, this time, XYZ prevails at Step 2. The trial moves to Step 3, and MBJ must prove that she was denied any reasonable alternatives. Remember Jack? He did not offer her any alternatives. MBJ now asserts that she should have been allowed to substitute some other technology-based work (e.g., the use of lessons infused with technology and the development of an electronic gradebook).

In this scenario, MBJ prevails again. XYZ is unable to show that the alternatives would be less effective than the original requirement. We summarize the reasons for MBJ's victory in Box 10.3.

Box 10.3. Why MBJ Wins in Scenario #2

Job-relatedness still works; the electronic gradebook would have been an appropriate, job-related alternative to an e-portfolio for the decision based on authentic tasks in the classroom. Most schools currently use electronic gradebooks, but few teachers have to prepare electronic portfolios.

Scenario #3:

All of the contextual elements are the same as in Scenario 1; however, MBJ is non-Hispanic Caucasian. Although females are a protected class, she knows that the statistics would not support a discrimination claim under Titles VI and VII. She does, however, have a due process claim under the Fourteenth Amendment. She asserts that the bachelor's degree in elementary education is a property right of which she has been deprived without either substantive or procedural due process. The court finds MBJ's rights to substantive due process were abridged on the same issues of content validity as described in Scenario #1 and this is sufficient for her to prevail.

The procedural due process claim introduces new problems for XYZ. The court finds in MBJ's favor again on procedural due process because Jack's decision was not fair. MBJ was given no alternatives and no opportunities for an appeal. He just said no. XYZ also takes no precautions against cheating and has no written policies about the assistance that faculty and peers can provide. Therefore, an unfair advantage is provided to some students who have multiple opportunities to revise their work and submit their portfolios, study with faculty who know how to use the technology and enjoy it, and receive substantive assistance from others. We summarize the reasons for MBJ's victory in Box 10.4.

Box 10.4. Why MBJ Wins in Scenario #3

Procedural due process resulting from various factors, the most important of which were a lack of appeals procedures and no written policies.

PSYCHOMETRIC ISSUES
AND LEGAL CHALLENGES

We have raised the specter of legal challenges, and it is time to address the challenges that can be faced in any certification test, be it large-scale or small-scale, state-administered or institutionally designed and administered. Legal challenges are based on the convergence of federal law and psychometric properties. It is difficult, if not impossible, to separate the two.

A review of the research written about legal challenges indicates that there are four basic legal issues in employment testing: two challenges under the 1964 Civil Rights Act (Title VI and Title VII) and two challenges under the Fourteenth Amendment to the United States Constitution (due process and equal protection). Title VI supplements Title VII by reinforcing the prohibition against discrimination in programs or activities that receive federal funding, which includes most teacher education program colleges and departments through grants and financial aid. (McDonough & Wolf, 1987; Mehrens & Popham, 1992; Pascoe & Halpin, 2001; Pullin, 2001; Sireci & Green 2000).

Precedent-setting cases come from a variety of employment situations, both within and outside the field of education. Many challenges introduce psychometric issues, the chief of which is validity. The applicable guidelines and standards governing the psychometric properties of the test and the decisions made using the test, whether or not it be in the field of education, are based in educational psychology and measurement as well as employment guidelines. The two most influential resources that provide operational direction for these legal decisions are the 1999 AERA, APA, and NCME *Standards for Educational and Psychological Testing* and the 1978 *Uniform Guidelines on Employee Selection Procedures* (Pascoe & Halpin, 2001). Perhaps you now see why we have pounded away at those AERA, APA, and NCME *Standards* throughout this book!

Regarding the Civil Rights Act of 1964, Titles VI and VII forbid not only intentional discrimination on the basis of race, color, or national original, but also practices that have a disparate impact on a protected class. Courts use a three-step process in which the burden of proof shifts back and forth from the plaintiff to the defendant. We used these three steps in our analysis of the Mary Beth JoAnne case. In the first step, the plaintiff must prove discrimination. The discrimination could either be intended or coincidental, but it is clearly the responsibility of the institution to ensure that unintended discrimination (disparate impact) does not occur. This is why the results changed from scenario to scenario, dependent on MBJ's ethnic background. She was a member of a minority group that was less successful than the majority population in the first scenario.

If discrimination has occurred, the defendant (SCDE or district) must demonstrate that the test was valid and is necessary, and this is most often linked to the job-relatedness (or the business necessity) of the test. It is in this second step, where the legal and psychometric issues converge (Scenario #1 of MBJ). If the defendant proves in court that the test is valid, the plaintiff has one more chance to prevail. If he or she can prove that the defendant could have used an alternative test with equivalent results, the defendant will lose (Scenario #2).

There are two basic requirements in the U.S. Constitution's Fourteenth Amendment that apply to this context: equal protection and due process. For a plaintiff to win under the equal protection claim, it must be shown that there was intent to discriminate. This is difficult and, therefore, rarely used. The due process provisions, however, have become relatively common. They forbid a governmental entity from depriving a person of a property or liberty interest without due process of law. (The *Debra P. v. Turlington* [1984] case established the diploma as a property right.) There are two kinds of these claims: substantive and procedural due process. Substantive due process requires a legitimate relationship between a requirement and the purpose. This is much easier to establish than the business necessity requirement of the Civil Rights Act. Procedural due process requires fairness in the way things are done, and these include advance notice of the requirement, an opportunity for hearings/appeals, and the conduct of fair hearings. Psychometric properties are excluded from this claim. MBJ prevailed on both types of due process in Scenario #3. (Mehrens & Popham, 1992; Sireci & Green, 2000).

Thus, the linkage between legal rights and psychometric properties can occur in two places, opening the Pandora's Box of validity and reliability. First it can occur within the context of Step 2 of a discrimination claim under Title VI and/or Title VII of the Civil Rights Act, where there is intended discrimination or disparate impact on a protected class. Second, it can occur within the context of a lack of a legitimate relationship between a requirement (e.g., a test) and a purpose (e.g., protecting the public from unsafe teachers) that constitutes a violation of substantive due process rights as assured by the Fourteenth Amendment of the U.S. Constitution.

> **DISCLAIMER**
>
> The authors hold degrees in measurement, not law. We express here our opinions and analyses as measurement experts and researchers, not lawyers.

There are other potential legal challenges as well, but they are beyond the scope of this chapter. Worth mentioning in passing, however, is the potential for challenges by faculty who are asked to conduct extensive work, without remuneration, outside of their regularly assigned course-based teaching assignments (Sandman, 1998). This is, of course, particularly problematic with portfolios completed and reviewed outside of the regular course teaching/assessing process.

LEGAL ISSUES AND PRECEDENTS

It is difficult to remain informed about current legal practice with regard to professional licensure, but it is important (Pascoe & Halpin, 2001). There are four sets of applicable laws and guidelines which we discuss in this chapter. They are listed in Box 10.5.

> **Box 10.5. Applicable Laws and Guidelines**
>
> - First and Fourteenth Amendments of the U.S. Constitution
> - Titles VI and VII of the Civil Rights Act
> - 1999 AERA, APA, & NCME *Standards for Educational and Psychological Testing*
> - 1978 *Uniform Guidelines on Employee Selection Procedures*

The courts have granted governmental authorities wide latitude as long as they have taken reasonable steps to validate the tests and the cutoff scores. Whether the plaintiffs are minorities or members of the majority population, other steps that the courts have considered include (1) providing ample prior notice before implementation of the high-stakes phase, (2) allowing accommodations in the administration of the tests for the disabled, and (3) allowing retesting and, to the extent feasible, remediation (Zirkel, 2000).

Courts recently have been supportive of performance measures (Lee & Owens, 2001; Rebell, 1991). As far as teacher educators are concerned, Pullin (2001) notes that the courts have been generally reluctant to second-guess educators' judgments of educational performance based on subjective evaluations. This is of some comfort to the teacher education community. She goes on to say that in situations in which the individual stakes are not as high, such as during an educator preparation program or during a probationary period of employment, then fewer procedural protections are required. If the decision making seems to be based on the purely evaluative judgments of qualified professionals, courts may be reluctant to intervene. On the other hand, how can we be sure?

Lemke (2002), too, offers an opinion. She reviewed court decisions concerning the dismissal of college students from professional programs and determined that courts upheld school decisions when the institution followed its own published processes and the students' rights had been observed. This, too, provides for a high degree of comfort. If students are told what is expected of them in clear terms, colleges are safer. But Lemke also found that there is a lack of information about what the judicial system finds to be appropriate and inappropriate admissions and dismissal procedures. She looked at the decision of *Connelley v. University of Vermont* (1965), in which the federal district court ruled that it is within the purview of academic freedom for faculty to make decisions about students' progress. Faculty and administrators were described as uniquely qualified to make these decisions. In those days, though, certification was still the purview of the state. Lemke also reviewed eight cases of students filing against institutions. In these cases, the institutions had the right to make decisions about a student's academic fitness as long as it followed its advertised processes. Reasons for dismissals that were upheld included the use of subjective assessments in clinical experiences, time requirements for program completion, comparison of test scores between the plaintiff and peers, GPA, and absenteeism.

Educators in Florida, though, have seen that the PK–20 system is not so safe. The groundbreaking *Debra P. v. Turlington* case (1984) begins to reduce the level of comfort engendered in the previous two citations. This was a diploma sanction case, bringing educators back to the issue of content validity. It is generally conceded that a state has the constitutional right to use a competency test for decisions regarding graduation. A diploma is considered a property right, and one must show some evidence of curricular/instructional validity, or what is also called *opportunity to learn* or *adequacy of preparation*. In this case, both due process and the equal protection clauses of the Fourteenth Amendment were found to be violated by Florida officials, who were using a basic skills test for diploma denial at the high school level. In appeals, additional issues were raised about whether the test covered material that was adequately covered in Florida's classrooms, and this has become the major precedent for looking at "instructional or curricular" validity. The judge ruled that, "What is required is that the skills be included in the official curriculum and that the majority of teachers recognize them as being something they should teach" (Mehrens & Popham, 1992). In our MBJ example, XYZ required candidates to prepare their portfolios outside of their regular courses, thereby increasing their risk of challenge based on the principle of opportunity to learn.

The continuing shift in responsibility to SCDEs from DOEs for more and more of the burden of making certification decisions can easily result in successful claims by unhappy students who are denied their career dreams. The diploma denial challenges, combined with the challenges based on denial of a teaching certificate by a state agency, provides for a natural leap to challenge diploma/certificate denial from an SCDE.

McDonough and Wolf (1987) identified five issues around which litigation against educational testing programs occurs: (1) the arbitrary and capricious development or implementation of a test or employee selection procedure, (2) the statistical and conceptual validity of a test or procedure, (3) the adverse or disproportionate impact of a testing program or selection procedure on a "protected group," (4) the relevance of a test or procedure to the identified requirements of the job (job-relatedness), and (5) the use of tests of selection procedures to violate an individual's or group's civil rights.

Courts have generally required evidence that the cut score selected for a test be shown to be related to job performance. In the Alabama case against National Evaluation Systems (NES) (Groves v. Alabama State Board of Education, 1991), the assessment designers, the court found that the company engaged in practices "outside the realm of professionalism" and that it violated the minimum professional requirements for test development. Among the problems found were decisions in test development that resulted in test scores that were arbitrary and capricious and bore no rational relationship to teacher competence. There was a similar finding in Massachusetts against the same company (Ludlow, 2001). In *Groves v. Alabama Board of Education,* the court found in 1991 that the arbitrary selection of a cut score without logical or significant relationship to minimal competence as teacher had no rational basis nor professional justification. As such, it failed to meet the requirements of Title VI and was not a good-faith exercise of the professional judgment. Evidence should be available that the cut score for a test does not eliminate good teachers from eligibility for teaching jobs (Pullin, 2001).

The California Basic Education Skills Test (CBEST) was challenged in 1983 under Title VII by the Association of Mexican-American Educators. The state won the case based on a job-relatedness study (Zirkel, 2000). In 1984, Florida lost a challenge to the Florida Performance Measurement System (FPMS) when the question of the validity of the decision about a teacher's certificate removal was successfully raised (Hazi, 1989). Georgia's Teacher Performance Assessment Inventory (TPAI) challenge was won by the plaintiff based on due process and validity challenges (McGinty, 1996). The U.S. Department of Justice sued the State of North Carolina in 1975 under Title VII based on results on the National Teacher Examination from the Educational Testing Service. They won the claim when the court found the test to be unfair and discriminatory because a validation study had not been conducted and the passing score was arbitrary, thereby denying equal protection. A second similar claim was filed against the State of South Carolina, but in this instance the state prevailed based on a proper validation study causing the test to be deemed fair and appropriate (Pascoe & Halpin, 2001). There are many such discussions in the literature. The point is that tests, even those written by major test publishers, can be successfully challenged.

Many college administrators believe that academic freedom will protect their decisions about denying admission or graduation to teacher candidates (Milam, 2006). As long as the context is academic freedom, almost any criteria deemed important by faculty or the institution can be used for admission, grading, or completion requirements, including physical-motor skills *(Southeastern Community College v. Davis, 1979)*, disabilities (*Ohio Civil Rights Commission v. Case Western Reserve University*, 1996), interaction with instructors (*Richmond v. Fowlkes*, 2000), inability to interact (*Lunde v. Iowa Board of Regents*, 1992), maturity (*Van De Zilver v. Rutgers University, 1997)*, cooperation (*Stretten v. Wadsworth Veterans Hospital*, 1976), lack of judgment (*University of Michigan v. Ewing*, 1985), personality (*Kirsch v. Bowling Green State University*, 1996), harmony (*McEnteggart v. Cataldo*, 1972), and even personal hygiene (*Board of Curators of University of Missouri v. Horowitz*, 1978).

Unfortunately, there are some recent challenges where academic freedom appears to provide less of a safety net (R. Wilson, 2005). In *McConnell v. Le Moyne College* (2006), the appellate court ordered admission of Mr. McConnell after he had been dismissed from the program for having values inconsistent with those of the university. (He believed in corporal punishment and disavowed multiculturalism.) Although university officials contended that it was their expert opinion that he did not have what it takes to be a teacher, the university did not have a standards-based process to assess him, nor did they have policies and procedures in place to tell him they were measuring his values and that he could challenge their decisions. The court held that Le Moyne had violated his rights to due process and had to take him back.

Due process for students affords a guarantee of basic fairness (Linder, 2006). Common issues in due process cases involve a right to appeal or public hearing, *reliable* evidence to prevent cruel and unusual punishment, and the restriction of a person's life, liberty, or property. Even though the quality of evidence as trustworthy and reliable originates in criminal cases, there is a possibility that a civil plaintiff would attack a poor assessment under due process, particularly given the act of teacher certification as a result of the program.

We have already described an assessment process that provides evidence that is valid, reliable, and fair (CAATS model), and we have described two that do not (XYZ and Le Moyne Universities). One was truth and one was fiction. By combining the use of stated and accepted professional standards as the basis for a measurement system, the provision of opportunities to learn and to remediate, and the accessibility of a hearing that can challenge decisions, an institution or district can feel more secure if challenged on due process. Institutions will tend to prevail on cases of academic freedom when they can support the expert judgment of faculty. But what about cases where the judgment is not based on expertise but rather whim and different treatment of teachers? We suspect that a lack of high-quality assessment evidence may be the ultimate test in academic freedom and due process cases. Imagine the forensic expert who claims there is evidence of the guilty party, but cannot describe the evidence or the process of collecting the evidence.

It now appears that colleges of education or school districts who act as agents of the state to certify teachers are less entitled to the protections of academic freedom

VALIDITY VS. RELIABILITY

Validity trumps reliability. Lawyers and measurement folks agree. As scary as that may be to all of us, it means you can't skip validity in favor of inter-rater reliability!

and more liable for violation of due process. In writing about the Le Moyne case, we concluded (Wilkerson, 2006) that:

> If the data collected have the potential to provide useful information to advise, diagnose, and remediate, it is clearly well worth the time and resource investment for colleges of education to develop good measurement devices from which solid decisions about candidates' skill-based values surface. The colleges can prevail in court, be accredited, and produce better teachers at the same time.

The same holds true, perhaps even more so, for competencies.

END NOTE

We end this work with a parting note about planning. We teach our students day after day that they should never enter a classroom without a lesson plan, a unit plan, and a classroom management plan. There's always a plan. Sometimes we call it something else, like a concept map. We would never hire a builder without an architect or try to put together a computer desk without a plan or set of instructions. Yet somehow, many of us have deluded ourselves into thinking that planning is less important in our world of teacher assessment.

In this book, we have attempted to demonstrate how solid planning not only gives us the data we need in a systematic way, but it gets us there safely. We hope that you have found our discussions useful, our model informative, and our worksheets invaluable. But even more important, we hope that we have convinced you that failure to measure competencies systematically and with integrity will surely leave some children behind.

We fear that the failure to measure professional and pedagogical skills may well leave some teachers behind, too. As we watch the advocates of measuring subject area knowledge in lieu of teacher skills or with a paper-and-pencil test that purports to measure teacher skills (Darling-Hammond & Sykes, 2003), we wonder what will happen to all the teachers who come through alternative routes and then cannot compete with the younger generation of teachers trained in pedagogy. They may find themselves across the hall from each other, both applying for National Board Certification, one with the skills to prepare a portfolio and one without. What will be the long-term impact of this frustration on the children these teachers teach?

It is obvious that bad measurement can lead to uninformed or incorrect decisions that can have dire consequences. We cannot tell if a hospital that has a lot of deaths is a poor hospital or one that does a good job of treating the worst patients. Should we close the hospital because of death rates, or pour money into it to do better what it already does well? If we look closely at the practice of each physician, we will make the right decision about quality and funding for that hospital. Frustrated legislatures propose teacher pay for performance that is simplistic (Schroeder, 2006) or horribly complicated value-added statistical models (McCaffrey et al., 2003). As a community of practitioners, we need to acknowledge that quality assessment at the local level is the effort we have failed to produce, which has led to the tidal wave of interventions and perceptions of ineffective teacher education.

We hope we have given you some of the tools you need to make good assessment happen. For all of our sakes, Hamlin just *must* be a medieval fairytale village.

P.S.: Here's one for the road:

Story Ender

We're down to just one:

Your boss, Dr. Nohaydinero (find a Spanish-speaking friend if you don't get this one), says: "We just need to keep the board, the state department, or NCATE out of our hair. This Wilkerson/Lang CAATS model is just too darned expensive. Cut the junk, and just do the minimum. Give 'em a test on content and have 'em write a lesson plan, and be done with it.

You say . . .

NOTE

1. The authors thank the editor of *Education Policy Analysis Archives* for permission to adapt portions of material previously printed as an article in the journal, an open-access, refereed education journal available at http://epaa.asu.edu.

Appendix A

Tasks Developed for Florida Alternative Certification Program Assessment System

These tasks were developed for the Florida Alternative Certification Program Assessment System sponsored by the Florida Department of Education. They are coded to the Florida Educator Accomplished Practices (FEAPs), which parallel the INTASC Principles.

FEAP #1 and INTASC #8: Assessment

01A: Unit Exam/Semester Final Assessment

01B: Alternative Assessment

01C: Classroom Assessment System

01D: Case Study of a Student Needing Assistance

01E: Demonstration of Positive Student Outcomes

FEAP #2 and INTASC #6: Communication

02A: Written Communication From the Teacher

02B: Evaluation of Videotaped Teaching

02C: Interaction Between Teacher and Students

FEAP #3 and INTASC #9: Continuous Improvement

03A: Professional Development Plan

03B: School Improvement Team Involvement

FEAP #4 and INTASC #4: Critical Thinking

04A: Questioning Using a Taxonomy

04B: Lesson(s) to Teach Critical and Creative Thinking

04C: Portfolio of K–12 Student Work

04D: Critical-Thinking Strategies and Materials File

FEAP #5 and INTASC #3: Diversity

05A: A Demographic Study of Your Students and a Plan to Meet Their Needs

05B: Documentation of Diversity Accommodations

05C: Individual Planning for Intervention

05D: Observation for Diversity

FEAP #6 and INTASC #9: Ethics

06A: Analysis of Slippery Situations

06B: Multiple Jeopardies and Infraction Penalties

06C: Potential Infractions and Teacher Responses

FEAP #7 and INTASC #2: Human Development and Learning

07A: Assessing Developmental Characteristics

07B: Assessing Learning Modalities

07C: Student Attitudes About School Learning

FEAP #8 and INTASC #1: Knowledge of Subject Matter

08A: Interdisciplinary Unit

08B: Portfolio of K–12 Student Work (cont.)

08C: Integrating Literacy Skills in Instruction

08D: Integrating Mathematics Skills in Instruction

FEAP #9 and INTASC #5: Learning Environment

09A: Classroom Management System

09B: Cooperative Learning Activity

09C: Case Study on Classroom Management and Motivation

09D: A Productive Classroom Environment

FEAP #10 and INTASC #7: Planning

10A: Semester/Year Curriculum Plan and Individual Unit Plan

10B: Semester Planning Record and Analysis

10C: Comprehensive Resource File

FEAP #11 and INTASC #10: Role of the Teacher

11A: Open House and Other Professional Involvement Plan

11B: Parent/Teacher/Student Conference

11C: Kids in Crisis

11D: Case Study of a Student Needing Assistance (cont.)

FEAP #12: Technology

12A: Computer-Enhanced Instructional Delivery

12B: Computer-Enhanced Management of Instruction

12C: Resource Materials From the Web

Appendix B

Glossary

Alignment

Alignment is a judgmental process by which we analyze two sets of like elements (e.g., standards) and position together the ones that are similar. Because it is a judgmental process, not all people will agree on every alignment.

> *Guiding Question: "Does the standard I am reading sound a lot like another standard or standards? Is this just wordsmithing?"*

Analytical Scoring

When raters score analytically, they think about and rate each of the criteria in the rubric. The ratings are then summed or aggregated in some way, and the teachers have feedback on what they did correctly and what they did not do correctly?

> *Guiding Question: "Do I want to give my teachers feedback on what was right and what was wrong so they can fix it, or is a global single score adequate to the purpose?"*

Common Format

A common format is helpful for writing tasks and includes, at a minimum, detailed instructions and scoring rubrics written in the same style.

> *Guiding Question: "How can I provide adequate instructions to teachers and scoring rubrics for raters that will yield high-quality and consistent data?"*

Competency

We use the word *competency* in this book to mean knowledge and skills—Bloom's cognitive domain. Competency may be defined differently by various groups. Competency as assessed for certification can be at a minimal level or restricted to subject matter knowledge, while competency for career advancement (e.g., NBPTS or promotion) can be at a much higher level.

> *Guiding Question: "What does the teacher need to know and be able to do?"*

Conceptual Framework

The conceptual framework is the content and philosophy that guide teaching and assessment. It is drawn from standards, research, professional experience, and vision.

> *Guiding Question: "What do I want to include in my system?"*

Construct

The concept or characteristic that a test or assessment system is designed to measure. In this work, we name it *teacher performance.*

> *Guiding Question: "What's the big picture idea of what we are assessing?"*

Construct Irrelevant Variance

Construct irrelevant variance is any extraneous factor that distorts the meaning or interpretation of a score. A common form of this variance is measuring the wrong thing.

> *Guiding Question: "Have I mixed some other stuff into the decision I am trying to make?"*

Construct Under-Representation

Construct under-representation occurs when we do not have enough data to make a decision about the construct because we haven't sampled well.

> *Guiding Question: "Do I have enough stuff to decide well?"*

Content

The content is the set of topics or matter with which we are going to work. Content includes, at a minimum, the standards for teaching—institutional or district, state, and national. The content defines precisely what material will be assessed and requires good sampling procedures once defined.

> *Guiding Question: "What will we assess?"*

Content Domains

Content domains consist of each grouping of standards that have been aligned because they are all similar and convey the same basic set of ideas.

> *Guiding Question: "Does this set of standards and indicators hang together to form a body of content that can be assessed?"*

Content Validity

Content validity is a form of validity evidence that ensures that the test measures the construct comprehensively and appropriately, and does not measure another construct instead of, or in addition to, the construct of teacher performance on the job.

> *Guiding Question: "How do I know that the decisions I will make about teachers will be based on adequate coverage of the construct of teacher performance and nothing else?"*

Context

The context defines and describes the conditions that surround us and influence our work. They may be institutional, state, or national. Some contextual factors are helpful and some are not.

> *Guiding Question: "What are the factors that will help or hinder implementation of the envisioned assessment system?"*

Credibility

Believability. Reasonable, practical, and useful.

> *Guiding Question: "Is there any evidence that this stuff is right?"*

Criteria

Criteria are the aspects of a performance task that will be judged in the scoring rubric. They help separate high-quality and low-quality work.

> *Guiding Question: "What will I look for to judge the quality of this task?"*

Critical Skills

Critical skills are the aspects of performance that a teacher should not be able to miss. They are the most valued aspects of job performance. A critical skill for pilots is landing the plane. The pilot who can't land the plane should not be a pilot.

> *Guiding Question: "What do the teachers absolutely have to do, and if they can't do it, they shouldn't be teachers?"*

Crosswalks

Crosswalks are charts or tables that align courses (or assignments in courses or staff development workshops) and standards.

> *Guiding Question: Not recommended; there is no question.*

Cut Score

The cut score determines who passes and who fails. Teachers below the cut score are not allowed to continue on the program. It may be reported as a raw score, percent correct, or scaled score derived through classical or item response theory.

> *Guiding Question: "At what point is the total score so low that we are comfortable saying to a prospective teacher, 'You cannot be a teacher because you do not have the minimal skills required and you might harm children'?"*

Data Aggregation

Data are compiled in ways to make different decisions. Decisions at a criterion level could be based on a rubric and then combined (or aggregated) to reach a task level score (e.g., raw percent or scale) or a decision related to a standard (demonstrated/ not demonstrated). Data continue to be aggregated for the standard across tasks and then for the certification decision itself. Data can be combined for individuals in this way and subsequently for programs as a whole.

> *Guiding Question: "How can I combine decisions throughout my system in a way that is useful for decision making?"*

Data Analysis

The analysis of data often starts with a philosophy that dictates a technical choice of a statistical technique.

> *Guiding Question: "What kind of data analysis, item analysis, or statistical reports do I need?"*

Differential Item Functioning (DIF)

DIF is a statistical process that seeks to determine if there are meaningful differences in the way *subgroups* perform, particularly groups that are classified as protected— women and minorities. It is okay for the performance to be different, as long as it is not because of *problems in the construction or administration* of the assessment itself.

> *Guiding Question: "Are minorities and women doing worse on the assessments because they are minorities and women?"*

Differential Person Functioning (DPF)

DPF is a statistical process that seeks to determine if there are meaningful differences in the way *item subsets* perform, particularly patterns that are classified as a certain type— representing a subconstruct. It is okay for the performance to be different, as long as it is not because of *problems in the persons* such as anxiety, cheating, guessing, or test strategy.

> *Guiding Question: "Are any item patterns demonstrating that a person's score needs individual interpretation?"*

Directions

Directions are the same as instructions. They tell teachers precisely what evaluators are looking for so that they can complete the task successfully.

> *Guiding Question: "What do I want teachers to do in this task?"*

Empirical Evidence

Evidence based on numbers and scores that the assessment is credible.

> *Guiding Question: "What do the numbers tell us about credibility?"*

Fairness

Fairness ensures that rights are protected and that test takers are not penalized because they are a member of a protected group, or because they don't have adequate opportunities to learn and succeed, or because the criteria and tasks have language or contexts that are offensive to them, or because their rights to due process were violated.

> *Guiding Question: "Do all teachers have an equal opportunity to complete the tasks successfully, regardless of gender, ethnicity, or handicapping condition, and is there an appeals process in place?"*

Formal Assessments

Formal assessments provide data for decision making and are typically highly structured with scoring keys or rubrics and can be either objective or subjective.

> *Guiding Question: "What tests, tasks, or performances will give me concrete data to use for confident decision making?"*

Formative Assessments

Formative assessments are used primarily to conduct a kind of status check during which we make decisions about what immediate improvements in instruction are needed so that our students can achieve our goals better. They occur during instruction and may be formal or informal, traditional or informal in nature.

> *Guiding Question: "How can we track students' growth in ways that allow us to help them learn what they missed?"*

Frameworks

Frameworks are two-way grids that help one conceptualize a balanced and appropriate set of assessments.

> *Guiding Question: "What do I have in my system that fits a selected set of planning criteria (e.g., timing, standards, Bloom's taxonomy)?"*

Growth Portfolios

Growth portfolios contain evidence collected over time so that users can determine if growth is as expected, greater than expected, or less than expected. They are formative in nature and help us determine next steps—keep going, change direction, remediate, quicken the pace.

> *Guiding Question: "What artifacts will help me track improvement over time?"*

Holistic Scoring

Scoring guides that are holistic in nature lead to a single decision (e.g., a 6 or a "satisfactory"). While raters think about multiple criteria, they do so all at once and do not systematically rate each criterion. They make a single, global judgment instead—based on the criteria they keep track of informally or in their heads. This method provides no feedback for improvement to teachers unless comments are provided.

Guiding Question: "Do I want to give feedback for diagnostic purposes or is a summative single score adequate for the purpose?"

Indicators

Indicators are statements or subparts that give specific examples or meanings to standards. We would call them *substandards,* but that might be misinterpreted!

Guiding Question: "What are the details of the standards that help me understand what the standard is intended to mean?"

Inferences

Inference levels are controlled by the level of difficulty in making a decision or judgment. They range from no judgment (low inference), as in a correct/incorrect response, to extensive judgment requiring professional expertise to interpret a response.

Guiding Question: "How hard will it be to make a decision about quality—or how much subjectivity is there in this decision?"

Informal Assessments

Informal assessments tend to be loosely constructed and analyzed but are important to give users an overall sense of strengths, weaknesses, or important issues for moving forward or remediation. One of the most common strategies is casual observation of the class.

Guiding Question: "Do students appear to be learning or understanding or behaving in the way we expected?"

Inter-Rater Reliability

Inter-rater reliability is an index of consistency across raters calculated using correlations. Raters' scores should consistently go up or down across students. When one rater rates a student high, the other rater should rate him/her high. Low ratings should also be consistent across raters. If some raters score students high and the other raters score the same students as low, then the ratings are not consistent or reliable.

Guiding Question: "Are scorers consistent in their ratings?"

Job Analysis

A job analysis requires that we identify all of the important things a teacher is expected to know and do to be able to perform the job well.

Guiding Question: "What does a teacher have to do on the job to ensure that children learn?"

Judgmental Evidence

Judgmental evidence relies on expert opinion rather than numbers.

> *Guiding Question: "What do the experts say?"*

Management or Tracking System

The management or tracking system is the process used to keep track of scores in the system so that reports can be generated for decision making. It may be kept by hand or on a computer.

> *Guiding Question: "What procedures and materials do I need to have in place to retrieve data?"*

Maintenance System

The maintenance system is the set of procedures and plans used to keep the system going and to make updates and changes as needed.

> *Guiding Question: "How will I know what needs to be changed, when, and by whom?"*

Measures

The scientifically determined amount of any predetermined construct expressed in equally defined units.

> *Guiding Question: "How well did I do? How much do I know?"*

Product- and Performance-Based Tasks

Tasks are the things we ask teachers to do to show evidence of their competence. They result in a tangible product (e.g., a classroom management plan) or a live performance (e.g., a class session in which children are working well together to learn).

> *Guiding Question: "What things can I have teachers do to prove they can do the job?"*

Proposition

Propositions are what we believe to be true that influence the way we will develop the assessment system. They are the agreed-upon givens we hold to be self-evident. They are based on our values and beliefs about teaching and assessment.

> *Guiding Question: "What are the fundamental truths about teaching and assessment that guide our thinking?"*

Psychometric

Psychometric is a big word that refers to the measurement of aspects of people, such as knowledge, skills, abilities, or personality.

> *Guiding Question: "What do the data tell me about validity, reliability, and fairness in this test?"*

Psychometric Integrity

Psychometric integrity, like other forms of integrity, is about doing what is right—in this case when we assess teachers. It is making sure people (children and teachers) don't get hurt by design rather than by accident.

> *Guiding Question: "Will I be able to sleep at night if I make these decisions?"*

Purpose

The purpose is the reason for establishing an assessment system. It is the end, not the means.

> *Guiding Question: "Why are we assessing our teachers?"*

Reliability

Reliability is the degree to which test scores are consistent over repeated applications of the process and are, therefore, dependable or trustworthy.

> *Guiding Question: "If students took the same test again under the same conditions (or a similar version of the test), would they score the same scores?"*

Rubric

A rubric is a set of scoring guidelines that facilitate the judgment-making process. They typically include a set of criteria and a mechanism (rating scale or checklist) to determine and record levels of quality.

> *Guiding Question: "How will I decide whether or not teachers did the task well?"*

Ruler (Logistic Ruler)

A construct of imaginary but defined equal units or intervals. Physically, the unit may be inches or centimeters. With teacher performance measures, the unit is generically called a *logit*.

> *Guiding Question: "How can I determine the level of teacher knowledge and ability in a scientific way?"*

Sampling Plan

There are bunches of things a teacher could do to provide evidence of competence, and there are bunches of indicators collected in the domains made up of various standards. The sampling plan selects the most important tasks and indicators from the domains being assessed. It must include a representative sample from each domain. It would not be a good sampling plan if the teacher had to create 30 lesson plans and no assessments, or if the teacher was assessed on only 3 of 30 indicators or 6 of 10 standards.

Guiding Question: "What tasks will I pick to cover all of the standards?"

Scores (Raw Scores)

The count of items correct or rating of judges on items in tests or assessments.

Guiding Question: "How many did I get right?"

Showcase Portfolios

Showcase portfolios are used to share best work, so that creators can take pride in their accomplishments and/or showcase their work to parents or prospective employers.

Guiding Question: "What artifacts can I have my students assemble in a folder or computer file that will make them feel proud of themselves or impress someone else?"

Standards Sets

Lots of groups have written or rewritten standards. Each set of standards written by one group is a standards set. Examples include INTASC, Florida Accomplished Practices, and National Council of Teachers of Mathematics.

Guiding Question: "Whose standards count for me?"

Summative Assessments

Summative assessments help us draw conclusions about what students actually learned from our instruction. Summative assessment occurs after instruction has concluded and is typically formal but can be either traditional or alternative in nature.

Guiding Question: "Did students learn what we taught?"

Task

A task is something you ask a teacher to do to demonstrate competency. The task may be in the form of a written product (e.g., a lesson plan) or a skill (e.g., that lesson plan delivered).

Guiding Question: "What things can I ask a teacher to do that will show competence—or lack thereof?"

Use

The use of the system is the decision or set of decisions to be made about teachers. It defines what will be done with the data collected.

Guiding Question: "What decisions will we make with our data?"

Utility

Utility of data refers to usefulness. There's no point in collecting a bunch of stuff to fill a filing cabinet if you have no expectation of using it.

> *Guiding Question: "Will the data I collect give me useful information so I can have better teachers and programs?"*

Validity

Validity is the extent to which assessment measures are truthful about what they say they measure or the degree to which evidence and theory support the interpretations and use of a test or assessment process.

> *Guiding Question: "Does this test really measure what it says it measures? Does the assessment system provide adequate coverage of the standards?"*

References

American Educational Research Association, American Psychological Association, and National Council of Measurement in Education. (1999). *Standards for educational and psychological testing.* Washington, DC: American Educational Research Association.

Andrich, D., & Wright, B. D. (1994). Rasch sensitivity and Thurstone insensitivity to graded responses. *Rasch Measurement Transactions, 8,* 382.

Angoff, W. H. (1971). Scales, norms and equivalent scores. In R. L. Thorndike (Ed.), *Educational Measurement* (2d Ed.) (pp. 508–600). Washington, DC: American Council on Education.

Baker, F. B., & Kim, S. (2004). *Item response theory: Parameter estimation techniques* (2d Ed.). New York: Marcel Dekker.

Barnard, G. A. (2001). "Logit," "Log," and Log-odds." *Rasch Measurement Transactions, 14*(4), 785.

Barrett, H. (2004). *Differentiating electronic portfolios and online assessment management systems.* Proceedings of the SITE Conference. Retrieved June 13, 2005, from http://electronicportfolios.com/systems/concerns.html

Bayley, S. (2001). Rasch vs. tradition. *Rasch Measurement Transactions, 15*(1), 809.

Berk, R. A. (1986). A consumer's guide to setting performance standards on criterion-referenced tests. *Review of Educational Research, (56)*1, 137–172.

Berk, R. A. (1995). Standard setting: The next generation. In *Perspectives in Teacher Certification Testing* Amherst, MA: National Evaluation Systems. Retrieved August 30, 2006, from http.nesinc.com/pub1995_frameset.htm/1995_05Berk 3.pdf

Berk, R. A. (1996). Standard setting: The next generations (where few psychometricians have gone before!). *Applied Measurement in Education, 9,* 215–235.

Berk, R. A. (2002). Teaching portfolios use for high-stakes decisions: You have technical issues! In *How to find and support tomorrow's teachers, 2002.* Amherst, MA: National Evaluation Systems. Retrieved September 9, 2006, from http://www.nesinc.com/PDFs/2002_06Berk.pdf

Bezruczko, N. (2005). *Rasch measurement in health sciences.* Maple Grove, MN: JAM Press.

Bloom, B. S., & Krathwohl, D. R. (1956). *Taxonomy of education objectives: The classification of educational goals, by a committee of college and university examiners.* New York: Longman, Green.

Board of Curators of University of Missouri v. Horowitz, No. 76–695, SUPREME COURT OF THE UNITED STATES, 435 U.S. 78; 98 S. Ct. 948; 55 L. Ed. 2d 124; 1978 U.S. LEXIS 64, Argued November 7, 1977, March 1, 1978.

Bond, T. G., & Fox, C. M. (2001). *Applying the Rasch model: Fundamental measurement in the human sciences.* Mahwah, NJ: Lawrence Erlbaum.

Bontempo, B. D., Marks, C. M., & Karabatsos, G. (1998, April). *A meta-analytic assessment of empirical differences in standard setting procedures.* Paper presented at the annual meeting of the American Education Research Association, San Diego, CA. (ERIC Document Reproduction Service No. 422 352)

Braun, H. I. (1988). Understanding scoring reliability: Experiments in calibrating essay readers. *Journal of Educational Statistics, 13,* 1–18.

Cannell, J. J. (1989). *The 'Lake Wobegon' report: How public educators cheat on standardized achievement tests.* Albuquerque, NM: Friends for Education.

Cohen, J. (1960). A coefficient of agreement for nominal scales. *Educational and Psychological Measurement, 20,* 37–46.

Connelly v. University of Vermont and State Agricultural College, 244 F. Supp. 156 (D. Vt. 1965).

Cureton, E. E. (1950). Validity, reliability, and baloney. *Educational and Psychological Measurement, 10*(1), 83–95.

Darling-Hammonds, L., & Sykes, G. (2003). Wanted: A national teacher supply policy for education: The right way to meet the "highly qualified teacher" challenge. *Education Policy Analysis Archives. 11*(33). Retrieved September 9, 2006, from http://epaa.asu.edu/epaa/v11n33/

Darling-Hammond, L., & Youngs, P. (2002). Defining "highly qualified teachers": What does "scientifically-based research" actually tell us? *Educational Researcher, 31*(9), 13–25.

Debra P. v. Turlington, 730 F.2d 1405 (11th Cir. 1984).

Dollase, R. H. (1998). When the state mandates portfolios: The Vermont experience. In N. Lyons (Ed.), *With portfolio in hand: Validating the new teacher professionalism* (pp. 220–236). New York: Teachers College Press.

Earley, P. M. (2001, November). *Title II requirements for schools, colleges, and departments of education.* (Report No. ED. 460124). Washington, DC: ERIC Clearinghouse on Teaching and Teacher Education. Retrieved March 23, 2006, from http://www.ericdigests.org/2002-3/title.htm

Earley, P. M. (2000, January and March). Finding the culprit: Federal policy and teacher education. *Educational Policy, 14*(1), 25–39.

Ebel, R. L. (1972). *Essentials of educational measurement* (2d ed.). Englewood Cliffs, NJ: Prentice Hall.

Elder, C., McNamara, T., & Congdon, P. (2004). Rasch techniques for detecting bias in performance assessments: An example comparing the performance of native and non-native speakers on a test of academic English. In E. V. Smith & R. M. Smith (Eds.), *Introduction to Rasch Measurement* (pp. 419–444). Maple Grove, MN: JAM Press.

Embretson, S. E., & Reise, S. P. (2000). *Item response theory for psychologists.* Mahwah, NJ: Lawrence Erlbaum.

Flanders, N. (1970). *Analyzing teaching behavior.* Reading, MA: Addison-Wesley.

Florida Department of Education. (2002). *Florida's alternative certification program: Assessment system.* Florida Department of Education, Tallahassee, FL: Author. Retrived October 15, 2006, from http://altcertiflorida.org/AssessmentSystem.htm

Florida Education Standards Commission. (1996). *Florida Educator Accomplished Practices.* Tallahassee, FL: Florida Department of Education.

Frels, K., Cooper, T. T., & Reagen, B. R. (1984). *Practical aspects of teacher evaluation: Annotated guide to a practical approach in the legal setting for evaluation of teacher performance.* Topeka, KS: National Organization on Legal Problems of Education. (ERIC Document Reproduction Service No. ED251989).

Gerrold, D. (1973). *The trouble with tribbles: The birth, sale, and final production of one episode.* Dallas, TX: BenBella Books.

Girod, G. R. (Ed.). (2002). *Connecting teaching and learning: A handbook for teacher educators on teacher work sample methodology.* Washington, DC: American Association of Colleges of Teacher Education.

Gollnick, D. (2001). *NCATE/state site visit team training.* Presentation to National Council for Accreditation of Teacher Education, St. Petersburg, FL, and Florida Department of Education, Washington, DC.

Gollnick, D. (2006, February) *Preconference—Unit assessment data.* PowerPoint presentation at the annual meeting of the Association of Teacher Educators, Atlanta, GA. Retrieved April 17, 2006, from http://www.ncate.org/public/presentations.asp?ch=37

Groves v. Alabama State Board of Education, Civil Action No. 88-T-730-N, UNITED STATES DISTRICT COURT FOR THE MIDDLE DISTRICT OF ALABAMA, NORTHERN DIVISION, 776 F. Supp. 1518; 1991 U.S. Dist. LEXIS 14890, October 3, 1991, Decided, October 3, 1991, Filed.

Guttman, L. (1944). A basis for scaling qualitative data. *American Sociological Review, 9,* 139–150.

Hambleton, R. K. (1998, January). *Setting performance standards on achievement tests: Meeting the requirements of Title I.* A commissioned paper for the Council of Chief State School Officers, Washington, DC.

Hambleton, R. K. (2001). Setting performance standards on educational assessments and criteria for evaluating the process. In G. Cizek (Ed.), *Setting performance standards: concepts, methods, and perspectives* (pp. 86–116). Mahwah, NJ: Lawrence Erlbaum.

Hambleton, R. K., Jaeger, R. M., Plake, B. S., & Mills, C. N. (2000). *Handbook for setting standards on performance assessments.* Washington, DC: Council of Chief State School Officers.

Hambleton, R. K., & Plake, B. S. (1995). Using an extended Angoff procedure to set standards on complex performance assessments. *Applied Measurement in Education, 8*(1), 41–55.

Hazi, H. M. (1989, Spring). Measurement versus supervisory judgment: The case of Sweeney v. Turlington. *Journal of Curriculum and Supervision, 4*(3), 211–229.

Higher Education Reauthorization Act of 1998, Pub. L. No. 105–244. Retrieved August 30, 2006, from http://thomas.loc.gov/cgi?bin/bdquery/D?d105:1:./temp/~bdn75F::l/bss/d105query.html

Impara, J. C., & Plake, B. S. (2000, April). *A comparison of cut scores using multiple standard setting methods.* Paper presented at the annual meeting of the American Educational Research Association, New Orleans, LA.

Ingebo, G. S. (1997). *Probability in the measure of achievement.* Chicago: MESA Press.

Ingersoll, G. M., & Scannell, D. P. (2002). *Performance-based teacher certification: Creating a comprehensive unit assessment system.* Golden, CO: Fulcrum Publishing.

Interstate New Teacher Assessment and Support Consortium. (1992). *Model standards for beginning teacher licensing, assessment, and development: A resource for state dialogue,* Washington, DC: Council of Chief State School Officers. Retrieved August 30, 2006, from http://www.ccsso.org/content/pdfs/corestrd.pdf

Interstate New Teacher Assessment and Support Consortium. (1995). *Next steps: Moving toward performance-based licensing in teaching.* Washington, DC: Council of Chief State School Officers.

Jaeger, R. M. (1982). An iterative structured judgment process for establishing standards on competency tests: Theory and application. *Educational Evaluation and Policy Analysis, 4,* 461–476.

Jaeger, R. (1989). Certification of student competence. In R. L. Linn (Ed.), *Educational measurement* (3rd Ed.). (pp. 485–514). New York: Macmillan.

Jaeger, R. (1995, May). *An approach to the design of pilot tests for National Board for Professional Teaching Standards Assessments.* Greensboro, NC: National Board for Professional Teaching Standards, Technical Analysis Group, Center for Educational Research and Evaluation, University of North Carolina-Greensboro.

Karabatsos, G. (1999). Rasch vs. two- and three-parameter logistic models from the perspective of conjoint measurement theory. Paper presented at the annual meeting of the American Education Research Association, Montreal. *Rasch Measurement Transactions, 12*(4).

Kirsch v. Bowling Green State University, No. 95API11–1476, 1996 Ohio App. LEXIS 2247 (Ohio C. App. May 30, 1996).

Koretz, D. (1994). *The evolution of a portfolio program: The impact and quality of the Vermont portfolio program in its second year (1992–1993).* Report from the National Center for Research on Evaluation, Standards, and Student Testing, Los Angeles, CA. Washington, DC: Office of Educational Research and Improvement.

Lang, W. S. (2005, February). Analysis of disposition measures of consistency with INTASC principles: Results of an initial study. In Wilkerson, J. (Chair), *Measuring teacher dispositions with credibility: A multi-institutional perspective.* Symposia presented at the Annual Meeting of the American Association of Colleges of Teacher Education, Washington DC.

Lang, W. S., & Wilkerson, J. R. (2006, February). *Measuring teacher dispositions systematically using INTASC Principles.* Paper presented at annual meeting of the American Association of Teacher Educators in San Diego, CA.

Lawshe, C. H. (1975). A quantitative approach to content validity. *Personnel Psychology, 28*(4), 563–575.

Lee, W. W., & Owens, D. L. (2001). Court rulings favor performance measures. *Performance Improvement, 40*(4), 35–40.

Lele, M., & Sheth, J. (1991). *The customer is key: Gaining an unbeatable advantage through customer satisfaction.* New York: Wiley.

Lemke, J. C. (2002). Preparing the best teachers for our children. In *No child left behind: The vital role of rural schools.* Annual National Conference Proceedings of the American Council on Rural Special Education (ACRES). 22nd, Reno, NV, March 7–9, 2001.

Linacre, J. M. (1994). *A user's guide to FACETS.* Chicago, MESA Press.

Linacre, J. M. (2003). *A user's guide to Winsteps and Ministep: Rasch-model computer programs.* Chicago: Winsteps.

Linacre, J. M. (2004). Rasch model and the quest for perfection. *Rasch Model Transactions, 18*(3), 983.

Linder, D. (2006). The due process rights of students. In *Exploring Constitutional Law.* Retrieved September 10, 2006, from http:www.lang.umkc.edu/faculty/projects/ftrials/conlaw/dueprocesstudents.htm

Livingston, S. A., & Zieky, M. J. (1982). *Passing scores: A manual for setting standards of performance on educational and occupational tests.* Princeton, NJ: Education Testing Service.

Ludlow, L. H. (2001). Teacher test accountability: From Alabama to Massachusetts. *Education Policy Analysis Archives, 9*(6). Retrieved September 9, 2006, from http://epaa.asu.edu/epaa/v9n6/.html

Lunce, S., Lunce, B., & Maniam, S. (2002). *A model for strategic enrollment management in a regional university.* Retrieved on June 27, 2005, from http://www.sbaer.uca.edu/research/swdsi/2002/Papers/02swsdi037.pdf

Lunde v. Iowa Board of Regents, 92–365, SUPREME COURT OF THE UNITED STATES, 506 U.S. 940; 113 S. Ct. 377; 121 L. Ed. 2d 288; 1992 U.S. LEXIS 6643; 61 U.S.L.W. 3301, October 19, 1992.

Lyons, N. (1998). *With portfolio in hand.* New York: Teachers College Press.

McCaffrey, D. F., Lockwood, J. R., Koretz, D. M., & Hamilton, L. S. (2003). *Evaluating value-added models for teacher accountability.* Santa Monica, CA: RAND Corporation. Retrieved September 10, 2006, from www.rand.org/pubs/monographs/2004/RAND_MG158.pdf

McConnell v. Le Moyne College, CA 05–02441 , SUPREME COURT OF NEW YORK, APPELLATE DIVISION, FOURTH DEPARTMENT, 2006 NY Slip Op 256; 25 A.D.3d 1066; 808 N.Y.S.2d 860; 2006 N.Y. App. Div. LEXIS 330, January 18, 2006, Decided, January 18, 2006.

McDonough, M., & Wolf, W. C. (1987). Testing teachers: Legal and psychometric considerations. *Educational Policy,* 199–213.

McEnteggart v. Cataldo, SUPREME COURT OF THE UNITED STATES, 408 U.S. 943; 92 S. Ct. 2878; 33 L. Ed. 2d 767; 1972 U.S. LEXIS 1985, June 29, 1972.

McGinty, D. (1996). The demise of the Georgia teacher performance assessment instrument. *Research in the Schools, 3*(2), 41–47.

McKibbin, M. (2001). One size does not fit all: Reflections on alternative routes to teacher preparation in California. *Teacher Education Quarterly, 28*(1), 133–149.

McMillan, J. (2003). *Classroom assessment* (3d Ed.) Boston, MA: Allyn & Bacon.

Mehrens, W. A. (1991). *Using performance for accountability purposes: Some problems.* Paper presented at the annual meeting of the American Educational Research Association. Chicago, IL. (ERIC Document Reproduction Service No. ED 333008)

Mehrens, W. A., & Popham, W. J. (1992). How to evaluate the legal defensibility of high-stakes tests. *Applied Measurement in Education, 5*(3), 265–283.

Mellnick, S., & Pullin, D. (2000). Can you take dictation? Prescribing teacher quality through testing. *Journal of Teacher Education, 51*(4), 262–275.

Messick, S. (1995). Validity of psychological assessment: Validation of inferences from persons' responses and performances as scientific inquiry into score meaning. *American Psychologist, 50,* 741–749.

Milam, S. (2006, February). *Legal issues in assessment of dispositions.* Paper presented at the annual meeting of the American Association of Colleges of Teacher Education. San Diego, CA.

Miller, G. (2001). Preparing the next generation of teachers: Title II of the Higher Education Act. *Policy Perspectives, 2*(5), 1–4.

Mitchell, K. J., Robinson, D. Z., Plake, B. S., & Knoles, K. T. (Eds.). (2003). *Testing teacher candidates: The role of licensure tests in improving teacher quality.* Washington, DC: National Academy Press.

Myford, C. V., & Wolfe, E. W. (2004). Detecting and measuring rater effects using the many-facet Rasch measurement: Part I and Part II. In E. V. Smith & R. M. Smith (Eds.), *Introduction to Rasch measurement* (pp. 460–574). Maple Grove, MN: JAM Press.

National Board for Professional Teaching Standards. (1986). *Five core propositions.* Arlington, VA: NBPTS. Retrieved August 30, 2006, from http://www.nbpts.org/about/coreprops.cfm

National Commission on Excellence in Education. (1983). *A nation at risk: The imperative for educational reform.* Washington, DC: NCEE. Retrieved August 30, 2006, from http://www.ed.gov/pubs/NatAtRisk/index.html

National Commission on Teaching and America's Future. (1997). *Doing what matters most: Investing in quality teaching.* New York: Author. Retrieved September 9, 2006, from http://www.nctaf.org/documents/DoingWhatMattersMost.pdf

National Commission on Teaching and America's Future. (2003). *No dream denied: A pledge to America's children (Summary & full report).* Washington, DC: NCTAF. Retrieved August 30, 2006, from http://www.ecs.org/html/Document.asp?chouseid=4269

National Council for Accreditation of Teacher Education. (2002). *Professional standards for the accreditation of schools, colleges, and departments of education.* Washington, DC: NCATE. Retrieved November 4, 2004, from http://www.ncate.org/2000/unit_stnds_2002.pdf

National Council for Accreditation of Teacher Education. (2006). *Program standards and report forms.* Washington, DC: NCATE. Retrieved September 9, 2006, from http://www.ncate.org/public/programsStandards.asp?ch=4

National Research Council. (2001). *Knowing what students know: The science and design of educational assessment.* Washington, DC: National Academy Press.

Nedelsky, L. (1954). Absolute grading standards for objective tests. *Educational and Psychological Measurement, 11*(1), 65–80.

Nweke, W., & Noland, J. (1996). *Diversity in teacher assessment: What's working, what's not?* Paper presented at the annual meeting of the American Association of Colleges for Teacher Education, Chicago, IL. (ERIC Document Reproduction Service No. ED 393828)

Office of Federal Contract Compliance Programs. (1978). *Uniform Guidelines on Employee Selection Procedure* (Section 60-3). Washington, DC: Author.

Ohio Civil Rights Commission, et al. v. Case Western Reserve University, 666 N.E. 2nd 1376, 1386 (Ohio, 1996).

Pascoe, D., & Halpin, G. (2001, November). *Legal issues to be considered when testing teachers for initial licensing.* Paper presented at the annual meeting of the Mid-South Educational Research Association: Little Rock, AR.

Paulson, F. L., & Paulson, P. (1994, April). Assessing portfolios using the constructivist paradigm. Paper presented at the annual meeting of the American Educational Research Association, New Orleans, LA. In Fogarty, R. (Ed.). *Student Portfolios: A collection of articles.* (ERIC Document Reproduction Service ED392542), Palatine, IL: IRI/Skylight Training and Publishing.

Plake, B. S., Hambleton, R. K., & Jaeger, R. M. (1997). A new standard-setting method for performance assessments: The dominant profile judgment method and some field-test results. *Educational and Psychological Measurement, 57,* 400–411.

Popham, J. W. (2003). *Classroom assessment: What teachers need to know* (3rd Ed.) Boston, MA: Allyn & Bacon.

Popham, J. W. (2004). All about accountability: Why assessment illiteracy is professional suicide. *Educational Leadership, 62*(1), 82–3.

Pullin, D. C. (2001, July). Key questions in implementing teacher testing and licensing. *Journal of Law and Education, 30*(3), 383–429.

Rasch, G. (1960). *Probabilistic models for some intelligence and attainment tests.* Copenhagen: Danish Institute for Educational Research. Expanded edition with foreword and afterword by B. D. Wright. (1980). Chicago: University of Chicago Press.

Rebell, M. A. (1991). Teacher performance assessment: The changing state of the law. *Journal of Personnel Evaluation in Education, 5,* 227–235.

Regents of University of Michigan v. Ewing, No. 84–1273, SUPREME COURT OF THE UNITED STATES, 474 U.S. 214; 106 S. Ct. 507; 88 L. Ed. 2d 523; 1985 U.S. LEXIS 149; 54 U.S.L.W. 4055, October 8, 1985, Argued, December 12, 1985, Decided.

Richmond v. Fowlkes, No. 99–4162, UNITED STATES COURT OF APPEALS FOR THE EIGHTH CIRCUIT, 228 F.3d 854; 2000 U.S. App. LEXIS 24822, June 15, 2000, Submitted, October 2, 2000, Filed.

Ricker, K. L. (2003). *Setting cut scores: Critical review of Angoff and modified-Angoff methods.* Edmonton, Alberta, Canada: Center for Research in Applied Measurement and Evaluation. Retrieved August 30, 2006, from http://www.education.ualberta.ca/educ/psych/crame/files/RickerCSS2003.pdf

Rudner, L. M. (2002). *Measurement decision theory.* Graduate Management Admission Council and LMP Associates: College Park, MD. Retrieved May 28, 2004, from http://edres.org/mdt/home3.asp

RUMM. (2003). *Rasch unidimensional measurement models.* Duncraig, Western Australia: RUMM Laboratory.

Salzman, S. A., Denner, P. R., & Harris, L. B. (2002). *Teacher education outcomes measures: Special study survey.* Washington, DC: American Association of Colleges of Teacher Education.

Sandman, W. (1998, November). *Current cases on academic freedom.* Paper presented at the annual meeting of the National Communication Association, New York.

Schroeder, C. (2006). *Florida State Board of Education Approves First STAR Plan.* Tallahassee: Florida Department of Education Press Release. Retrieved October 24, 2006, from http://www.fldoe.org/news/2006/2006_10_17-2.asp

Sireci, S. G., & Green, P. C. (2000). Legal and psychometric criteria for evaluating teacher certification tests. *Educational Measurement: Issues and Practice, 19*(1), 22–24.

Smith, E. V., & Smith R. M. (2004). *Introduction to Rasch measurement.* Maple Grove, MN: JAM Press.

Smith, R. M. (2004). Detecting item bias with the Rasch model. In E. V. Smith & R. M. Smith (Eds.), *Introduction to Rasch measurement* (pp. 391–318). Maple Grove, MN: JAM Press.

Southeastern Community College v. Davis, 442 U.S. 397, 99 S. Ct. 2361, 2371 (1979).

Southern Association of Colleges and Schools, Commission on Colleges. (2001). *Principles of accreditation: Foundations for quality enhancement.* Decatur, GA: Author.

StatSoft, Inc. (2006). *Electronic statistics textbook.* Tulsa, OK: StatSoft (http://www.statsoft.com/textbook/stathome.html).

Stemler, S. E. (2004). A comparison of consensus, consistency, and measurement approaches to estimating interrater reliability. *Practical Assessment, Research, Evaluation, 9*(4). Retrieved April 16, 2006, from http://PAREonline.net/getvn.asp?v=9&n=4

Stenner, A. J. (1996, February). *Measuring reading comprehension with the Lexile framework.* Paper presented at the Fourth North American Conference on Adolescent/Adult Literacy: Washington, DC.

Stiggins, R. (1998). *Student centered classroom assessment.* Upper Saddle River, NJ: Prentice Hall.

Stiggins, R. (2000). *Specifications for a performance-based assessment system for teacher preparation.* Washington, DC: National Council for Accreditation of Teacher Education. Retrieved June 15, 2004, from http://www.ncate.org/resources/commissioned%20papers/stiggins.pdf

Stretten v. Wadsworth Veterans Hospital, No. 75–2309, UNITED STATES COURT OF APPEALS FOR THE NINTH CIRCUIT, 537 F.2d 361; 1976 U.S. App. LEXIS 11283, May 18, 1976.

Stone, G. E. (2004). Objective standard setting (or truth in advertising). In E. V. Smith & R. M. Smith (Eds.), *Introduction to Rasch measurement* (pp. 445–459). Maple Grove, MN: JAM Press.

Technology Standards for School Administrators Collaborative. (2001). *Technology standards for school administrators.* North Central Regional Technology in Education Consortium. Retrieved September 9, 2006, from http://cnets.iste.org/tssa/

Texas Education Agency. (2005). *Technical digest for the academic year 2004–2005: A collaborative effort of the Texas Education Agency, Pearson Educational Measurement, Harcourt Educational Measurement and Beck Evaluation and Testing Associates.* Retrieved April 15, 2006, from http://www.tea.state.tx.us/student.assessment/researchers.html

U.S. Department of Education. (2004, March). *Overview: Fact sheet on the major provisions of the conference report to H.R. 1, the No Child Left Behind Act.* Washington, DC: Author. Retrieved March 24, 2006, from http://www.ed.gov/nclb/overview/intro/factsheet.html

Van de Zilver v. Rutgers Univ., CIVIL ACTION NO. 97–806, UNITED STATES DISTRICT COURT FOR THE DISTRICT OF NEW JERSEY, 971 F. Supp. 925; 1997 U.S. Dist. LEXIS 11213, August 1, 1997, Decided, August 1, 1997, ORIGINAL FILED.

Vestal, S. (2005). WSU takes hit on free speech: Disposition assessment for teachers draws criticism. *Spokesman Review,* October 22. Retrieved August 30, 2006, from http://thefire.org/pdfs/32027f641aa53ba0fdd1fbfa73444c35.pdf

Walter, R. A., & Kapes, J. T. (2003). Development of a procedure for establishing occupational examination cut scores: A NOCTI example. *Journal of Industrial Teacher Education, 40*(2), 25–45.

Wilkerson, J. R. (2006, April). Measuring teacher dispositions: Standards-based or morality-based? *Teachers' College Record.* Date Published: April 20, 2006, http://www.tcrecord.org ID Number: 12493, Date Accessed: February 10, 2007.

Wilkerson, J. R., & Lang, W. S. (2003, December). Portfolios, the Pied Piper of teacher certification assessments: Legal and psychometric issues. *Education Policy Analysis Archives, 11*(45). Retrieved February 15, 2004, from http://epaa.asu.edu/epaa/v11n45/

Wilson, M. (2005). *Constructing measures: An item response modeling approach.* Mahwah, NJ: Lawrence Erlbaum.

Wilson, R. (2005). We don't need that kind of attitude. *The Chronicle of Higher Education, 52*(17), 8.

Wolfe, E. W., & Mapuranga, R. (2004). South Carolina High School Assessment Program (HSAP) 2003 field test evaluation: A report to the Education Oversight Committee. Retrieved April 15, 2006, from http://www.sceoc.org/PDF/HSAPFinalReport.pdf

Wright, B. D., & Linacre, J. M. (1989, November). Observations are always ordinal; Measurement, however, must be interval. *Archives of Physical Medicine and Rehabilitation, 70,* 857–860.

Wright, B. D., & Masters, G. N. (1982). *Rating scale analysis.* Chicago: MESA Press.

Wright, B. D., & Stone, M. H. (1979). *Best test design.* Chicago: MESA Press.

Wright, B. D., & Stone, M. H. (2004). *Making measures.* Chicago: Phaneron.

Zirkel, P. (2000). Tests on trial. *Phi Delta Kappan, 8*(10), 793–794.

Index

CORWIN PRESS

The Corwin Press logo—a raven striding across an open book—represents the union of courage and learning. Corwin Press is committed to improving education for all learners by publishing books and other professional development resources for those serving the field of PreK–12 education. By providing practical, hands-on materials, Corwin Press continues to carry out the promise of its motto: **"Helping Educators Do Their Work Better."**